The reading public outside Sweden knows little of that country's history, beyond the dramatic and short-lived era in the seventeenth century when Sweden under Gustavus Adolphus became a major European power by her intervention in the Thirty Years War. It is also known how Sweden lost her status after the dramatic confrontation between the warrior king Charles XII and Peter the Great of Russia.

In the last decades of the seventeenth century another Swedish king, Charles XI, launched a less dramatic but remarkable bid to stabilize and secure Sweden's position as a major power in northern Europe and as master of the Baltic Sea. This project, which is almost unknown to students of history outside Sweden, involved a comprehensive overhaul of the government and institutions of the kingdom, on the basis of establishing Sweden as a model of absolute monarchy. This book gives an account of what was achieved under the direction of a distinctly unglamorous, but pious and conscientious ruler who was convinced of his Christian duty to secure the welfare of his kingdom and the subjects God had placed in his care. It also shows why a seventeenth-century European might well see royal absolutism as an acceptable way to govern a society, and why Charles XI enjoyed the support of most of his subjects.

CAMBRIDGE STUDIES IN EARLY MODERN HISTORY

Edited by Professor Sir John Elliott, University of Oxford
Professor Olwen Hufton, European University Institute, Florence
Professor H. G. Koenigsberger, University of London
Dr H. M. Scott, University of St Andrews

The idea of an 'early modern' period of European history from the fifteenth to the late eighteenth century is now widely accepted among historians. The purpose of Cambridge Studies in Early Modern History is to publish monographs and studies which illuminate the character of the period as a whole, and in particular focus attention on a dominant theme within it, the interplay of continuity and change as they are presented by the continuity of medieval ideas, political and social organization, and by the impact of new ideas, new methods and new demands on the traditional structure.

For a list of titles published in the series, please see end of book

Charles XI and Swedish Absolutism

Charles XI on his horse 'Brilliant' at the battle of Lund, 4 December 1676,
by D. K. Ehrenstrahl, 1682.

Charles XI and
Swedish Absolutism

A. F. UPTON
University of St Andrews

CAMBRIDGE
UNIVERSITY PRESS

PUBLISHED BY THE PRESS SYNDICATE OF THE UNIVERSITY OF CAMBRIDGE
The Pitt Building, Trumpington Street, Cambridge CB2 1RP, United Kingdom

CAMBRIDGE UNIVERSITY PRESS
The Edinburgh Building, Cambridge, CB2 2RU, United Kingdom
40 West 20th Street, New York, NY 10011–4211, USA
10 Stamford Road, Oakleigh, Melbourne 3166, Australia

First published 1998

Printed in the United Kingdom at the University Press, Cambridge

Typeset in Postscript Ehrhardt 10 on 12 pt [VN]

A catalogue record for this book is available from the British Library

Library of Congress Cataloguing in Publication data

Upton, Anthony F.
Charles XI and Swedish absolutism / A. F. Upton.
p.   cm. – (Cambridge studies in early modern history)
Includes bibliographical references and indexes.
ISBN 0 521 57390 4
1. Sweden – Politics and government – 1660–1697.   2. Charles XI,
King of Sweden, 1655–1697.   I. Title.   II. Series.
DL727.U67   1998
948.5'03–dc21   97–25197   CIP
ISBN 0 521 57390 4 hardback

Contents

Illustrations

Swedish words used in the text

indelningsverk   This was a system long practised in Sweden, whereby an institution or an individual public servant drew income from a revenue source, usually land rent or taxes, which had been permanently assigned for that purpose in the state budget. The recipient would collect the income directly at source. Part of the reform plan under Charles XI, in the first place for financing the armed forces, was to universalize this method of payment for public services.

knektehåll   A system used in Sweden for maintaining infantry soldiers. The king entered into a contract with the peasantry of a province, whereby they undertook to maintain a specified number of soldiers in constant readiness for service, in return for the crown giving up its traditional right to call for conscription. Peasant farms grouped into rotas, and recruited the soldier, provided a cottage with an allotment, or alternatively board and lodging, basic clothing and a wage. These contracts were regarded as legally binding and irrevocable.

reduktion   This is a legal process, based on the principle of the inalienability of the crown's lands and revenues. The principle meant that even if a ruler made a grant to a subject in perpetuity from these lands and revenues, he, or his successors, could recall the grant at any time on grounds of public necessity. It was the principal means used in the reign of Charles XI to fund his reform programme.

Riddarhus   This is strictly the building, first used in the Diet of 1680, as the permanent meeting place for the Estate of the Nobility – *ridderskap och adeln* – and to house the archives of the Estate, including the Matriculation Register of its members. The term is also commonly used, as in this text, to denote the Estate of the Nobility in the Diet.

Currencies in use in Sweden

In the seventeenth century there were three main types of currency in use.

1   The *rixdaler*, denominated in the text as rd. This was the silver thaler of the Holy Roman Empire being used as an international currency.

2 The *daler silvermynt*, the Swedish silver daler, denominated in the text as dsm. This was the internal money of account, and there was a silver currency in use, though there was no actual coin of that denomination, and the copper coinage was used in most contemporary cash transactions.

3 The *daler kopparmynt*, the Swedish copper daler, denominated in the text as dkm. It was an intrinsic value copper coinage that circulated in the kingdom. This meant that high denominations were minted slabs of solid copper – *plåter* – too heavy for an individual to carry. It had been intended that the silver and copper coinage should be of equivalent value, but in reality silver coins enjoyed a substantial premium over copper of the same face value.

Dates

Seventeenth-century Sweden used the Julian calendar, like the rest of Protestant Europe, and in consequence the dates in the text are Old Style, unless otherwise indicated.

Comparative chronology

1609 Truce between Spain and the United
Provinces.

1611 Accession of Gustav II Adolf; Axel
Oxenstierna appointed Chancellor. Sweden
at war with Denmark, Russia, Poland.

1613 Peace of Knäröd with Denmark,
status quo maintained, but Sweden pays a
large indemnity.

1617 Peace of Stolbova with Russia. Russia
cedes Kexholm and Ingermanland to
Sweden.

1618 Bohemian revolt begins the Thirty
Years War.

1618 Sweden renews the offensive against
Poland.

1620 Battle of the White Mountain;
Bohemian revolt crushed.

1621 Sweden captures Riga and control of
Livland.

1622 Olivares made First Minister in
Spain.

1624 Richelieu comes to power in France.

1625 Wallenstein employed by the
emperor, war moves into north Germany.
Denmark enters the war in the Protestant
interest.

1629 Edict of Restitution; Denmark leaves
the war, defeated.

1629 Sweden concludes a truce with
Poland; left in possession of Livland
provisionally.

1630 Sweden decides to enter the war in
Germany in the Protestant interest and
sends an army into Pomerania.

1631 Sweden makes subsidy treaty with France. Sweden wins major victory over the Imperialists at Breitenfeld.

1632 Gustav II Adolf killed at the battle of Lützen. Accession of Christina; regency government led by Axel Oxenstierna and the Council of State.

1634 Murder of Wallenstein.

1634 Swedish army defeated by the Imperialists at Nördlingen; Sweden concludes new treaty with France as junior partner in the Thirty Years War. Swedish Diet accepts Oxenstierna's draft for a Form of Government for the kingdom.

1635 France officially enters the war against the Imperialists and Spain.

1643 Death of Louis XIII; accession of Louis XIV and a regency.

1643 Sweden launches preventive war on Denmark.

1645 Denmark defeated; concludes Peace of Brömsebro; cedes provinces of Jämtland, Härjedalen, Halland and the islands of Gotland and Ösel.

1648 Peace of Westphalia; year of widespread revolts through Europe.

1648 By the Peace of Westphalia Sweden acquires the German provinces of Pomerania, Bremen Verden and Wismar from the Empire. King of Sweden made a guarantor of the treaty and Sweden gets the status of a major international power. The king of Sweden becomes a prince of the Empire, represented in the Imperial Diet.

1650 Post-war financial crisis in Sweden results in confrontation between the commoner Estates and the Riddarhus and Council of State in the Diet. The commoners put forward a request to Christina for a general reduktion of crown donations to the nobles.

1653 End of the *frondes* in France. Mazarin becomes First Minister.

1654 Abdication of Christina; accession of Charles X Gustav, father of Charles XI.

1655 Swedish Diet agrees a scheme of partial reduktion; king and Council agree to embark on a war of conquest against Poland. Birth of future Charles XI.

1656 Sweden attacks Poland; Russia attacks Sweden.

1657 Sweden launches preemptive attack on Denmark; causes the defeat of Denmark and the Peace of Roskilde; Denmark cedes the provinces of Skåne, Bohuslän and Blekinge.

1658 Sweden renews the attack on Denmark with a view to achieving total annexation; United Provinces and the emperor intervene to save Denmark, and the attack is repulsed.

1659 Peace of the Pyrenees ends the French–Spanish war.

1660 Restoration in Britain; Louis XIV begins his personal rule; Denmark becomes an absolute monarchy.

1660 Charles X Gustav dies; regency for Charles XI led by the queen-mother and the magnate Magnus de la Gardie as Chancellor; the Form of Government reinstated as the basis of the regency regime. Peace of Copenhagen with Denmark, Sweden retains the three ceded provinces. Peace of Oliva with Poland; Livland formally ceded to Sweden; end of the dynastic feud between the Swedish and Polish Vasas.

1661 Peace of Kardis between Sweden and Russia on the basis of the status quo. End of Sweden's imperial expansion. Regency adopts a policy of defensive consolidation. Gustav Bonde draws up a balanced national budget.

1665 Anglo–Dutch War begins.

1667 Louis XIV launches his first war of conquest geared to the Spanish succession.

1668 The 'Blue Book', a report commissioned by the Council, reveals the failure to observe the budget guidelines, and exposes a structural deficit in the public revenues.

1672 Louis XIV's Dutch War begins.

1672 In response to the international crisis, de la Gardie persuades the regency to pursue a balancing position for Sweden, and to ease the budget problem by concluding a subsidy treaty with Louis XIV; Sweden committed to station troops in Pomerania. Diet of 1672 declares Charles XI of age and he assumes the government. Attempts in the Diet by a magnate faction to impose a restrictive accession Charter rebuffed by all four Estates. Charles XI retains de la Gardie as Chancellor.

1674 Preliminary negotiations for Charles XI to marry the Danish princess Ulrika Eleonora. Pressure from Louis XIV forces Sweden to mobilize an army in Pomerania.

1675 Swedish army moved into Brandenburg; defeated at Fehrbellin; defeat triggers a general attack by Sweden's neighbours, except Russia. Denmark, United Provinces, the emperor and Brunswick-Lüneburg join Brandenburg. Denmark invades Skåne.

1676 Peace negotiation begins at Nijmegen.

1676 Swedish navy overwhelmed by Danish and Dutch fleets; Sweden's German provinces overrun. In Skåne, Charles XI leads his army to a decisive victory over the Danish invaders at Lund. Charles XI blames de la Gardie and the regency for the disasters; takes Johan Gyllenstierna as his chief adviser.

1678 Peace of Nijmegen.

1678 Swedish Diet meets and sets up a Commission to investigate the conduct of the regency government, with the approval of Charles XI.

1679 Following the Nijmegen settlement, Sweden makes peace with the emperor and the United Provinces. Louis XIV pressures Brandenburg, Brunswick-Lüneburg and Denmark to make peace on the basis of the restitution of conquered territory. Planning conferences at Ljungby on post-war reconstruction; Gyllenstierna negotiates a political and marriage alliance with Denmark as the basis for a new foreign policy.

1680 Louis XIV embarks on policy of *réunions* at the expense of the Empire.

1680 Charles XI marries Ulrika Eleanora. Gyllenstierna dies, no new chief minister appointed. Bengt Oxenstierna, as Chancery President, assumes direction of foreign policy. Diet of 1680; driven by joint pressure from royalist nobles and the commoner Estates on the regency magnate families. On the basis of the report from the Commission on the regency sets up a Tribunal to assess the alleged illegal gains of the regency government and force repayment. Diet authorizes a broad reduktion of crown donations since 1632. Issues a formal declaration that Charles XI as an adult, Christian king has absolute power to rule his kingdom at his discretion, according to law and custom. Budget Office established. Military reforms begin on the basis of the indelningsverk, funded by the proceeds of the reduktion.

1681 Charles XI and Bengt Oxenstierna begin the change of foreign policy from a French alliance to alliance with the emperor and the United Provinces to constrain Louis XIV.

1682 Council of State purged and downgraded to King's Council. Tribunal on the regency assesses heavy financial penalties on the regency government. Diet of 1682 again sees pressures from the commoner Estates on the Riddarhus. Diet approves change from conscriptions to the knektehåll system for raising infantry for the new model standing army. Diet issues a formal recognition that the king has unlimited powers to legislate without the confirmation of the Estates.

1683 Turkish siege of Vienna.

1683 Sweden, now in the anti–French camp, threatened with attack from Denmark, supported by a French fleet; Sweden's German neighbours discuss joint war of conquest while Sweden is weak. Their mutual rivalry and distrust obstruct the design.

1684 The Truce of Ratisbon.

1684 Denmark challenges Sweden by the seizure of the lands of the duke of Holstein-Gottorp. Charles XI backs off from confrontation, looks for allies in the Empire.

1685 Revocation of the Edict of Nantes.

1686 The League of Augsburg against Louis XIV.

1686 Sweden joins the League of Augsburg; in return emperor sets up the conference of Altona for the restitution of Holstein-Gottorp. Diet of 1686 accepts king's new Church Law without debate; pressed by the king to relieve the public debt; in spite of stubborn opposition agrees to an extensive repudiation, which concludes the legislation of the reduktion. Diet authorizes the king to undertake a general revision of Swedish law.

1688 Louis XIV begins the Nine Years War in the Palatinate; the Glorious Revolution in Britain.

1689 Because of deadlock at the Altona conference, Charles XI prepares to use force against Denmark. Diet of 1689 agrees to grant supply; gives the king an open authorization to raise funds in case of war with Denmark. Diet issues a public repudiation of the offensive protocols in the minutes of earlier Diets and Council debates, which implied the powers of the king were subject to limitation. Sweden mobilizes against Denmark. Denmark gives way and agrees to full restitution of the duke of Holstein-Gottorp. Sweden's international position strong as the only major power uncommitted to the general war; solicited by all the belligerents. Charles XI resolved to keep his involvement to the minimum consistent with his existing engagements.

1692 Peak of success for Louis XIV, war begins to turn against him.

1692 Abortive attempt by pro-French faction in Sweden to change Sweden's alignment; Charles XI continues his support of Bengt Oxenstierna's policies.

1693 Death of the queen. Funeral Diet

used to publicize the achievements of the reign. King declares the budget in surplus, extraordinary taxation no longer needed in peace time; promises early completion of the reduktion. Diet empowers the king to raise whatever funding may be needed in the event of war, without the consent of the Diet. The Diet Resolution incorporates a 'Declaration of Sovereignty'. This confirms that kings of Sweden are absolute, Christian rulers, answerable for their actions to God alone. Subjects have an unlimited duty to yield full compliance with the king's commands. The Diet affirms that the king's achievements are to be regarded as permanent and inviolable. Any public criticism of the king's actions by a subject is sedition.

1693–7 In the last years of his reign Charles XI continues to exploit the full legal possibilities of the reduktion, despite the undertaking to the Diet of 1693 to bring the process to a conclusion. The indelningsverk and the knektehåll substantially completed. Charles XI declines wider involvement in the war; protests vigorously effects of Anglo-Dutch blockades on Swedish commerce.

1693 Belligerents accept Charles XI as mediator for a general peace.

1695 Peace negotiations begin at Rijswick.

1696 Charles XI instructs the Law Commission to prepare a new draft royal law, based on the absolute sovereignty of the king. Draft near completion at the king's death.

1697 Peace concluded at Rijswick, nominally under mediation of Sweden.

1697 Death of Charles XI at age forty-two from cancer. Accession of Charles XII at age fifteen, regency appointed under terms set out in Charles XI's Testament.

The structure of government before and after 1680

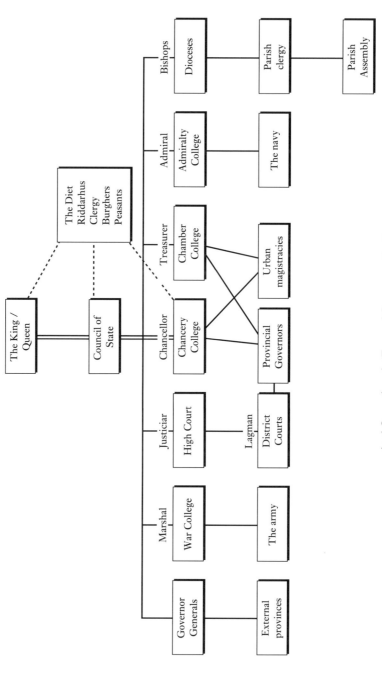

Axel Oxenstierna's 'Form of Government', 1634

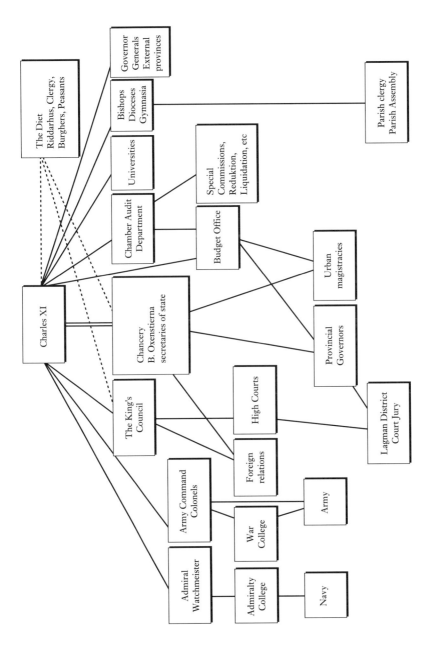

Government after 1680

Foreword

The research from which this book has developed was begun with the intention of writing a definitive account of the construction of a royal absolutism in Sweden during the reign of Charles XI. But I soon discovered that someone like myself, who was a full-time university teacher throughout the period when the book was being researched, and who was based in Scotland, could not realize the original intention. There is a belief among many historians that the records of the reign of Charles XI were substantially destroyed in the great fire of Stockholm Castle in 1697. This was not the case, and the sheer volume of the surviving primary materials conserved in Swedish archives is such that a single researcher, working from a foreign base, could not hope to master them; they could only be sampled. The problem is then compounded by what may appear to an outside observer to be a neglect of this reign by Swedish historians. The historiographical situation resembles that which once applied to the history of the early Stuart period in England. There the historians, even after nearly a century have to start from the monumental multi-volume narrative of S. R. Gardiner, which has never been bettered or displaced. In the case of Charles XI, there is a similar narrative, written at almost the same time as Gardiner and which is a monument to the achievements of that generation of archive-based historians working in the late nineteenth century. This is F. F. Carlson's, *Sveriges historia under konungarna af Pfalziska huset*, which has never been replaced as the basic scholarly narrative. However, the notes and bibliography in this book show how much excellent work has been done, since Carlson wrote, mainly by Swedish and Finnish historians. But this seems to have left wide gaps where not much systematic research has been undertaken. The obvious example is the history of the reduktion, the radical repossession of crown land revenues, which provided most of the resourcing for all Charles XI's projects. There are several good studies of what the royal policies were and how they were applied by the administration. But there is little detailed overview of what the actual impact of the policy was on Swedish society, although the whole economic position and lifestyle of the Swedish nobility were radically affected by it. This constitutes an historical black hole. We can affirm that despite the eloquent lamentations of contemporary observers and of the victims, the nobility survived the experience and continued to be the hegemonic ruling elite in Swedish society and we can note that, when, after 1718, they had the possibility of reversing the reduktion, they chose not to do so. But there are only a few scattered studies of what the actual experience of affected individuals was.

This book is not therefore the definitive history but a survey which has been written in the first instance for students of early modern European history who cannot read the Swedish language, but who share my own view that this unusual political experience has a significance that extends beyond the limits of Swedish domestic history. Since the publisher has wisely set a firm word limit for the book I have been obliged to leave out some aspects of the story which I would have been glad to include. Finland was legally and constitutionally part of the kingdom and fully integrated into it, but it has distinct experiences of its own and unfortunately there was not the space to do them justice here. Two other features of the book require a brief justification. I have deliberately inserted a considerable number of quotations from contemporary sources into the text, as a means of illustrating the thought processes of these early modern Europeans in the most direct way possible. Most of these quotations were originally in Swedish and the translations are my own and I take full responsibility for the results. I have never enjoyed any academic training in the Swedish language and realize that an amateur linguist may not achieve a high standard of elegance in making translations and will certainly make a few errors. I also considered how far it was useful to employ Swedish words and expressions in the text. The decision was to keep these to a minimum and use them only where there is no acceptable English equivalent. Thus the word Diet is well understood and can be used instead of *riksdag* to describe meetings of the Swedish Estates. But there is really no suitable English word to convey the meaning of reduktion, or indelningsverk. I have therefore provided a list of the very restricted number of Swedish words or phrases which appear frequently in the text.

It is not possible to mention by name all those who have given help and encouragement over the years, without which nothing could have been accomplished. It would include many academic colleagues in the United Kingdom and in Sweden, who showed interest and gave advice. But I would like to give particular thanks to Professor Göran Rystad, Professor Herman Schück and Dr Alf Johansson for their assistance. I would then like to thank the numerous members of staff in libraries and archives, but especially those in the Riksarkivet and the Kungliga Biblioteket in Stockholm, and the University Library at Uppsala, who were very patient in assisting a foreigner to find his way through their collections. In France I am indebted to the Ministère des Relations Extérieures for the permission to consult the official archives at the Quai d'Orsay. My research has been supported financially by grants from the British Academy and by the Court of the University of St Andrews, which granted research leave and gave financial assistance through its travel and research funds. My wife has been supportive throughout, and gave assistance with the preparation of the text. Finally I must give a special mention of our friends Lea and Sven-Erik Leffler, whose open-ended hospitality made it possible for me to stay in their home in Sweden during extended periods of research.

Abbreviations

KB   Kungliga Biblioteket (the Royal Library), Stockholm

RA   Riksarkivet (the State Archive), Stockholm

UUB   Uppsala Universitetsbibliotek, (the University Library), Uppsala

PR   L. Thanner, ed., *Prästeståndets riksdagsprotokoll*, IV: *1680–1714* (Nor-rköping, 1962) (Minutes of the Estate of the Clergy)

SRARP   *Sveriges riddarskaps och adels riksdags-protokoll*, XIII: *1680* (Stockholm, 1896); XIV: *1682–3* (Stockholm, 1898); XV: *1686, 1689* (Stockholm, 1899); XVI: *1693, 1697* (Stockholm, 1900) (Minutes of the Estate of the Nobility)

HT   *Historisk tidskrift* (Historical Journal)

KFÅ   *Karolinska Förbundets Årsbok* (Caroline Society's Yearbook)

Map of Sweden in the reign of Charles XI

Introduction: the historical background to Sweden's seventeenth-century crisis

The kingdom of Sweden, which then included Finland, had a rich historical past. It was unusual in early modern Europe in having a written constitution, the Land Law of Magnus Eriksson. Some time in the early fourteenth century this king had ordered the collection of the kingdom's provincial laws and customs and formed them into a comprehensive national code of laws, which was in public use by 1352. The Land Law stated that there was a unitary kingdom, 'a kingdom called Sweden', and that 'over all Sweden there shall not be more than one crown or king'. The king held his kingdom in trust for he could not alienate any of his rights, but he was the executive ruler and 'all those who live and dwell in his kingdom shall yield him obedience, conduct themselves according to his command and be at his service, especially to defend the kingdom'. The kingdom was elective and not hereditary and it was contractual. At the election of the kings the incoming ruler exchanged oaths with his subjects. The king's oath was sworn to all who dwell in the land, confirming that all the inhabitants were free subjects of the king and protected by his laws. The limits of royal power were specified: 'he shall be true and faithful to all his subjects, and he shall not harm anyone poor or rich, except according to law and after legal process'. The king would live off his assigned revenues and would not seek additional taxation except for specified contingencies and by negotiation with the subjects. The king was to uphold 'all the ancient Swedish laws which the subjects have adopted'. The reciprocal oath from the subjects pledged them to obey and support the king and to pay their taxes freely and without prevarication.[1]

The Land Law stated that there was to be a Council of native-born clerics and noblemen, chosen by the king but holding office for life and the king governed the kingdom 'with the advice of the Council'. The Council also acted as a guarantor of the constitution, while their main function was 'to advise the king what they know before God to be useful and advantageous for him and his realm', and to do this without fear or favour. They were also to assist the king to keep his oath to the kingdom and the subjects to keep their oath to the king. The Law stated further that for major policy decisions over war and peace, changes to the laws, or supplementary taxation, the king should seek the advice and consent of the

---

[1] Å. Holmbäck and E. Wessen, eds., *Magnus Erikssons Landslag: i nysvensk tolkning*, Rättshistoriskt bibliotek 6 (Lund, 1962), 3. Konungsbalken, pp. 1–6.

community of the realm. Thus, Sweden was a community with a strong executive kingship, which could command the unquestioning obedience of its subjects, was sustained by independent revenues, but was controlled by a rule of law which protected the rights of the subjects, and prescribed consultation between the king and his subjects on major policy decisions. The Land Law stood as a rule-book of government which the whole community accepted as a fundamental law. The effect of the Land Law was reinforced in 1608 when an official text was printed and became generally available in the authorized version.[2]

The social reality behind this formal political structure was that Sweden was a peasant society to a degree that was unusual even in early modern Europe. In France, peasant agriculture supported some 70% of the population; in Sweden it was 95%. Sweden had a small population spread thinly over a large geographical area. A typical settlement was of three to six farmsteads with a fringe population of cottagers, labourers and farm servants attached. The Swedish peasant was always a tenant, but there were three main types of tenure: tax-peasants, crown peasants and nobles' peasants. The tax-peasants were virtually freeholders, since provided they met their fixed obligations to the crown they had security of tenure and could sell, lease or mortgage their holdings; it required three successive years of default before they could be legally evicted from their farms. They were a large sector of the peasant population, about a third overall. Because of their favourable conditions their farms tended to be larger and more affluent than the other categories and they were the natural leaders, providing peasant society with its spokesmen, office holders and jurymen. The other two categories were tenants at will of the crown and the nobility respectively and rendered dues in money, produce and labour services, which were negotiable but often established by local custom. As tenants at will they were more exposed to exploitation by their landlords, but this was constrained by other aspects of Swedish conditions. Economic circumstances meant that there was little inducement for landlords to engage in demesne farming so that nearly all productive land was let out to peasant farmers. Labour services were most commonly used for building work and transportation. Then Sweden was very thinly populated with about 1 million inhabitants in 1600 rising to a little under 2 million in 1700. The evidence points to a general shortage of manpower and since all peasants were legally free men their bargaining position relative to landlords and employers was relatively favourable. The great European population boom had had limited impact on Sweden, and the frequency in the crown's books of untenanted farms and the persistent complaints of all kinds of employers about the difficulty of hiring labour further suggest that the common man had a fairly good bargaining position.

Thus economic realities underpinned the status of the Swedish peasant as a free subject of the crown. Axel Oxenstierna remarked in 1642 that 'in Sweden our peasants are born free so that it is an honour to be the son of a peasant'. His fellow

---

[2] *Ibid.*, p. 8.

magnate, Krister Bonde, complained in 1652: 'it is strange that people whom God has created for service, should be regarded as free'. However, it was public policy, to maintain peasant rights: Charles XI wrote in his instructions for the provincial Governors: 'you shall at all times be diligent and unremitting in hearing the grievances of the people and help them to secure justice, so that none may have reason to complain that he was not listened to or assisted in what is right and feasible'.[3] Then there were in Sweden institutions which assigned an active role in government to the common people. Two were at local level, the district court (häradsting) and the parish council (sockenstämma), and at national level there was the Peasant Estate in the Diet. The district court was a populist institution which handled civil and criminal cases and in addition took a broad range of local administrative decisions. Its formal core was the jury (nämnd) of twelve local householders presided over by a crown official (lagman), appointed after local consultation. The jurymen were chosen or emerged by various processes and could be deselected, but were generally an elite group of local worthies. The general public attended the court sessions and much evidence suggests they could make their opinions known to the jury. These peoples' courts, which settled disputes between subjects and between them and crown officials and landlords gave common folk a voice in government and the rulers had to take them into account. Even in the Catholic period Swedish parishioners had been consulted over the appointment of the parish priest. In the Lutheran period the clergy had chosen to develop an element of popular participation through the parish council of all the householders. This too had a core body, a jury (*sexmän*), but the council made most of the decisions. The parish priest, who presided in the council, was not freely elected, both the bishop and the crown and sometimes the local nobleman had powers to nominate or veto candidates, but in all cases it was accepted that the parishioners too had a voice and candidates were expected to present themselves for a trial performance before the parish. It was perhaps more important that the parish council controlled the economic administration of the parish. They decided such matters as poor relief, maintaining the fabric of the parish buildings and participated with the priest in upholding religious discipline. Offenders against the prevailing moral codes were accused and had their cases determined in the parish council which also decided the penalties. The Swedish Church, like established churches everywhere in Europe, was one of the main instruments of social control, discipline and indoctrination and it was important that it had this element of popular participation built into its structures. Finally the Swedish peasants participated in the national representative institution, the Diet of four Estates. The delegates who formed the Peasant Estate were elected at the district court and were answerable to it. The crown had tended to uphold their right to free elections. In 1680, Charles XI, in response to petitions from the Estate, ruled that crown officials

---

[3] E. Ingers, *Bonden i svensk historia*, 2 vols. (Stockholm, 1949), I, pp. 275, 312.

must not interfere in the freedom of choice and the peasants were allowed to use 'their own pleasure and discretion'. It will be seen that the Peasant Estate took a realistic view of its role; they tenaciously sought to fend off new burdens on their constituents, but in matters of high politics tended to evade involvement on the grounds that they were poor, uneducated folk who were not qualified to judge. Their most useful power was the right to present grievances. These were initiated in the election meetings and then collated at the Diet as the corporate grievances of the Estate. The crown was obliged to return a formal public response which became a matter of record. Here too Charles XI favoured free expression; he ruled that the peasants 'cannot be denied at a general Diet to present all their grievances and complaints'. There were ways by which the crown and the ruling elites could seek to subvert the legal protections enjoyed by the Swedish peasants, but their rights were sufficiently entrenched in ancient law and custom, and in functioning institutions to protect the peasants from the extremes of exploitation that were the common experience of their fellows in less favoured parts of Europe, a fact of which the Swedish peasants were well aware.[4]

Above the peasantry there was a thin layer of the groups who constituted the ruling elites of the society. First were the clergy. The Catholic Church had developed in Sweden on the patterns laid down in Rome and over the years it had acquired a large landed endowment and was further sustained by its income from tithe and fees. It had a place in government and its bishops shared power with the nobility in the Council. In 1523 some 20% of peasant farms were assigned to the Church. The commercial and industrial component of Swedish society was marginal. There was a primitive mining industry exploiting deposits of silver, copper and iron, while trading, particularly foreign trade, was mostly in the hands of aliens, who dominated such urban centres as existed. The burghers were an exotic element in a society that really consisted of a cluster of local subsistence economies generating little exchange of goods and services, but they were recognized as an Estate and it was the consistent endeavour of the crown to encourage and expand the urban, trading sector in society. Finally there was the emergent landed nobility – those who enjoyed *frälse* status, and who were exempted from taxation in return for the obligation to cavalry service. Anyone who qualified could claim the status, which was not hereditary and could be lost if the condition were not fulfilled. But the crown had developed a policy of donating land as a reward for public service; this too was in principle revocable if the service ceased, but the recipients tended to treat these grants as allodial property and through this process there had emerged a small elite of leading landed families which competed among themselves for control of the royal government and its patronage. In 1523 the number of peasant farms held by this nascent nobility roughly equalled the 20% held by the Church.[5]

---

[4] S. Grauers, *Sveriges Riksdag: förre avdelningen: Riksdagens historia intill 1865: fjärde bandet, Riksdagen under den karolinska tiden* (Stockholm, 1932), p. 206.
[5] Holmbäck and Wessen, eds., *Landslag*, p. 9; Ingers, *Bonden*, p. 173.

During the later middle ages the strong executive monarchy described in the Land Law failed to develop because Sweden–Finland was joined with Denmark–Norway in a loose Scandinavian Union with the king of Denmark as its head, which put Sweden under a series of regents and blocked the development of a national monarchy. This all began to change after 1523 when the leader of a major magnate family, Gustav Vasa, was elected king of Sweden and waged a successful war of independence from Denmark. To sustain his efforts he took advantage of the Reformation to break with Rome and reendow the crown with the assets of the Church; all its landed property and two-thirds of tithe income were transferred. Gustav Vasa used the prestige and resources he had acquired to reassert the primacy of the king in the government of the realm. He defied the Land Law by employing aliens in his government and told the peasants of Uppland in 1539 not to interfere with his government since 'We as a Christian king will set commands and regulations for you and all other Our subjects, and will that you, if you wish to escape Our severe punishment and wrath shall be attentive and obedient to Our royal commands in both secular and religious affairs.' He went on to crush the last major political revolt of the commoners, under Nils Dacke, in 1542–3, using his German mercenaries to defeat the rebels, and in 1544 he secured the agreement of the Estates to make the kingship hereditary in the Vasa family. This act of 1544 was the turning point in the history of Swedish monarchy, for all educated Europeans acknowledged that an hereditary king was truly king by the grace of God and all Christian subjects owed him unreserved obedience as a religious duty. The servants of Charles XI would repeatedly emphasize the significance of the act of 1544, which they presented as liberating the kingdom 'from the dangers and uncertainties of elective monarchies'.[6]

It was an irony of history that the achievement of Gustav Vasa was nearly undone by the rivalries of his three sons. The dynasty embarked on a policy of eastward expansion at the expense of a disintegrating Muscovy and the collapse of the Teutonic knights. Sweden acquired in the outcome the provinces of Kexholm, Ingermanland and Estland, giving her full control of the eastern Baltic. But the policy also created a major problem. Johan III married his son Sigismund to a Polish princess and then secured his election as king of Poland with the idea of establishing a Polish–Swedish union that could establish hegemony in eastern Europe. However in 1593, after decades of ambivalence, the Swedish Church adopted the Augsburg Confession and the Diet made the evangelical Lutheran faith the exclusive national religion. This led to civil war between Sigismund, now a committed Catholic, and his uncle Charles, acting as regent. Sigismund's faction was defeated and he was deposed and Charles eventually became king as Charles IX. This created a standing feud between the Swedish and Polish Vasas that was not resolved until 1660. The weakened monarchy was then challenged by a

---

[6] Ingers, *Bonden*, p. 160.

resurgence of the nobility. By the early sixteenth century the traditional informal acquisition of noble status by cavalry service began to be supplemented by the issue of formal letters of recognition from the crown, which conferred on the grantee and his descendants noble status in perpetuity. This was followed in 1563 by the institution of titles of count and baron, which were conferred on an elite of noble families. These titles were endowed with grants of crown lands, over which they were given quasi-seigneurial powers, thus distinguishing the holders from the more numerous, untitled noblemen. In the political instability of the 1590s some leading families put forward claims for the recognition of the nobility as a third force in society, entitled as of right to the senior offices in the kingdom, and acting as mediators between the king and the commoners. Charles IX had met this challenge by adopting a style of chauvinistic, populist kingship. He forced a confrontation and with the help of the three commoner Estates had his leading aristocratic opponents judicially murdered at the Diet of Linköping in 1600. This was a dramatic reassertion of the power of the crown, but was also deeply divisive.

The accession of Gustav II Adolf in 1611 resulted in a healing of this division. The king established a partnership with the magnate leader, Axel Oxenstierna, who became his Chancellor and intimate friend, and after the king's death in 1632, was effectively regent for his daughter Christina. The first step was the grant of a generous charter of privileges to the nobility in 1612. This confirmed their exemption from taxation and gave them priority in selection for the higher public offices, which were to carry regular salaries. In 1627 the nobility were formally incorporated as an Estate by the establishment of the Riddarhus, which was to be their chamber during sessions of the Diet and would house the register of noble families, with their titles and precedence. In future, nobility would be conferred exclusively by royal letter, but this in turn had to be recognized by a vote of the Riddarhus to include the new entry into the register. The nobility was also formally divided into three Classes, first the titled nobility, second all other noble families who had had a member on the Council of State and third the rest of the untitled nobility. The Riddarhus voted by Class, not by head, so that the magnate families in Classes I and II could generally dominate the Estate. These developments had confirmed that the nobility were the ruling elite in Swedish society but at the same time institutionalized the oligarchic structure of this elite. Studies have shown how, prior to the accession of Charles XI, a group of nine families, distinguished by their wealth and tenure of the highest offices, and an outer group of twenty-three families with whom they intermarried, dominated public life in Sweden.[7]

The next stage was to take Sweden into a phase of predatory, militaristic expansion and to engage the nobility as partners in the enterprise with the crown.

[7] B. Asker, *Officerarna och det svenska samhället 1650–1700* (Uppsala, 1983), p. 14; K. Ågren, 'The rise and decline of an aristocracy: the Swedish social and political elite in the 17th century', *Scandinavian Journal of History*, 1 (1976), pp. 63–75.

The Swedish armed forces were remodelled as a professional force of native conscripts, drilled to execute new tactics which, for a time, enabled Swedish armies to dominate the battlefields of northern Europe. This was underpinned by a further factor, that war should pay for itself by being fought on foreign territory from which the necessary resources could be extracted, either as subsidies from clients and allies, or requisitions from occupied enemies. The policy seemed to work. The conflict with Muscovy was settled at Stolbova in 1617. Accounts were then settled with the Polish Vasas, bringing Sweden the city of Riga and the province of Livland in 1629; this cleared the way for the intervention in Germany after 1629. It can be argued that the German enterprise was initially a defensive strategy to forestall the establishment of a Habsburg naval presence in the Baltic, but it soon turned into a policy of predatory expansion. This was brutally demonstrated in 1643 when Sweden turned on Denmark. Christian IV of Denmark had naturally seen the rise of Swedish power with apprehension and contemplated means of restraining it. So in 1643, Swedish armies invaded Denmark and at the peace of Brömsebro in 1645 forced Denmark to cede territory to Sweden. This proved that Sweden had now replaced Denmark as the leading Scandinavian power, but it left Denmark a humiliated and implacable enemy. The culmination came with the treaties of Westphalia in 1648, in which Sweden stood with France as a co-guarantor of the settlement and was recognized as an international power. Sweden received a huge monetary indemnity and the king of Sweden became a prince of the Holy Roman Empire, invested with the territories of Bremen-Verden and Pomerania with Wismar. This made Sweden a force in north Germany and gave her control of most of the southern shore of the Baltic.

The domestic component of these policies was a reorganization of government led by Oxenstierna. This was established by the Form of Government of 1634, which purported to have been worked out and confirmed by Gustav II Adolf before his death. The preamble claimed that the king had recognized a need for clear rules of government and had consulted the Council about this and 'the other Estates who are concerned, and thus after timely consideration, advice and consent caused to be set up an ordinance and statute, which shall be observed and taken into account for ever more'. It has never been proved that the king had consented to the Form of Government, certainly no subsequent ruler gave it formal confirmation. It has been argued that the scheme was only intended to operate during a regency, though the text of 1634 does not give that impression. The Form of Government described a fully bureaucratized structure of central and local government, centred in Stockholm and run by salaried public servants. Justice was centralized by a system of High Courts presided over by the Justiciar. The administration was divided among four collegiate ministries, the Chancellery, the Chamber, the War and Admiralty Colleges presided over by the Chancellor, Treasurer, Marshal and Admiral respectively. The kingdom was divided into provinces, each of which was supervised by a royal governor. The whole structure was overseen by the Council of State, composed of native-born noblemen, who would include the five great officers of state, and would have permanent representation in each of the governing colleges. The old concept of a governing council of landed magnates, serving part time, had been changed to a standing executive of full-time administrators. Although the Form of Government was never fully implemented, it gave Sweden a systematized and professional government machine, which was far in advance of her rivals and was a major factor in her rise to power. There was provision for meetings of the Diet, although it was envisaged that these would be infrequent and it affirmed that the Estates, jointly with the king, had a sovereign authority, 'through its resolutions, which none may question, since king and kingdom are subjected to them with obedience and loyalty'.[8]

There was a final dimension to Oxenstierna's reform programme. The bulk of crown revenue was derived from rents and taxes on its landed estate, a large proportion of them paid in kind. But it was believed that an effective military machine demanded cash revenues. So a policy was instituted of granting away crown land for cash advances or as reward to office holders. It was claimed the whole kingdom would benefit since the properties would be more profitably developed in private hands. The lost income was to be replaced by modern monetary taxes, like excises on trade and commerce, and by intensive development of the mining industries, yielding a royalty to the crown. The disposal of the crown estates by grant or sale was pursued so vigorously that by 1650 about two-thirds of the peasant farms were under the nobility, doubling their holdings since 1600. The compensatory tax revenues that should have been generated were slower to come through. The reality was exposed by the peace of 1648. Sweden's great power status depended on hiring out her services as a mercenary hit man to other powers. With the coming of peace her services were no longer needed and despite the war indemnity and the revenues of the newly acquired territories the revenues of the kingdom could not sustain her international status. This basic truth would drive the policies of Charles XI.

The problem was articulated by a remarkable document, a petition of the three commoner Estates to Queen Christina in the Diet of 1650. What was extraordinary in this 'Supplication' was that the commoners openly challenged the hegemony of the nobility and the policies it had promoted, and advanced their own alternative.[9] They began by denying any intention to challenge the authority of the queen, stating that they did not allow 'that any shall speak as though we seek to prescribe anything to your royal Majesty, and infringe your royal authority, which God preserve us from, acknowledging that your royal Majesty's full kingly power and authority is the foundation of our liberties, and they hang so together that they

---

[8] E. Hildebrand, ed., *Sveriges Regeringsformer 1634–1809* (Stockholm, 1891), Regeringsform 1634, Preamble; Regeringsform 1634, para. 45.

[9] S. Loenbom, ed., *Handlingar til konung Carl XI:tes historia*, 8 vols. (Stockholm, 1763–7), IV, collection X, p. 70.

similarly must stand or fall'. They revealed how, in the thinking of commoners, a strong kingship was a protection of their liberties, not a threat. They claimed that the whole community had sacrificed for the wars, yet they had received little return, but a select few had taken all the profit, 'as if we had fought and striven for them, and not for the best interests of the Fatherland'. They set up a strong case, beginning with Scripture, for reversing the policy of dispersing the crown estates and urged that it should be stopped and that the crown must recover its endowment. The queen did not accept the Supplication in 1650, but she did not reject it either, so that it stood on public record. The commoner Estates did not claim any power to enforce their desires, they accepted that only the queen could act, but they had shown that if she, or a successor, decided to reclaim the crown estates through *reduktion* they would give support.[10]

The nobility made a vigorous defence of their position. One of the best known of the contemporary tracts, by an anonymous nobleman, took the form of a conversation between a peasant, a priest, a burgher and a nobleman and was written soon after the Diet of 1650. It naturally concluded with the nobleman persuading the other three that the commoners had been mistaken. The nobleman argued that the nobility had earned their rewards and that the whole community benefited because the lands became more productive in private control. But the main thrust was that the behaviour of the commoners had been unacceptable in a well-ordered society. They were reminded that Sweden was not the United Provinces, or Switzerland or republican Rome, but a Christian monarchy. Whatever the commoners might pretend they were violating their duty of obedience, because 'they who will censure a king's actions and judge whether he does right or wrong and issue a correction, are presuming that they have the rights of sovereignty and some higher power over the king's'. The nobleman warned them of the awful consequences if they were to succeed: 'the whole government will fall into confusion and be overturned. All kingly respect and authority will be trampled down and violated, there will be disunity, distrust, desperation between the Estates.'[11]

The debates of 1650 illustrated basic features of Swedish society. They showed that it was well integrated; all the participants asserted that they were 'patriots' and would sacrifice everything for the 'Fatherland'. On this basis they could agree that the aim of the debate must be consensus, as the nobleman had put it, to maintain 'all good friendship, unity and trust' between the Estates. Because it was a society of Estates, each with its specific functions, there were demarcation disputes between them. The Law sought to avoid these by prescribing the rules of intercourse between the Estates and to give it effect there was the king, endowed by God with sovereign power to judge and resolve. He could best do this impartially if his

---

[10] *Ibid.*, pp. 93–6.
[11] KB, Rålambska Manuskriptsamlingen: Fol. Nr. 5: 1680 års riksdagsärenden, chapter 3, 'Samtaal emellan Junker Pär, Mäster Hans, Nils Andersson Bårgare och Jann i Berga Danneman hållen . . . i Lindköping Ao 1650'.

authority was unfettered. The 1650s did see a crisis in Sweden's public affairs but the position of the monarchy in society was no part of it, despite the traumas of Christina's abdication in 1654. In the thinking of seventeenth-century Swedes, the monarchy was not the problem but the solution.[12]

The personal crisis of Christina was resolved by her abdicating in favour of her cousin, who succeeded as Charles X Gustav. On his initiative a new consensus on policy was forged. At the Diet of 1655 the commoners were offered a partial reduktion, the recovery by the crown of a quarter of all lands donated since 1632, with the assurance to the nobility that the settlement was definitive. The nobility would find compensation in a new round of predatory warfare, first against the Polish Vasas and then against Denmark. In the treaties of Roskilde in 1658 and Copenhagen in 1660, Sweden won further territory and established her modern border in Scandinavia. But when Charles X Gustav died unexpectedly in 1660, the regency for the five-year-old Charles XI was fortunate to be able to disengage from the remaining conflicts without loss – in the settlement with Poland at Oliva, which ended the dynastic dispute and with Russia at Kardis in 1661. However, the problems created by Westphalia remained unresolved. Sweden by herself did not have the resources to sustain her international status, and now there would be no adult king able to implement solutions for a further twelve years.

[12] *Ibid.*

2

The formative years: regency and war, 1660–1679

The international position of Sweden in 1660 was superficially secure but actually precarious. Sweden's border with Denmark–Norway was now fixed and the control of the Sound, the main exit from the Baltic, was shared. But the inhabitants of the new Swedish province of Skåne were loyal to Denmark and resented their transfer to the Swedish crown. The enmity of the crowns was compounded by the Holstein-Gottorp problem. Parts of the mainland territories of the Danish crown were shared with a feudal vassal, the duke of Holstein-Gottorp. Danish kings wished to subdue or absorb this dangerous vassal; the Swedish crown tried to sustain his autonomy. In addition to Sweden–Finland, the Swedish crown ruled over three groups of territories, all distinct from one another and all provoking external hostility. The eastern border provinces of Kexholm and Ingermanland had been seized from Russia and cut her off from the Baltic. Sometime Russia would certainly challenge this. The two Baltic provinces of Estland and Livland were sovereign possessions of the crown, both areas where enserfed Estonian and Lettish natives were exploited by German landlords and urban settlers who had colonized them in the middle ages. The German settlers accepted Swedish protection because the alternatives, Polish or Russian domination, were unattractive. The German territories of Bremen-Verden and Pomerania with Wismar had a guaranteed legal status as parts of the Holy Roman Empire, with rights of appeal to the imperial courts and the emperor and representation in the imperial Diet. Their very existence was an offence to the Habsburg emperor to whom they symbolized defeat in the Thirty Years War. The emperor had no incentive to help Sweden establish control there and plenty of legal opportunities for making difficulties. This was compounded by Sweden's status as Guarantor of the Westphalia settlements, with rights to intervene in defence of the Protestant-Evangelical members in the Empire. This ensured more confrontation with the emperor. Sweden's claim to Pomerania, on dubious dynastic grounds, was contested by the Hohenzollern Electors of Brandenburg, who regarded it as rightfully theirs. Bremen-Verden had been coveted by Denmark, which saw Swedish control as a threat, and by the Brunswick-Lüneburg dynasty, an upwardly mobile princely family in search of an Electorate, to whom all territorial acquisitions were welcome. The reality was that Sweden in 1660 was ringed by potentially hostile neighbours, victims of past aggressions and looking for revenge. The mitigating factor was that their complex mutual hostilities made it unlikely they would unite against her. Even so, defence of the provinces required the upkeep of fortifications and garrisons, and the maintenance of a sufficient field army at home and of a navy capable of convoying it to any point on the perimeter that was attacked. This must be reinforced by a diplomacy that built up alliances, isolated enemies and if possible earned Sweden financial subsidies.

Charles X Gustav had provided for a regency in his Testament of 1660, concentrating power in the royal family.[1] This was overturned by the Estates in the two Diets of 1660. On 3 November 1660 the Diet approved an Additament to the Form of Government, laying down how the regency would be conducted.[2] It was vested in the queen-mother and the five great officers of state, but they would be advised by the Council of State and unless they were unanimous could be directed by its votes. Since this gave effective power to the magnate families who constituted the Council, the Estates had insisted on imposing restrictions. All appointments to the regency must be ratified by the Diet. There were attempts to control the extensive patronage which would be wielded by the magnates which reflected the changes in the governing bureaucracy in consequence of Oxenstierna's reforms. The additional posts, particularly at the lower levels, could not be filled with noblemen, and talented commoners who had acquired university training through the deliberate expansion of the university system had been recruited. As the ablest of them moved up the hierarchy of office it became customary to confer nobility when they reached the qualifying rank. This was changing the structure of the Riddarhus. A new nobility of promoted public servants, of humble social origins and with little or no landed estate, concentrated in Class III. Their values and aspirations differed from the magnates of the titled nobility, whose families mon-polized the higher public appointments and shared disproportionately in the rewards handed out by the crown. While the Riddarhus could still unite as an Estate against outsiders, on some issues these Class III nobles were prepared to work with the commoner Estates. This coalition wrote into the Additament clauses limiting the number of offices held by one family, and prescribing open access to posts: 'in all appointments to offices the person's abilities and merits shall be considered and none excluded for lesser birth or promoted for social standing'.[3]

The Additament gave an enhanced role to the Estates during the regency. They were to meet every three years and receive a report on what had been done. All major policy decisions needed 'the knowledge and agreement of the Estates'. The regency was to conduct the government, 'as they shall answer before God, his royal Majesty and all the kingdom's Estates'.[4] During the regency the Estates appeared to

---

[1] T. Nilsson ed., *Den svenska historien* vol. VII: *Karl X, Karl XI, Krig och Reduktion* (Stockholm, 1978), p. 30.

[2] Hildebrand, ed., *Regeringsformer*, Additament till Regeringsform af 1634, p. 63.

[3] *Ibid.*, Additament, para. 8; U. Sjödell, *Infödda svenska män av riddarskapet och adeln: kring ett tema i Sveriges inre historia under 1500- och 1600-talen* (Västerås, 1976), p. 55.

[4] Hildebrand, ed., *Regeringsformer*, Addittament, para. 14.

claim a role in government more like that of an English parliament. They debated policy, called ministers and officials to account and refused grants of supply. But the apparent shift of political power to the Diet was deceptive: the clue lay in the explicit statement in the Additament that its provisions were only operative during the regency. After that traditional royal government would resume.

The regency period looked like a repeat of 1632, a government of magnate families led by the wealthiest nobleman in the kingdom, Count Magnus Gabriel de la Gardie. Like Oxenstierna he was Chancellor, but where Oxenstierna had been one of the leading statesmen of seventeenth-century Europe, de la Gardie was a lesser figure. He was experienced, intelligent, cultured and power-hungry. But his weaknesses were exposed by poor decision making. His family were parvenus; as the anonymous *Anecdotes de Suède* put it: 'la Famille estoit regardé de travers par les Anciennes Gentilshommes' ('the family were looked down on by the established gentry'). On the other hand he was a gifted communicator, 'il estoit d'une merveilleuse présence d'esprit, et très èloquent, il luy estoit aisè de refuter ceux qui s'opposeroient à ses sentiments; ce qui faisoit naistre à plusieurs la pensée qu'il vouloit s'attribuer tout le gouvernement, et s'élever infiniment audessus des autres Senateurs' ('he had a marvellous presence of mind, and was very eloquent, it was easy for him to refute the arguments of those who opposed his views; which gave rise to the impression with many that he wanted to take the whole of government on himself, and raise himself far above the other Councillors'). With all his gifts, de la Gardie had independent colleagues to contend with, men like Per Brahe, C. G. Wrangel (the Marshal) and G. Bonde (the Treasurer), and at critical points would lose his nerve and retire to the country, leaving the government to his rivals in Stockholm.[5]

The regency government was inherently weak and plagued by a standing budget deficit. In June 1661, the Treasurer, G. Bonde, produced a report for the Council. The deficit must be eliminated so that 'the kingdom can subsist independently and not need continually to seek help from others'. Therefore the first priority was the avoidance of war. Public expenditure could then be reduced with the aim, which was to be taken up by Charles XI after 1680, of a settled budget, 'where every item has a secure assignment year after year'. The government would be able to pay salaries and not burden the community with taxation. Bonde argued it was in the interest of the crown that subjects should be prosperous. The nobility, 'which as the foremost is established to assist the king in governing', had two basic needs: 'that they should be employed in the kingdom's service and have land and farms to live off as well as salary'. The clergy were comfortable, provided the bishops did not ordain more than could be employed, for if clergymen became discontented they

---

[5] Anon., *Les anecdotes de Suède ou histoire secrette des changemens arrivèes dans ce royaume sous le regne de Charles XI* (Hesse-Cassel, 1718), pp. 116–17; G. Wittrock, 'Valda bref till M. G. de la Gardie från fränder och vänner 1656–1678', *HT* 33 (1913), pp. 308–12; R. Fåhreus, *Magnus Gabriel de la Gardie* (Stockholm, 1936), pp. 186–9.

'go beyond their office, interfere in politics and government, as has been happening in the kingdom in the Diets and elsewhere'. Burghers had a vital role in enriching the community and the government should support their enterprises, but must stop ennobling rich businessmen, who then gave up trade. As for the peasants, 'the priority is that we uphold them with law and justice the same as the other Estates'. It was important to avoid putting new burdens on them, 'since it is better to milk the cow than hit it on the head'.[6] Bonde's memorandum was a faithful reflection of the mind of early modern Swedes. It assumed a consensus society built round the concept of four Estates, each with its distinct functions, working together harmoniously under a rule of law maintained by the royal government. Bonde's programme was readily accepted and a budget on the lines suggested was drawn up in 1662.

It failed to work; the Diets of 1664 and 1668 heard embittered complaints from the lesser nobility that salaries were not being paid and the Council ordered an official report on what was going wrong, which appeared in June 1668. This document, known as the 'Blue Book' was in effect a damning criticism of de la Gardie's administration. Basically the budget of 1662 had not been applied. It listed fifteen practices which evaded the controls, and used creative accounting: 'in the budget resources had been set down and payments ordered on them which could in no way be honoured'. It recommended a list of expenditure cuts, starting with the royal court which they claimed would cut expenditure by 10%. The granting of donations by the crown must cease, and the proposed *reduktion* of 1655 be fully implemented.[7]

The 'Blue Book' was effectively suppressed by de la Gardie in the Diet of 1668, as was an attempt in 1670 to implement it during one of his absences in the country. In principle Bonde's programme of 1661 would have worked, but in practice it could not be applied without hurting the interests of the magnates who ran the government. They were not exceptionally corrupt by early modern standards; given the power they held, they showed themselves public spirited and restrained. But the enforcement of the 1662 budget would have hurt them and a weak government could not enforce it. Instead it looked for help from the international situation. This had changed in 1667, when Louis XIV's aggression in the Netherlands opened his bid for French hegemony. Sweden might hire herself out to one side or the other. De la Gardie preferred France, though in 1668, during one of his absences, a faction on the Council led by Sten Bielke took Sweden into the anti-French coalition, the Triple Alliance, in return for a Spanish subsidy of 480,000 rd.[8] After de la Gardie returned he swung the Council back. In a debate in 1671 on the international crisis, they agreed Sweden should aim at a balancing position, and seek foreign subsidies to maintain an army in Pomerania to make it

[6] G. Wittrock, 'Riksskattsmästaren Gustav Bondes politiska program 1661', *HT* 33 (1913), pp. 42–53.
[7] S. Loenbom, ed., *Historiskt archivum innehållande märkwärdigheter, upplysningar och anecdoter i Svenska historien* (Stockholm, 1774), pp. 30, 35, 36, 37, 38, 46, 85.
[8] G. Landberg, *Den svenska utrikespolitikens historia, 1:3 1648–1697* (Stockholm, 1952), pp. 161–4.

credible. Louis XIV made the best offer, 400,000 rd. a year. The force would intimidate the north German princes into staying neutral, so that Sweden would not actually have to engage. This French subsidy treaty of 1672 was the last and most fatal error of a weak and struggling government.[9]

In 1672 the Diet met to prepare the end of the regency and the assumption of the government by the young Charles XI. It was the last chance for interested groups to seek to secure their interests under the new regime, particularly through the drafting of the coronation oath. Older accounts used to suggest a confrontation between the Council magnates led by de la Gardie and an absolutist faction of lesser noblemen led by Johan Gyllenstierna, who had made a reputation as a critic of the regency government. The reality was much more confused than such a scenario suggests. There was a faction of young noblemen active in 1672. It had a military wing, Mårten Reutercrantz, Gustav and Christopher Gyllenstierna, and the Wachtmeister brothers, Hans and Axel. A civilian wing including Gustav Taubenfeldt, Johan Olivekrantz and a group of recently ennobled civil servants, Henrik Hoghusen, Joel Örnstedt, Erik Lindschöld, Johan Rehnskiöld. What they all had in common was a critical attitude to de la Gardie and an active place in the entourage of the king. De la Gardie complained to a diplomat in 1672 how the king spent too much time with these people, 'from which he can learn nothing and can easily be misled by the young peoples' foolishness or their intrigues'.[10] They tended to urge the king to assert himself and prepare to emulate the glorious deeds of his ancestors. Still it was confusion, rather than a confrontation. De la Gardie, who should have led the magnates in efforts to entrench their power in the Council, and use it to restrain the king, had no such intention. He had reason to expect the young ruler to retain him in office and looked forward to consolidating his position as head of government, with the added authority and backing of a ruling monarch.

One skirmish of 1672 was between the magnates of Classes I and II and an aggressive band of Class III noblemen over preference for appointments. The lesser nobles wanted to write into the coronation oath that appointments should be made on merit, not birth or title, and that official precedence should be determined by office. De la Gardie wanted to fudge this explosive issue; he told the Council that 'senior offices ought to go before rank and birth, but if this should apply to all offices, I do not know'. Since the king was pressing for the Council to resolve the issue it could not be wholly evaded, but it is interesting that the magnates in the Council did not assert the precedence of birth, but grasped de la Gardie's compromise. They resolved that the precedence of senior office holders was decided by their function; for the rest, 'status, birth, venerable age, seniority of office and other relevant considerations' would all apply. Since the senior posts were likely to be held by magnates they had neatly side-stepped the demands of the Class III

[9] *Ibid.*, pp. 170–2.
[10] A. Åberg, *Karl XI* (Stockholm, 1958), pp. 46–7, 52; G. Rystad, *Johan Gyllenstierna, rådet och kungamakten: studier i Sveriges inre politick 1660–1680* (Lund, 1955), pp. 65–6.

nobles.[11] But on a different issue there was a different alignment. In 1671 the Council had issued a decree on the disciplinary powers of noblemen over their tenants – *gårdsrätt*. This was vigorously attacked by the Peasant Estate in 1672 on the ground that it was invalid without the consent of all the Estates. They easily persuaded the Clergy and the Burghers to support them; the decree was 'prejudicial to all government'. In the discussions a burgher reminded them that in Denmark in 1660 king and commoners had joined to restrain the nobility. He did not add that the outcome had been a royal absolutism, but his audience knew this. The commoners demanded that the decree be referred to the king for consideration and the nobility, united on this in defence of their class interest, were unhappy, but could not deny the basic principle that 'a law which concerns all should be approved of by all'. The issue was referred to the king and he subsequently annulled the decree. The commoners had signalled their readiness to work with the king in restraining a united nobility.[12]

The key debate in 1672 arose over the coronation oath. Discussion is hampered over this because the draft text of an oath proposed in the Riddarhus is lost and its content must be inferred from the discussions. The Council chose not to put forward a draft of its own, which suggests that de la Gardie was not seeking any restrictions on the powers of the crown in the new reign. It was a Riddarhus committee which reported a ten-point proposal for the oath on 28 September. The spokesman for Class III was critical; he said: 'it seems, even so, as if we want to tie the king's hands by this'. In Swedish public discourse, 'to tie the king's hands' was unacceptable. It would be a direct negation of the authority vested in the king by God, and the concept became the focus of the ensuing debates. The Riddarhus referred their draft to the Council for comment and they began to discuss it on 1 October.[13] It can be inferred from the discussion that the draft contained two potentially restrictive provisions, presumably reflecting the views of a magnate faction. One was to provide that in making appointments to public office the king should be bound to take advice from the Council and the government Colleges. This had prompted the Class III protest and in Council de la Gardie opposed the 'innovation'. The Marshal of the Nobility, who did support it, was defensive about binding the king's hands. He said: 'God forbid anybody should presume that; our idea is no more than to ease the king's burdens.' J. Rosenhane added that even if the king did consult, 'still the decision remains with the king alone'. The second controversial point was apparently a requirement that the king should promise to confirm the Form of Government 'as a law that shall be observed here in the kingdom for all time'. The effect of this would be to apply the restraints imposed on the regency, through the Council and the Diet, on the government of a reigning

[11] U. Sjödell, *Kungamakt och hög aristokrati: en studie i Sveriges inre historia under Karl XI* (Lund, 1966), pp. 60–3; Rystad, *Rådet och kungamakten*, 65–6.
[12] Grauers, *Sveriges Riksdag*, pp. 17–19; Nilsson, ed., *Svenska historien*, p. 82.
[13] Rystad, *Rådet och kungamakten*, p. 62; Sjödell, *Kungamakt*, p. 66.

monarch. This would have been a significant reduction of royal power, mainly in favour of the magnates; in Council the Marshal was defensive and urged that it would be better to put the matter to the king by way of petition after he assumed the government. It seems the Council was divided over the proposals and they recommended that the nobility should confer with the other Estates. The meeting took place on 4 October, and although the Marshal introduced the proposals cautiously they met with an instant rebuff from the commoners. They insisted on using the oath of 1654, taken by Charles X Gustav, and they said they had heard that the nobility was seeking 'to tie the king's hands'. The Marshal told the Riddarhus they were immovable: 'you see gentlemen how the three commoner Estates have got together'. The veto of the commoners was decisive and all the Estates asked the Council to draft an oath based on that of 1654.[14] The Council did try to include an undertaking by the king not to bypass the Council by resorting to private advisers, and de la Gardie and the queen-mother were commissioned to persuade him to agree, but in one of his first major decisions Charles XI refused. De la Gardie told the Council, tactfully: 'he is well informed about everything, more than people believe'. G. O. Stenbock made a more perceptive comment: 'that was not his own idea'.[15]

On 29 November all the Estates approved the new draft by acclamation. The text was traditional. The king would swear: 'We will rule and direct the kingdom in every respect according to the king's oath'; he would fill offices 'with Swedish men of the nobility' and rule with the advice of the Council. When major policy decisions had to be made, 'then all such shall be made and pursued with the advice of the Council of State and the knowledge and consent of the Estates'. This episode in the Diet of 1672 was crucial for what followed in revealing the power structures in Swedish society. A group of magnates, led by the Marshal and not by de la Gardie, had tried to fix restraints on the powers of the new king through the coronation oath because they felt their hegemony was under threat from a coalition of Class III nobles and the commoner Estates. But the attempt had only served to expose the political impotence caused by the disunity of their Estate and had been dismissed with contemptuous ease. The defeat was followed by another ominous occurrence. The regency had asked the Diet for a subsidy to ease the budget problems. This met with an unequivocal refusal by the commoner Estates and the Class III nobles in the Riddarhus on the grounds that until the reduktion agreed in 1655 had been fully implemented 'they exempt themselves from further taxes and urge on the reduktion'. During the Riddarhus debate on this Hans Wachtmeister remarked that 'that which has been given away under the regency must also be recovered'. This was a sharp reminder that the budgetary problems were still unresolved and that the solution supported by most of the community was still reduktion. This threatened to undercut the

---

[14] Rystad, *Rådet och kungamakten*, pp. 80–96; Nilsson, ed., *Svenska historien*, p. 81.
[15] Rystad, *Rådet och kungamakten*, p. 39.

whole position of the magnate class and it was no wonder they viewed the future with apprehension.[16]

Everything would now turn upon the new king whose majority was seen as a cause for universal rejoicing. The rising civil servant, Erik Lindschöld, who also ranks as a respectable poet, composed this congratulatory verse:[17]

> We have long waited and at last reached the day
> Which rejoices the Earth and pleases the Heavens.
> On which a king of Sweden, son of a victorious king
> Takes on the government of his kingdom and enters on his throne,
> Himself to rule his people, to lead his people.

The seventeen-year-old youth was an unknown factor in 1672 and reports and rumours about him were mixed. One that has persisted into modern times alleged that he was barely literate which any familiarity with the records, containing his own written comments, shows to be false. The main source of negative impressions is the *Anecdotes*, which claim that the incompetence of his tutors left his natural talents undeveloped and put him off academic studies, so that he was solely interested in sports and outdoor activities, in which he was allowed to indulge in the company of wild and irresponsible young noblemen. His companions then poisoned his mind against the regency government and the magnates. Claes Rålamb, in a more measured assessment, made a similar charge. He wrote that there 'was a great neglect of the king's education, those involved failing from the beginning to instil in him the right, true principles of government'.[18] The reality seems to be that Charles XI was a loner as a child, without father or siblings, and his mother played the key role in his upbringing. She was a cultured woman, with whom the king developed a close relationship that lasted all his life, but she was no intellectual and inclined to be indulgent of her only child. He had a conventional set of tutors, an aristocratic governor, whom most contemporaries regarded as incompetent and lazy, a team of academic tutors, among whom Edmund Gripenhielm, criticized as too academic, won his pupil's affection and seems to have made the learning process a pleasant one. Olav Svebilius, the future archbishop, had charge of his religious instruction. The boy did have learning difficulties; he was temperamentally disinclined towards academic pursuits, a characteristic that persisted all his life, but he was also dyslexic and a slow reader. He was reputed to have been a sickly child: a Danish ambassador reported he was 'of weak constitution' and his mother refused to allow the tutors to press him too hard, while encouraging his innate disposition to outdoor activities. At age nine a report to the regency conceded that his reading was not fluent, and rumours of his poor attainments caused a debate in the Diet of

---

[16] Nilsson, ed., *Svenska historien*, p. 82; Grauers, *Sveriges Riksdag*, p. 14.

[17] Åberg, *Karl XI*, p. 55.

[18] KB, Rålambska Manuscriptsamlingen: Fol. Nr. 5: 1680 års riksdagsärenden; Anon., *Anecdotes de Suède*, pp. 101–10.

1668.[19] He spoke only one foreign language, German, and attempts to teach him French and Latin failed, while two terms at Uppsala University seem to have had little effect.

Outwardly, the young Charles XI was a fairly typical young nobleman, surrounded by companions of the same type, the clique who were active in 1672. They did undoubtedly influence him against the regency government, since they saw their own futures as bound up with the king asserting his personal authority. Even the queen-mother became alarmed at their influence and tried to introduce him to public affairs and interest him in Court entertainments, such as ballets and masques, but in this she failed completely. Instead the king and his companions indulged their taste for hunting, field sports and military exercises, which remained a constant feature of the king's lifestyle. These activities were filled with violence and danger. The French ambassador, Isaac de Pas, Marquis de Feuquières, reported in January 1681 how the king had encountered 'un ours d'une prodigieuse grandeur' ('a bear of prodigious size') which he had wounded, and he had survived the encounter. He stressed that, 'ce prince était seul, et à pied' ('the prince was alone and on foot'). He had already commented a year earlier on the king's vigorous style of outdoor activity.

Les ordinaires divertissements sont à la chasse, et aux jeux de mains: ce prince est toujours bien monté et déterminé cavalier, il saut de grandes fosses, et les fait sauter aux autres, qui quelques fois aussi cassent un bras ou un jambe, et quelques fois courent hazard de noier. Quand il se trouve un cavalier devant lui en beaux debut, il pousse son cheval de grande force, at en passant il met sa jambe sous celle de l'autre, et lui donne un gros coup de poing dans l'estomac qui ordinairement le fait tomber rudement à terre.
The ordinary relaxations are hunting and horse-play: the prince is always well mounted and a relentless horseman, he jumps big ditches, and makes others do the same, who sometimes break an arm or a leg, and sometimes run the risk of drowning. When he finds a rider in front of him, he urges his horse on with maximum force, and when overtaking he puts his leg under that of the other and hits him hard in the stomach with his fist, which usually causes him to fall violently to the ground.

It is not advisable to take such anecdotes at face value; Feuquières was not invited on the king's hunting trips and derived his stories from malcontents in Stockholm but the basic image is consistent with other evidence.[20] The king's enthusiasm extended to all things military and he was assiduous in staging realistic training exercises in which participants got killed. The Danish minister, Jens Juel, reported on manoeuvres held in 1674: 'the manoeuvres which were conducted by the king

---

[19] Nilsson, ed., *Svenska historien*, p. 92; A. Losman, 'Tre Karlars studier', in K. Holmqvist, ed., *Tre Karlar: Karl X, Karl XI, Karl XII* (Stockholm, 1984), pp. 16–19; O. Sjögren, *Karl den elfte och svenska folket på hans tid* (Stockholm, 1897), pp. 13, 18, 93.

[20] Åberg, *Karl XI*, p. 47; Losman, 'Tre Karlars studier', pp. 16–19; Archive du Ministère d'affaires étrangères: Correspondance diplomatique, Suède: vol. 63, Feuquières to Louis XIV 19 Feb. 1680, p. 136; vol. 64, Feuquières to Louis XIV 22 Jan. 1681, p. 30.

are finished: various minor incidents occurred: the king had a horse shot dead under him, a boat blew up with twenty men and ten barrels of powder, a bridge collapsed with some cavalry on it and several of them were injured'.[21] This was nothing unusual in Charles XI's war games.

The king was immensely proud of his martial ancestors and in early life spoke of emulating their glorious deeds. The experience of real war between 1675 and 1679 cured him of this and left him a keen militarist, who developed his armed forces to the maximum efficiency, but who knew the uncertainties of war and always sought to avoid it. His acceptance of physical violence was unquestioning and his disregard of personal safety total. The king's conduct during the war was consistent with his behaviour in the hunting field; he instinctively sought out the heaviest fighting and plunged into it.

There is little evidence about the king's inner personality; he was a very private man. His one hobby and indulgence was a passion for horses. This caused a rare example of him patronizing the arts when he commissioned the Court painter, D. K. Ehrenstrahl, to paint his favourite animals in a series running from 1673 to 1689.[22] Haqvin Spegel, a royal chaplain, noted how in February 1676, when the war was going badly, the king took a day off with his horses, 'so as to have some little relaxation after a whole week of great and persistent troubles'. It was the Italian traveller, L. Magalotti, who noticed how the king was a changed man on a horse.

The king looks like a person who is embarrassed and nervous about everything. He seems as if he did not dare look anyone in the eye, and he moves all the time as if he were treading on ice. When he sits on a horse, he seems an entirely different person, and then he really looks like a king . . . is lively in expression and freed from all the oppression that sometimes hangs over him indoors.[23]

There is general contemporary agreement that the king had no social graces. When he paid a visit to his mother's appartments he would retire again without speaking to her court ladies; when he heard that a delegation was coming from Stockholm magistracy to present their compliments, the king left the castle hastily by a back door. Feuquières found him difficult to talk to, though the king's inability to speak French cannot have helped: 'il ne s'ouvre guère, et les conversations se passent ordinairement en termes généraux' ('he never begins conversation and usually it is carried on in generalities'). One critical source asserted that 'il est même incapable de répondre avec quelque élégance aux compliments qu'on lui fait' ('he is even incapable of responding gracefully to the compliments he is paid'). It is a matter of record that he did not make public speeches on ceremonial occasions.[24] It seems a

---

[21] A Fryxell, ed., *Handlingar rörande Sveriges historia ur utrikes arkiver samlade*, 4 vols. (Stockholm, 1836–43), I, Jens Juel to the king of Denmark 17 Sept. 1674, p. 303.

[22] R. Josephson, 'Karl XI och Karl XII som esteter', *KFÅ* (1947), p. 16; S. Hildebrand, ed., *Haqvin Spegels Dagbok* (Stockholm, 1923), p. 8.

[23] Sjögren, *Karl den elfte*, p. 96.

[24] Correspondence diplomatique: vol. 63, Feuquières to Louis XIV 20 Mar. 1680, p. 215; vol. 64, Feuqières to Louis XIV 22 Jan. 1681, p. 44.

reasonable deduction that Charles XI found verbal contact with other people difficult. This could be one cause of his occasional, terrifying outbursts of rage; the stories that he physically assaulted ministers and advisers cannot be verified, but the anger could be an expression of the frustration of a man who found self-expression difficult.

One piece of evidence about the king's inner world is the diary that he kept, an entirely private record that suggests he could not even talk to himself. The *Almanack* is a source of frustration to historians. The entry on the battle of Lund, in December 1676, one of the most significant events of the king's life, first noted the date and that it was a Monday and then added a religious platitude: 'through God's assistance we had a fortunate victory over the Danes . . . let God be eternally honoured and thanked for it'. The entry for his wedding in May 1680 runs: 'the 6, which was a Thursday, I was at Skottorp and met the Princess and the same day my wedding took place. On the 8 we came here to Halmstad.' In the year 1685, the king experienced the loss of three infant sons in succession. In each case the diary records the date, the day of the week, the time of day and adds the formula: 'it pleased almighty God to call to Himself out of this transitory world into eternity my dear son'. The *Almanack* only comes to life recording trivialities, particularly his own travels, where the exact distance and the time taken were meticulously recorded and whether this established a new record for the distance. The *Almanack* suggests a mind that never reflected independently on the world but responded to experience in internalized platitudes. Scholars will tend to deplore the narrowness and lack of imagination, the total absence of intellectual curiosity in Charles XI, yet it may be that his conventional and clichéd ideas served him well in the position to which he had been called.

The king's world view was built on the one part of his education that was wholly successful, his indoctrination into Lutheran piety. This was the work of his tutor, Bishop Olav Svebilius. The evidence of the king's unremitting performance of his religious duties, the early morning prayers and bible reading, the regular attendance at public services, his lifelong desire to compel his subjects to follow the same godly lifestyle, his utter absence of doubt about his religious belief is abundant. There was nothing spiritual in Charles XI's faith, he summed it up in the *Almanack* on the centenary of the adoption of the Augsburg Confession in Sweden in 1693. 'Let God be eternally praised, who has allowed us to enjoy His saving Word, pure and clear in this hundred years. Lord God, favour us, Sweden's children, that we may keep this, his pure Word until the end of the World.' For Charles XI, God presided over the creation which was moving towards its predestined end. God had given men an explicit set of rules in Scripture which were to be followed unswervingly, and would bring them to salvation if rightly observed. The actual world was transitory and without value, a testing ground for believers which if negotiated successfully prepared men for a future of eternal bliss with God. The duty of kings and magistrates was set an example of godly behaviour and enforce it on the subjects. This enables the historian to deal briefly with the king's sex life – he did not have one. None of the reports linking Charles XI with various females can be substantiated. The evidence on the other side is clear: he sowed no wild oats in youth; the hostile author of the *Anecdotes* wrote: 'On n'a jamais aii dire qu'il eust aucun penchant à la galanterie, et un de ses domestiques, qui a couché seize ans dans sa chambre, m'a juré qu'il n'avoit jamais connu d'autre femme que la Reine' ('It has never been said that he has any inclination to gallantry, and one of his servants, who had slept in his bedroom for sixteen years, swore to me he had never had intercourse with any woman except the queen'). A diplomat reported: 'I believe he would rather spend the night with a veteran Major General than the most beautiful woman in the capital.' The king did his duty; he showed towards women, especially his mother and his wife, the affection and respect required by God's law and he kept his wife constantly pregnant. That was the story of Charles XI's relations with women; he took a functional view of sex, it was for procreation, otherwise it was sin.[25]

Charles XI's world view was one of simple black and white certainties derived from his Lutheran upbringing. Papists were by definition corrupt and untrustworthy. Louis XIV and the whole French nation were unreliable, for if they perceived some worldly advantage, 'they would become Turks, for his conduct in recent times is little better'. Calvinists, though they counted as Evangelical, were almost as bad and the king wholly supported the refusal of his clergy to grant them more than the most grudging toleration. The Lutheran Evangelical religion embraced the whole of God's truth and any deviation from it was destructive and subversive.[26]

It was on this rock of faith that Charles XI constructed his conception of his kingly function. It is easy simply to label this as absolutist. A sermon by Andreas Nohrmoraeus, which the king ordered to be printed in 1673, stressed the duty of absolute obedience; God and the king stood together, 'two great monarchs', and the subject who 'does not obey Your word in that you command us, he shall die'. This seems clear enough, yet the Swedes had a model of a true absolutism over the water in Denmark and they repudiated it. In 1658 the king's father had told the Council that Danish practices were not suited for Sweden, while Charles XI wrote to Nils Bielke in 1687: 'in no way do I conduct myself according to what the king of Denmark does in his kingdom, but I will have a free hand to command in my kingdom, just as he does'. Charles XI's view rested on the concept of hereditary kingship as a trust from God. His personal salvation lay in the conscientious fulfilment of that trust and it was an eternal, not a personal glory that he sought. In a rare letter in his own hand he wrote to Bielke in 1687:

[25] S. Hildebrand, ed., *Karl XIs Almanacksanteckningar: från original ånyo utgivna* (Stockholm, 1918), pp. 9, 68, 105, 106, 110, 260; Anon., *Anecdotes de Suède*, p. 194; Sjögren, *Karl den elfte*, p. 95.

[26] O. Malmström, *Nils Bielke såsom generalguvernör i Pommern 1687–1697* (Lund, 1896), p. 20; O. Malmström, ed., 'Karl XIs bref till Nils Bielke', *Historiska Handlingar*, 18, no. 2 (Stockholm, 1900), p. 76.

I desire nothing more here in the world than to get a blessed relief from this wearisome world, since after all everything done here is vain, for which I pray daily to God, at the same time to set the kingdom entrusted to me from God in the condition, that my successors and loyal subjects may have from it enjoyment and security.

This was not an isolated expression; when he was seriously ill in 1679 the king told Spegel that because of his youth it was assumed 'that I shall desire to live longer, but because of sin and evil I have long been weary of life and am long assured out of God's word of a more glorious and better one'. In 1672 he declared, through de la Gardie, that no deserving subject who approached the throne should go away uncomforted or unhelped. In order to realize this ideal, God had conferred supreme power on the king. When, in 1674, the senior High Court – the *Svea hovrätt* – protested at a royal order to submit its judgements to review, the king reminded them that their authority derived from him and he would never yield 'the right and superiority to be the supreme judge, which belongs to Us alone'. The point was repeated in 1676 when the Danes published an intercepted letter from Louis XIV, which said: 'le gouvernement de Suède soit sur le point de prendre une autre forme' ('the government of Sweden is about to take a new form'), by which 'ce jeune prince . . . se rende maître absolu de la conduite de son état' ('this young prince will make himself absolute master of the direction of his state'). Charles XI issued a declaration, denying any intention to innovate, but said the supreme power was from God, 'through whose grace we exercise the government of the kingdom, after our forefathers, kings of Sweden'. When his Palatine relative, Duke Adolf, claimed personal exemption from the reduktion laws in respect of his Swedish properties, he was told this was unacceptable because of the king's supremacy, the fundamental laws of Sweden and 'also jura communia gentium et regnorum which do not tolerate a state within a state'.[27] Charles XI had learned from his education the essence of hereditary kingship, which was that the final power of decision and judgement within the kingdom was vested in the ruler personally, by the grace of God, and could not be challenged. This was not because of any personal merit of the ruler, but, because he could not discharge his trust to defend the security and welfare of all his subjects without it. If this reading of the king's thinking is correct it is necessary to re-examine the proposition that after 1680 Sweden was changed from a power-sharing constitution to one based on royal absolutism. The king believed no such change was needed; the kind of transformation that had happened

---

[27] C. E. Normann, *Prästerskapet och den karolinska enväldet: studier över det svenska prästerskapets statsuppfattning under stormaktstidens slutskede* (Lund, 1948), p. 219; L. Thanner, '1680-års statsförklaring', *Historiskt arkiv 11* (Lund, 1961), p. 61; Malmström, ed., 'Karl XIs bref', pp. 24, 35; Loenbom, ed., *Handlingar*, I, collection II, Spegel to G. O. Stenbock 26 Mar. 1679, pp. 67–70; Sjögren, *Karl den elfte*, p. 104; S. Lindegård, *Consistorium regni och frågan om kyrklig överstyrelse: en studie i den svenska kyrkoförfattnings teori och praxis 1571–1686* (Lund, 1957), p. 222; E. Ingers, *Erik Lindschöld: biografisk studie* (Lund, 1908), p. 194; G. Barudio, *Absolutismus – Zerstörung der 'Libertären Verfassung': studien zur 'Karolinscher Eingewalt' in Schweden zwischen 1680 und 1693* (Wiesbaden, 1976), p. 45; UUB, N884, Nordiska Samlingen, Charles XI to Duke Adolf, 6 Feb. 1685.

in Denmark in 1660 was not needed, for in Sweden the king's absolute authority was fully established and grounded in Swedish law and custom. The Diet of 1672, which deliberately refused to consider imposing legal restrictions on the powers of the new king, suggests most of his subjects shared his view and those Council magnates who sought to promote limitations were an unpopular and discredited faction.

The king's assumption of the government in 1672 appeared to make little difference, for de la Gardie retained his confidence and was left in charge of policy. The king indulged his taste for hunting and war games. His immediate entourage was still dominated by critics of de la Gardie and the regency, but this did not stop the king issuing a formal discharge to the regents in 1672, freeing them from any further accounting in the most comprehensive terms. The king was the natural focus for malcontents who wanted change, but he was making no commitments. During this period, however, several men destined to play a major role in the reign were coming to the king's attention. Most came from magnate families, like Count Bengt Oxenstierna, a rising diplomat already identified by Feuquières as anti-French, 'il n'y a un meilleur espagnol en toute Castille' ('there is not a better Spaniard in all Castile'), or Carl Sparre, a rising soldier. Others were outsiders; the most important was the arrival of the promoted commoner, Erik Lindschöld, who became a Chancery secretary, and was an articulate advocate of absolutism. The foreign mercenary, Rutger von Ascheberg, later acknowledged by Charles as his principal tutor in war, was establishing his position, and promoted his commoner friend Erik Dahlberg, a gifted polymath, who was to become the king's expert on fortifications. But despite the intensity of the factional manoeuvring around the king, nothing significant developed.

This fact supports the argument that the later developments of the reign were not part of a preconceived design, already formed in 1672, but were driven by the problems exposed when Sweden became involved in war. De la Gardie's policy, which was to accept French subsidies, but avoid hostilities in order to play a part as mediator, broke down when Louis XIV, faced with war with the Empire, required Sweden to mobilize a deterrent force in Pomerania. An army was mobilized under the aged Field Marshal Wrangel but the effort exposed the deterioration of Sweden's military capacity since 1660. Even with French subsidies the army could not be maintained in Pomerania and in 1675 moved into Brandenburg to live off occupied territory. During the summer it suffered defeat at the hands of the Great Elector at Fehrbellin and the Swedish position fell apart. It had been sustained by the myth of Swedish invincibility. Fehrbellin was the signal for all Sweden's enemies to fall on her, except the Russians who were otherwise occupied. Denmark led by declaring war and was supported by the United Provinces. Dutch naval squadrons joined the Danes and swept the Swedish navy from the seas. That meant the German provinces were lost, the emperor declared war and authorized Brandenburg and Brunswick-Lüneburg to sequester them. With loss of naval control,

Denmark was able to invade the lost province of Skåne, where her troops were received as liberators by much of the populace. In face of Danish regulars and peasant guerrillas, the Swedish defenders had to withdraw. The military disasters of 1675 were the making of Charles XI's kingship. He was turned from a naive adolescent into a mature warrior king. He had left Stockholm to take personal command of the army and established a headquarters at Ljungby in the far south, which became the seat of the wartime government. War suited the king; he had able professional advice and was a natural fighter, and after years of playing war games relished the reality. The turning point was the battle of Lund in December 1676 where the Danish field army suffered decisive defeat and retired into its fortified bases for the rest of the war. The king spent the battle in the thick of the fighting and emerged with a new image in the eyes of his subjects, a true hero-king in the manner of his ancestors and the saviour of the Fatherland. Enjoyment of war could have been the ruin of Charles XI, but his religion steadied him. Spegel noted that he was never bloodthirsty and after 1679 his desire to avoid war in future was a driving force of his foreign policy. Religion also sustained him in defeat. In June 1676, at the lowest point of the war when the Swedish navy had suffered shattering defeat, he wrote to de la Gardie:

We accept . . . with humility God's decree in the disasters, which We and Our arms have so far encountered . . . However We take heart from them because they proceed from the all powerful hand, which can reverse them as quickly as He has despatched them to us, and therefore in a humble confidence in the Highest and the justice of our cause, courage and our hands must not be lowered.[28]

During the war Sweden had two centres of government, geographically far apart. At Ljungby were the king, his military commanders and most of the Chancery secretariat. In Stockholm were the Council, the governing Colleges and the financiers, men like Joel Gripenberg, who farmed the taxes and advanced loans and provided the cash flow that sustained the war effort. It soon became apparent that the real power was at Ljungby. An extensive literature, contemporary and modern, has debated whether this situation arose from an absolutist plot to eliminate magnate power, or was a pragmatic response to the demands of war. The disasters of 1675–6 shocked the whole community and led to a search for scapegoats. At the Diet of 1675 there was a concerted effort to put the blame on de la Gardie and the regency. The critics were vocal in the Estates of the Nobility, the Clergy and the Burghers, and were supported from within the Council by dissidents like Johan Gyllenstierna, Sten Bielke and Claes Rålamb. The Estates asked

---

[28] O. Varenius, *Räfsten med Karl XIs förmyndarstyrelse*, 2 vols. (Uppsala, 1901–3), I, pp. 44–7; Sjödell, *Kungamakt*, pp. 110–15; A. A. Etienne-Gallois, ed., *Lettres inédites des Feuquières tirées des papiers de famille de madame la duchesse Décazes*, 5 vols. (Paris, 1845–64), III, Feuquières to Pomponne 19 Sept. 1674, p. 42; J. Helander, *Haqvin Spegel: hans lif och gärning intill år 1693* (Uppsala, 1899), p. 39; E. Hildebrand and C. Grimberg, *Ur källorna till Sveriges historia under nyare tiden*, I: *1520–1721* (Stockholm, 1911), p. 184.

for a full investigation into the financial administration of the regency. De la Gardie opposed and at first had the support of the king who disliked the idea of the Estates having access to Council records. But the king shifted his position during the Diet and a royal commission was issued on 12 October 1675 for an investigating committee of the Estates, 'in consideration of the weak condition which at present is being experienced everywhere'.[29] This signalled that the king had aligned himself with the position that the Council magnates were answerable for the current disasters. The magnates were now defenceless against a populist attack, from which only the king could save them. A key factor in the king's position was his growing frustration with the poor administrative performance of de la Gardie and the now demoralized and divided Council. At the end of the Diet, the king returned to Ljungby and instructed the Council members to stay in Stockholm.

The next major development was a summons to Johan Gyllenstierna, a fierce and longstanding critic of the regency, to come to Ljungby. The royal letter of 6 July 1676 said he was needed because 'We now, especially in Our present circumstances, need you near to Us so that you can serve Us much better with your well known loyalty, prudence, diligence and commitment to furthering the best for Us and the kingdom.' Gyllenstierna was an enigmatic man, characterized by ruthless energy and a forceful, even brutal personality. Once established at Ljungby he dominated the administration and was recognized as chief minister. There is little evidence of personal warmth between the king and Gyllenstierna, but their political cooperation was intimate and Gyllenstierna was the dominant partner. A Danish diplomat summarized the relationship in 1680:

The king found in him great enthusiasm for his service, good outcomes from his advice, firmness in his projects, so that what he set out to do, he would seek to bring to a conclusion by any means, was disinterested in all his actions . . . In military affairs, where the king himself will keep control, he always listened to him, and nothing happened without his advice . . . he had general disposition over internal affairs and nothing was done unless he approved.

Gyllenstierna's rise widened the gulf between the king and the Council, signalled by the king's growing enthusiasm for the regency investigation. By October 1676 the king asserted: 'before the matter is resolved there will have to be a legal tribunal'. He was now thinking in terms of calling the regency government to account.[30]

In May 1677 the Council tried to reassert its authority by writing to the king and reminding him of his obligation to govern with the advice of the Council. Gyllenstierna felt it expedient to yield and a delegation from the Council was invited to Ljungby for conferences at which the whole range of policies was debated. The

---

[29] Varenius, *Räfsten*, pp. 139–56.
[30] Hildebrand and Grimberg, *Källorna*, p. 184; O. Malmström, *Anteckningar rörande drottning Ulrika Eleonora D.Ä. och Karl XIs hof* (Lund, 1898), p. 51; Varenius, *Räfsten*, p. 91.

king formally accepted the Council's advice to summon a Diet in 1678. This proved to be a misjudgement by the Council magnates, for the Diet which met at Halmstad gave no comfort to Gyllenstierna's critics. The Estates were united in support of a final Resolution which the king undertook to implement and which clearly fore-shadowed the agenda of 1680. The Estates wanted full, even extended, application of the 1655 reduktion, 'without any consideration of who may be involved'. They called for a speedy conclusion of the investigation into the regency. The most significant discussion was in the Riddarhus, where Gyllenstierna's brother-in-law, Mauritz Posse, and Claes Fleming, an embittered enemy of the magnates, rallied the lesser nobility in support of further reduktion policies. They argued that the donations of crown properties had been monopolized by a few magnate families, while working officers and civil servants struggled on with their salaries unpaid, and while the whole nobility had to surrender its tax exemptions to fill the deficits. The Resolution of the Halmstad Diet showed that if Charles XI chose to implement a radical reform of the public finances, by recovering from the magnates their alleged depredations from the public revenues, and beyond that to enforce an extended reduktion, he could count on the full support of the commoner Estates and substantial support in the Estate of the Nobility.[31]

By late 1678 the war in Europe was ending and Sweden's conflicts were the main problem unresolved. The Danish attempt to recover Skåne had failed, but in Germany all Sweden's possessions were lost, and with the navy destroyed there was no way they could be recovered. Fortunately for Charles XI, Louis XIV was prepared to insist on the restitution of nearly all Sweden's losses, partly out of a sense of obligation to an ally, partly out of a calculation that Sweden's presence south of Baltic could still be useful, partly to show Europe that France was the arbiter of its affairs. The French king knew that Charles XI was a difficult client. He wrote to Feuquières in January 1679: 'ce prince ne peut attendre de moi que des choses possibles' ('this prince cannot expect more from me than what is possible'); he would do his best and the king could be assured 'que la conservation de ses intérêts ne m'est pas moins chère que celles des miens propres' ('the preservation of his interests is no less dear to me than of my own'). Louis then made agreements with Brunswick-Lüneburg for the restitution of Bremen-Verden, with a small cession of territory, undertaking that Sweden would agree. This patronising position infuriated Charles XI and was compounded when he did the same with Brandenburg to secure the return of Pomerania. Even the peace with Denmark, which Gyllenstierna negotiated on the basis of the status quo ante, was in fact secured by Louis XIV who issued a formal declaration in August 1679 that he expected a settlement based on total restitution. But the worst offence had occurred in May 1679 when Louis XIV ordered that the subsidy money be paid directly to the Swedish commander in Livland. This was the supreme insult, to pay Charles'

[31] Rystad, *Rådet och kungamakten*, pp. 163–9, 171–3, 179, 182; Loenbom, ed., *Handlingar*, III, collection VIII, pp. 45–61; IV collection XI, p. 33.

own subjects over his head. Feuquières was told the French action 'lui ferait préjudiciable à sa rèputation parmi les étrangers qui le jugerait incapable de gouverner ses propres affaires, et lui ferait perdre le respect de ses sujets, principalement les gens de guerre, qui s'attachent toujours à celui qui les paie' ('would damage his reputation with the foreigners who would judge him incapable of controlling his own affairs, and would lose him the respect of his subjects, above all the military, who always adhere to the one who pays them'). By the end of 1679 Sweden had settled with all her enemies, although the United Provinces was demanding a commercial agreement that both the king and Gyllenstierna regarded as too harsh, and for the moment the king withheld ratification. The emperor was willing to settle for the status quo ante.[32] Charles XI's dissatisfaction with the peace settlements imprinted on him two attitudes which underlay all his subsequent policies. The specific was a growing personal dislike of Louis XIV, which led him to reconsider Sweden's traditional alliance with France. The general was a determination that Sweden should never again find herself in humiliating dependency on a foreign power. He resolved to make Sweden strong enough to pursue her own, independent policies and to this end any sacrifices would be justified.

With the end of hostilities the interest of both contemporaries and historians fixed on the projects of Gyllenstierna, who continued to enjoy the confidence of Charles XI until his unexpected death in June 1680. Contemporary testimony agreed that the king would do nothing without Gyllenstierna's advice, and that when Gyllenstierna was absent the king avoided contact both with the diplomats and his own subjects.[33] The problem for both contemporaries and historians is then to discern what Gyllenstierna's policies were, for he was a man fond of trying out ideas on others, and on his record was a pragmatist and perhaps an adventurer. Feuquières was baffled: 'Jean Gullenstiern m'en a parlè, mais confusement à son ordinaire avec un mélange de deux milles choses, vraisemblables et fausses, parmi lesquelles il est si difficile de trouver la vérité' ('John Gyllenstierna spoke to me, but confusedly, as he usually does, with a mixture of two thousand topics, credible and false, among which it is difficult to find the truth'). There was wild speculation, with at one extreme the conspiracy theories, found in Rålamb's writings and the *Anecdotes*, that he was intending to get rid of king, while building up a personal power base in Skåne, where he was Governor General. There is no supporting evidence for this. Feuquières had a more widely accepted view that 'le dessin principal de Gullenstierna est de rendre son roi absolu' ('Gyllenstierna's main intention is to make his king absolute'). But there is little clear indication of this either. It is established that during December 1679 there was a series of conferences at Ljungby, with Gyllenstierna, a team of Chamber officers led by his brother Göran, the secretaries and the Admiral, Hans Wachtmeister, participating. As

---

[32] Gallois, ed., *Lettres inédites*, IV, Louis XIV to Feuquières, pp. 278, 283, 311, 377; Correspondance diplomatique: vol. 61, p. 83; vol. 63, p. 245.

[33] Correspondance diplomatique: vol. 63, pp. 124, 134, 135, 361; Malmström, *Ulrika Eleanora*, p. 51.

there is no surviving record of these, it can only be surmised that they discussed the post-war situation and decided to raise financial resources by a penal tribunal on the regency magnates and an enlargement of the reduktion, and that these would be spent on restoring Sweden's military capabilities; this after all is what did happen. Feuquières reported there was an actual plan signed by the king: 'j'apprends, Sire, qu'il a fait signer au roi le projet de tous les changements qu'il a fait dans toute la royaume' ('I am told, Sire, that he has got the king to sign a schedule of all the changes which he has made in the entire kingdom'). If there ever was such a document it has vanished without trace. When Gyllenstierna died the king ordered Erik Dahlberg to secure his archive, 'since it is especially important for Us that his writings and papers may be secured . . . immediately sealed and kept in safety'. But although Dahlberg obeyed, these papers too have vanished. So Gyllenstierna's intentions remain enigmatic.[34]

There is one significant episode on record from January 1680. In that month the marriage treaty with the Danish princess Ulrika Eleonora was concluded, and Secretary Örnstedt reported this to the Treasurer. The Treasurer states that 'I replied that the Council could do no less, in all humility than to remonstrate if they have something to say, particularly since it says that it is concluded with the advice of the Council of State.' So the Council wrote to the king with their observations on the treaty. The king sent a severe response: 'We do not remember having . . . committed the matter to you to discuss', and accused them of seeking to dictate to him. The Council hastily denied any such intention and regretted that their intervention was 'ungraciously received'. They did remind the king that their action was consistent with their oath of office, and the king's coronation oath, 'that their Excellencies may remonstrate humbly, unasked, about what they know the welfare and prosperity of the kingdom demands'. The Council was indeed stating an established legal and constitutional position and clearly perceived a tendency in the king to override this. But they did not venture to pursue their claim in face of the king's expressed displeasure. This showed that the king had nothing to fear from the Council magnates: they did not like what was happening but they had no stomach for a confrontation with the king.[35] There is one further, known facet of Gyllenstierna's plans. They involved a radical foreign policy shift based on alliance and collaboration between Sweden and Denmark. There is some indication that Charles XI had reservations over this, but he went along with the treaty of alliance and cooperation that was negotiated by Gyllenstierna in Copenhagen and the marriage that was part of it. The problem for the historians is to understand what Gyllenstierna expected of this alliance. He knew as well as anyone the animosities and distrust between the two kingdoms that made any genuine partnership between

---

[34] Correspondance diplomatique: vol. 63, pp. 118, 239, 314, 361; KB, Rålambska Manuskriptsamlingen: Fol. Nr. 5: 1680 års riksdagsärenden, chapter 6; Anon., *Anecdotes de Suède*, pp. 152–63; UUB, E470, Kongl. brev till Greve Erik Dahlberg, 16, 25, 27 June 1680.

[35] RA, Rådsprotokoll 1680, vol. 72, Lillieflycht, 10, 12, 31 Jan. 1680.

them improbable in the longer term. The idea of the two Scandinavian kingdoms presenting a common front against all third parties, to their mutual advantage, was attractive in principle but unworkable in practice. Yet Gyllenstierna wrote of dictating the terms of Baltic trade to the United Provinces, or pursuing joint expansion of their joint interests in northern Germany. The selling point with the king may have been that reported by Feuquières, that the policy would 'délivrer le roi son maître de la nécessité de s'engager à aucune alliance par la consideration d'un subside' ('free the king his master from the need to enter into any alliance for the sake of a subsidy').[36] This had now become one of the fixed principles of the king's view of foreign policy. In the end Gyllenstierna's foreign policy designs remain as impenetrable as the domestic programme. What is certain is that when he died in June 1680 he was never replaced by any other chief minister; henceforth Charles XI took charge of the whole range of policy making.

[36] G. Landberg, *Johan Gyllenstiernas nordiska förbundspolitik i belysning av den skandinaviska diplomatierns traditioner* (Uppsala, 1935), pp. 121–8, 134; Correspondance diplomatique: vol. 63, p. 232.

3

The defining of the absolute monarchy

Traces of preparations for holding a Diet can be found from January 1680, but the first clear evidence came on 30 June when the Council was asked whether it should be called in the autumn or postponed. Since the Council of State was the only power base of a potential opposition, which might wish to influence the timing and the agenda, this could have been a risky procedure. But the Council showed no desire to seize the initiative, Rålamb, one of the king's most consistent critics, recommended referring a decision back to the king: 'no one can know better than the king himself if the business can bear any delay'. The Council recognized that the financial situation was dire and in the end resolved unanimously to recommend calling the Diet for 1 October. That summer Stockholm was full of rumours that there would be an absolutist coup when the Diet met; the ambassadors picked them up and there was a lively pamphlet war. One supposed dialogue between a foreigner and a Swede began: 'Does not your king wish to be wholly absolute? – It may well happen if he has several years. – It will be difficult for him to master this task – He will be helped by every honest Swedish man.' Juel reported to Denmark that the commoner Estates 'intend to offer the king the sovereignty at the coming Diet'. Yet there is no conclusive evidence for any coup plan. Reports of unusual troop movements near the capital cannot be substantiated; it was true that three potential dissidents, Rålamb, L. Sperling and H. Falkenberg, were given overseas postings at the end of 1679, which would keep them away, but the appointments themselves were reasonable ones. Feuquières, who was an assiduous reporter of gossip, decided at last that there was no plan and told Louis XIV they must wait and see, noting that Charles XI 'fulmine contre ceux qui disent qu'il veut changer la forme du gouvernement' ('storms against those who say he wants to change the form of government').[1]

A Swedish Diet was not an open forum for debate. It met in response to the royal summons to advise the king on a set agenda, the Propositions. Each Estate discussed these by itself and then worked out a consensus with the other Estates, which when confirmed by the king, became the Resolution of the Diet. It was an

[1] RA, Rådsprotokoll 1680, vol. 72, Lillieflycht, 30 June 1680; UUB, N897, Handlingar till Sveriges politiska historia 1677–80, *Veritas odium*; Correspondance diplomatique: vol. 61, pp. 415, 424; Fryxell, ed., *Handlingar*, I, pp. 393–4, 400; J. Rosen, 'Johan Gyllernstiernas program för 1680 års riksdag', *Scandia* 16 (1944), p. 163.

unresolved question whether, if three Estates outvoted a fourth, that would constitute a binding consensus. The crown had the initiative in setting the agenda and had two powerful means of shaping the responses. It appointed the Marshal of the Nobility, who presided over the Riddarhus, and became *ex officio* chairman of the Secret Committee. This was a body of delegates from three Estates, since the Peasants were excluded. It had been set up to handle confidential foreign policy discussions, but since 1660 began to consider the domestic agenda too. The Secret Committee got a more detailed agenda, the Secret Propositions, and was the main forum where the consensus was forged, prior to consideration and confirmation in plenary sessions of the Estates. Normally the king chose the delegates to the Secret Committee and in 1680 he had selected the Marshal and the delegates in advance. The Marshal was Claes Fleming, a young member of a major magnate family which had been consistently critical of the regency government. On the other hand the Council of State was in attendance in the Diet, available for consultation by the Estates and actively involved in framing the Resolution. The Council was a potential rallying point for opposition, but little dissent was expected to the royal programme set out in the Propositions, which on the domestic side consisted of four points:[2]

1 How could the security of the kingdom be secured for the future?
2 How could the navy be strengthened?
3 How could the land forces be strengthened?
4 How could the problem of supply be met?

This programme contained no hint of constitutional change, which suggests the royal government did not see that as an issue, however hot the discussion might be in the salons and taverns of Stockholm. In 1680 it is difficult to identify who the principal royal policy directors were. The servicing of the Diet was in the hands of the secretaries and the chancery officials, but decision making had to be referred back to the king, who was resident in the Castle in close proximity to the meeting places of the Estates. It is clear that the king and his floor managers were in constant contact, and in the Riddarhus, besides the Marshal, the two leaders were the Wachtmeister brothers, Hans and Axel, currently the king's close companions. A letter of 23 October noted: 'his Majesty is in the Castle all week, until Saturday evening when he travels to Jakobsdal and has no one in the coach with him but the Wachtmeisters'.[3] The proposal for a massive rebuilding of the armed forces was unlikely to be opposed by anyone after the wartime experience, and nobody did. It did not say where the money would come from, but everyone knew, since the ground had been gone over in the Diets of 1675 and 1678. There would be a Tribunal to recover the alleged financial malversations of the regency. This would

---

[2] *SRARP*, XIII, p. 255.
[3] Rosen, 'Johan Gyllenstiernas program', p. 164.

focus on the leading magnate families and in one blow should recover large sums of money, while paralysing the victims politically, since once condemned their only hope of mitigation would be to seek the protection of the king. Secondly there would be an extension of the reduktion beyond the limits set in 1655.

One advantage of this agenda was that the king would not need to be directly involved; he could stand aside and let it happen. The Estates had been pressing for the Tribunal since 1675; a Commission had been investigating and its report was ready in 1680. Nobody would rally to defend the discredited oligarchs of the regency. Reduktion was a more complex issue. The commoners had every reason to support it, they did not have any donations and could expect their taxes to be reduced. The nobility had a difficult calculation to make. As always the bulk of the donations were held by the magnate families, but there was a numerous group below them who had enjoyed small grants from the crown. And there was a major threat beyond that. Nobody knew precisely what properties had once belonged to the crown, and a general inquisition into titles could have unforeseeable consequences and weaken property rights. Even a poor nobleman might worry about that. On the other hand a majority of noblemen were in crown service, mostly in the armed forces, and they could expect improved career prospects and the regular payment of their salaries, something that had not happened in living memory. That was why numerous noblemen would be prepared to work with the commoners to carry an extended reduktion in the Diet.

The Propositions were read on 5 October and business began. The Marshal told the Riddarhus the basis of the programme. 'We must be thinking of such resources as can put the kingdom in the position that it can subsist of itself, and rather find its security within itself than with others.' This can be taken to encapsulate what Charles XI was aiming to do after 1679. Hans Wachtmeister steered the discussion towards a Tribunal and asserted that it would recover so much wealth 'that no, or very little taxation will be needed thereafter'. This was a delusion, and if Wachtmeister knew that, it was a cynical deception. But he was a career naval officer, not a politician; indeed 1680 was his only appearance as a political leader. He could easily have believed it. The Riddarhus listened to him because they knew he was a man close to the king. The Commission report was given to the Secret Committee and the Estates quickly agreed to ask the king for a Tribunal. This caused a debate in the Riddarhus where Wachtmeister assumed the remit of the Tribunal would be to assess penalties on men already found guilty. A group, led by the magnate P. Sparre, wanted a proper legal process allowing the accused to defend themselves. Tempers rose until one of Sparre's supporters claimed threats were being uttered that those who opposed 'will be noted to the king and Wachtmeister'. His faction did not bother to deny it. On 15 October the king wrote to the Estates that he approved of a Tribunal and each Estate should appoint members to it.

This alarmed some in the Riddarhus who, like most of the commoners, wanted the king to appoint the judges and assume responsibility for condemning some of the greatest families in the kingdom. The king wanted to involve the whole community in the process. Sparre tried to reopen the question, but the Marshal insisted they could not vote because the king had decided: 'how can we vote on that which the king has commanded?' This makes clear why Charles XI did not need any constitutional change in 1680. In the minds of his subjects, even the most exalted, the express command of the king could not be questioned. Sparre's challenge was futile. The Estates therefore agreed to establish a Tribunal – the Great Commission – composed of delegates from each Estate, with the remit of assessing and enforcing the penalties due from those responsible for government under the regency. The first item in the crown's agenda had been secured.[4]

The second item, to establish the budget so that income would cover expenditure, was more difficult. The matter was under discussion in the Council from 15 October, where proposals aimed at limiting any extension of the reduktion were considered. But the main forum was the Secret Committee. The Secret Committee minutes for 1680 are lost, but the diary of a clergy delegate for 17 October recorded that 'we began a discussion in the Secret Committee about means for making good the budget'. If the Committee had been intended to get a solution, then by 20 October it had failed; the diary entry for that day says the members agreed to adjourn to their own Estates.[5] The reason was that the Peasant Estate had taken the initiative and proposed reviving the full reduktion programme of 1650. Since there are neither minutes nor any other record for the Peasant Estate the origins of the initiative remain obscure. Historians have generally assumed that the chancery officials who provided the secretarial services to the Estate had prompted it, but the Peasants themselves undoubtedly supported the proposal. On 15 October they had gone to the Burghers and called for a united approach by the commoners. By 19 October the Clergy had joined the discussions, but while the Burghers were immediately supportive, the Clergy had reservations; the archbishop told the Burghers the Clergy agreed in principle but needed time to discuss the implications.[6] The Riddarhus was discussing budgetary possibilities, apparently ignorant of what the commoners were doing until Carl Gyllencreutz raised the alarm in the Secret Committee and urged the nobility to forestall the attack. He had realized the full danger in the proposal, 'there are few properties which have not at one time or another been in the hands of the crown and there will be almost no family in Sweden which will not suffer seriously through this'. He suggested the major recipients of donations should offer voluntary surrender of part of their properties. On 23 October the Clergy yielded to pressure and agreed, reluctantly, to join the Peasants and the Burghers in a joint letter to the king urging a full reduktion of all donations. The Council now recommended to the Nobility that they should

[4] *SRARP*, XIII, pp. 3, 6, 15, 19, 33, 35–40.
[5] RA, R 5956, Riksdag-journal, 1680, af Erik Benzelius, 17, 20 Oct. 1680.
[6] UUB, N879, Anon. riksdag-dagbok, 1680, 15, 20, 22, 23 Oct. 1680; RA, R 5956, 18, 19, 20, 21, 23 Oct. 1680.

publicly justify their position, and went to the king to protest at the move of the commoners. The king side-stepped this by saying he left it to the Council and the Riddarhus to resolve what was best for them. The Marshal reported this response to the Riddarhus, where Sparre and his supporters led a vigorous denunciation of the commoners for an attack on the privileges of the Nobility and persuaded the Riddarhus to start drafting a formal protest.[7]

The royal policy was blocked as long as the dispute between the Estates continued. This deadlock was broken in a dramatic session of the Riddarhus on 29 October. Hans Wachtmeister had a new proposal which he had clearly discussed with the king, but it was obvious that the Marshal had not been informed so that he and Wachtmeister were working at odds. This created chaos in the Riddarhus. The Estate began discussing its remonstrance against the commoners. Wachtmeister attacked this as futile; the commoners had acted in the public interest and what the Nobility must do was to forestall them by a proposal of its own. They should accept reduktion in principle, but petition the king to give relief to the poorer benefici-aries, so that those 'who have not got much and could perhaps have 10 to 20 or a few hundred silver dalers income, might keep it'. It was a blatant invitation to the Class III nobles to break ranks. It succeeded; Sparre and his supporters urged the need to safeguard their privileges, claimed the commoner proposal infringed the royal prerogative and said in any case it was out of order, since in the Propositions, 'the king says nothing about reduktion and there can be no proposition except from the king'. The noisy argument exposed the underlying tensions within the Nobility; one group shouted, 'the poor have done most and have to pay contributions, but the great and the rich, who have made away with the country's property, they have done nothing'. Conrad Gyllenstierna asserted: 'all serve without pay, and a few sit around and enjoy the kingdom's lands'. They began to argue about whether or how to vote: Wachtmeister tried to claim that on an issue that concerned the welfare of the whole kingdom, voting was improper and they should proceed by acclamation. Others called for a formal vote by Classes and others for a ballot of individuals. It then emerged they did not have a valid motion, since only the Marshal could frame a proposal and he had not done so. In the arguments Reutercrantz wanted Wachtmeister's proposal written into the minute, as coming from the king and specifying an exemption of 600 dsm. income from the general reduktion. Wach-tmeister agreed, saying: 'my speech can be a proposition'. The Marshal had completely lost control of the proceedings, vainly trying to read out the standing orders and at last the Classes separated to deliberate. Class III announced that they supported a general reduktion and then Axel Wachtmeister claimed that Class II concurred, though immediately two of its members, Ulf Bonde and Axel Ståhlarm, challenged this and claimed they had not known what was being proposed. Class I

---

[7] *SRARP*, XIII, pp. 55–8, 287, Almogens skrifvelse, 295; *PR*, IV, pp. 21, 24–6, 26–9, 30; UUB, E491, Handlingar till Sveriges politiska historia 1680–6, Gyllencreutz's speech to the Secret Committee 21 Oct. 1680; RA, Rådsprotokoll, vol. 72, Lillieflycht, 22 Oct. 1680.

was polarized round Sparre and Wachtmeister, and eventually Wachtmeister announced that those who supported him should gather round and go up to the king. Sparre responded that his group would also go up to the king and they walked out, ignoring the Marshal's pleas to return. The Marshal then ruled that it seemed the Riddarhus had approved a general reduktion in principle and they appointed a committee to draft a specific proposal.[8]

In this manner the reduktion was approved, though the proceedings in the Riddarhus were certainly irregular and disorderly and were arguably invalid. Even so it looks as though once the Nobility had split, the commoner proposal was unstoppable, which was why the king himself had been able to stand aloof. Sparre was right; the king had made no proposition, only insisted the budget must be balanced, and the Marshal remarked on 29 October that nobody had advanced any viable alternative way of achieving this. When Sparre and his group got to the king, they had already given in for they said that what they had objected to was being coerced by the other Classes, when they had been prepared to make a voluntary surrender of their donations. The king seized the opening; he was sure that everyone had been acting for the best and now urged the nobility to show moderation and unity, 'so that the king shall not be troubled with making decisions'. The king managed to make it appear that the reduktion had not been his policy but the free choice of his subjects.[9]

At this point the Council, which remained opposed to reduktion, had its last chance to try to prevent it. The Riddarhus followed convention in deciding to ask the Council for its opinion on what it was proposing. Sparre certainly clung to the hope that the Council might have an alternative proposal, 'which would work better, so that the king's intentions would be satisfied'. The Council did have such a proposal, but decided to suppress it when they met the Riddarhus since it would do them no good with the king if they succeeded in making the nobility reconsider. They met a Riddarhus delegation on 2 November and lectured them on their disorderly conduct and solemnly urged that in future they adhere strictly to the rules of procedure. But they did agree to remonstrate directly to the king about 'the many bad consequences that could follow', as Gustav Sparre put it. These were legal and constitutional; principally the commoners' attack on the privileges of the nobility was an infringement of the king's authority, and that the granting of donations was an exclusive royal prerogative and the Estates had no competence over it. Thus the Council avoided attacking the principle of reduktion itself. Sten Bielke led the Council to speak to the king and they received a sharp rebuff. The king replied: 'It is only with astonishment that I perceive the Council wishes to advise me on that which all four Estates have approved, and I have promised to support them in it, and how should it be safe for me to do anything contrary to what the four Estates have advised?' Bielke hastily affirmed that the Council had had no

---

[8] *SRARP*, XIII, pp. 65–77.
[9] *Ibid.*, p. 80.

thought of being divisive, and the king replied: 'so I have not understood correctly, and that is good'. The Council's intervention had failed completely. Since the Riddarhus continued to press the Council for its opinion on the reduktion decision itself, the Council did issue a petulant response, pointing out that their advice had only been sought after the decision was made. 'The Council had been of a quite different opinion. We wish with all our heart that what is resolved and decided will tend to the honour of God, the power and service of the king, the welfare of our dear fatherland.'[10] In this way the Council squandered its opportunity to intervene effectively after the confusion of 29 October. It seems clear that the members, although opposed to what was being done, lacked the will or the intention to lead a resistance to it.

The Riddarhus worked out its reduktion proposal on 4 and 5 November. It fell short of the full reduktion demanded by the commoners. Crown donations to sustain the titled nobility were recalled unconditionally. All other donations made since 1632 were liable to recall, subject to the reservation that holders could retain up to 600 dsm. annual revenue. Finally this settlement was to be definitive and permanent. The commoner Estates were unhappy at the limitations; for a time the Peasants were threatening to refuse to sign the Diet Resolution, but it became the agreed decision. But when the Riddarhus proposed to pursue their protest at the commoners' attack on their privileges, they got a message from the king, through the Marshal, to drop it; the king wanted no further argument on the subject.[11]

The Diet then proceeded to its formal close without further incident, but in a manner that demonstrated the underlying strength of royal authority. If the Estates hoped that they had done enough the king was quick to disabuse them. He needed supplementary taxation as well. When the Marshal informed the Riddarhus, 'there was like a brief silence in the chamber'. But there was no word of protest and a committee was set up to consider means. The Burghers were told that the king needed a grant double that of 1678 and 'unanimously declared their humble willingness to support the common good'. The archbishop had told the Clergy on 17 November that despite his pleas of poverty the king needed a grant and he recommended submission. There was talk of sending a deputation to the king but nothing came of it. They calculated it was wiser to agree; Master Grubb remarked: 'I agree to keep the king's favour, however burdensome it may be.'[12] The Diet of 1680 showed how secure the king's control of his kingdom was. A few hints and guiding words from him had sufficed to steer the programme through the Diet. The controversies which did arise were within Estates and between Estates. The king could preside over them as an impartial umpire. The Diet was formally ended with the ceremonial entry of the queen into Stockholm and her coronation.

---

[10] RA, Rådsprotokoll, vol. 73, Wattrang, 3, 4 Nov. 1680; *SRARP*, XIII, pp. 97, 321.
[11] *SRARP*, XIII, pp. 102, 118, 121.
[12] *Ibid.*, p. 126; Stadshistorisk Institut, *Borgarståndets Riksdagsprotokoll före Frihetstiden* (Uppsala, 1933), p. 208; *PR*, IV, pp. 84, 86.

It was followed by an apparently unplanned epilogue which produced the first formal constitutional declaration of the reign. The Regency Tribunal, consisting of thirty-six members drawn equally from the four Estates, was starting work and had issued citations to the members of the regency after 1660, or in most cases, their heirs. But they also cited the Council of State collectively, since by the terms of the Additament, the regency had been bound to seek the advice of the Council. The Council refused absolutely to accept the citation. On 6 December the Marshal told the Estates that the king required them to remain in Stockholm and resolve this issue. The Riddarhus adjourned after a long discussion which showed the members were baffled. So a conference was held between delegates of three Estates, excluding the Peasants, and the Council. The Council asserted that it had no responsibility for the actions of the regency, but even if it did, different members had taken part in different decisions and they could not be accused collectively. Further, 'since the Council of State is a separate Estate, like the other Estates in the kingdom . . . it is not at all reasonable that the whole body of the Senate shall stand answerable for what only concerns a few'. The following day was given over to several meetings in which general confusion prevailed, but some participants showed a desire to raise basic constitutional questions. In the Riddarhus R. Lichton, for no apparent reason, asked if, since the Additament specified that the government must take the advice of the Council, the same applied under a reigning king, and could the Estates overturn what a king had resolved, citing the breaking of Charles X Gustav's Testament in 1660. Hans Wachtmeister surprisingly thought that had been all right; in 1660 authority had rested in the Estates. Sometimes kings were expected to consult the Estates, at others not. At this point the secretary lost track of the discussion, noting they were so discursive and uttered so many different opinions, 'that I could not catch any more'.

The confusion was resolved during 8 December by the king posing some specific questions to the Estates. The Marshal had conferred with him the previous evening and the king had framed his questions, either because he felt there were genuine uncertainties about the limits of royal authority, or because he perceived an opening for asserting a basic constitutional principle. The Marshal put the questions first to the Riddarhus. Was the king bound by the Form of Government? This caused no problem; it had been stated in the Additament that it applied only during a regency. Then, was the Council a separate Estate, alongside the other four Estates? The Marshal said: 'the king thinks there are only four Estates in the realm'. Nobody disagreed with that, especially after Wachtmeister suggested that as an Estate, the Council might claim to be mediator between the king and the subjects and 'one would hope no mediators are needed between the king and the Estates'. The core issue was what the Land Law meant to say when it said that the king governs with the advice of the Council. The Marshal set out what was presumably the king's position: 'the king certainly uses the advice of the Council, but the decision remains with the king'. Wachtmeister put in a cryptic comment here: 'not in every case, for the Estates also have authority'. He made two similar comments later, when Sparre said sometimes the king consulted the Council, sometimes not, but it did not matter since in either case the decision was the king's. Wachtmeister objected: 'in some things the king must hear them'. And when the Marshal suggested that they petition the king to draw up a Testament now and lay down directions for a regency, Wachtmeister said: 'but it must be agreeable with Sweden's laws'.[13] It is apparent that in the open discussion there was no confrontation between absolutists and Council constitutionalists. The speakers were genuinely uncertain; they spoke in platitudes and, like Wachtmeister, seem to have been bouncing ideas off one another to see how they sounded. There were no real disagreements and when the Marshal went to the Burghers and Clergy he could report a consensus in the Riddarhus that, 'since the king is sworn to the law and the privileges, so the king cannot be bound to anything else'. As for the advice of the Council, 'this must be understood, that the Council of State may well express their opinions and thinking in matters which his royal Majesty pleases and finds necessary to propose to them, but the decision and the execution of it remains with the king alone'. Neither the archbishop nor O. Thegner, for the Burghers, raised any objection to this.[14]

A consensus was reached in the Estates which was published on 12 December as *The Declaration of the Estates*, formally accepted by the king. This stated 'that your royal Majesty, as an adult king who rules the kingdom according to law and lawful custom, as your own hereditary kingdom granted by God, is solely responsible to God for your actions'. It went on to deal with the issues raised by the king and affirmed that the Form of Government had no force in the reign of an adult king; that the Council was not an Estate of the realm, nor a mediator between king and subjects; and that the king took the advice of the Council as he saw fit, but the final power of decision rested with the king alone. It can be argued that the *Declaration* of 1680 made no substantial difference. What it said about the status of hereditary, Christian princes was a platitude that would have been accepted in most parts of early modern Europe. The specific points concerning Sweden are at least plausible interpretations of the existing law. The key issue about the advice of the council developed from the ambiguity of the Land Law. This had never specified that in taking the advice of the Council, the king must do so in every case, much less that the advice was binding. On the other hand the Councillor's oath in the Land Law required the Council to proffer advice unasked if the Council believed that the welfare of the kingdom required it. The *Declaration* did not exclude this possibility, though saying that the king takes advice as he sees fit would seem to discourage it.[15]

The *Declaration* was sent to the Council in a letter from the king and although this did not call for an answer the members agreed with de la Gardie that 'it would

---

[13] RA, Rådsprotokoll, vol. 72, 4 Dec. 1680; *SRARP*, xiii, pp. 206, 207, 220, 225–31.
[14] *SRARP*, xiii, pp. 231–5.
[15] *Ibid.*, p. 374.

be damaging for the Council to stay silent and make no answer'. So they debated it at length on 22 and 29 December. There were long discursive discussions, not fully minuted, and the overwhelming impression left by them is of the reluctance of the Council members to enter into confrontation. The one issue that preoccupied them was the obligation in their oath. They accepted all the other points, even that the king was not bound by their advice. But the oath seemed inescapable. Bielke put their dilemma clearly: 'the Council stands as between two fires in that the Estates do not free them from their oath, and so they must humbly remonstrate what belongs to his Majesty's service, even if it were not pleasing to the king, it will at least please God'. They could not agree on an answer on 22 December and got no further on 29 December. G. O. Stenbock wondered if the *Declaration* had not released them, since it purported to be a clarification of the Law and 'it stands in our power, together with the Estates to make new law and interpret previous constitutions'. But others, like Knut Kurk, were not persuaded. In the end they did not make any reply to, or comment on, the *Declaration.*[16] In all these discussions the real constitutional issue was never mentioned. It is necessary to go to the private papers of Rålamb to find this discussed. He saw precisely the issue raised by the *Declaration.* 'The authority of the Council, which had been the other foundation on which the kingdom's rights and the Estates' liberties had previously been secured, was overturned and broken.' He realized that the Land Law had given the Council a share with the king in governing the kingdom, through the requirement to take the Council's advice. When the *Declaration* reduced this requirement to an option to consult, it eliminated the one institution empowered to question publicly the king's conduct of the government. Most contemporaries either failed to see this, or were unconcerned because they saw the episode as political, not constitutional. The issue was not whether Charles XI was a king with unrestricted power to rule his kingdom; nobody doubted that, provided he ruled according to law. The issue in December 1680 was whether members of the Council could use their constitutional position to block the intended working of the Regency Tribunal and this was still unresolved.[17]

By the end of the Diet in 1680 observers could see that Charles XI had now taken personal control of the government. A contemporary wrote: 'the king goes on as before, with his great sword at his side, dressed as in the camp. He is undisturbed by all dangers which surround him and does all that he does on his own. Only a few have access to his person and there is no one who has power over his mind.' His habit at this time was to spend as much time as possible in the country, mostly at Kungsör, and to forbid anyone, ambassadors or suitors or officials, to follow him there. He secluded himself with his immediate helpers and made irregular visits to Stockholm to move things forward in the capital. The main concern was the reconstruction of the armed forces. Hans Wachtmeister, after his brief foray into

---

[16] RA, Rådsprotokoll, vol. 72, 22, 29 Dec. 1680.
[17] F. F. Carlson, *Sveriges historia under konungarna af Pfalziske huset*, 7 vols. (Stockholm, 1855–89), II, pp. 175–7; KB, Rålambska Manuskriptsamlingen: Fol. Nr. 5: 1680 års riksdagsärenden, ch. 3.

politics, spend the rest of the reign working on the navy, rebuilding it and establishing it in a new southern base, built on a greenfield site to be called Karlskrona. The main army appointment was held by Ascheberg, appointed Governor General in Skåne on the death of Gyllenstierna. He was a man with his own ideas and had been empowered to depart from Gyllenstierna's plans, 'to review all that, as you may judge necessary for Us and the kingdom, according to changing times'. The king himself took direct charge of most military administration. This deprived the War College, under G. Baner, of most of its functions; he noted: 'there remains here in the College nothing left'. The king ruled that all regimental colonels reported directly to himself and their cashiers answered directly to the Chamber. The king personally handled all appointments, promotions and dismissals. The College was not abolished; in December 1680 it got new regulations. Baner became President of the reduced institution; P. Sparre, for all his role in the Diet, remained Master of the Artillery; two crown officials, Secretary Hoghusen and B. Gyllenhoff were assigned to maintain a skeleton collegiate structure but all real autonomy had ended. The central tool of the king's policies was budgetary control. On 11 December 1680 the king ordered the Treasurer, Sten Bielke, to set up a Budget Office – *Statskontoret* – linked to the Chamber, but under an independent Commissioner of the Budget. It would control all public revenue and expenditure by drafting an annual budget, which the king would sign each year. This would then become mandatory, not to be exceeded in any circumstances and binding on the king himself. If the king issued an order contrary to the budget it was void: 'the king's Majesty will himself in no way exceed its dispositions'. The budget became the king's ultimate assurance of complete overall control.[18]

The next priority was revenue enhancement. Two initiatives were launched for this. The first was the Reduktion Commission. This had been appointed in the Riddarhus to execute the new reduktion law. It was dominated by committed Class III nobles like U. Bonde, Jakob Fleming, Erik Lindschöld and Jakob Gyllenborg, with the previous Marshal, Claes Fleming, as President. Its remit was to identify and recover the properties covered by the new law. It was naively supposed this could be completed by the end of 1681; in reality the task was still unfinished at the king's death in 1697. The second initiative, whose activity dominated the years 1681–2, was the Tribunal. The idea was to raise very large sums of money by convicting the members of the regency government of large-scale misuse of public funds. That was why, to make the returns worthwhile, it was necessary to involve not just the members of the government, but the Council of State as well, and possibly officials of the Colleges who had given advice. The process should fatally

[18] Carlson, *Historia*, II, p. 193; UUB, E472, Kongl. brev till Fältmarskalken Rutger von Ascheberg 1656–90, the king to Ascheberg, 13 July 1680; B. Steckzen, *Krigskollegii historia*, I: *1630–1697* (Stockholm, 1930), pp. 460, 463, 464, 468–71; N. Eden, *Kammarkollegiets historia: från Gustav Vasa till Karl XIIs död 1539–1718* (Stockholm, 1941), pp. 137–9; C. G. Styffe, ed., *Samling af instructioner görande den civila förvaltningen i Sverige och Finland* (Stockholm, 1856), pp. 124–8.

undermine the political, economic and social power of the magnate families. The Council had shown no willingness to defend its political status but members put up a prolonged defence of their property, starting by the refusal to recognize the competence of the Tribunal, which had precipitated the events of December. The original idea was to issue a general indictment of the government and the Council and to require the individuals involved (or their heirs, since many were dead by 1681) to respond to it. By March 1681, the king, guided by Fleming, accepted they must issue individual indictments, specifying what each must answer for. At first the Tribunal was slow; there were members who were unenthusiastic about the whole process, but in May the king ordered the issue of indictments and appointed the zealous J. Gyllenborg as prosecutor. In a general observation the Tribunal ruled that between 1660 and 1672 there had been no reason why the official budget was exceeded and put the excess at 12 million dsm., equivalent to about three years' normal revenue. This was then apportioned between some sixty individuals or their heirs. By 27 May 1682 this process was complete and the king discharged the Tribunal with a personal letter of thanks to the thirty-six deputies who had served on it. The obvious tactic for the accused was to submit and seek to negotiate a favourable personal settlement. J. G. Stenbock had led the way in this, closely followed by Bielke and Bengt Oxenstierna, but this was a complex bargaining process and it was 1689 before most of the deals were concluded.[19]

Some Council members had continued to resist the indictments on the grounds of their status as councillors and by the autumn of 1681 Charles XI seems to have seen this as a challenge to his authority and he determined to reduce the Council to its proper position in government. He made it known that he now wanted a formal reply by the Council to the *Declaration*. On 6 October 1681, Oxenstierna, now Chancery President and chairman of the Council, recalled that in December a few of them had drafted and signed a letter from the Council to the king accepting the *Declaration*. The text was of humiliating submissiveness and concluded with an undertaking to deserve the king's confidence and 'with faithfulness and loyalty in dutiful submission perform what befits an honest Council member and is owing to your royal Majesty and the kingdom'. Oxenstierna suggested to his colleagues that they all sign this, 'unless some of them were perhaps of a different opinion'. Four more members agreed at once but two, Knut Kurk and Gustav Sparre, refused. They were bullied into submission by threats of legal proceedings. Then in December came the first appointments to the Council for many years, Claes Fleming, Ascheberg, Hans Wachtmeister and Christopher Gyllenstierna. Even so relations with the king remained uneasy; the Council ventured to complain that it had not been consulted on a new treaty with the United Provinces and got this crushing response from the king: 'I shall let all the world know that you do not have

---

[19] Carlson, *Historia*, II, pp. 196, 216, 220, 231, 248; R. Blomdahl, *Förmyndarräfstens huvudskede: en studie i Stora Kommissionens historia*, 2 vols. (Stockholm, 1963), pp. 182, 205, 230; H. Schück, 'Karl XI och förmyndarräfsten', *HT* 84 (1964), pp. 276–9.

the smallest share in my power, and you are my Council, which I can consult or not at my will.'[20]

During the beginning of 1682 the issue between king and Council was finally resolved. The indictments of the Tribunal showed Council members how grave their danger was, while the new members indicated the king wished to change the title from 'Council of State' to 'King's Council'. An exchange of letters in February brought a full submission. On 28 February, the Council apologized for not making clear that their status as described in the Land Law had been modified in consequence of the Reformation and the institution of hereditary kingship. The change of name became official. In March the king ordered the cessation of public prayer for the Council of State; hereafter it was to be called 'Our Council, since between Us and the kingdom there is no separate or special interest, but there is a union, which in itself is completely inseparable and can in no way be divided or distinguished'. This absolutist rhetoric finally snuffed out any idea of an independent Council that shared sovereign power with the king. As the Tribunal indictments were finalized they were used to complete the process of neutering the Council. Fleming hinted to Council members that if they confessed their guilt and offered to retire, the king might mitigate the penalties. A draft letter was presented, recognizing the justice of the indictment and concluding: 'therefore I beg that mercy may go before justice and that I may be allowed to spend my remaining years in the country'. This enabled the king to reconstitute the new King's Council. The four recent appointees were joined by the Justiciar, de la Gardie, the Admiral, the Treasurer and four other members of the old Council, Oxenstierna, Stenbock, Lars Fleming and Göran Gyllenstierna, all active in royal service. The other eight retired and went out of public life. It must be said they were cheated, for when they did seek mitigation of their penalties the king regretted he 'could in no way discharge them from repaying the sums, to which they have been condemned by the Tribunal'. Thereafter Charles XI steadily recruited the Council, which developed an active role in the machinery of government.[21]

It was decided to convene the Diet for October 1682. The new vigour of royal government was shown in the careful advance preparations. Royal letters indicated members of the Estate of Peasants whose presence the king required, a sign of the active role the Estate was to play in the Diet. The Council was given a role, but was uncertain of its position, for when the king asked for comments on the Secret Propositions, they sent Oxenstierna to the king to ask 'that the king will instruct the Council what it is the king wishes the Council to undertake'. They were taking no chances. The most obvious innovation of the 1682 Diet was the way all business was worked out in the Secret Committee and then referred to the full Estates for

[20] RA, Rådsprotokoll, vol. 73, Wattrang, 6 Oct. 1681, 7 Dec. 1681; Carlson, *Historia*, II, pp. 334, 342–6; H. A. Olsson, 'Ständernas förklaring år 1682 rörande lagstiftningen', *KFÅ* (1971),p. 65; RA, Lagkommission 1686–1736: protokol: the Council to the king 28 Feb. 1681, the king to the bishops 11 Mar. 1682.   [21] Sjögren, *Karl den elfte*, pp. 319, 321.

what was intended to be formal ratification. The Committee members were carefully chosen, and the king required that for some business the Peasants should join it. The Marshal, Fabian Wrede, was a reliable and experienced royal official, and was seconded in the Riddarhus by the Secretary Erik Lindschöld and R. Lichton as floor leaders. This Diet also had a special role for O. Thegner, the Burgomaster of Stockholm, who had the job of coordinating the commoner Estates when they were needed to put pressure on the nobility.[22] The agenda contained in the Secret Propositions was to ratify the work of the Tribunal, to make arrangements for providing the manpower for the reformed military establishment, to find further long-term funding to balance the budget and reduce the debt and to grant short-term, extraordinary taxation to meet urgent current needs. The Riddarhus was understandably nervous in light of what had happened in 1680. Per Sparre, Carl Oxenstierna and the lawyer Anders Lilliehöök headed a group critical of some aspects of the agenda. They tried to take preemptive action at the beginning by asking the Marshal for assurances that Secret Committee decisions could be discussed in plenary meetings, that the standing orders would apply and that ballot voting would be used where appropriate, while Lilliehöök suggested that the minute should omit the names of the speakers. Wrede assured them everything would be done in due order.[23]

Army recruiting was taken first; it was announced that the king meant to form the infantry into territorial regiments of 1,200 men based on a particular province. The Secret Committee was asked the best way to recruit these and options emerged: either the Estates give the king open-ended authority to conscript the necessary men, or the king could negotiate contracts with the peasantry in each province, whereby peasant farms would club together and undertake the permanent provision of a soldier, in return for the permanent abolition of conscription. For this proposal to work all peasants would have to take part on an equal footing. This was denounced by the nobility as an attack on a basic privilege: the right of their tenants to lower rates of taxation and liability to conscription than crown and tax peasants. Further under conscription the nobleman decided who should go, which was a powerful disciplinary weapon. The issue was referred back to the Peasant Estate and the Riddarhus. When debate opened in the latter on 16 October, the Secret Committee delegates had already talked to the Council, who recommended: 'leave it to the king's own discretion to hold conscriptions without calling the Diet'. It emerged that everyone preferred conscription, but some realized that the need for it was a main reason for assembling Diets, and suggested the grant of discretion for a limited period, preferring four years. A member said: 'it was not so good to abandon the calling of the Estates altogether'. Some Class III nobles retorted that for them Diets were an expense they could not

---

[22] *Handlingar rörande skandinaviens historia*, 40 vols. (Stockholm, 1816–60), XXIX, p. 231; *Handlingar rörande Sveriges historia*, 3rd series, new edn, vol. XI (Stockholm, 1983), p. 206; Carlson, *Hitoria*, III, pp. 5–11. [23] *SRARP*, XIV, pp. 11–12.

afford, and they would be glad to give the king a free hand. There were calls for a ballot vote, but the Marshal insisted instead that those in favour of a time-limited grant stand up and be counted. Since no one did, he declared the Riddarhus had agreed to unlimited conscriptions. At the same time, after consultation with the king, Thegner was organizing the commoners. Their three Estates declared in support of the contract system, with tenants of the nobility contributing equally. When a delegation of the Peasants came to the Riddarhus the Marshal challenged them whether they were proposing to override the privilege of the nobility and they replied that in choosing the contract 'we are conforming to the king's Majesty's wishes'. This compelled the Riddarhus to reconsider, and they resolved to leave it to the king to choose the option he preferred. But they also drafted a protest to the king at the commoners' infringement of their privilege. However, they did not put individual names to it, and when the Marshal took it to the king he looked it over, 'and when he saw it was unsigned, the king expressed himself in some ungracious terms' and advised the Marshal to tell the Riddarhus not to send any more anonymous memoranda. In this first round, the king had demonstrated his mastery, the Nobility had exposed their divisions and their unwillingness to confront the king and they had been easily outmanoeuvred by Thegner.[24]

The pattern was repeated over raising fresh resources to reduce the debt. Thegner and the archbishop worked together and got the king's authorization for the Peasants to send a delegation to the Secret Committee. On 31 October, Thegner, 'in a beautiful speech', introduced the eleven-point programme which the commoners had worked out, as though the Peasants had devised it. It called for the vigorous pursuit of those condemned by the Tribunal and a further extension of the reduktion, including the abolition of the 600 dsm. exemption of 1680. In the Secret Committee, the nobility 'expressed great passion' at this and demanded an adjournment while their Estate discussed it. The discussion in the Riddarhus opened on 4 November, and the king sent a warning. They had intended to go into committee, where discussion was unminuted, but the Marshal announced the king wanted the debate in plenary session. They began a prolonged debate on the commoner programme and the key issue became whether they should insist on the legal force of the Diet Resolution of 1680, which had confirmed the reservation and laid down there would be no further reduktion proposals. Carl Oxenstierna led the group which advocated this; Lindschöld and Lichton argued it was dangerous: 'we must not argue with the king'. On 13 November the Marshal brought a message from the king: the Riddarhus must decide and he wanted a roll-call vote to see who supported what. The Marshal advised them they could safeguard their interests better by compliance than by standing on their legal rights, and Oxenstierna

---

[24] J. H. Liden, ed., *Handlingar om Riksdagen 1682* (Norrköping, 1788), Diary of Erik Duraeus, pp. 14, 17–18, 23; *SRARP*, XIV, pp. 16, 23–5, 27, 44.

conceded defeat, 'since we perceive it is the king's will', then any reference to the Resolution of 1680 should be left out.[25]

The king had won the immediate issue, but decided to exploit it for further gain. On 13 November the Estates were informed that the king perceived that the commoners and the nobility differed over how far a king could make donations or recall them so he presented questions to the Secret Committee. The main point was whether a king had a general power to make donations and recall them 'without the consent and voluntary agreement of the Estates in general, any Estate in particular or any individual beneficiary', and cited the Land Law in support of the view that he had. This set off a round of discussions within and between the Estates, and between the Nobility and the Council. Thegner had no difficulty uniting the commoners in full support of the king. This position contained the paradox that a king could make a grant in perpetuity, but it would be as much subject to recall as any other. The Nobility and the Council wanted to establish that a king could make a valid grant in perpetuity, but could find no support for this in the Land Law, and decided they must acknowledge the king's powers were unlimited, but added a petition that the king would remember the need to conserve his nobility so that they could do him service. On 17 November the king was handed two replies, one from the commoners and one from the Nobility. He asked whether there was a difference and the Marshal said it was just a matter of wording, but Thegner asserted 'the difference was not just in the wording, but was real enough'. The drafts were sufficiently close for the king to accept both, and combine them in his own final resolution which confirmed there were no limits on the king's power, but did not say that grants in perpetuity were always void, only noted it was the wish of the Estates that they should not be made. The king had now completely unblocked the reduktion process; he could pursue it as far as found expedient. The Nobility had been outflanked on two sides, by the king and by Thegner, and had wisely given in, and it must be said that although the Land Law had its ambiguities, it does seem to say that the royal patrimony is inalienable and can only be granted out conditionally. Even so, the Nobility had some grounds for feeling they had been cheated when the 1680 settlement, supposedly definitive, collapsed about them. It was natural they sought revenge and pointed out that the Clergy and the Burghers had endowments which were equally liable to reduktion. The Secret Committee erupted into mutual recrimination, but it came to nothing. Bishop Carlson told the Clergy 'that we should not answer the Nobility'; the king had let it be known he did not wish the argument to continue and it was dropped. The king went on to a further demonstration of his predominance. When the Estates came to consider the Proposition about extraordinary taxation, which was in principle a free gift from the subject, the king told the Secret Committee, through the Marshal, exactly how much each Estate must give. He said: 'the king had said that the Estates will not get

---

[25] Liden, ed., *Riksdagen 1682*, pp. 33, 35; *SRARP*, XIV, pp. 51, 77–9; Carlson, *Historia*, III, pp. 56–7.

away from here before they produce the sum'. In the end they did, quarrelling acrimoniously among themselves what each should contribute, but never thinking for a moment that they might simply have said no.[26]

The most dramatic episode of the Diet of 1682, which occasioned a major constitutional shift, seems to have occurred by accident and stands out in a session that was otherwise planned and controlled. In the Riddarhus debate of 4 November on the commoner programme, Anders Lilliehöök, an experienced lawyer and crown official, queried the rules being applied by the officers enforcing the existing reduktion. He asked if they had ever been referred to a Diet. On being told not, but that they had been in regular use for twenty years past, he burst out: 'God preserve us from the precedent: if they are a law, they should be adopted with the consent of the Estates: otherwise it is no law.' Lilliehöök, for no obvious reason, had challenged head on a vital royal prerogative. Somebody, presumably the Marshal, reported the speech to the king, who took it very much to heart as a direct criticism of the sovereign by one of his subjects. On 7 November the king sent a message to the Riddarhus and demanded answers to seven questions about Lilliehöök's speech. The questions left no doubt what the expected answers should be. The king regarded the speech 'as a great presumptuousness and an attack on his rights and authority'. He asked whether Lilliehöök spoke for himself, or acted in concert with others, whether the Riddarhus agreed with the speech and whether the Riddarhus claimed a right to discuss retrospectively 'that which the king has done and approved, or if anyone has the intention to tie the king's hands, so that the king may not make laws and regulations in his kingdom . . . and that they are invalid without the Estates?' This went to the heart of the constitution and asked was the king in any sense answerable to his subjects for what he had done and could they restrain him? The expression 'to tie the king's hands' or its analogue, to 'prescribe' to the king, were central to Swedish political discourse. Both were absolute tabus. The point was reinforced in the sixth question, whether any subject had the right to judge the king's power, 'where it is used to the honour of God's name, and the profit and best interest of the kingdom'. The final question asked if anyone had the right to question how the law was applied and 'either mislead others with superfluous memoranda, or anger the king with improper reproaches'. He concluded by asserting the king's actions were solely for 'the general security and welfare of the kingdom, which is the only thing the king seeks and intends, not the advantage of one, or a few, but of all'.[27]

The Diet, for the questions went to the commoner Estates as well, was confronted with a basic question about its power in relation to the king. Did they wish to assert that they had the right, to any extent, to constrain the king's actions? And did they as the representatives of the community claim the right, assigned to them in the Land Law, to share the legislative power with the king? The Riddarhus was constrained;

---

[26] Carlson, *Historia*, III, pp. 77–83; Liden, ed., *Riksdagen 1682*, pp. 44, 51, 62–4, 93; *SRARP*, XIV, pp. 80, 108, 109, 110, 131, 134, 236, 239.
[27] *SRARP*, XIV, pp. 49, 52, 53–5, 62, 227, 239; Carlson, *Historia*, III, pp. 70–1.

already attempts to vote by ballot had been blocked by royal intervention. Most of them seem to have accepted a survival strategy of seeking royal protection to preserve their preeminence in society, rather than to assert their legal rights. Still it is difficult to accept that if a majority of the Riddarhus had wanted to defend Lilliehöök on the ground that he was only stating their clear right to share in law making, they could have done so. The debate showed that no such will existed. The spokesmen for all three Classes competed in condemning the speech, only some in Class I ventured to say in exculpation 'that he did it with a good intention'. Ståhlarm ventured to assert that 'we know Hr Lilliehöök for an honest man'. On the question whether a subject could judge the acts of his sovereign, P. Sparre, the critic of 1680, declared: 'it is the kind of question which horrifies; he would be a scoundrel who had such ideas'. The minute adds: 'everyone was of the same opinion'. On the question of participation in legislation, it was clear that the Riddarhus wanted to claim a voice, and they eagerly took up Lindschöld's formula that Lilliehöök had been talking about administrative rules applying only to a few. 'But if it had been a general law, it should have been communicated to the Estates.' The Secretary could be assumed to reflect the king's thinking and a committee set to drafting a reply. Lilliehöök was recommended to throw himself on the king's mercy. The committee produced a draft with surprising speed, which has led some historians to suggest the whole episode had been carefully orchestrated, though it is difficult to see how that could be. What is clear is that in committee, Lindschöld's clear distinction between regulations and general laws was so watered down that the right of the Estates to participate in legislation almost vanished. The distinction was retained; the king could issue regulations by virtue of his 'rightful Christian and proper sovereignty' and it would be 'unreasonable' to require they be submitted to the Estates. But if it was a general law, 'like Sweden's law, which is the concern of the whole kingdom and of all the Estates collectively', the king could issue such laws and have them scrutinized by experienced lawyers of his own choosing. But the Estates were confident that, as a gracious king, he would also impart them to the Estates,

in no way so that the Estates may or should prescribe to your royal Majesty, but expect it of your royal Majesty's own gracious pleasure, when and how your royal Majesty finds it good, so that they may have the opportunity, humbly as faithful subjects, to present their general thoughts, without any presumption and without the least detriment to your royal Majesty's right and authority.

They went on to affirm that no subject could judge or limit the king's powers and that the nobility detested such ideas, 'when, where, or by whom' they were expressed. It is difficult to conceive of a more grovelling form of words, even allowing for the extravagances of Baroque style. The Estates' reply was incorporated in the Resolution of the Diet.[28] Lilliehöök came to no harm. After submission

---

[28] Carlson, *Historia*, III, pp. 71–3; *SRARP*, XIV, pp. 63–6, 229.

he was pardoned and within a year was given a senior office: Charles XI did not bear personal grudges against men willing to serve. The episode therefore did not represent a deep ideological divide in Swedish society. The Riddarhus would have wished to claim a share in legislating, but saw no point in contesting the issue, once the king's position was clear. Further, the declaration of the king's rights, however dramatically worded, was in fact cosmetic and had little real repercussion on the world of affairs. It does show that Charles XI had an obsessive concern to assert his sovereignty, whenever it appeared to be challenged, and he showed it again in the last significant episode of the Diet of 1682.

In 1680 the Estates had asked the king to draw up a Testament, to regulate the succession and set rules for a regency. In 1682 the king and Council recommended to the Estates that the succession should follow the male, and then the female, line. In the Riddarhus this was accepted by acclamation. Then the Council and the Secret Committee were informed that the king had drafted a Testament, but were told to send delegations to meet the king, who had discovered in minutes from the Diets of 1660, 1664 and 1672 matter which might impugn the validity of the Testament and he wanted this expunged. Nobody questioned that this must be done. Alongside the negotiations over taxation, delegations from the Council and the Estates began reading the offending material. On 13 December, the king conferred with the delegations and said he wanted a formal statement to be included in the Diet Resolution. Things had been said in 1660 and 1664 'which were not fit for any honest patriot'. The Riddarhus heard next day from Charles X Gustav's secretary what a stickler he had been for legality and how shamefully his Testament had been attacked, while the Marshal affirmed it was essential 'that the arrangements which the king has now made may not be in any uncertainty'. All Classes made abject repudiations of the condemned speeches, and begged the king to blame the individuals and not impute them to the Estate as a whole. A draft was offered for all to subscribe. The Marshal said, pointedly, 'the king will not force anyone to sign'. In fact the pressure was intense; the archbishop told how when he was talking to the king about the criticisms of his father, 'he was aroused to so much passion that the tears began to run from his eyes'. This is a rare account of Charles XI showing emotion, but he was devoted to the memory of the father he had never known. The official declaration ordered that the offensive records be purged, and anyone who spoke publicly about a king in such terms in future would be guilty of sedition.[29]

The actions of the two Diets of 1680 and 1682 had cleared the way for the king's reforms, politically, financially and constitutionally. They affirmed the king's authority as an hereditary, Christian prince and neutralized potential restraints on his freedom of action. Then the most powerful Estate in the realm, the Nobility had exposed themselves to large-scale asset stripping, through the Tribunal and the

---

[29] *SRARP*, XIV, pp. 131, 140, 141, 143–8, 149–52, 159, 161; Carlson, *Historia*, III, pp. 85–8; Liden, ed., *Riksdagen 1682*, pp. 76, 78, 88, 91, 97, 98, 100, 106.

reduktion, that could have brought them to economic ruin. They got little in return except the hope of the king's benevolence and the promise of salaried careers in the royal service. Rålamb had no doubt what had happened. The Nobility had been ruthlessly intimidated by an unholy alliance between the king's entourage and the commoner Estates. He wrote of 1682: 'the Nobility, with the Senate, were so humiliated and discouraged, that nobody could any longer utter a free word'. The king was the tool of his entourage, particularly the Fleming connection, led by Claes Fleming, 'who was then in great credit with the king'. Wrede was his brother-in-law, Thegner was a client of long-standing, the archbishop and his son-in-law, C. Carlson, bishop of Västerås were allies. They had got the king worked up over his father's Testament. Such conspiracy theories do not satisfy, nor is the evidence of bullying and intimidation, solid though it is, enough to explain why a once hegemonic oligarchy surrendered power, almost without a struggle. They were internally divided and open to manipulation, but the reasons must go deeper than that. The root is a loss of confidence. Their period in power had ended in the disasters of the war, their policies had manifestly failed, but they offered nothing credible in their place. Against this there was the young, unchallenged, hereditary king, short on personal charisma, but a proven hero on the battlefield and a vigorous organizer, offering the prospect of a reinvigorated kingdom, with a secure and honourable status among the powers, in consequence of the painful sacrifices he was demanding of all his subjects. It was an unequal contest.[30]

The comments of the Danish minister, H. Meyer, are interesting. He wrote how Charles XI was now powerful in 1682: 'the king is no longer bound by any law, but become sovereign, because he no longer needs the consent of his subjects in the most important matters'. He alleged there had been intimidation: 'in every Estate the debates and meetings are known to the king's secretaries and minuted; in the Riddarhus there is also a guard from the Life Guards, so that no one can speak against'. Yet he remained uncertain about the long-term outcome.

The nobility is unwilling to abandon oligarchy, and all the officers are natives and the Senators interrelated, and thus in hope of taking part in such a government; but if there is a minority, or the king were out of the kingdom, a change could take place. Also, as long as the Diet is not wholly abolished, the one Diet can repeal the resolutions of another.

The structure appeared solid enough, and it was unlikely the king's personal authority would be challenged from any direction, but contingency could still bring the whole structure down, as ultimately it did.[31]

---

[30] KB, Rålambska Manuskriptsamlingen: Fol. Nr. 5: 1680 års riksdagsärenden, III, Angående några särskilta A.80 Åhrs Rikd. Generaliter: ch. 5.

[31] Fryxell, ed., *Handlingar*, II, Meyer to the king of Denmark, pp. 192, 207.

4

The financial reconstruction

The basis of the reforms pursued in Sweden after 1680 was a major reallocation of resources. It was stated in the Propositions put to successive Diets, down to the last of the reign in 1693, that there must be an increase of public revenues and a reduction of the public debt. Two processes were pursued which involved transferring resources from private hands to the public domain. The Regency Tribunal would secure restitution from those identified as having caused losses to the public treasury by their maladministration. The general reduktion of crown properties alienated by donation, mortgage, sale or exchange was authorized within limits in 1680, and without limits when the Diet of 1682 accepted that kings could make donations as they saw fit, but they or their successors could revoke them, if the good of the kingdom required it. These two processes ran parallel, but were legally quite distinct. The Tribunal was seeking a single cash settlement from a small group from the highest levels of Swedish society, the actual members of the regency government and of the Council of State which had advised them, together with the directors of the governing Colleges. It was not a criminal process but the recovery of debts owed to the crown. The aim of the reduktion was to recover properties that had once belonged to the crown, so that they would become additional sources of permanent public revenue. This process could involve most of the noble families in the kingdom, if they had ever acquired such properties. The two processes overlapped in that everyone pursued by the Tribunal was also affected by the reduktion, though the majority of families which lost property under the reduktion were not involved with the Tribunal.

Since the processes were legally distinct they have to be examined separately. The Tribunal – in Swedish, *Stora Kommissionen* – was elected by the four Estates, who were formally responsible for its actions. This got round the problem that in 1672 the king had given a full discharge to the regents. The Form of Government, however, stated that a regency was answerable to the king and to the Estates, so the latter were free to proceed. This signalled, from the very beginning, the dubious legality, to say nothing of the equity, of the whole process. The *Anecdotes* claimed that the Tribunal was carefully selected by the king, despite the elections, and that 'on avoit choisi des gens dont pas un n'avoit assez de scavoir pour se faire les scrupules à l'égard de leur Commission, mais qui étoient seulement propres à suivre aveuglément leurs Ordres et Instructions' ('they had chosen men, none of whom had enough knowledge to develop scruples about their commission, but who were fit only to follow their orders and instructions blindly'). As for the Peasant members, 'ils ne manquoient guere de s'endormir tranquillement pendant qu'on examineroit les Comptes, estant assoupis par les fumées de vin brulé qu'ils avoient eu la précaution de prendre le matin' ('they never failed to sleep peacefully while the accounts were being examined, being drowsy with the fumes of aquavit which they had taken the precaution of drinking in the morning'). This description is viciously partisan, but the Danish minister reported in 1682 that on each verdict the Peasants declared: 'Devil take him, he shall pay.'[1] Rålamb left a more measured judgement on the Tribunal. He asserted that the commoners had been seeking the ruin of the nobility since 1650, and therefore their members were not impartial judges, as the law required. Several noble members were known enemies of the regency and similarly biassed. Therefore the Tribunal was 'against all legal process . . . acting simply on authority, and securing for itself confirmation and approval from higher hands for everything it might undertake'. It was the case that the Tribunal was under constant pressure from the king to maximize the returns, and that Claes Fleming, his closest adviser, had a family grudge against the regent families that had excluded his father from office in 1660. Further, Thegner, a client of Fleming's father, was active in mobilizing commoner support for the process.[2]

The Danish minister reported in October 1681 that Charles XI 'is so busied with the Great Commission' that he had no time to give audiences, and he had no doubts about the justice of the proceedings. When Bengt Oxenstierna put to him the objections that were being voiced, the king replied that neither he nor his advisers

have any other purpose than to put the kingdom and Fatherland in that prosperity, and in that security, which the self-interest and self-will of some people has hindered and set back until now, whereby our enemies profited and the whole country in general, and every honest Swedish man has suffered and been penalised in his honour and well-being.

This is one example of evidence that by 1680 the king was convinced that the regency was responsible for the wartime disasters and was therefore unsparing in pursuit of the defaulters.[3] In reality the Tribunal was not a wholly compliant tool in the king's hands. The commoner members made no difficulties, but some nobles were unhappy, like Axel Ståhlarm and Ulf Bonde, and sought to restrict the scope of its activity. The king had to drive hard from the beginning to enforce rulings that had not been part of the Diet Resolution. It was the king who insisted that the inquest would not be confined to the actual regency government, men who had held

---

[1] Blomdahl, *Huvudskede*, pp. 59–74; Anon., *Anecdotes de Suède*, pp. 178, 179; A. A. von Stiernman, ed., *Alla Riksdagars och Mötens beslut*, 2 vols. (Stockholm, 1729–33), II, p. 1707; Fryxell, ed., *Handlingar*, II Meyer to the king of Denmark, p. 152.

[2] KB, Rålambska Manuskriptsamlingen: Fol. Nr. 5: Book 2, 'Om Stoora Commissionens for-farande . . .', ch. 1.

[3] Fryxell, ed., *Handlingar*, I, p. 470; Loenbom, ed., *Handlingar*, I, collection II, p. 118; Carlson, *Historia*, II, pp. 250, 252.

one of the five great offices of state between 1660 and 1672, but should extend to the members of the Council who had advised them and the executive officers of the Colleges that carried out their orders. This greatly increased the numbers involved and hence the potential returns. It was reinforced by a second ruling that where those responsible were dead, and this was the case with all but two of the regents and many members of the Council, their heirs, as beneficiaries, were responsible for the debts. The justice of this did worry members of the Tribunal, who thought that to pursue the heirs for actions, for which they had no conceivable responsibility, was straining the limits of equity. On 3 February 1681 the king wrote to the Tribunal dismissing such scruples and ordered enforcement of the rule. Without this rule, and with so many of the participants dead, the returns would have been severely restricted.[4]

It was clear from the first that those affected intended to resist; that had caused the attack on the Council by the King at the end of the Diet. Their tactic was to combine refusal to recognize the legality of the Tribunal with a further denial of any collective responsibility. The Tribunal had intended to issue collective charges against the regents, the Council and the Colleges and having asserted responsibility apportion the damages among their members. The Tribunal was loath to get involved in the complexities of making up individual charges. Since the Council stuck to its refusal to accept a collective charge, it fell to the king to make a ruling. He was clearly out of his depth dealing with legal technicalities, and he was vigorously lobbied by all parties, resulting in several changes of mind on his part. The break came in March 1681, when J. G. Stenbock and S. Bielke, who had led the Council in rejecting collective charges, agreed to answer as individuals for their own actions, if the collective charge were dropped.[5] The proceedings then began to move forward erratically, driven by pressure from the king, and delayed by the stubborn defences of the accused and the anxiety of Tribunal members to preserve legal appearances.

The basis for the main charges was that the state budget of 1662 represented a norm that should not have been exceeded. Thus all public expenditure in excess of this budget was chargeable and the Diet Commission had estimated the sum involved was approximately 12 million dsm., and the damages were divided under twenty-seven separate heads. They covered making improper grants, donations, tax exemptions, pensions and gifts. There were also false expense accounts and advantageous debt settlements with the crown. These were covered by twelve of the heads, the clearest being a salary increase of 600 dsm. a year, awarded to the Council by the regents. This would be repayable in full, with interest. Another distinctive item was to classify the international dispute over Bremen in 1665 as an avoidable expenditure, put at 2 million dsm. The last fifteen heads all concerned

---

[4] Carlson, *Historia*, II, pp. 201, 204, 209, 216.
[5] Blomdahl, *Huvudskede*, pp. 175–84, 191–205, 228, 230, 231; Schück, 'Karl XI och förmyndarräfsten', pp. 273–7.

maladministration in the Colleges. The slow progress with pursuing the charges was rooted in the reluctance of the Tribunal's own prosecutors to press them. They sent in a letter on 30 April 1681 protesting that all the evidence had been collected by the Diet Commission, set up in 1675, 'so that not the least part should or can be said to be worked out by us'. This clearly implies that they thought the evidence was unreliable.[6] As the replies to the charges began to come in, it was clear there was wide scope for obstruction, ranging from flat denials to elaborate justifications and the shuffling off of personal responsibility. Some accused replied to the Tribunal, some still challenged its legality and wrote directly to the king. De la Gardie sent in the most detailed and formidable defence. It was weakened by the unconvincing claim that he had never wanted to be a regent, that his offices were 'a general slavery' and that he had gained nothing personally, compared with his sacrifices for the public service. But he went on to expose obvious contradictions; he was accused simultaneously of increasing defence expenditure and neglecting the kingdom's defences. He asserted the figures were quite unrealistic and that in reality the public revenues had not diminished at all under the regency. The unhappy prosecutors, H. Fägerstierna and D. Talas, wrote to the Tribunal that de la Gardie's response was 'a substantial and well-grounded document', and virtually conceded that their evidence was so unsatisfactory that it was unsafe to proceed on it. The Tribunal agreed with them and wrote to the king for guidance. The royal reply was an order to go ahead, and the Tribunal responded with a long adjournment.[7]

The king reacted vigorously to this clear obstruction. He appointed a new prosecutor, Jakob Gyllenborg, who then became the main driving force with the Tribunal. Gyllenborg was an apothecary's son who had made a career in the Chamber, and was ennobled in 1680. He was Thegner's son-in-law and an implacable opponent of the regency magnates. He was a zealous supporter both of the Tribunal proceedings and later of the reduktion. On 8 June 1681 the Tribunal got a letter from the king, which Gyllenborg had drafted, reprimanding them for their slow progress, and ordering them, 'without any further delay or consideration', to carry out the royal instructions. But the Tribunal was not intimidated; they turned on Gyllenborg, who admitted 'his tongue had run ahead of his reason' and protested to the king. He had to back down and assure the Tribunal he had 'always considered them as honourable men and upright judges'. So the manoeuvring resumed, the king nagged, the Tribunal hesitated, the defendants obstructed. It was almost a year after starting work, 14 October 1681, that the first judgements were pronounced on G. Baner, J. Rosenhane, L. Kagg, J. G. Stenbock and J. Ribbing, who was cleared. The others got off lightly, except Baner, judged to have taken an improper donation worth 36,000 dsm. which he had to repay with interest. Stenbock, who had been negotiating a settlement directly with the king, was almost cleared, except he had to repay his 600 dsm. salary

---

[6] Blomdahl, *Huvudskede*, pp. 192–205, 210.
[7] *Ibid.*, p. 274.

increase.[8] Progress remained slow and resistance often paid off. For example on 6 February 1682 the Tribunal began considering 637 cases of doubtful donations. After looking at 230 of these, over two-thirds of which they decided had been legitimate, the Tribunal abandoned the rest. Similarly an original estimate of sums paid out in excess of the 1662 budget and due for repayment had been 2.8 million dsm. The definitive charges approved by the Tribunal for these items amounted to 730,000 dsm. Three-quarters of the first estimate had been abandoned or written off, while the 2 million dsm. costs of the Bremen crisis were not pursued at all in the end.[9]

The king had done his utmost to keep up the pressure on the Tribunal but they proved surprisingly resistant. He wrote on 18 January 1682 suggesting that they could speed up the work by sitting all day, morning and afternoon. The President declined, saying among other reasons that 'those who must judge are much fresher when they rest for a while and everything goes more easily and with more consideration'. By the summer of 1682 a critical point was reached, for the king wanted the work of the Tribunal completed, so that it could be ratified by the forthcoming autumn Diet. It was now deep into the question of charges against the Colleges, which constituted nearly half the total. On 26 April 1682, the Tribunal tried a collective charge against the Reduktion College, established to carry through the reduktion of 1655. The officials of the College were uncooperative and the Tribunal spent three days debating how to fix responsibility. In the end it gave up, and told the king it would take an unacceptably long time to pursue the charges against the Colleges. The king followed a recommendation of Gyllenborg on 16 April that the Tribunal would only issue general charges to the Colleges, and a separate commission be set up in the Chamber to work out the charges against individuals. On 25 May the king appointed 'the Liquidation Commission for the Great Commission's judgements on the Colleges'.[10] This cleared the way for the Tribunal to report that its work was concluded. Their letter of 20 May reiterated the principle on which they had operated. All those responsible in the regency and the Council, 'so far as they themselves, or their forefathers were obstructive and neglectful with their resolutions, instructions, orders and votes, they should begin to compensate and repay his Majesty and the crown all the damage and neglect which the public good had suffered thereby . . . together with 6 per cent yearly interest'. Ten days later the king replied in a letter naming all the members of the Tribunal, which declared that he 'graciously confirms and approves' all that they had done. It continued: 'therefore We have graciously wished hereby to proclaim this Our gracious confirmation'. He promised them his continuing protection. In the Diet of 1682 the report of the Tribunal was considered at length in the Secret

---

[8] O. Lindqvist, *Jakob Gyllenborg och reduktionen: köpe-, pante-, och restitionsgodsen i räfstepolitiken 1680–1692* (Lund, 1956), pp. 5, 12; Blomdahl, *Huvadskede*, pp. 285, 289, 396–9.

[9] Blomdahl, *Huvudskede*, pp. 478, 528, 552–4.

[10] *Ibid.*, pp. 482, 562, 575, 595.

Committee and endorsed by the Estates in the Diet Resolution. All suggestions to mitigate the Tribunal's judgements were rejected.[11]

The work of the Tribunal had not ended; it was just getting started. It had, except for the Colleges, identified the responsible individuals and how much they owed. But each individual financial settlement had to be negotiated in the general Liquidation Commission, set up in 1680 to investigate the crown's debts. This work was not wound up until 1700 due mainly to two factors. It proved immensely complex to work out the personal liability; most of those charged had counter-claims against the crown for items like unpaid salary, and these had to be inves-tigated by the Liquidation Commission which had other remits and was seriously overloaded. Then there was the factor of poor motivation among the officials involved and a reluctance to persevere. The king was repeatedly involved, and though he generally sought to maximize the returns, he was open to persuasion by advisers who were less committed than he was. He also lacked the professional expertise to dominate the advisers. For example, there was a review of progress in the Council on 31 December 1687, but the minute shows the king made few interventions and these sometimes exposed his deficiencies. Claes Fleming had supplied much of the driving force until his death in 1685, after which Gyllenborg carried on his activist line. The kind of resistance they faced can be illustrated from the efforts of the special Liquidation Commission on the Colleges.[12]

This body decided to begin with the Chamber and met a barrage of legal objections that the College had only acted on instructions from the regents, as it was obliged to do by law. Fleming and Gyllenborg led an investigation of contracts which the Chamber had negotiated on terms alleged to have been disadvantageous to the crown. By 1684 Fleming and Gyllenborg were ready to admit defeat. Their own experts warned of the consequences of a retrospective review of contracts: 'what sort of an outcry could there be in the country? Who will want to make a contract with the crown after that?' When the issue went to the king he was persuaded to drop it; he ruled it was necessary that 'public faith and credit be maintained in this'. After eighteen years of attempts to pin charges on the Chamber there was little or no real return. An attack on the Chancery was stalled up to 1685 by the stubborn resistance of de la Gardie, compounded by the obvious reluctance of the prosecutor, Fägerstierna, to press the case. Gyllenborg tried to reopen the case against the Chancery after 1687 but failed. The College of Mining had its president, S. Bielke, sitting on the Liquidation Commission and proceedings there were fruitless. The Tribunal had charged the Admiralty College over 4 million dsm. Fägerstierna was the prosecutor in charge and for five years after 1682 no progress was made. The king demanded more vigorous action in 1687, but so little

[11] *Ibid.*, pp. 611–16; UUB, E491, Handlingar till Sveriges politiska historia 1680–6, 'Riksens Ständers Deputerade utslag', 20 May 1682: king's letter to the Tribunal, 30 May 1682.
[12] R. Blomdahl, *Förmyndarräfstens ekonomiska resultat* (Stockholm, 1973), pp. 1–4; R. Blomdahl, *Förmyndarräfstens slutskede* (Stockholm, 1968), pp. 104, 107–10.

headway was made that in 1689 he was recommended to abandon proceedings. In this instance the king insisted on going on, and in 1695 a group of specific charges emerged. The three successful cases yielded 3,021 dsm.; seven others were dropped. It is clear that despite the pressures from the king, and the commitment of advisers like Fleming and Gyllenborg, the bureaucrats had closed ranks to protect their institutions. While in the Liquidation Commission itself, key members like J. G. Stenbock and the two prosecutors Fägerstierna and Talas were lukewarm. In the case of the War College, Talas eventually recommended dropping every case he took up. The king attempted to revive the process in 1687 when he appointed Gyllenborg to preside over a 'Commission on the office of prosecutors'. It was to review the whole position over the prosecution of the Tribunal's judgements. At first it was ordered to send weekly progress reports to the king, subsequently altered to monthly. The evidence suggests no reports were ever made and within months the new Commission was merged back into the Liquidation Commission. It was a weakness of Charles XI that being a workaholic himself, he would not allow for the overload on officials who carried multiple responsibilities, so that this initiative, and two subsequent attempts by the king, prompted by Gyllenborg to reinvigorate this process all failed. One official, P. Snack, remarked of it that it 'seems to be an ocean we sink into'. The king's lack of expertise was a factor; J. G. Stenbock once told colleagues wishing to refer a matter to the king: 'it is not worth it, he will only answer that we must judge impartially'. In this case Charles XI discovered that an established bureaucracy has a will of its own that even the most absolute of kings could not override.[13]

It is possible to estimate the results of the Regency Tribunal with some confidence. Charges were considered against about 1,200 individuals, but only about a fifth of these were actually prosecuted, 58 members of the Council and 226 other public officers. In money terms the charges that were pursued added up to 6.5 million dsm., of which 4 million was charged to members of the Council. It is possible to account for about 4.66 million dsm., so that it seems some 1.5 million was never collected. Thus the actual receipts fell far short of the original estimates of 12 million.[14] The experience of individuals varied widely. It could be expected that Claes Fleming escaped lightly, the charge on his father, 78 dsm., was the smallest of all and appears not to have been paid. Those who collaborated, like Sten Bielke, got off with 26,000 dsm. So did J. G. Stenbock, who paid only 17,000 dsm. Those who chose to resist could gain by it; G. O. Stenbock got his original charge of 300,000 dsm. reduced to 100,000 by vigorously pressing his counter-claims. There were successful lobbyists, like Henrik Horn, with access to the king, who attended a royal breakfast, and 'as I found the king in a good humour, I gave the king my humble petition, which was graciously received'. He paid 24 *daler* on his charge of 19,679 dsm.; the king remitted the rest. On the other hand Rålamb was driven into

[13] Blomdahl, *Slutskede*, pp. 57, 60–2, 64, 69, 72, 83, 86, 88–91, 92–8, 99–102, 120.
[14] Blomdahl, *Ekonomiska resultat*, pp. 90–1, 97–8.

bankruptcy, and Per Sparre, the dissident spokesman of 1680, had to pay the whole of his charge of 26,789 dsm. The best-known case was that of the richest man in Sweden, Magnus Gabriel de la Gardie. His pathetic letters to the king, which suggested he had been reduced to beggary, exaggerated. In reality, the king had left him a substantial estate at Vängarn; he had his salary as Justiciar; and his wife was assured, in a letter from the king, that she was secure in her estate of Höjentorp. But when he asked the king for cash, to prevent the Bank repossessing his Stockholm residence, the king refused. He wrote: 'the ready money which would have been required for that was needed to satisfy the budget: we have scarcely got so far that office holders can get their salary for the year, much less what they ought to get for previous years'.[15]

It is an open question whether the money recovered through the Tribunal, equivalent approximately to a full year's revenue, though it took twenty years to collect, was really worth the political odium and the bureaucratic effort that it cost. It was a substantial contribution to the overall budget balance that was achieved in the reign, but it may be that the political consequences were more significant. The bulk of the payments fell on the exclusive group of magnate families that had dominated government in Sweden between 1611 and 1680. Fifteen of these families were actually bankrupted, though that was almost certainly the result of the additional burdens imposed by the reduktion. Even de la Gardie, the worst hit with a charge of 505,000 dsm., could have survived but for that. Certainly, at the end the old oligarchy was publicly discredited, and so severely damaged economically that it never recovered its power. This had been the intention of Fleming, Thegner and Gyllenborg; whether it was the conscious intention of Charles XI can only be a matter of speculation. Some of his utterances suggest that he saw their conduct as moral delinquency, and his actions over the Council in 1680–2 show him conscious that they were potential claimants to a shared authority with the crown. On the other hand he knew from experience by 1680 the political impotence of the magnates when faced by an adult ruler. From the point of view of the power structure, the blows dealt by the Tribunal were redundant.

Charles XI set harsh rules for himself and his subjects. The budget was sacrosanct and personal favours, even to the most deserving, low on his list of priorities. The experience of Bengt Oxenstierna, President of the Council from 1680, virtually foreign minister for the rest of the reign, was instructive. In 1681 he had written a long letter to the king about the Tribunal and asked, 'for all these reasons, through a gracious resolution in my favour, to be dismissed and cleared from these proceedings'. The king refused to consider this, and Oxenstierna was charged 71,362 dsm. He continued to plead his disastrous financial situation until in 1686, the king remitted the charge. But Oxenstierna had also been hit by the

---

[15] *Ibid.*, pp. 11–74; Munthe, 'Ett stycke karolinsk vardag. Ur Henrik Henriksson Horns dagboksant-eckiningar . . . januari 1684–juli 1685', *KFÅ* (1946), p. 26; Sjögren, *Karl den elfte*, p. 345; KB, Engströmska samlingen: B.II.I.12, king's letters, 17 Mar. 1685, 7 Apr. 1685.

reduktion and the begging letters continued. The main Oxenstierna estates in Ingermanland were taken, and he asked if he could keep them on a lease at a favourable rent. He claimed that they were all he had left after forty years' public service. The king made some concession, but not as much as Oxenstierna had wanted. The king had explained his attitude in a letter to Oxenstierna on 27 June 1687, in which he had sympathized with his financial difficulties, 'and that I cannot help the councillor in everything as I would dearly like to do'. He recognized the value of Oxenstierna's services in generous terms; he had kept the kingdom at peace, 'which I account to the conduct and enlightened intelligence of the Councillor alone, next to God'. But the public debt was still such that he could only promise to consider any specific reduktion case that Oxenstierna might raise, 'so that I shall expect that the Councillor can be satisfied'.[16] The king was not by nature a dissimulator; it is likely he really did sympathize with his minister's problems, but the need to balance the kingdom's budget always had priority, and even a successful and devoted servant like Oxenstierna could not be exempted from the resultant austerities.

The reduktion was a process of a different order of magnitude. Most obviously it affected a far wider circle of families. At the end most of the families of the nobility of 1680 were drawn into it. There were three reduktions in Sweden in the seventeenth century. That of 1655 had been limited in time and required the return of a limited category of properties, while the rest of the donations would yield one quarter of their rents and taxes to the crown. This had been far from complete by 1680, and was confirmed in the Diet Resolution, but in effect merged into the second reduktion of 1680. This retained the restriction to donations made after 1632, but added a much larger category of properties to be surrendered unconditionally from whatever date they were made, and then included the reservation of 600 dsm. income to all grantees. The third reduktion was that of 1682, based on the recognition of the Estates that crown lands were inalienable, and kings could make donations or recall them at will. Gyllenborg stated this principle during the debates: 'they who drafted the law have established by it that the kingdom should be perpetual and have its resources, so that the one king may be able to reward his subjects as well as another'. Reduktion was now a qualitatively different process. The Estates had given up any claim to regulate it, it was open-ended at the king's discretion; as Lindschöld said: 'the Estates do not have the right to give or to take . . . or to decide that which depends on the king's Majesty'. A further reduktion Commission was added to that set up by the Estates in 1680, its authority based solely, 'on what belongs to the kingly office'. The merging of the two Commissions was considered but rejected; however, at first Claes Fleming presided over both. The king was extremely active in intervening to drive the process forward. By

[16] Blomdahl, *Ekonomiska resultat*, p. 53; Carlson, *Historia*, IV, p. 144; RA, Skrivelser till konungen, Karl XIs tid, Bengt Oxenstiernas skrivelser till KM, 26 Feb. 1681, 29 June 1687; Loenbom, *Handlingar*, I, collection I, p. 122.

January 1683 he had bypassed his own Commission by sending lists of properties to be recovered directly to the provincial governors. They controlled the evidence on which the whole process rested: the provincial land books, an early achievement of Swedish bureaucracy, kept since Gustav Vasa's time. These books listed every property in the kingdom and recorded its status, rental, tax obligations, with the name of its tenant and whether the landlord was the crown or a nobleman. The provincial governors were ordered to extract from these books 'everything under the heading of donation, allodial or granted under certain conditions'. They were to notify the grantees and set a day for them to produce their titles, 'and then what is pure donation shall be immediately resumed'. Only doubtful cases need be referred to the Commissions, while individual petitions should go directly to the king. Even so the Commissioners were hard pressed. The king instructed them to work an eight-hour day and avoid excessive holidays, yet in the early years they were not even assured of their full salary. The king wrote to the Commissions about pay in 1684: 'since they have received it for 1681 and 1682, so they must be satisfied with this for 1683 and 1684'. The king was not at first aware of all the complexities of the process and his interventions could be counter-productive; as Fleming remarked in 1681, it was difficult for the king to make rulings, 'because he did not find himself sufficiently informed about the matter'.[17]

In principle the reduktion process was simple. After 1682 it was enough to identify a property as having once belonged to the crown, after which it could be recovered. In practice, as is usually the case with titles to property, there were unending complexities and uncertainties. These were compounded by the king's propensity for changing the rules when some new complication was revealed, and then demanding that previous cases that had been settled should be reexamined in the light of the new ruling. The most feared and hated aspect of the reduktion was the unending uncertainty it created over rights to property. J. G. Stenbock, who was a member of the Commission, but an opponent of excessive enforcement, spoke in the Council in 1684 on how 'the insecurity that we live under creates a great diffidence among the people'. It was a complaint that occurred in the grievances of the Nobility in successive Diets down to 1697, with a plea that the process be wound up so that they could know with certainty what was their own.[18]

The prospect of a winding-up was dangled before the Nobility at intervals throughout Charles XI's reign. The Council was given a full progress report by Fleming in 1684, in which he claimed that good progress had been made. There is a first-hand account of the sessions held on 30 June and 1 July by H. Horn. After hearing Fleming's lengthy and detailed report, the Council was asked if they wished to comment. Horn wrote that it 'was very difficult for us to comment

[17] Carlson, *Historia*, III, pp. 182, 200; Lindqvist, *Gyllenborg*, pp. 44, 61; RA, Lagkommissionen 1686–1736: protokol, 'KMs Reduktions Stadgar', 2 Dec. 1682.
[18] Carlson, *Historia*, III, p. 201; KB, Engströmska samlingen: B.II.I.12, Riddarhus petition, 10 Dec. 1697.

straight away on such an important matter . . . And since this same undertaking was based on Diet Resolutions, and other royal decrees and resolutions, which do not now allow any contradiction, so it was all too late and without effect to make any comment, therefore everybody refrained.' The underlying feeling in the Council, that the reduktion was beginning to run out of control, was apparent in the Diet of 1686. There were two further categories of former crown properties in private hands in addition to the donations. One was the mortgaged properties, granted in return for loans to the crown. The revenues from these constituted the interest on the loan. The second category was the straight sales of crown properties for cash. Royal officials had been investigating both categories, but as the law stood, unless some fault could be found in the original contracts, they were immune from reduktion. The more enthusiastic royal officials, like Lindschöld and Gyllenborg, responding to the king's known desire to get these properties back, were looking for legal devices to make this possible, but down to 1685 they were restrained by Fleming, who was a moderate on reduktion, in contrast with his aggressive stance in the Tribunal. It seems that the king, for all his personal militancy, had complete confidence in Fleming, and stated in a letter of September 1684 that he had Fleming to thank, 'for what has happened for my own and the kingdom's best advantage'. With Fleming dead, J. G. Stenbock led the moderate faction on the reduktion, but he was not as influential with the king as his predecessor. This enabled Gyllenborg and Lindschöld to prepare a programme for the Diet of 1686.[19] The particulars of this will be discussed in a later chapter, but broadly the king opened the way by insisting to the Diet that further steps be taken to reduce the public debt, and then Lindschöld and Gyllenborg introduced and got accepted a scheme depending on juggling with interest rates, which enabled most mortgages to be liquidated, as they were by 1697, and the properties recovered. This was followed by a scheme for recovering the purchased properties, which involved a reinterpretation of the original sales contracts. It was legally so dubious that the Council, when consulted, advised the king against it, to his considerable displeasure. Even Lindschöld had doubts; at least he told the Riddarhus that 'this was a quite different matter from the mortgaged properties, because they involved only a few people, but this concerns almost every nobleman'. But it too was driven through because of the known will of the king.[20]

After 1686 the reduktion entered on its final phase. This was marked in December 1687 when the king set up a new enforcement agency, the Deputation for the reduktion, with Gyllenborg as its president. It was based on the assumption that the process was almost complete, and what remained was to finalize the accounts. The Deputation would rule on all points of difficulty and the Chamber officials could then work out the settlements. This was hopelessly optimistic; even Gyllenborg conceded that the complications were such that it could take the

[19] Munthe, 'Ett stycke karolinsk vardag', p. 135.
[20] Lindqvist, *Gyllenborg*, pp. 94–8, 121, 133–43.

Deputation fourteen days continuous work to resolve a single case. Yet the king, who repeatedly expressed his concern at the slow rate of progress, would not consider proposals from his advisers to sacrifice some potential gains to speed it up. In a case in 1689 where the Deputation recommended such a concession, the king expressed his astonishment that they should advise him to forgo the crown's legal rights, and demanded to know what members of the Deputation had supported it, threatening to call them to account. The threat was not pursued, but the king got his way.[21] There was a progress report given to the Secret Committee in the Diet of 1693 which illustrated the scale of the problem. The king actually expressed his regret that the reduktion had not yet been concluded; he said, in a massive understatement: 'various questions arise, which not only increased the work but have also extended the time'. For example, the report listed seven different types of purchase properties, with the special problems belonging to each one. This was meant to account for the slow progress being made. The report did recognize the factor of overload on the officials involved, 'almost all have their ordinary offices and commitments to perform, which give them enough to do'. Yet though this was advanced as a further reason why the reduktion was not yet complete, the promised solution which, it was claimed, 'at last, and within a short time, can bring about a final end to the remaining reduktion business', was yet another Commission of Chamber officials, with a quite unrealistic remit. The Commission would produce definitive lists of all the purchase properties, with the details of each contract, and of any that remained to be settled. They would also make a definitive register of all the crown farms and their revenues, and note those remaining in private hands, and a register of all the exchanged and substituted properties accepted in satisfaction of the crown's claims, and finally they would compile a register of all the properties legitimately held by the nobility. Thus the admittedly unbearable uncertainties over titles to property would be resolved. It is no surprise that this ambitious programme was never executed in Charles XI's lifetime – nor was it likely to be. Such an ambitious bureaucratic project was well beyond the working capacity of the civil service of seventeenth-century Sweden.[22]

The history of the reduktion has still not been written, and perhaps it never will be because of the complexities of the task. For although the rules and procedures can be described, the results of their application could only be determined by examining the documentation of individual cases. It would be a formidable undertaking to do this even for a representative sample. For when a property had been identified as liable to be recovered, that was only the beginning of the process. It started a negotiation with crown officials, often interspersed with direct reference or appeal to the king, to establish a settlement. Despite the clear basic principle, after 1682, that any property that had once belonged to the crown could be taken back without compensation, the possible complications were many. The grantee

[21] *Ibid.*, pp. 165, 195, 197, 200, 209, 210.
[22] RA, R 2378, Secreta Utskottets Protocoll 1693, session of 11 Nov. 1693.

could claim for improvements made to the property while in his possession. He might also have outstanding claims on the crown, the commonest being unpaid salary. There was no legal right to set these against his loss through reduktion, but a petition, submitted with due humility and submission for the exercise of royal favour, could produce concessions. Those who tried to bargain, rather than petition, were swiftly discouraged. Field Marshal O. W. Königsmarck tried it in 1686, and got a royal command to desist. 'We enjoin those involved to perpetual silence about this', on pain of 'Our highest displeasure.' The king's relative, Duke Adolf Johan claimed exemption because he was a prince of the Holy Roman Empire. The king deeply resented the style of the duke's letters, as if 'he were not bound by any obedience or loyalty in the kingdom of Sweden . . . it is not becoming to Us to allow any of Our royal rights and jurisdiction in Our kingdom to be argued over or contested'. The duke would get the same justice as any other subject. The king was adamant that all concessions and exceptions from the reduktion rested solely on his sovereign authority. Thus when in 1686 it was drawn to his attention that a ruling he had issued in 1682 seemed to restrict his absolute discretion, it was explained that 'the king's meaning has never been to tie his hands by this, but rather to maintain for himself the right and freedom, which are due and belong to the royal Majesty, in this as in other cases'.[23]

The objects of the exercise of the royal discretion were diverse. One of the worst complications was that caused when a crown donation had changed hands by sale or exchange with a third party. If it had been done with crown permission, and was therefore legal, the current owner might be allowed up to ten years further possession to recover his investment. If it had been done without permission, he lost the property and had to seek redress from the seller through the courts. One of the most important areas of discretion was to permit the grantee to offer alternative property of equal value to that being recovered. This was acceptable in general to the king, because his interest was not in the actual property, but the revenue it produced. This kind of exchange could do something to mitigate the harshness of the reduktion process on noble families. The core of a noble estate was the manor, where the family residence was located. Manor farms enjoyed the highest rates of exemption from tax and conscription, and were therefore the most valuable. If outlying properties were offered in substitution for manor farms liable to reduktion, there could be a substantial advantage, and there is evidence to suggest that many families used this strategy. As a final resort the nobleman could simply petition for mitigation on compassionate grounds, and this often succeeded. There is a contemporary folklore about noble families ruined by the reduktion being evicted from their homes and begging a crust of bread from their former tenants. None of these lamentable anecdotes has ever been proven true, and it would have run contrary to the king's policy. One of the commonest forms of royal intervention

---

[23] Carlson, *Historia*, III, p. 195; RA, Lagkommissionen 1686–1736: ÄK 15:8, king's instruction to Stiernhöök 17 May 1681, king's letter to Adolf Johan 6 Feb. 1685; Lindqvist, *Gyllenborg*, p. 190.

was to prevent the total impoverishment of noble families. A royal instruction to the reduktion officials in 1685 says that in the last resort a statutory subsistence allowance is to be made. The king would also, in deserving cases, allow grantees to lease back their properties for a moderate rent, or grant possession for a period of years, or for life, to soften the blow. This can be illustrated from the experience of Edvard Ehrensteen, a successful career civil servant, though as he had once been personal secretary to the king's father, he was not a typical case. Ehrensteen told how in 1680 he had a claim of 24,000 dsm. for unpaid salary, which the Chamber officials bargained down to 12,000 dsm., though he adds, writing in 1687, 'that is still unpaid'. He surrendered properties in the reduktion of 1680, and further properties after 1682. But then, to his surprise, as he says, in 1683 the king appointed him to the new King's Council, and, in view of his previous services, was granted a lifetime tenure of some of the lost property. He says that being old in 1683, he would have preferred to be retired on a pension, 'but since God's merciful providence, and my gracious king have wished to order otherwise, so I thanked the king in this present writing, and pray God for a gracious support'. Ehrensteen's patient submission is surely connected to the bitterness he expresses against those who called themselves 'the old families', who had consistently scorned and resented men like himself who had risen on merit.[24]

Since the state of research makes a general description of the effects of the reduktion impractical, the historian is reduced to using individual experiences to illustrate its consequences. There are claims of drastic impoverishment. In 1684 the widow of the magnate Treasurer, Sten Bielke, petitioned the king for protection because officials were threatening to seize her furniture and household effects. In 1683 the de la Gardie family put in a collective petition, asserting they were being stripped bare. This was certainly exaggerated in respect of the former Chancellor, and the alleged impoverishment did not prevent the younger generation pursuing successful public careers after 1680. Axel Leijonhufvud was a member of an old magnate family who fared less well. He had followed a normal career path and in 1680 was an Assessor in the Commerce College. But when the College was merged with the Chamber in 1680 he lost his post, and did not get another appointment for the rest of the reign. His memoirs suggest he was a victim of a personal feud, 'the hostility and jealousy of certain persons was a major cause of that change'. He lost properties through the reduktion and lamented: 'what loss and deprivation the subjects had from the reduktion, everyone who was affected well knows. I and my house got a heavy share of it . . . The breach and loss which I had to suffer in my little dwelling and household from this same reduktion was so heavy, that subsistence for our numerous family was sadly much diminished.' His efforts to get a new appointment brought nothing but empty promises. He claimed that his experience was not uncommon: 'what arguments, quarrels, hardship and difficulty many

---

[24] S. Loenbom, ed., *Anecdoter om namnkunniga och märkwärdiga svenska män*, 3 vols. (Stockholm, 1770–5), I, section IV, pp. 80–134.

decent subjects had to undergo under all that, could scarcely be expressed in a whole volume'. Leijonhufvud took pride in his endurance, though he had to sell much of his inheritance to survive. But he did survive, and managed to educate three sons, all of whom entered successful military careers, while after the fall of the absolutism in 1718, he himself reentered public life. Leijonhufvud suggests that the reduktion could hit hard, but also it could be survived.[25] Survival could be helped by skilful lobbying. It was noted how Henrik Horn used his access to the king, as a member of the Council, to lobby him. Horn also approached Bengt Oxenstierna and tried to interest Lindschöld by sending him 200 ducats, but it was not accepted. The veteran Field Marshal, C. G. Wrangel, who had major problems over his settlement approached Johan Rosenhane, a fellow magnate who was securely based in the Court of the queen-mother in 1681. 'I would be glad if you could be so good as to write to Claes Fleming and put to him all our case; I am sure it would have a great effect.' Later, still in pursuit of relief from the king, he asked Rosenhane to try Lindschöld: 'Lindschöld can do a lot for the business if he is willing . . . in this time in which you cannot win anything by moderation'. It is clear that some of the officials who were working on the reduktion process could be influenced to help achieve favourable settlements, but it was a hazardous business, because the king insisted on full and rigorous enforcement. Only after that would he consider exercising his prerogative. The king wrote one of his rare letters in his own hand to the reduktion commissioners on 24 January 1688:

If any of you, against all expectation, shall presume to arbitrate or follow other principles than what the Diet Resolutions, the reduktion regulations, the royal resolutions and letters contain, We reserve the right, for ourselves and our successors, now and in all times to call him to answer for it: since the right of sovereignty knows no limits of time, but remains open for ever.

Charles XI was warning his servants not to bend the rules, for the royal retribution would catch up on them in the end.[26]

One case that has been studied in some detail is that of J. G. Stenbock, a magnate who held two offices, Marshal and head of the War College and royal Stable Master. In 1680 he had enjoyed a revenue of 14,860 dsm. from his extensive properties, 12,159 dsm. from lending out surplus funds, much of them in mortgages to the crown, for which he got up to 20% interest, and 9,878 dsm. in official salary, which, exceptionally, was paid up to date. It has been noted how Stenbock managed to keep abreast of the Tribunal by being a member of it, and then sitting on the Liquidation Commission, eventually becoming its President. This must be

---

[25] RA, Skrivelser till konungen, Karl XIs tid, D, Gustav Adolf de la Gardie to the king, 10 Mar. 1688; UUB, E491, Margarete Bielke to Claes Fleming, 6 Oct. 1684; Loenbom, ed., *Anecdoter*, I, section IV, pp. 23, 26, 29, 34.

[26] Munthe, 'Ett stycke karolinsk vardag', pp. 136, 137; UUB, E518, Brev till Johan Rosenhane, II 1668–81, Wrangel to Rosenhane, 13 Aug. 1681; RA, Lagkommissionen 1686–1736: ÄK 15:8, king to Reduktion Commissioners, 24 Jan. 1688.

part of the reason why his Tribunal charges were moderate, and he was not pressed hard to settle. His weak point was the threat of a collective charge against the Chamber, and in 1687 this became urgent because the king and Gyllenborg had opened a new drive to maximize the returns from the Tribunal. So Stenbock ducked out by offering the king a quick final settlement of all outstanding charges, noting that the king had 'granted many subjects settlements, and they in consequence escaped all further charges for a fixed sum'. He offered a large landed property in settlement and the king accepted. In 1690, Chamber officials tried to reopen this settlement, on the grounds it had been unduly favourable to Stenbock, but the king ordered the matter to be dropped. This was one of several royal interventions in Stenbock's favour, which saved him from the fate of less fortunate, or well-placed sufferers, who commonly found settlements they had supposed to be final being challenged by the crown's officers, with the encouragement of the king. Stenbock's money lending did suffer, both from the 1686 rulings on mortgaged properties, and defaults by private debtors in consequence of the reduktion. He may have lost 90,000 dsm. in bad debts. But he did do well in settling his own reduktion account by way of exchange of properties. He used sharp practice, for instance putting a tenant into a deserted farm in order to offer it in exchange, so that, as his bailiff wrote, 'no complaint may arise when it is exchanged or given up to the crown'. For another exchange the bailiff suggested 'those poor and untenanted and wretched vacant farms, which no peasant can live on'. By the 1690s the shape of Stenbock's operations had been transformed. He was getting out of land and his income from it had halved, and he gave up lending on the security of property, so that by 1699 his income from this sank to 44 dsm. The official salary now became more important; since 1683 it had been 10,640 dsm., usually paid in full, and in 1688 the king upgraded the salary of Council members, which raised his official salary to 14,000 dsm. He was also one of a group of favoured officials who got a 12,000 dsm. bonus, out of recovered properties in 1694, in effect a new donation, though it was in cash, not property. Overall, Stenbock's income in the late 1690s was almost what it had been in 1680, though now nearly 60% came from salary and none from money lending. It must be concluded that Stenbock had survived the Tribunal and the reduktion unscathed. He was, of course, about as untypical of an ordinary nobleman as could be, but he does suggest the reduktion could be survived; some of his techniques were open to others, and losses in donations and mortgage properties could be partly offset by the regular receipt of official salary. That was probably the main reason why the reduktion was not the major disaster for the nobility that it could have been.[27]

The one serious attempt to estimate the outcome of the reduktion nation-wide is based on counting tenancies in the land books. It is generally accepted that in 1600, two-thirds of peasant farms were under the crown, one third under the nobility;

[27] A. Kullberg, *Johan Gabriel Stenbock och reduktionen: godspolitik och ekonomiförvaltning 1675–1705* (Uppsala, 1973), pp. 25, 37–8, 43–4, 49–51, 52–3, 62, 79, 80, 128, 129–30, 133.

that by 1680 these proportions were reversed; and by 1700 the earlier distribution had been restored. This would suggest that the reduktion had cost the nobility half its properties, a very serious loss indeed. But the loss was not evenly distributed, since in 1680, 60% of all donations belonged to magnate families.[28] These figures are too unspecific to reveal very much, but there is a study of the province of Uppland which offers more precise information. There, in 1680, 29% of peasant farms were ancient noble property; 59% were farms alienated by the crown, which retained the remaining 10%. This gave the Uppland nobles a solid base in their ancient properties, which were beyond the reach of the reduktion. Further, only half the alienated farms were pure donation, the others had come by purchase or exchange and in 1718 two-thirds of these properties were still in the possession of the nobility. The average holding of alienated farms by Uppland nobles was nine. On the other hand three magnate families had nearly 600 between them. All this suggests that the ordinary Uppland noble family's exposure to loss through reduktion was limited. Further, it is now established that when the crown alienated a farm, it had often reserved part of the income; in Uppland this seems to represent about a quarter of the rents and taxes, so the loss of income through recovery was reduced. Since the salary from the kind of appointments to which nobles could aspire was around 1,200 dsm., and this would now be paid in full, the trade-off between reduktion and official salary could have been reasonable for the average family.[29]

There are two further aspects of the reduktion to be considered. The Uppland study exposes the central importance of the manor, with its favourable tax status, for the noble economy. Legally each family could claim only one manor on which it registered its official residence. The evidence shows that down to 1680 there had been a major increase in the number of manors. This was a widespread phenomenon, and was causing so much loss to the revenue that in 1678 the king had ordered an investigation. In Uppland this resulted in one third of the existing manors being declared unlawful and suppressed. It was followed up in 1686 by a royal ordinance prohibiting the establishment of new manors in perpetuity. The purge and freezing of manors was an economic blow to the nobility, parallel with the losses by reduktion.[30] The other aspect concerns the position of the tax-peasants, the backbone of the Peasant Estate because they were quasi-freeholders. Part of the commoner case for reduktion had been that when alienations placed tax-peasants under the nobility their status would be subverted by the noble landlords, who would try to take their farms into the manors and use their labour service to cultivate the manorial demesne. The grievances of the Peasant Estate

---

[28] E. F. Heckscher, *An economic history of Sweden* (Cambridge, Mass., 1954), p. 127; L. Magnusson, *Reduktionen under 1600-talet: debatt och forskning* (Malmö, 1985), pp. 19–20, 33, 35, 36.
[29] J. A. Almqvist, *Frälsegodsen i Sverige under storhetstiden: med särskild hänsyn till proveniens och säteribildning*, 2 vols. (Stockholm, 1931), I, pp. 87, 89–90.
[30] Holmqvist, ed., *Tre Karlar*, p. 39; Almqvist, *Frälsegodsen*, I, p. 85; Ingers, *Bonden*, p. 290.

asserted repeatedly that this was happening, and it seems such an obvious strategy for the noble landlord that it was assumed it must be true. It was then suggested that one motive for Charles XI to embark on reduktion was to weaken the nobility by reestablishing the independence of the tax-peasant. But all attempts to verify this scenario by research have failed. Such detailed studies as exist show that a tax-peasant on an alienated farm retained his legal status, could defend it in the courts if threatened, and that where landlords did incorporate tax-peasant farms in a manor, it was by purchase or exchange in most cases. And when reduktion brought the farms back under the crown, the regime was harsh and exacting, since the whole purpose of the reduktion was to maximize the crown revenues. Charles XI was in truth always vigilant to uphold the legal rights of peasants, but he did this on principle, as part of his kingly duty to uphold the law. Nothing he said or wrote suggests that the reduktion policies were driven by a desire to rescue the peasants from oppression.[31]

The reduktion under Charles XI is an almost unique phenomenon in early modern history. A well-established nobility submitted peacefully to a massive attack on its income and its property rights. Some suggestion must be made, and it can only be a suggestion, to explain why the nobility was unwilling or unable to defend its position. A united Riddarhus should have been able to block, or at least to modify, policies so threatening to its status and economic welfare. The solution suggested is that the policies could not be resisted because they were the king's command, and because basically they were legal. Rålamb tried to argue the contrary, but despite ambivalences in the Land Law, the basic principle that the public lands were an inalienable patrimony of the crown was almost universally accepted. When Charles XI formally asserted this in the Diet of 1682, nobody was prepared to contest it. For most Swedish noblemen that was the end of the matter. The king had declared his will, the Estates had confirmed it and there was no more to be said, at least in public. E. J. Meck, a loyal, long-serving officer in the artillery, was pursued by the Chamber for claims arising from his father-in-law's inheritance. In his diary he lamented the 'terrible charge' which would 'lead to the ruin of all the parties concerned'. He had to travel from Skåne to Stockholm in order to petition the king for relief, but his only comment was: 'we must accept God's Providence and the Ruler's pleasure with patience, and consider besides, the Lord gave and the Lord takes, may His name be blessed'. Men whose whole political culture was built round the rule of unquestioned obedience to the powers that be, sanctioned by God, which was the general culture of seventeenth-century Sweden, could not contemplate resistance.[32]

At another level, after 1680 there was no dispute about the need to find resources to rebuild Sweden's military capacity; the arguments were about means, not ends,

---

[31] Ingers, *Bonden*, pp. 291–3; Holmqvist, ed., *Tre Karlar*, pp. 42, 130.
[32] F. Arfwidsson, ed., *Erik Johan Mecks dagbok 1644–99* (Lund, 1948), p. 99; KB, Rålambska Manuskriptsamlingen: Fol. Nr. 5: 1680 års riksdagsärenden, ch. 7.

and the nobility were genuinely divided over this. Most modern studies have presented this as a choice between reduktion and taxation. If the nobility were to retain their donations they would have to submit to being taxed on their incomes, and surrender their exemption from taxation enshrined in the Privileges of 1611, the main distinguishing mark of their status. It was true that the Privilege had been breached almost as soon as it was confirmed, but this did not weaken its symbolic value. The Riddarhus had to choose between reduktion and taxation, and between keeping their donations and receiving regular payment of their salaries. Since more families held official posts than enjoyed donations, the attraction of assured payment of salary was strong. These were choices which the individual had to make; they cut across Class lines and stood in the way of the Estate uniting round a common policy. To this must be added structural changes in the nobility, promoted by Charles XI. In the course of the reign he enlarged it substantially by 500 new creations, at a rate of twenty a year after 1680. At the same time he diluted the titled nobility by generous promotions within the Estate, creating 46 new counts and 111 new barons, and these promotions were almost exclusively for service. The king also diluted the social exclusivity of the nobility. Before 1680, 90% of men promoted to the nobility were already landed proprietors; after 1680 this proportion fell to 30%; able commoners were sometimes promoted directly into the titled nobility. This development fuelled the precedence disputes, whether status was determined by office or birth, which split the nobility throughout the century. The lower nobility argued for an official Table of Ranks and after 1680 Charles XI granted one. There were forty-one ranks, with equivalents in the army, the navy and the civil service, and this institutionalized a meritocratic system, based on service. In general a commoner who reached the rank of army captain, or its equivalent, was likely to be ennobled. In 1600 the Swedish nobility had been a small, exclusive elite of hereditary landowners, some of whom pursued careers in the public service. By 1700 it was a much larger, professionalized service nobility which was unlikely to come out in opposition to the king.

It was inevitable that the Regency Tribunal and the reduktion engendered bitter resentments and hatred. Feuquières, writing in January 1681, showed a grasp of why, even so, the nobility would not resist. 'La nation est indolente, elle se flatte que la plus grande mal est passé . . . La noblesse ruinée ne le peut guère troubler parcequ'elle est décréditée aussi, et qu'elle ne consiste qu'en une trentaine de races' ('The nation is complacent, it flatters itself that the worst troubles are over . . . The ruined nobility can scarely trouble him because it is discredited as well and it only consists of some thirty families'). It is easy to illustrate hostile talk. J. Svedberg went to dinner with a wealthy family, and was shocked when the guests 'began during the meal to talk about the reduktion and the liquidation proceedings and such like which gave the children no positive ideas about the king'. Ambassadors' reports and hostile pamphlets show the depth of feeling aroused. A tract issued in Amsterdam in 1694 described seeing a procession of five carts, followed by weeping women and children, that carried to auction the last possession of a ruined noble family. Everything the king had done was decried. The writer lashed out at a sycophantic clergyman, 'un des adorateurs de l'avarice royale' ('one of the admirers of the royal greed'), who preached submission and added: 'on n'en doute autrement qu'il ne fera fait évêque à la première occasion' ('besides there is no doubt he will be made a bishop at the first opportunity'). The royal ministers were blackguarded: Stenbock had 'une vanité extraordinaire' ('an extraordinary vanity') and was 'l'esclave de son ventre' ('the slave of his stomach'). Lindschöld was 'mignon de la fortune et favorit de l'avarice royale'; ('a slave of chance and favoured by the royal avarice'); Lichton was stupid; J. J. Hastfer was 'un véritable ignorant et âne' ('a real ignoramus and an ass'); Hans Wachtmeister was compared to Caligula's horse, and finally, 'ce petit homme boiteux que tu vois . . . portant grande épée et petit chapeau, qui a la mine bizarre est le roi, il est brave, avaricieux ennemi des gens de naissance, ignorant et peu son faute qu'il n'est véritable tyran' ('this little lame man that you see . . . wearing a big sword and a little hat, with the bizarre appearance is the king, he is brave, avaricious, an enemy of the well born, uneducated, and it is scarcely his fault if he is not a true tyrant').[33] The resentment is manifest, yet there is no evidence of any serious attempt to resist the king's policies. Indeed, it is not easy to see how it could have been achieved. The magnates faced a divided nobility and the solid royalism of the commoners. Since 1611 they had themselves been imbued with a public service ethos under Gustav II Adolf and Axel Oxenstierna, and they were not feudatories who could mobilize retainers from their estates. Once the magnates surrendered the Council of State, their only institutional power base, they had the choice of withdrawing into private life or collaborating and most chose the latter, serving on the meritocratic terms now on offer.

[33] Correspondance diplomatique: vol. 64, p. 14, Feuquières to Louis XIV, 1 Jan. 1681; G. Wetterberg, ed., *Jasper Svedbergs lefwernes beskrifning*, 1 Text (Lund, 1941), p. 130; UUB, N886, MSS *Le Dessein*.

5

The indelningsverk and the rebuilding of the armed forces

The most enduring legacy of Charles XI was the restructuring of the armed forces on a basis that lasted unchanged into the mid-nineteenth century. The foundation was the provision of adequate and assured funding through the indelningsverk, combined with the knektehåll system of contracts with the localities to support the rank and file of the infantry and the seamen for the navy. By 1697 the system provided, in Sweden–Finland, fifteen infantry regiments of 1,200 men and ten cavalry or dragoon regiments. These were supplemented by specialist units of mercenary, professional soldiers, the royal Life Guards, the fortress garrisons and the artillery. The total army establishment, including the troops in the overseas provinces, was 61,100 men. The navy had thirty-one capital ships, twelve smaller fighting ships and some galleys for use in the archipelagos. The cost to the crown was 2,800,000 dsm. out of a gross annual budget of 4,576,129 dsm.[1] This represented the near completion of plans which the king had conceived in 1679 and reflected his strategic thinking. Sweden was faced by hostile, predatory neighbours who were a permanent threat to its security. A ring of fortifications, permanently garrisoned, would hold off initial attacks, while the field army in Sweden–Finland was kept in constant readiness for rapid mobilization to move wherever it was needed and the navy was strong enough to secure its passage overseas if necessary. The strategy was defensive, though tactically an aggression would be met by a crushing counter-attack and the tactical thinking was offensively orientated. Charles XI thought of his army as a deterrent, so formidable that it would not need to be used. The one part of the plan still unfulfilled in 1697 was the fortress building programme, which required heavy capital expenditures and was held back by budgetary constraints.

The indelningsverk was a method of funding public expenditure by allocating to each item a permanent source of public revenue. It had been practised in Sweden and in other European countries for a long time past; what made Charles XI's use of it distinctive was the scale and consistency of its application. The reduktion had been a precondition for finding sufficient properties to make the system viable. The first phase was directed to establishing the cavalry and dragoon regiments. The units of the field army were territorially based, so properties with a suitable yield in

---

[1] G. Arteus, *Den gamla krigsmakten: en översiktlig beskrivning av den svenska förvarsorganisationen 1521–1901* (Stockholm, 1985), p. 17; J. Cavallie, *Från fred till krig: de finansiella problemen kring krigsutbrottet år 1700* (Uppsala, 1975), p. 34.

rents and taxes had to be identified in the right area and then allocated in perpetuity. The officers and non-commissioned officers (NCOs) of each unit were provided with a farm, suited to their rank and status, that constituted their residence and main source of income. For as long as they remained in service they were the landlord of the property and were required to live there, for it was part of the reforms that the commanders should 'live with their men', so that they could keep them 'under the proper training and exercises'. Higher-ranking officers needed an augmented income provided from neighbouring crown farms, but on these they were not landlords, but the collectors of their dues. The implementation of a comprehensive indelningsverk had been signalled in 1679, when P. Cronhielm and L. Eldstierna were appointed Commissioners, with the remit of securing 'the total stabilization of the cavalry regiments'. Their remit was extended to cover the infantry and B. Gyldenhoff was added to the Commission, and a separate Commission was set up for Finland, which had special local problems, under C. Falkenberg.[2] These Commissions did the groundwork of selecting suitable properties. The cavalry troopers were provided by the more affluent crown tenants, usually tax-peasant freeholders, who undertook *rusthåll*. The tenant agreed to provide a cavalry trooper, his horse and equipment on a permanent basis in exchange for complete tax exemption. The trooper lived on the farm, got a wage and accommodation, and when not on duty would work for his employer. The *rusthåll* tenants were carefully selected and came in time to form a peasant elite in local society.

The process was lengthy and complex and it was 1687 before the cavalry allocations were declared completed. The king was personally closely involved in choosing properties. In a typical intervention in 1687, when it was proposed to take a crown hunting-lodge for the indelningsverk, he wrote: 'it is much more acceptable to Us to have a good and well-endowed cavalry farm in the country, for the defence and security of the kingdom, than a hunting-lodge for vain appetites and pleasure'. Charles XI was very clear about his priorities, and also about the permanence of the new system. It was laid down in 1679 that there would be 'a new *militiebok*' kept in each parish, which listed the assigned properties, what they were assigned for and exactly what the obligations were on each one. Copies would be held centrally in the Chamber. A royal letter in 1687 stressed that it was 'a work that We have once and for all put on such a firm foundation and sound basis for the service and security of the kingdom, that it shall be maintained for all time to come for Us and successive Swedish kings'. There was a warning that severe punishment awaited anyone who sought to infringe the allocations.[3] It was ironic that it was realized almost immediately that the settlement was defective, and it was comprehensively reviewed by a new Commission between 1688 and 1697, when it was once

---

[2] S. Ågren, *Karl XIs indelningsverk för armen: bidrag till dess historia åren 1679–1697* (Uppsala, 1922), pp. 11, 14, 57.

[3] *Ibid.*, pp. 65, 74, 75, 76, 77; *Handlingar rörande skandinaviens historia*, XIV, p. 223, king to Ascheberg 16 Oct. 1687.

more declared complete. The problem was that unrealistically high assessments had been put on some properties, making the allotted revenue unreliable. It was noteworthy that the king, who had a reputation for meanness with public revenues, did not hesitate to order a general revaluation, which lowered many rentals and required him to assign additional properties to compensate. For example he told a provincial Governor, G. Duvall, that officers in his province had complained their allocations were insufficient. He was to review them and make any necessary changes. In a letter to Eldstierna in 1691 the king insisted how important it was to get the cavalry indelningsverk right. It must have priority until 'the cavalry are completely clear and settled'.[4]

The infantry regiments were different, since although the support of the officers and NCOs was put on the indelningsverk, like the cavalry, the soldiers had traditionally been raised by conscription. Conscription was not an efficient way to secure recruits; it was massively unpopular, resulting in evasion or flight to avoid being taken. It was further weakened by the exemptions enjoyed by the tenants of the nobility. An official memorandum conceded that 'the common man greatly abhors it'. There was the alternative system, adopted in the border wilderness of Dalarna since 1611, and taken up in two other border provinces: recruitment by contract – the knektehåll. Under this the local peasants, in exchange for the ending of conscription, undertook to band together to recruit and maintain a quota of infantrymen at their own expense. There were few noblemen resident in these border provinces, but elsewhere noblemen were wholly opposed to the knektehåll because it undercut the advantage their tenants enjoyed, and their ability to control their tenants. The Marshal had told the Riddarhus in 1652: 'it is certain that the only means to keep the peasants under control is conscription'. In the Diet of 1680 the Peasant Estate had expressed interest in the knektehåll and the king had responded positively. After the Diet he made soundings in Värmland province and the local nobility circulated a memorandum of protest, claiming that 'conscription has always been a deterrent to the peasants, whereby they are to some extent forced into obedience: if they are freed from it, there is reason to fear that neither God's nor the world's law will compel them to keep themselves in bounds'. They warned the burghers and the clergy, whose servants were also exempt from conscription, that with its removal they would be unable to find servants.[5]

It has been shown above how in the Diet of 1682 the king had announced his intention to raise provincial infantry regiments of 1,200 men and asked how the recruits were to be provided. The Peasant Estate had declared its preference for the knektehåll and were able to claim that the king shared their view, and further he had told the Värmland peasants that it must mean that the tenants of the nobility participate on equal terms. He had said: 'the one as well as the other derives the

---

[4] Ågren, *Indelningsverk*, p. 79; S. F. Gahm-Persson, ed., *Kongl. stadgar, förordningar, bref, och resolutioner, angående Swea Rikes landt-milicie til häst och fot*, 4 vols. (Stockholm, 1762–1814), II, p. 457.
[5] Ågren, *Indelningsverk*, pp. 93–7, 102, 110, 111–13; *SRARP*, XIII, pp. 156–7.

same advantage from the peace and security which, with God's help, is to be expected from a standing army'. The nobility were outflanked in the Diet of 1682; the nominal compromise that the peasants in each province could choose knek-tehåll, but the nobility could keep conscription for their tenants, was unworkable. Conscription was so unattractive to the tenants that in almost every province where the knektehåll was adopted, the nobility agreed that their tenants take part. As the king put it, the nobility had discovered that 'their peasants cannot, without major damage, be separated from the others and therefore they have willingly joined in equally'.[6] After the Diet the king's officials had to negotiate contracts province by province for providing their quota of men in perpetuity. The peasants formed a rota, usually based on two full-value peasant farms, and paid the enlistment money and wage for the soldier, and also provided his civilian clothing and either lodged him on the farm or provided a cottage and an allotment for the upkeep of himself and his family. The king usually supplied the uniform and equipment and paid his wage when he was on service. When not on duty the soldier was obliged to work on the farm for wages. If the soldier died, or deserted, the rota was obliged to replace him at their own expense. In the early years the provinces of Småland, Västergöt-land, Österbotten and much of Finland chose to keep conscription, but eventually the knektehåll was universally adopted. The reason was the security it gave to both parties. The peasants undertook the obligation on top of their existing liabilities to tax and services, but in return they were liberated for all time from the deadly lottery of the conscription. The king was guaranteed the manpower he needed for his standing army at minimal cost to his Treasury. This was set out in the king's letter confirming his acceptance of the Diet scheme in 1682. He welcomed the 'establishment of a certain and permanent quota of soldiers', and in return he promised the peasants that 'in all time to come they shall have the benefit of it in all respects and be protected and no one who should be included by force of the aforementioned agreement shall be permitted to exempt themselves from this establishment of soldiers to the detriment or prejudice of others'.[7]

The process of negotiating separate contracts for each province took some years to complete, but the bargaining was genuine and considerable local flexibility was allowed. Småland, for example, got its quota reduced to 1,100 men. The actual contracts were solemn and binding. The guarantee against conscription in future was comprehensive; it included the peasants, their children and servants, and covered 'conscription and all the services connected with it, whatever name they carried, together with demands for doubling and forced enlistments, now and for the times to come'. Everywhere the local nobles tried to secure favourable terms for their tenants to join, but were defeated by the crown tenants and the king, and won no significant concessions. The actual rota arrangements had to be negotiated with

---

[6] *SRARP*, xiii, pp. 118, 120, 125, 145.

[7] *Ibid.*, pp. 134–41; RA, Kongliga concept: vol. 287, king to Axel de la Gardie, C. Gyllenstierna, C. Fleming 5 Dec. 1682.

the provincial governor, and again there was flexibility around the norm of two farms to a rota. The king was amenable, provided the required numbers were provided for the army. In each rota the wealthiest farm acted as manager of the rota, paid the soldier and provided the accommodation, but also had first call on his labour. There were problems of adjustment; at first recruits were demanding excessive enlistment money, as much as 500 dkm., but this soon settled down to the rate recommended by the king, of 100 dkm. In the same way, the original annual wage of 35 dkm., suggested in the Diet Resolution of 1682, was too high and upset local wage rates, but eventually settled down to a norm of 20 dkm. The king clearly regretted the absence of uniform wage rates, but in his instructions of 1686, he accepted there could be different local rates. The wage rate was moderated by the power given to the rotas to recruit any masterless men compulsorily. However, as the system settled down, the soldier came to have recognized status in rural society and there was an early tendency for the position to become hereditary. It was a reasonable career option to landless labourers, or surplus sons, combining a measure of economic security with a way of life that was civilian for most of his time.[8] Once the knektehåll contract had been finalised for an infantry regiment, farms and dwelling houses had to be provided, in the locality, for the officers and all NCOs above the rank of corporal through the indelningsverk. The parish *militiebok* could be written up and the whole scheme, in all its details, entered on the official Muster Roll, which was usually signed and sealed by the king. There would then be a ceremonial muster held, at which all the documents were read out in front of the troops before being lodged in the archives.[9]

Charles XI's military reforms lasted for nearly two centuries in Sweden, and their longevity rested on their essential rationality. They solved two basic problems at once: how to sustain a professional standing army in a poor country like Sweden, and how to exploit a public revenue, much of which was paid locally in produce, not cash. A standing army is normally parasitic, economically, on the community it serves. But this army remained part of the productive process. The officers and NCOs were farmers of their allotted property; the troopers and infantrymen, in peacetime, were employed as farm labourers and contributed to production. This made the burden of supporting the army tolerable, especially when combined with removing the debilitating effects of conscriptions. The problem over the tax revenues was also solved. The *militiebok* put a monetary value on the farms allocated through the indelningsverk. The tenant's obligations were usually specified in quantities of produce, and he could either hand these over, or pay the cash equivalent at local market prices. Until 1684, if the cash equivalent was below the valuation, the officer could claim a cash supplement from the crown. The new

---

[8] Ågren, *Indelningsverk*, pp. 157–9, 160–2, 164–6, 175; Gahm-Persson, ed., *Stadgar*, I, p. 498; II, pp. 1, 8, 11, 26.

[9] Ågren, *Indelningsverk*, pp. 75, 199–200; F. Lagerroth, *Statsreglering och finansförvaltning i Sverige till och med frihetstidens ingång* (Malmö, 1928), pp. 74–7.

regulations of 1684 laid down that the officer must accept the market value of his entitlement. If it was above the official valuation he could keep the surplus, if it fell below he must carry the loss. It was 'reasonable and in conformity with the king's Majesty's command and will' that he take the rent in kind in full settlement, since over time his profit and loss would balance out. Most evidence suggests that the allotments did yield the officers somewhat more than their official entitlements, and that the problem of how to pay wages to the army from revenues received in produce was resolved.[10]

The great attraction of the system for all parties to it was the security it offered. The mutual obligations were fixed for all time; the peasants were guaranteed that their basic rents and taxes would not be increased. If the peasants, or the officers and NCOs on their home farms managed to improve them and raise the yield, they kept the surplus themselves. This was underpinned by various insurance schemes. Fire was a constant hazard of early modern living, and clearly if a farm burnt down, the local arrangements were disrupted. A royal order of August 1685 required the summoning of regimental meetings, where each company would enter agreements for 'mutual help and assistance . . . so that one will help the other if any farm burns down . . . in this way Our service is more secure and their burdens easier'. In 1690 royal instructions to the Commissioners for the indelningsverk required that each cavalry farm must pay a premium of 3 dsm. annually into a regimental insurance fund to replace unexpected losses of equipment. There were similar mutual assurance schemes for the rotas against sudden heavy costs, like replacing the soldier if he died or absconded, or replacing equipment.[11]

There were problems arising from the scheme. An essential feature was that the command personnel lived on their home farm, so that the rankers were under constant supervision and training. An early difficulty was where the farm did not have a suitable dwelling house. After some years of struggling to identify properties that did have proper accommodation, the usual rationalization followed. In January 1687, the king ordered plans made of model dwellings appropriate to each rank. These would then be constructed wherever necessary, a policy that endowed the Swedish countryside with a stock of these regulation houses. Then there was the problem of ensuring that the soldiers took good care of their properties. This was covered by orders for thorough inspections and inventories of all properties, which should have taken place every three years. These were based on sets of detailed rules about upkeep, which could list such particulars as how much fencing and ditching should be done over a three-year cycle, or what area of roofing-shingles must be renewed. Endless official vigilance, combined with sanctions, was necessary to make the system work. In March 1688 the king ruled that incompetent tenants of cavalry farms could be investigated and replaced, and a month later ruled that command personnel who neglected their home farms could have the cost of

---

[10] Ågren, *Indelningsverk*, pp. 83–7.
[11] Gahm-Persson, ed., *Stadgar*, I, p. 563; II, p. 343; Nilsson, ed., *Svenska historien*, p. 176.

repairs deducted from pay. An order of 1689 dealt with the special problems of NCOs, who were often young and inexperienced and could not run a farm properly. The regimental colonels were to look into this, and while on principle the king wanted them left free to manage their properties, those obviously incapable should be persuaded to accept lodging and a money rent from the peasants.[12]

The extensive documentation that has survived shows how the need to adjust the scheme generated an endless stream of royal orders, exhortations and adjudications down to the smallest details. For example the priest's widow, Catherine Gudelius, described as 'poor and indigent' was tenant of a property allocated to the army. The royal order was that the soldiers must be found alternative support while she lived. This illustrates the basic competence of the Swedish bureaucracy that, given time, could sort out the myriad details of such a complex process, while also showing some real regard for the rights of the poor and the weak. Charles XI was adamant in demanding that the peasants must deliver their services in full and on time. But he was equally fierce against officers and officials who exhibited the age-old tendency of elites to disregard the rights of common folk. A royal letter to provincial governors in September 1683, in response to peasant complaints of abuse by the officers on their allotted properties, declared: 'We cannot tolerate and permit such misbehaviour and bad conduct any longer.' Officers must be instructed 'that they are not in the slightest to take from the peasant more than he is legally obliged to render'. Offenders 'shall as a well-deserved punishment for the first offence forfeit their year's pay'. For any further offence they would be dismissed and compelled to compensate the peasants for their losses. This order was to be read out in churches throughout the kingdom. The struggle was continuous; two years later the king issued a set of rules for the allotted properties, which took eight lengthy paragraphs to list and forbid the prevalent abuses, from demanding unreasonable labour services to trying to cheat the peasants over cash equivalents for corn rents. The effectiveness of the king's efforts is difficult to assess, but his sincere intention was beyond doubt. Charles XI knew that one of his duties to God was to uphold impartial justice for all subjects.[13]

The indelningsverk and the knektehåll were to be applied in Finland, but not in the overseas provinces. There were special difficulties in Finland which explain why the Finnish peasants were initially unenthusiastic, basically because in a much poorer part of the kingdom the king's proposals seemed excessive. There was a further problem that some of the Finnish territorial troops were employed on garrison duty in Livland, and generally had to stay there because, as the king explained, 'transport of men to and from the garrisons would be so expensive for the king's Majesty'. The province of Österbotten was so determined to keep conscription that the king gave up trying to persuade its peasants. But he persisted

---

[12] Nilsson, ed., *Svenskahistorien*, p. 179; Gahm-Persson, ed., *Stadgar*, I, p. 328; II, pp. 21, 96, 129, 295.
[13] RA, Riksregistraturet 357, 1682, 21 Jan. 1682; 367, 1683, Circular to *landshövdingar* 10 Sept. 1683; Gahm-Persson, ed., *Stadgar*, I, p. 516.

in requesting 6,000 men from the other provinces, and in 1691 ordered the provincial governors to try again. They replied that in Finland there were not enough farms to sustain the rotas, suggesting that being generally poorer in Finland, four farms would be needed instead of two. They pointed out that if the peasants were pressed too hard, they might migrate into Russia. The king decided to offer inducements: if the rotas would find a recruit and provide housing, the king would pay the annual wage. The king clearly felt the officials in Finland were not really trying; he insisted there were enough farms, and they should put aside their tendency to defend local interests and 'have Our interests and service in the matter as your priority aim'. In the end the king got the knektehåll established in most Finnish provinces, but had to offer more concessions: he told the governors they could accept 1,000 men instead of 1,200, and as a last resort go down to 800. Finland offers an interesting glimpse of a king who was theoretically absolute entering into genuine negotiation with his subjects and making real concessions to get agreement.[14]

There was an example of Charles XI's obsessive drive to maximize his military potential in his campaign to revive noble cavalry service. The status conferred on men who served on horseback, or provided a man at their own expense, had been the origin of nobility in Sweden–Finland. When, in the sixteenth century, nobility was conferred by patent, cavalry service became a property tax and the more affluent owed multiple service. But it was clearly obsolete as a method of raising cavalry and was irregularly enforced in the seventeenth century until it caught Charles XI's attention. It was a resource that, if fully exploited, would yield some 600–700 horsemen at no cost to the crown. In 1684 the king ordered a general muster of the contingents of the nobility throughout the kingdom which revealed multiple deficiencies; at some musters the equipment provided was rejected as inadequate in 98% of cases. Reorganization began on the basis of one horseman for every 250 marks of rental income and for fractions of this quota noblemen could join together to make it up. This naturally alarmed the nobility and they petitioned for a definitive law at the Diet of 1686. This was conceded by the king and regulations were published in November 1686. The basis was halved to one horseman for 500 marks rental, with the same provision for consolidating fractions. The requirements were closely defined, the type of horse and the precise equipment required were specified, and the soldier should be experienced or, 'some other reliable man'. Nobles must make a return of their rentals in February of each year so the rolls would be up to date, and there would be a full inspection of the contingent, by companies, every three years. Any complaints were to be referred directly to the king, 'since in this matter We will rule what We find to be reasonable'. An anachronistic feudal survival had been harnessed to a modern military system; it did emphasize the personal bond of service between a nobleman

---

[14] Gahm-Persson, ed., *Stadgar*, I, pp. 436, 653; II, p. 560; III, pp. 53, 97, 318, 385, 1018.

and his sovereign, and it yielded 636 horsemen in 1684 and 672 at the next muster in 1689. That was the last of the reign. The cycle of three-yearly musters could not be sustained; the bureaucracy was always over-strained, and the king's aspirations to build a smooth-running machinery exceeded its capacity. The nobility very clearly saw cavalry service obligations as a grievance, but there was no legal ground on which they could refuse.[15]

In the Diet of 1686 the king announced his intention to extend the indelningsverk to the civil service as well, so that the civilian budget in all its branches would derive 'its yearly salary and entire support from settled property rents'. This programme was unfinished in 1697; the central government departments were still paid cash salaries, but a start had been made. The province of Uppland got its indelningsverk in 1686 and it was spreading steadily to cover further areas of government, including the Church, the education services, hospitals and the costs of municipal government. The basic scheme was the same as for the military budget, except the insistence on permanence was omitted from the civil budgets, which were usually annual.[16]

The king's drive to upgrade his armed forces did not stop with finding the resources to sustain them. He wanted an army that would be qualitatively superior to any potential enemy. In the seventeenth century, as in most periods of history, the armed services were recruited from the rejects and outcasts of society, often by force. Their lives in the services tended to be nasty, brutish and short. Charles XI wanted a different kind of army. Under the new system the typical Swedish soldier was a native volunteer, serving under native officers. The king was obsessive about the importance of national identity. He wrote many letters and orders on this subject. When Nils Bielke was raising a regiment in Pomerania in the 1690s, the king urged that he 'will always try to secure Swedish officers in his regiment, because I prefer to have my own subjects under superiors who are Swedish', though he conceded subjects from the Baltic or German provinces were acceptable. The king's attention was not confined to the officers; in 1692 Colonel Cronhjort was rebuked by the king after an inspection revealed he had a Pole in his regiment, who was both illiterate and a Catholic, and was quite unacceptable. The king wanted quality soldiers and that meant God-fearing soldiers. The Articles of War of 1683 made this quite clear: 'Since all blessings come from God, and all people should worship Him, as He has revealed in His Word, therefore all ungodliness is hereby forbidden.' Undesirables were to be excluded; blasphemers, drunk or sober, would suffer death, 'without any pardon'. Enforcement was stressed in a general order of 1685 on the need for godliness in the army. The common soldiers especially must be 'bound to a true fear of God'. They would be instructed 'in the articles concerning their Christianity, and thereby can be led

---

[15] P. K. Sörensson, 'Adelns rustjänst och adelsfanans organisation', *HT* 42 and 44 (1922 and 1924), *passim*; Gahm-Persson, ed., *Stadgar*, I, p. 44.

[16] Eden, *Kammarkollegiets historia*, p. 150; Lagerroth, *Statsreglering*, pp. 82, 83, 84.

and directed from lives of wilfulness and selfishness to a true knowledge of the Highest'. The soldiers must take religious instruction from the parish priest and secure a certificate of religious knowledge, or face punishment. The king then went on to negotiate a scale of fees to the clergy for their pastoral care of the soldiers, 12 *öre* for a soldier and his family. It was inevitable that there were complaints of clergy who tried to exceed this level of payment, and that when the king heard of it a letter went out to provincial governors and the bishops that it was absolutely forbidden to demand anything extra. A group of priests, who had been exposed, tried to claim they had not realized that soldiers' wives were included; the king dismissed the excuse: 'the regulation itself is clear'. He would however let them off their deserved punishment if they refunded twice the excess they had taken from the soldiers.[17]

It was characteristic of the king's attitude to his soldiers that he tried to protect them from the abuse by their social superiors, which was endemic in the armies of the day. In September 1692, a general order was issued and printed forbidding a range of oppressive actions by officers. These included interfering with the men's pay, or trying to exploit their labour for private advantage. In a letter to Nils Bielke in 1689 the king said: 'since it has come to Our ears that some officers should dare to engage in trade and commerce with their own soldiers . . . We find such conduct wholly intolerable'. Bielke was instructed to stamp this out in his command. Perhaps the most striking expression of the king's attitude was his reaction at learning that the Stockholm Guild of Surgeons accepted lower standards for candidates entering the forces. He wrote a condemnation, 'as if it were less important to choose and select well-trained surgeons for so many thousand of our brave officers and honest soldiers, who venture life and blood for the Fatherland'. The Guild was told: 'We note with grave displeasure this custom and bad practice.' Yet the king was a stern disciplinarian. The Articles of War, all 145 of them, were to be read out monthly in all units. They were draconian, and the judicial officers were reminded they were to be enforced to the letter. Otherwise they themselves would not 'avoid the punishment they are to expect, according to the circumstances of the case, if they behave otherwise'. The Articles were clear that obedience to superiors was unconditional at all levels and any refusal of orders was punishable by death, as was any cowardice in battle and serious moral offences, including all instances of rape. However, on balance it seems clear that Charles XI recognized that even the common soldiers were subjects with legal rights, who performed a vital service to the kingdom, and that it was his duty to defend their rights against abuse by the ruling elites. The soldier in Sweden's standing army was not a social outcast, but had a respectable position in the social structure. In the territorial regiments he could live at home with his family, assured of housing, subsistence and a regular wage, and could expect continuing social support if he were invalided out, or

[17] Malmström, ed., 'Karl XIs bref till Nils Bielke', p. 99; Gahm-Persson, ed., *Stadgar*, I, p. 591; II, pp. 401, 405, 553; III, pp. 232, 731, 763.

retired through old age, provided by various compulsory insurance schemes set up on the king's orders.[18]

The king showed equal care over the equipment and training of his troops. His aim was to have standard uniforms for officers and men, and standard, high-quality equipment. The contracts for army uniforms gave a considerable boost to Sweden's modest textile industry. In 1686 it was ordered that all uniforms were to be of domestic cloth and quotas were allocated to the different manufacturing centres. The king insisted that once issued, the uniforms be properly cared for, above all not used as work clothes. Except when the soldiers were on service, the uniforms were stored in locked chests of specified dimensions, and propped up above floor level to stop vermin getting in. The same care was taken with the equipment; it was kept in locked stores, so that in between training sessions the weapons would not be damaged, or worse sold. The king was active in promoting the armaments industries. When, in 1682, the king was told of an iron works in Jönköping, capable of making 12 and 24 pounder artillery pieces, he decided it must be encouraged, and orders went to the local governor to see they were supplied with oak for the gun carriages. The owner of a major harness-making business in Arboga declared his wish to retire on health grounds and the king organized a take-over to keep the business going, since 'Our service cannot bear, nor will We permit that the same shall become decayed and neglected.' Quality control was taken seriously; in August 1684 it was ordered that all cavalry weapons were to be purchased from Lars Fleming's works in Uppland, but were first to be tested and stamped. This followed earlier instructions specifying exactly what equipment the troopers should have. In 1865 the breast-plates being manufactured at Arboga were to be tested by trial shots, and given a certificate of satisfactory performance before issue. By the 1690s the king could expect all units to have standard equipment, and insisted that non-standard equipment be discarded, 'so as to achieve uniformity, so that all sets of equipment be alike in every item'.[19]

Training was an essential part of the reforms; in the territorial regiments each company held a training session once a month, and the regiment held a summer camp and manoeuvres, and every third year would face an inspection by the king. The king spent a large part of his working life on tours of the provinces, during which all the local military units were inspected. These royal inspections must have been a fearful ordeal; the volume of official correspondence which they generated shows that no detail was too small to escape the king's attention, and how easily the royal anger was kindled by evidence of slackness or neglect. Horn's diary for February 1684 gives a vivid description of the king conducting an inspection. On 12 February, 'the king began the review and passed six companies because he started

---

[18] Gahm-Persson, ed., *Stadgar*, I, pp. 227–9, 233–45, 489, 515, 516, 563; II, pp. 319, 330; III, p. 169; Malmström, ed., 'Karl XIs bref till Nils Bielke', p. 44.
[19] Nilsson, ed., *Svenska historien*, p. 62; Gahm-Persson, ed., *Stadgar*, I, pp. 449, 454, 563; II, pp. 345, 407; III, pp. 710, 733: RA Riksregistraturet 357, 1682, king's letter of 21 Jan. 1680.

remarkably early'. The next day he did the remaining two companies before the meal break, after which

all senior and junior officers went through their musket drills in the king's presence, which took up time, so it struck one before we could get to table. The mealtime was hurried and in the meantime the regiment was drawn up outside town, where the king proceeded and held all kinds of military exercises which lasted late into the afternoon . . . The mealtime was late in the evening, because the king was much occupied with the officers' residences and called in all the senior officers to inform himself about this . . . I left and went to bed without eating.

The day following the king watched each company do its exercises separately, and after leaving the commander orders to continue with the training, departed for Stockholm. The instructions for preparing an inspection of the newly recruited regiment for Närke and Värmland reveal the dual purpose of the inspection, to verify that the manpower was of acceptable quality and that it was properly trained. Similar instructions for Dalarna in 1685 stressed that all the allotted farms would be inspected, as would the recruits, and if any were found unsuitable the rota would be called to account. Elderly soldiers were to be replaced, with the reservation 'that the regiment is not filled up with a crowd of young and inexperienced soldiers through excessive discharge of old ones'. All the muskets would be checked and certified to be of standard pattern, and checks made to ensure that the various insurance funds had been set up. These instructions were formidable documents; the instruction of 1692 for general musters in Hälsingland and Jämtland contains twenty-five dense paragraphs of requirements.[20]

An essential part of the system was the careful planning for rapid mobilization and assembly of the army, mostly at ports of embarkation for service south of the Baltic. A basic plan was issued in February 1689. Previously, the costs of the feeding, transporting and billeting of troops on the march had fallen excessively on communities close to the main roads. Now the king declared that, 'while we still are in enjoyment of a time of peace', it was an opportunity to prepare. There was to be a cash levy on property throughout the kingdom. This would provide a fund so that in future all those involved in supporting marching troops would be recompensed promptly, in cash. The provincial governors would help to plan the routes in advance, calculate what transport and supplies were needed and establish the necessary stores along the route. The levy was not popular, and there were protests, but the king insisted on the principle that all must contribute. The modified march order of April 1696 justified this 'because all will enjoy the defence and security, there being nothing more reasonable in any matter intended for the whole kingdom's and especially each individual's security and peace, that all, each according to their condition, help to sustain the burdens involved'. Charles XI's mobilization plan was a model of meticulous bureaucratic planning,

---

[20] Munthe, 'Ett stycke karolinsk vardag', pp. 131–2; Gahm-Persson, ed., *Stadgar*, I, pp. 444, 565; III, p. 81.

based on a clear public service ethos. When it was activated in 1700 it worked to perfection.[21]

The king's tireless labours had created an army of high quality, recruited from native subjects, with its discipline based on professionalism and close ties between officers and men. It had sound equipment, realistic training and was backed by careful logistical planning. The accounts of the training programmes show they concentrated on the actual business of warfare; this was not a parade army. In 1694 the king issued a manual on tactics describing how this quality force would be used. The thinking was that while the strategy was defensive, the tactics must be offensive, since Sweden lacked the resources for prolonged warfare and must seek a speedy resolution through a decisive encounter. The tactics accepted the relative ineffectiveness of early modern firearms, except at very close range. Success would be achieved by the very rapid movement of highly disciplined units, whose sheer impact would break the enemy. The Swedish infantry, who still used the pike and carried swords, would advance and fire only twice, at seventy and thirty paces from the enemy, then draw swords and fall on. The cavalry advanced rapidly without firing at all.[22] It was a gamble on highly trained troops, well motivated and disciplined and moving with disconcerting speed, being able to break the average mercenary or conscript armies of the day. When it did go into action under Charles XII it had phenomenal success and justified a lifetime of laborious questioning and nagging and attention to detail by his father, and his proclaimed pursuit of equality of sacrifice from subjects in pursuit of the welfare of all.

Navies are essentially different from armies, but the same basic thinking drove the complete rebuilding of the Swedish navy after 1680. Charles XI never had the same input into naval affairs, lacking both expertise and enthusiasm, and the principal direction of the naval reforms was devolved on Hans Wachtmeister, who had uninterrupted control from 1679, with the king's influence operating at a distance. This was because it had been decided to relocate the fleet to a greenfield site south of Kalmar and move the Admiralty administration down from Stockholm. The site chosen was controversial; Dahlberg says that Wachtmeister wanted a site at Lyckeby, but after site inspections 'it was decided that a town be built at Trossön which was named and called Karlskrona'. It has remained the main base of the Swedish navy to the present day. The reason for the move was to increase the effectiveness of the navy. In a southern location it would be free of ice at an earlier date and the distance to the most likely area of operations, against Denmark, was much shorter. The negative side was a conservative reluctance to leave Stockholm for a province, Blekinge, recently acquired from Denmark, where the local population was of doubtful political reliability, and proved unwelcoming to incomers. At first the conditions at Karlskrona were equally unwelcoming; a letter of 1687 complained that the new Admiralty buildings leaked so that rain was

---

[21] Gahm-Persson, ed., *Stadgar*, II, pp. 343, 441; III, p. 879.
[22] Holmqvist, *Tre Karlar*, pp. 28, 56, 58–60; Sjögren, *Karl den elfte*, p. 365.

ruining the archives and called for the building to be weatherproofed as a matter of urgency. But the move came to be accepted, and the formal report of the Admiralty to the Diet of 1697 put it first in the list of improvements since 1680. The same report defined the remit of the navy. A strong navy was required because by right *dominium maris Baltici* belonged to the kings of Sweden. It concluded that 'it has always been proven necessary that your royal Majesty's kingdom must be equipped with such a substantial battle fleet, that the same *dominium maris* can be upheld at all times with appropriate force and your royal Majesty's provinces and territories sheltered and protected from hostile invasion, also that the free and unhindered flow of commerce be sustained as far as possible'.[23] This stated the obvious: without naval control, Sweden was vulnerable to attack, the territories south of the Baltic could not be defended at all and effective constraint of Denmark was impossible.

G. O. Stenbock, although he was discredited by wartime failures and deeply involved with the Regency Tribunal, held his post as Admiral until his death in 1685, but took no further part in naval administration. The Admiralty College in Stockholm lost authority, as Wachtmeister was appointed 'General Admiral' in September 1681 and shortly after was appointed to the Council of State. He held virtual monopoly powers over the navy and set about moving the administration down south. In 1683, as a result of a war scare, the king spent some time at Kalmar and in August restructured the naval command. The fleet was divided into three squadrons, each headed by an Admiral, and they were to share administrative responsibility, restoring a form of collegiate control, except that Wachtmeister alone controlled finance. His two colleagues were Hans Clerk and Eric Sjöblad, who were also made Governor over Kalmar and Blekinge provinces respectively, giving them civil control over the hinterland of Karlskrona, while Wachtmeister was made Governor General over both provinces. The king's letter of appointment urged harmony: 'the king has no doubt of good understanding between them and all good unity and trust, to the advantage of the common good . . . without intrigue or jealousy'. In fact the three admirals worked quite well together, but Wachtmeister engaged in a bitter feud with Gabriel Hilleton, whom the king appointed in 1684 as Commissary to supervise naval finance. Hilleton was outraged by Wachtmeister's accounting methods and the king agreed with him, engendering some outspoken correspondence between the admiral and the king. There is a series of royal letters of complaint to Wachtmeister and unapologetic replies from the admiral, which pointed out the administration was under-staffed and said bluntly that admirals could not be expected to be accountants. It became a war of attrition between Wachtmeister, essentially a fighting sailor, and the bureaucratically minded king.[24]

---

[23] Åberg, *Karl XI*, p. 95; Sjögren, *Karl den elfte*, pp. 368–9; E. Wendt, *Amiralitetskollegiets historia*, I: *1634–1695* (Stockholm, 1950), p. 410; Loenbom, ed., *Handlingar*, IV, collection XI, pp. 113–26.

[24] Wendt, *Amiralitetskollegiets historia*, pp. 302, 306, 313–15, 319, 320, 335, 340.

In 1689 Hilleton died; at the same time the fleet was mobilized and taken to sea. Wachtmeister sent letters from the fleet to highlight the supply problems that arose, which he blamed on Hilleton's interference: 'he processed contracts and assignments in his office, before the matters had been prepared and decisions taken in the College'. Wachtmeister then pointed out it was really the king's fault, 'since I most humbly petitioned that your Majesty would be graciously pleased to set up a proper College for the Admiralty'. He trusted that henceforth the king would show 'the gracious confidence that I, after so many years being involved in this business, may have grasped its nature'. Wachtmeister had sent a scheme for an Admiralty College, which eliminated the office of Commissary, in June 1688, but the king had been offended; it contained, 'doubtful expressions' and involved extra expenditure. He rejected it, telling Wachtmeister that if he and his colleagues did their jobs properly, they could manage 'with the numbers they had before this'. Wachtmeister is unusual among the king's servants for his outspoken criticisms, but he got away with it, presumably on the strength of their youthful intimacy, the admiral's professional credentials and the long distances that separated Karlskrona from Stockholm. 1690 was a rough year; the king visited Karlskrona and sent letters expressing anger at what he found: the naval budget for 1689 had been 138,204 dsm. overspent. Then the king sent down a set of operational instructions for the navy and Wachtmeister objected; they had been copied straight from British admiralty instructions. The king was infuriated by the 'mass of criticisms and comments' and concluded: 'it would not matter if it had been taken from a Turkish order, if it contributed to the advancement of Our service'. As the king saw it he had worked hard to see that the navy was adequately funded. A large block of land revenues in Finland, recovered through the reduktion, was allocated to the navy, and its basic allocation of 350,000 dsm. annually, set in 1685, was well secured. It is understandable why Charles XI was driven to fury by Wachtmeister's endless pleas for more funding. He wrote in 1686: 'you must make sure that the budget is observed and in no way exceeded . . . as We have established the ordinary budget in a condition that it shall become fixed, so We will not permit you to come in hereafter with memoranda and reminders concerning some addition'. Wachtmeister turned the Nelsonian blind eye to this and he won. In 1691 he had a supplementary budget of 129,048 dsm. By 1697 this had increased to 306,235 dsm., nearly as much as his ordinary budget. Yet in return Wachtmeister did create an effective, modern navy.[25]

Recruiting the navy was done on lines similar to that for the army. Traditionally the Burgher Estate, in return for exemption from conscription, had paid for a quota of seamen, which doubled in wartime. It could be supplemented by conscription from the countryside in maritime districts. But the move to Karlskrona created a

[25] *Ibid.*, pp. 343, 345, 347, 350, 351, 353, 362, 364, 368, 395, 438, 453, 455, 459, 468, 469; RA, Skrivelser till konungen, Karl XIs tid, Hans Wachtmeisters skrivelser till Kong.Mt. 1677–90, letters of 24 June 1689, 29 July 1689.

new problem. The local population was considered politically unreliable, and the transport of recruits over long distances from traditional recruiting grounds was costly and unreliable. Wachtmeister had discussed the problem with the king in 1679, and in 1680 it was decided that for the more remote regions of Norrland and Finland, the local communities would be invited to commute the obligation to supply seamen for cash. This worked; in the end they negotiated fifty-five separate contracts which cancelled the liability to conscription and substituted a money equivalent, which would double in wartime. An early modern navy did not need a full complement of men in peacetime, when the ships were not fully manned. So the next stage was to bring the men who were needed down to Blekinge, and billet them on peasant farms for a cash payment. By April 1685 contracts had been completed to billet 1,500 seamen in Blekinge, and 800 more in neighbouring Södre Möre, while as Karlskrona town developed, some could be lodged there. The remaining seamen were maintained in their homes by rotas of peasant households. In the only full mobilization of 1689, the locally based boatmen were supplemented by 6,200 more provided by the rotas. In addition the cash was used to hire mercenaries, and the total raised proved adequate.[26]

It was not possible to train the seamen on the pattern of the army for it would have been impossibly costly to mount summer cruises. For experienced petty-officers, the navy relied on mercenaries and experienced merchant seamen, though from 1692 there was a school for navigators and midshipmen. Commissioned officers were generally required to get experience as petty-officers, and the king instituted a basic qualifying test for officers, and encouraged them to gain experience in foreign service. The navy had a special requirement for skilled craftsmen, particularly for the new shipyard at Karlskrona. The period saw the development of a flourishing new shipbuilding industry in Österbotten, and favourable wages were offered to relocate skilled craftsmen to Karlskrona, with their families. This ran into many difficulties, but carried a bonus in that the newcomers settled in the existing communities and diluted the existing Danish orientated population.[27]

The report by the Admiralty to the Diet of 1697 has an obvious propaganda content and puts the best possible construction on what had been done. Five major achievements were claimed. The most important was the move to Karlskrona, since bringing the ships south put them so much nearer the likely area of operations that greater seapower could be projected with the same number of ships. Then the fleet had been rebuilt, the twenty-seven ships of 1680 had increased to fifty-two, and only nine of them were older than 1680. The concentration of the fleet in one station facilitated the build up of stores and services. The manpower requirements

---

[26] Wendt, *Amiralitetskollegiets historia*, pp. 410, 411, 416, 417; N. E. Villstrand, ed., *Kustbygd och centralmakt 1560–1721: studier i centrum-pereferi under svensk stormaktstid* (Helsinki, 1987), pp. 391, 400; *SRARP*, xv, p. 159; Lagerroth, *Statsreglering*, p. 411; J. Cavallie, *De höga officerarna: studier in den svenska militära hierarki under 1600-talets senare del* (Stockholm, 1981), p. 12.

[27] Wendt, *Amiralitetskollegiets historia*, pp. 417–19, 438; Villstrand, *Kustbygd*, pp. 367–8.

of the navy had been covered on a basis that was not excessively burdensome. Finally the Admiralty administration had been overhauled completely and its budget settled.[28]

The military reconstruction, which was the core project of Charles XI's reign, can be evaluated from two directions: as the creation of effective armed forces, adapted to Sweden's requirements and capacity, and as the cause of significant social developments. For common folk the reform did not bring much reduction of their contribution. The peasants in the rotas for the knektehåll or the contract boatmen had undertaken heavy obligations which the king enforced rigorously. While the tenants of farms included in the indelningsverk often found that their military landlords, who had every incentive to maximize their returns, and usually lived on the property, were more exacting than the former owners. What the common folk gained was a measure of security, liberation from a range of arbitrary demands in exchange for fixed, legally defined and enforceable obligations. Urban employers, clergy, peasant farmers and their hired labourers and servants were free from the hazards of conscription, free from arbitrary demands for the billeting and transport of soldiers and protected from the scourge of early modern society, the anti-social behaviour of a licentious soldiery. Charles XI's soldiers were not social outcasts, but disciplined servants of the crown, with a humble but recognized place in society, who could live on equal terms with the civil population. The one group excepted from these securities were the 'masterless men', who paid for their independent lifestyle by remaining subject to arbitrary direction by the authorities. It would be unhistorical to idealize the situation – the records are filled with complaints of failings and abuses – but those same records show the king and his officials working conscientiously to remedy abuse and achieve a rough equity, in which the unavoidable hardships of early modern living were shared out among different social groups, not of course equally, but according to their recognized status in society.

In the elite sector the central issue is how far the nobility were able to recoup the losses they suffered through reduktion and the heavy taxation they continued to pay, in spite of their privileges, by securing permanent, reasonably paid public employment. The change in the Swedish nobility, very broadly, from a small elite of aristocratic landlords, who also served the state, to a much more numerous open oligarchy of state servants, who were ennobled and also possessed some landed property, has been noted already. A recent study by Dr Asker has concluded that 'an ever growing proportion of landowners could rather be described as land-owning state servants than as landowners serving the state'. Analysis of the officer corps under Charles XI shows that the higher ranks, major and above, were almost wholly filled by noblemen. There were seventy-seven of them in 1699, and forty were of the high nobility, Classes I and II, and the remainder from Class III, apart

---

[28] Loenbom, ed., *Handlingar*, IV, collection XI.

from five foreign nobles. It is true that twenty-two of them were commoners by birth, but none of these got higher than colonel, and all had fathers who had been ennobled before they began army careers. There is a different distribution among the regimental officers, ensigns, lieutenants and captains. Figures for 1682 show over half of these were commoners. The salary structures too emphasize the differences between these categories. After the uprating of pay scales in 1690 a captain of infantry got 200 dsm. and a captain of cavalry 240 dsm. This was a modest salary derived wholly from his allotted farm. The status was equally modest; in Charles XI's revised Table of Ranks of 1696, which has forty grades, a captain ranked thirty-six. Then above the rank of captain, salaries were augmented because the higher ranks held multiple commissions. Thus a major drew a captain's salary in addition to his pay as major. As an example, in 1699 Lieutenant-General R. Rehbinder drew 1,800 dsm. as lieutenant-general, a further 1,500 dsm. as colonel and his 200 dsm. as captain. In addition officers of this rank got a large part of their pay in cash in addition to the allotted land rent. It seems clear that even after 1680 the upper nobility retained its predominance in the higher ranks of the armed forces, though there are signs that merit, rather than status, was carrying more weight in promotions. Whereas in an earlier period, L. Ribbing, a nephew of a field marshal, had been commissioned as ensign in January 1659, and was a lieutenant-colonel by April 1660 at the age of twenty-two, this ceased to happen under Charles XI. Once the son of a magnate could confidently expect to reach colonel by the age of thirty, but of the sixty-two sons of Council members who entered the army in 1682–97, only one got to colonel by that age. The key was that after 1680 all officer appointments were reserved to the king, and he gave them close attention and was looking for professional competence. Being of the nobility did carry some career advantage, for there were fast-track entry systems for noblemen, not open to commoners, which conferred advantage in a career increasingly based on seniority. A nobleman could enlist in the Life Guard as a ranker and get early commissioning, or he could get an appointment as page at the royal Court, and again move early into a commission, or he could get a university qualification and be commissioned on graduation. In each case he would gain some years career advantage over a commoner working up through the ranks. On top of that a nobleman, commissioned as ensign, was often able to skip the lieutenancy and get his first promotion directly to captain. This all helps explain the preponderance of nobles in the higher ranks by 1699. They were further helped by the king's desire to eliminate foreigners, illustrated by the sharp fall in numbers of foreign nobles in Swedish service. The few who did survive mostly served in the mercenary units stationed outside Sweden proper.[29]

---

[29] Asker, *Officerarna*, pp. 37, 43, 147–50; Cavallie, *Officerarna*, pp. 13, 14, 15, 17–24; M. Revera and R. Torstendahl, eds., *Börder, bönder, börd i 1600-talets Sverige* (Uppsala, 1979), pp. 224–32, 233–55; G. Rystad, ed., *Europe and Scandinavia: aspects of the process of integration in the 17th century* (Lund, 1983), p. 155.

The evidence analysed so far does seem to suggest that after 1680, noblemen could make an acceptable career in the armed forces, usually in the home-based territorial regiments, and could expect to be promoted to field rank, with a salary, perquisites and position in the Table of Ranks that would allow them to maintain a modest aristocratic lifestyle, with a country residence. The magnate families had lost much of their former advantage, since the patronage network had largely slipped away from them into the hands of the newly ennobled civil servants, who were best placed to influence the king's promotion choices. It can be observed that many of the these first generation nobles preferred to send their own children into military careers. The navy offered parallel opportunities, except that salary levels for equivalent ranks were lower there, which is one reason why at all levels in 1699 half the naval officers were commoners. It does therefore seem that Charles XI's reconstruction of the armed forces, largely out of the proceeds of the reduktion, brought compensating advantages for noblemen, as it did for commoners, in return for the sacrifices they had been forced to make.

6

The search for external security, 1679–1686

Thomas Hobbes, the English philosopher, told his readers that they could see what the State of Nature would be like – an endless war of each individual against every other individual in order to maximize his own power relative to everyone else, a struggle that ended only in death – if they looked at the contemporary system of international relations. The rulers of seventeenth-century Europe were locked into an open-ended power struggle, in which all the participants were trying to change the balance of power in their own favour. It was not an option to contract out of this struggle, for those who did not compete would be devoured by the predators. That was why the emerging early modern states were, primarily, war machines, Sweden being a very good example of this. It was a ruthless struggle with only one rule, that might was right and the winner takes all. There had long been attempts to civilize the system by introducing legal and moral concepts that would mitigate its brutal consequences. There had been the concept of Europe as Christendom, a community based on the acceptance by all its members of common moral values based on a shared religious faith, which should constrain their behaviour. This had been dealt a shattering blow by the Reformation, and such restraining value as it had exercised had been irreparably weakened. The seventeenth-century Europeans were trying to reinforce the old constraints, based on the law of God, with the more secular concept of a law of nations, based on the universal Law of Nature, accessible to all men through reason. The peace settlements of 1648 and 1660 were proclaimed as normative, an international law. They defined the parameters within which the European power struggle would be confined. By these settlements, the rulers of Europe and their ministers had tried to introduce moral restraints into the otherwise amoral world of competitive power politics.

Charles XI had to be personally involved in all matters of foreign policy, if only because international relations were still built around the personal interactions of sovereign princes, and largely conceived in terms of dynastic interest. Sweden was unusual because law and custom set some constraints on the ruler's conduct of foreign relations. The coronation oath bound him to consult the community of the realm over offensive war and the conclusion of peace. It was also long-established practice that the Council be consulted on matters of foreign policy. And every Diet session was given a report on international relations, in very general terms in the General Propositions, in considerable detail in the Secret Propositions, and in the

Diet Resolution the Estates, except for the Peasants who were considered too ignorant to participate, gave their considered views. Charles XI was scrupulous in consulting the Council on foreign policy, attending the meetings and participating in discussion. Yet there was a widespread contemporary impression that the king was poorly qualified and ineffective in foreign affairs, and thus a tool in the hands of his advisers. It was a fact that he knew nothing at first hand of the world outside Sweden's borders, that his only working foreign language was German, which limited his capacity for direct exchanges with foreign envoys. The Danish minister, M. Scheel, reported to his king how Charles XI seemed embarrassed by questions, kept his eyes down and was taciturn, 'so that there was little or nothing to conclude from it'. The French diplomat, Jean Antoine de Mesmes, comte d'Avaux, described him as 'a prince with few natural talents', so obsessed with getting money out of his subjects that 'he does not concern himself much with foreign affairs'. The Dane, Jens Juel, made a similar comment; the king was so immersed in domestic reconstruction that he left foreign policy to his diplomats, at least until such time as the reforms took effect, hence he concluded in 1681: 'there is little sign that Sweden, for some years to come, will really want to be engaged in any wars'.[1]

The king's apparent lack of concern about foreign affairs can also be explained by the existence among Sweden's ruling elites of a substantial consensus on the matter, which had prevailed since 1660. The basis of this was acceptance that the days of predatory expansion were over, and Sweden was now a satisfied power whose concern in international affairs was to uphold the status quo, as defined in the settlements of 1648 and 1660. For this there must be adequate armed strength, since otherwise the country was threatened by attack and dismemberment by her neighbours, all of whom had territorial ambitions at Sweden's expense. Denmark in particular had a succession of defeats and humiliations to avenge. This was not paranoia; the record shows that Christian V of Denmark always meant to recover Skåne for Denmark, to crush the duke of Holstein-Gottorp and ultimately to take Bremen-Verden from Sweden. So the Swedish policy makers also recognized that they needed an ally among the major powers, who was interested in maintaining stability in the Baltic, and would help keep the neighbours in check. Then, in the event of European war, Sweden could pursue a policy of armed neutrality, so as to come forward as mediator at a suitable opportunity.[2] This consensus analysis was shared by the three men who directed Sweden's foreign policy between 1660 and 1697: Magnus Gabriel de la Gardie, Johan Gyllenstierna and Bengt Oxenstierna, and accepted by Charles XI who had, therefore, no compelling reason to intervene.

[1] Åberg, *Karl XI*, p. 107; O. H. Wieselgren, ed., *Den Svenska utrikesförvaltningens historia*, I: A. Munthe, *Utrikesförvaltningen 1648–1720* (Stockholm, 1935), p. 157; Fryxell, ed., *Handlingar*, I, pp. 434, 643; R. Fåhreus, *Sverige och Danmark 1680–1682: ett bidrag till skandinavismens historia* (Stockholm, 1897), p. 56.
[2] B. Fahlberg, 'Den senare 1600-talets svenska utrikespolitik', *HT* 74 (1954), p. 103; K.-O. Rudelius, *Sveriges utrikespolitik 1681–1684: från garantitraktaten till stilleståndet i Regensburg* (Uppsala, 1942), p. 66.

Within the consensus there was still a need for tactical choices, for example which major power should be Sweden's patron and ally. Since the 1630s this had traditionally been France, for the kings of France had no interests of their own to pursue in the Baltic, but did appreciate having a powerful ally there, able to influence developments in northern Germany. The main rivals of France, the Habsburg emperors, were by comparison aggressively at odds with Sweden's claims to uphold the cause of Protestantism in the Holy Roman Empire, a role recognized in the Westphalia settlements, while the United Provinces were active commercial competitors with Sweden for the control of Baltic commerce. The consensus that France was Sweden's natural ally still held in 1680, though there was awareness that the connection had been the main cause of the recent unhappy war. When the Council discussed the matter in February 1680, they expressed dissatisfaction over French subsidy payments, but resolved not to press the issue, since 'their Excellencies find an alliance with France is absolutely necessary for us now'. Despite the dramatic shift of policy that began in 1680, this remained the view of much of the Swedish elite for the rest of the reign.[3]

When Johan Gyllenstierna had been in opposition, seeking to undermine de la Gardie, he had criticized the French subsidy treaty of 1672 and subsequently blamed it for the disastrous war. By 1679 Gyllenstierna controlled foreign policy and proposed a radical modification of the consensus line. This was built on a close alliance of Sweden and Denmark, formalized in the treaty of Lund in 1679. It had much to commend it in theory. It relieved both kingdoms of their most pressing security threat, attack by one on the other, and made them almost invulnerable to third parties, since between them they could dominate the Baltic Sea. They could jointly pursue their commercial grievances against the United Provinces, and jointly negotiate favourable terms of alliance with Louis XIV, who would lose the leverage he enjoyed by playing one Scandinavian monarchy against the other. In reality a Scandinavian alliance was a chimera because, for good historical reasons, the mutual confidence between Denmark and Sweden, essential for a working collaboration, did not exist. Rålamb expressed the traditional view in Council in 1680 when he said: 'we can place no reliance on Denmark, which has always abused our good faith'. Gyllenstierna shared this opinion; just before entering on the negotiation he had written to Nils Bielke what a good idea it would be if Sweden joined France in carving Denmark up: 'now is the favourable time, Denmark is deprived of all friends . . . How easy it would be to break into Holstein and the whole of Jutland.' More importantly, Charles XI, a natural traditionalist, shared the universal distrust. He warned Gyllenstierna, as he embarked on the new policy, that Denmark's sincerity was questionable and Sweden might 'neglect its former friends' and 'without one trustworthy friend, might fall between two stools, as they say'.[4]

---

[3] RA, Rådsprotokoll, vol. 72, meeting of 24 Feb. 1680.
[4] Fahlberg, 'Den senare 1600-talets svenska utrikespolitik', pp. 105–6; Landberg, *Utrikespolitikens historia, I.3*, pp. 203–4; Landberg, *Nordiska förbundspolitik*, pp. 117–30; Fåhreus, *Sverige*, pp. 5, 8, 11, 16, 28.

The treaty of Lund was negotiated in secrecy by Gyllenstierna and Secretary Joel Örnstedt for Sweden, and Jens Juel for Denmark. The public version was a simple defensive alliance. But a secret treaty provided for cooperation on a range of issues, in northern Germany, in jointly negotiating with Louis XIV and in maintaining a common economic policy against all third parties to ensure hegemony over Baltic trade. These economic plans seem to be the core of Gyllenstierna's project, and attracted Charles XI, who was then refusing to ratify an unfavourable commercial treaty with the United Provinces that had been part of the Nijmegen settlements of 1678. The distrust at the heart of the new alliance was apparent in the king of Denmark's instructions of April 1680, which suspected that Sweden would use the economic provision to do a favourable deal with the Dutch at Denmark's expense. But the worst sticking point was Holstein-Gottorp. Denmark demanded a free hand to deal with its troublesome vassal, and got a clause in the treaty that there should be no interference in internal affairs. This was a priority issue for Denmark, and Gyllenstierna fudged it by explicit personal assurances that Sweden would no longer intervene on the duke's behalf. The Danish envoy told his king that Gyllenstierna 'swore and affirmed that God should punish him eternally' if Charles XI intervened. Yet Gyllenstierna knew that the king regarded the protection of the duke as a question of honour, and would not shift from asserting the rights of the duke as enshrined in the treaties of 1660 and 1679. Further the queen-mother was a rabid Holstein partisan and influential with her son. It is unclear how Gyllenstierna persuaded the king to give him a free hand, as he did in a letter of September 1679, 'to do what you discover to be for the best interest and advantage of Us and Our kingdom'. The clue may be in the sentence that the duke could be protected 'through a good interpretation', in plain language, by cheating. The Holstein issue encapsulated the hollowness of the alliance: evidence suggests that Gyllenstierna and the king supposed that Louis XIV could be persuaded to insist on the rights of the duke as expressed in the peace treaties. But everything about Gyllenstierna's project is speculative; evidence is very sparse and he carried the secret to his grave in 1680. He may have believed cooperation could be made to work, or it could be he wanted only to neutralize Denmark while Sweden recovered her military potential. In any case once Gyllenstierna was dead, so was the alliance with Denmark. In February 1681 the Danish minister complained to Charles XI that Bengt Oxenstierna had told him that the alliance 'was, so to say, chimerical'. Later the same year Scheel told the Danish king: 'all your approaches are suspect to them . . . in every respect they have the doubt about your friendship that we could have of theirs'.[5]

There were two test issues in 1680–1 which showed that the alliance had failed. One was the question of making a commercial treaty with the United Provinces. Here Sweden behaved as the Danish king had feared; she concluded her own

---

[5] Landberg, 'Johan Gyllenstierna', pp. 128, 134; Fåhreus, *Sverige*, pp. 25, 27, 28, 30, 31; Landberg, *Utrikespolitikens historia*, pp. 206, 211; Fryxell, ed., *Handlingar*, I, pp. 434, 463; II pp. 128, 131, 135.

bilateral agreement, without consulting Denmark and at Denmark's expense. Before Gyllenstierna died, in February 1680, the Council had advised the king to ratify the treaty concluded in 1678, despite some unfavourable provisions. The king agreed, but was then dissuaded by Gyllenstierna. Thus when he died, the question of who would assume direction of policy was crucial. There was a choice, the Secretary Örnstedt was pro-Danish and was lobbied for by the Danish ministers. But the king's choice was Bengt Oxenstierna, who was appointed President of the Chancery College in place of de la Gardie. The College acted as Sweden's foreign ministry and Oxenstierna was in charge of foreign policy for the rest of the reign. It took the Dane, Jens Juel, by surprise; Oxenstierna was the head of the greatest magnate clan and a known enemy of Gyllenstierna. The minister reported: 'his character is quite different from the king's, being formal and sluggish, the only sympathy between them is that Count Bengt is also a great lover of horses'. But given that this was the king's one personal passion, Juel thought it could be the basis of a lasting relationship. In reality there was a more solid foundation than that: in a memorandum of 1696, Oxenstierna reminded the king that he had been instructed to ensure that 'the newly concluded peace could be preserved'. It was Oxenstierna's success in doing this that secured his position.[6]

Oxenstierna's first major decision was to carry through ratification of the commercial treaty, despite protests from Denmark that it would be regarded as a breach of the alliance. When the matter was debated in the Council again, in October 1680, the king expressed moral scruples, but Oxenstierna showed his strength by persisting, and in the end cut short the debate, 'since the matter is already resolved'. When ratification was announced publicly in February 1681, it was claimed to be consistent with the Danish alliance, and did in fact include some marginal concessions by the United Provinces that applied to Denmark as well. The Danish king was not deceived; he acquiesced in public, but his private view was that the agreement was a clear violation of the alliance treaty. The agreed joint negotiation with Louis XIV for a subsidy treaty proved equally hollow. Formal discussions were pursued in Paris, but both Sweden and Denmark maintained parallel bilateral approaches in secrecy. When the Council reviewed the policy, it gave lukewarm support; Nils Brahe expressed the mood: 'Denmark will always raise some objection to the French proposals, if they are such that they could be of advantage to us.'[7] It was well known that Oxenstierna was anti-Danish, but it then emerged that he was also anti-French and this caused a major policy shift. It was consistent with the consensus principle that Sweden's concern was to maintain the status quo. But while participating in the congress at Nijmegen, Oxenstierna had formed the view that now it was Louis XIV, with his aggressive *réunion* policy, who threatened

---

[6] Fryxell, ed., *Handlingar*, I, pp. 392, 393; Fåhreus, *Sverige*, pp. 28, 29; Munthe, *Utrikesförvaltningen*, p. 158; Loenbom, ed., *Handlingar*, I, collection I, p. 122.

[7] Landberg, *Utrikespolitikens historia*, pp. 217, 218, 219; Fåhreus, *Sverige*, pp. 58, 59, 60, 64, 67; RA, Rådsprotokoll, vol. 72, meeting of 11 Oct. 1680.

stability. He told the Council in October 1680: 'there can be no intention to conclude offensive alliances, because we have enough to do to defend the conquests Sweden already has'. In a letter of 1684 he was more specific: 'France wants war and grabs everything for herself under pretence of peace, and we want peace, so we must stick to those who have the same intentions as us.' He told the Council: 'since there are two main parties in Europe, the House of Austria and France, and one wants nothing more than to sit still, the other does not, so he believes that it would be easier for Sweden to hold with those who want to sit still than with the others'.[8] So Oxenstierna pressed for a change of tactics; Sweden should substitute agreements with the United Provinces and the emperor for the traditional alliance with France. He outlined the policy to the Council in 1680, arguing Sweden had two vulnerable points. One was the weakness of the navy, so that the support of a major naval power was needed. The other was the defencelessness of the German provinces, so 'Sweden must remain in good understanding with the emperor and the Empire, for the sake of the German provinces.' Since the majority in the Council never abandoned its traditional preference for France, it was essential for Oxenstierna to persuade the king. He was able to do this first because his policies worked but secondly by the weight and consistency of argument. Oxenstierna was a conscientious bureaucrat, who prepared careful position papers, and put them through a routine of debate in the Council, or the Chancery College, or informally in the king's chamber. On a day when Oxenstierna had had an audience, he might still send the king additional written communications. The sheer weight of argument seems to have stifled the opposition to his policy that certainly existed.[9]

Charles XI was open to persuasion too because of his growing personal resentment of Louis XIV. The roots of this, in the French behaviour over the peace settlements, have been discussed earlier. The king summarized his attitude in a phrase he used on several occasions: 'France has betrayed me once, so that I have been burnt and will come there no more.' The Danish minister, Scheel, reported in 1682: 'a particular aversion which the king has for the French character . . . that French friendship had brought them into peril in the first place, and that in their time, they never had a more insolent ally'. This was compounded by the question of the principality of Zweibrücken. Charles XI expected to inherit the principality as a prince of the Empire, and this became actual when its ruler died in 1681. But by then Zweibrücken had fallen victim to Louis XIV's *réunion* policy. It was occupied by French troops, its revenues were sequestered and its Protestant inhabitants subjected to harassment. For a prince with Charles XI's views and temperament this was a potent cocktail of grievances. He was offended as the lawful heir, as a prince of the Empire, as king of Sweden and guarantor of the Westphalia settlement and as a Protestant. This was exacerbated by the harsh reality that there was

---

[8] B. Fåhreus, 'Sverige och förbundet i Augsburg år 1686', *HT* 16 (1896), pp. 202, 203; O. Palme, 'Bazins besckickning till Sverige 1682', *HT* 30 (1910), pp. 2–4.
[9] Fåhreus, 'Sverige och förbundet', p. 203.

almost nothing effective that could be done about it. A memorandum from Oxenstierna in April 1681 admitted as much; it would be dangerous 'to speak emphatically before your Majesty has taken suitable measures for security, and on the other hand very prejudicial to stay completely silent'. He recommended the minister in Paris play it by ear until such time as they could devise a policy. Zweibrücken became an immovable obstacle to any agreement with Louis XIV, as Feuquières had twice reported in 1681. Louis XIV could not compromise his *réunion* claims; the best he could do was offer monetary compensation, which Charles XI disdained. The king referred this to the Secret Committee at the Diet of 1686, reporting the cash offer. A few pragmatic voices recommended the king to take the money: 'it would not be demeaning for the king's Majesty to take money from the king of France'. The Marshal, who was the pro-French Lindschöld, argued: 'it is better to temporize and do what is possible than to lose everything'. That was an argument unlikely to impress Charles XI; he preferred the Clergy recommendation, that because of the religious angle the king could not compromise, or Wachtmeister's blunt advice: 'as soon as the king departs from his right, then everything is lost'. The Committee referred the issue back to the king's discretion; in contemporary terms it was an insoluble problem.[10]

In the light of this it is not difficult to see why Oxenstierna won and the French alliance fell. The last straw was an incident discussed in the Council in 1686. There was a statue, though the king sometimes called it a painting, being installed at Versailles which caused apoplectic fury in Sweden, because it was said to insult Charles XI and his kingdom. When the Council discussed this they were unanimous that Sweden must express displeasure, since, as the king said, foreigners would think: 'if Sweden tolerates this indignity, it may well tolerate more'. It was decided that N. Lillieroot, the minster to Versailles, should be recalled, and as no successor was ever appointed this virtually broke off diplomatic relations. But this was only the climax of a steady deterioration, as Oxenstierna pushed on with his realignment of Sweden. After the commercial treaty, the United Provinces suggested a formal alliance and Charles XI agreed, but felt it must be kept secret from Denmark, since if news of negotiations leaked, Louis XIV might react. Feuquières knew his position was slipping in 1681; he described in July how the king secluded himself in Kungsör, with a group of advisers led by Axel Wachtmeister, and asserted: 'cet prince est continuellement obsédé par six hommes, hautement déchaînés contre la France' ('this prince is continually beset by six men, extremely hostile to France'). He did not include Oxenstierna, despite his recent marriage alliance with the Wachtmeisters, writing: 'je ne doute nullement de sa bonne intention dans son devoir' ('I have no doubt about his integrity in his post'). The alliance with the United Provinces was signed on 30 September 1681, and provided

---

[10] RA, Skrivelser till konungen, Karl XIs tid, Bengt Oxenstiernas skrivelser till KM, letter of 27 Apr. 1681; Correspondance diplomatique: vol. 64, p. 222, Feuquières to Louis XIV 25 June 1681, 30 July 1681; RA, R 2375, Secreta Utskottets Protocoll 1686, meeting of 16 Sept. 1686.

that the two powers would jointly uphold the settlements of 1648, 1660 and 1678. When it came to the Council on 18 October, Oxenstierna revealed that all powers, including France and Denmark, would be invited to adhere to the treaty. It was clear that a majority disliked the alliance, but realized the king had already decided. Oxenstierna was almost alone in his enthusiasm, but assured the others they could speak freely: 'we have now, God be praised, a reigning king, if we speak our opinions according to our best judgements and conscience, we have nothing to answer for'. J. G. Stenbock spoke for the opposition; he feared French retaliation, and warned of the danger 'when we change old guiding maxims'. Yet he voted for acceptance; only a few recorded formal dissent, including de la Gardie, Gustav Baner and Per Sparre. But the consent of the rest was obviously qualified and Oxenstierna was isolated in the Council.[11]

The reactions were quick to follow. Louis XIV mounted a campaign at The Hague to block ratification, and his agent, d'Avaux, spread derogatory propaganda against Sweden. Feuquières cultivated the pro-French faction in Stockholm; he reported in 1682 that he had been accused of 'donner les mauvaises impressions au Sénat et peuple du gouvernement et exciter les sujets contre le souverain' ('spreading bad impressions about the government among the Council and the people and inciting the subjects against the sovereign'). He admitted to talking critically about the Dutch alliance. When the four new Councillors were appointed in December 1681, everyone saw it as a reaction to the majority on the Council; Feuquières identified three of them as 'les plus signalés dans le petit nombre des ennemis de la France, et les plus entêtés qu'on puisse imaginer dans leurs sentiments' ('the most prominent among the small band of enemies of France, the most stubborn in their opinions that could be imagined'). The Danish king responded by discarding all pretence of cooperation with Sweden. In October 1681 he consulted his Council which, as such bodies usually do, recommended he keep his options open. The king ignored them; in January 1682 he made an agreement with Brandenburg, directed against Sweden, and in March concluded a subsidy agreement with Louis XIV. In return for subsidies, Denmark would support the French interpretation of the Nijmegen settlement, but also got assurances of support on the Holstein-Gottorp dispute. Denmark and Sweden now entered into a confrontation that lasted to the end of the decade.[12]

Oxenstierna then developed the second leg of his policy, rapprochement with the emperor. Gabriel Oxenstierna, another magnate collaborator, had been sent to

[11] RA, Rådsprotokoll 1686, transcript of Svanhielm's stenographic protocol, pp. 1708–18, meeting of 13 Mar. 1686; Correspondance diplomatique: vol. 64, pp. 263–70, Feuquières to Louis XIV 30 July 1681; Rudelius, *Utrikespolitik*, pp. 18, 24; Landberg, *Utrikespolitikens historia*, pp. 220, 221; RA, Rådsprotokol, vol. 74, meeting of 18 Oct. 1681.

[12] Rudelius, *Utrikespolitik*, pp. 28, 31, 35, 39, 43; Correspondance diplomatique: vol. 64, p. 368, Feuquières to Louis XIV 5 Nov. 1681, p. 427 Feuquières to Louis XIV 17 Dec. 1681; Fåhreus, *Sverige*, pp. 25, 27, 42, 43; Landberg, *Utrikespolitikens historia*, p. 222; Rudelius, *Utrikespolitik*, pp. 31, 39, 43.

Vienna in the summer of 1681, but his initial approaches won little response from the emperor. Then in February 1682, when the United Provinces ratified what became known as the Guarantee Treaty, the emperor agreed to negotiate with Sweden. An imperial envoy, Count von Althann, was sent to Stockholm, but as a first step the emperor would go no further than to join the Guarantee Treaty in May. Althann had reported that he found Oxenstierna and the king were the only committed supporters of the new policy, but that was deemed sufficient assurance, and in November the emperor did conclude a treaty of alliance with Sweden. In reality there was a difference of approach to the new policy between the king and Oxenstierna, which his enemies repeatedly tried to exploit. It emerged in January 1682 when Oxenstierna sent a long memorandum arguing for the transfer of Swedish troops to Germany: 'not only for the defence of your Majesty's own lands, but also for the common cause'. This would deter trouble makers, and encourage the United Provinces to offer additional financial and naval support to Sweden. The king was not responsive; he consistently viewed the Guarantee Treaty and its later variants as an arrangement for defending Sweden, and had little desire to commit forces for the 'common cause' of restraining Louis XIV. Oxenstierna had to point out repeatedly that Sweden would lose credibility as an ally if she held back on her obligations. The king was never really persuaded of this, which supports the idea that his conceptual grasp of international relations was defective. He could only see the situation from a narrowly Swedish perspective. Oxenstierna tried again in March and wrote to the king: 'we can have no security or profit from half an enterprise, but rather we shall be hated and evaded by both parties'. He was summoned to Kungsör for extended conferences from 7 to 19 April 1682 and emerged with the impression that the king did now fully accept his policy. He wrote to Wachtmeister: 'the king is also well satisfied with my work and understands the importance of it very well'. Yet in June, when Dutch proposals for military contributions to the alliance were discussed, the king pressed hard to reduce Sweden's proposed commitment by a third.[13]

Oxenstierna did succeed during 1682 in undermining his opponents by expelling French influence from Stockholm. A royal letter to the Council in March accused members of passing information to Feuquières. This was a preliminary to the purge of the Council in April and the renewal of its membership. Louis XIV was trying to avoid a rupture, Feuquières was being recalled and a replacement was sent in April, the Marquis Bazin de Baudeville with orders to keep a low, but friendly profile. Oxenstierna set out to prevent any rapprochement. Feuquières noted the growing hostility in June, when at an audience with the king and Oxenstierna, 'il les avait trouvés pour la première fois de mauvaise humeur' ('he found them for the first time in a bad temper'). He was told bluntly that Sweden had concluded the

---

[13] Palme, 'Bazins besckickning', p. 5; Landberg, *Utrikespolitikens historia*, p. 224; RA, Skrivelser till konungen Karl XIs tid, Bengt Oxenstiernas skrivelser till KM, letter of 28 Jan. 1682; Rudelius, *Utrikespolitik*, pp. 77, 78, 86.

Guarantee Treaty only 'après avoir recherché vainement, deux ans durant, la sécurité de son royaume dans le renouvellement de votre alliance' ('after having vainly sought the security of the realm through the renewal of your alliance for two years'). This was followed by a manufactured protocol dispute which meant Feuquières could not take his leave publicly, but had to accept a private audience on 16 July, when a furious quarrel developed, with Oxenstierna, who usually interpreted, refusing to speak French. Feuquières left Stockholm in a huff. Bazin stayed on, but reported he was being isolated: 'bien des gens, dont je puis savoir des nouvelles sures, retirent de chez moi, appréhendants que l'affection de me voir trop souvent ne les rendre suspects aux ministres' ('a lot of people, from whom I can get reliable information are avoiding my house, afraid that the reputation of seeing me too often will make them suspect to the government'). The protocol dispute was intensified until Bazin left Stockholm without any farewell audience and was not replaced. The pro-French faction, led by J. G. Stenbock, had hoped the difficulties would strengthen their hand, but they had the opposite effect on Charles XI. His report of the incidents to Lillieroot at Versailles shows that he had taken deep offence at the conduct of the French diplomats.[14]

The four years from 1682 to 1686 represent a transitional phase. At first Sweden was on the defensive against possible attackers, but her position improved gradually until, at the end of 1686 it seemed possible to take the initiative. At first it seemed Oxenstierna had blundered by choosing the losing side in Europe. Down to the Truce of Ratisbon in 1684, Louis XIV successfully asserted his hegemony over European politics, while the Habsburgs were paralysed by the Ottoman attack on Vienna. Sweden was involved on two different levels of international conflict: at the macro-level she was committed to the alliance, seeking to defeat the French supremacy, while at the micro-level she was engaged in an intense local power struggle in north-west Germany. There the competitors were Sweden, Denmark, Brandenburg and the two brothers, George William of Celle and Ernest Augustus of Calenburg, whose lands would form the future Electorate of Hanover. Contemporary usage called them the Brunswick-Lüneburg principalities. In this context, the duke of Holstein-Gottorp was a key player. It was a classic, early modern situation; all the participants had ends of their own which they wished to pursue at the expense of the others, and they combined and divided in all possible permutations as circumstances changed. In the late war, all the others had combined to seize Sweden's German provinces, and only the intervention of Louis XIV had forced them to disgorge. The risk that the king and Oxenstierna faced, in discarding French protection, was that the assault might be renewed.

The central issue was Holstein-Gottorp, for Christian V had decided to deal with the duke while Sweden was too weak to intervene. Charles XI had assured

---

[14] Palme, 'Bazins besckickning', pp. 10, 12–13, 17, 22, 32; Landberg, *Utrikespolitikens historia*, p. 223.

the duke's ambassador in 1682 that he was prepared 'allein dero gantz fortune und krone zu wagen' ('alone to venture his whole fortune and crown'). But this was bluff to stop the duke capitulating to Denmark. In the Council all agreed they must do something, but could not act militarily. Oxenstierna recommended asking the emperor to intervene, which in principle he was prepared to do, and he declared that the duke was a victim of injustice. It was, however, easy for Denmark to stall proceedings in the imperial courts; and further Slesvig, the territory immediately at issue, was not part of the Empire at all. When the Council looked at the problem in December 1682, the king was determined to reject Denmark's position that Slesvig was a domestic issue, but when J. G. Stenbock suggested seeking mediation, the king refused: 'it would be as though we were afraid of Denmark'. They decided to get help from Lüneburg, whose rulers did not want to see Denmark strengthened, but their price for assistance was that Sweden put troops into Germany. Oxenstierna argued strongly, in a memorandum of March 1683, for putting at least 2,000–4,000 men into Germany, but the king would not even consider it. His diplomats were in despair at his obtuseness. M. Wellingk, the envoy to Lüneburg, wrote in March: 'I hope that people in Sweden will think seriously about a transport, if we are to keep our German provinces . . . with our way of acting, we lose one favourable opportunity after another.'[15]

The real threat in 1683 developed from the agreement between Denmark and Brandenburg to attack Sweden's German provinces as soon as Louis XIV gave approval. The king and Council knew of the threat, which was one reason why in May the king reluctantly agreed to ratify the military convention of the Guarantee Treaty and reopen the negotiation with Lüneburg, but their condition was still that Sweden put 10,000–12,000 troops into Germany. The Council decided that could only be done if the United Provinces sent a naval force to convey them. Lüneburg rejected this, at which point the danger receded. Louis XIV decided that he did not want Sweden driven out of Germany and told Denmark and Brandenburg to drop their plans, suggesting instead that they combine to carve up Brunswick-Lüneburg. At that Brandenburg lost interest and the threat to Sweden collapsed. But it was artificially prolonged when Louis XIV, for prestige reasons, sent a French fleet into the Baltic, though its commander was instructed to keep the peace, and intervene only if Sweden tried to ship troops to Germany. The Dutch sent warships too, but they carefully stayed in the North Sea until the French withdrew in the autumn. Then they sailed into Gothenburg and offered to convoy Swedish troops into Germany, since Louis XIV had by then launched his attack on the Spanish Netherlands, but Charles XI refused to get involved. The war threat of 1683 was mildly farcical once Louis XIV had decided to stifle it. But Sweden did not know this, and when the French warships arrived, Charles XI insisted that his navy leave Karlskrona, which was still unfortified, and retire to Kalmar. In fact

[15] Rudelius, *Utrikespolitik*, pp. 163, 168, 196, 202, 213, 217; *Handlingar rörande Sveriges historia*, pp. 231, 312.

Sweden had survived the first year of the new foreign policy unharmed; the real danger came in 1684.[16]

In December 1683 the Council held one of its policy review meetings. It had a memorandum from Oxenstierna, whose theme was: 'the impossibility of enduring alone among such strong and considerable opponents'. Then he identified the most pressing danger as 'the duke of Holstein being under continual pressure and obliged to a damaging settlement for himself and Sweden'. He showed that Sweden currently had 2,500 men in Bremen-Verden and 1,500 in Pomerania and recommended they be reinforced. But when the king joined the debate, he opposed this and only Ehrensteen supported Oxenstierna's proposal; his consistent argument that Sweden's allies would not take her seriously without a strong military commitment got no understanding from Charles XI. In November, William III persuaded the Guarantee powers to set up a conference of ambassadors at The Hague in face of the renewed aggressions by Louis XIV. The king had agreed, reluctantly, to send N. Gyldenstolpe, but his instructions were to keep the peace if possible, and if not, ensure the guarantee was extended to the Baltic area. The presence of a Dutch fleet in the Baltic was a precondition for Sweden to send any further troops into Germany. But when, in March 1684, the Council took him up on this and proposed that 4,000–6,000 men be sent, if the condition were met, the king backed off; he insisted: 'we must tell Gyldenstolpe . . . what can be performed'. Charles XI was simply not mentally attuned to the politics of alliances. He thought that if the Dutch did send their navy into the Baltic, it should be used for an immediate knock-out blow at Denmark; the true purpose of the alliance, to restrain Louis XIV, would have to wait. The matter was academic, since Louis XIV's success in 1684, and the ascendancy of William III's Republican opponents at The Hague, put the alliance out of action.[17]

The collapse of the Guarantee Treaty in 1684 left Sweden dangerously weak and exposed in 1684. The central international event was the Truce of Ratisbon between Louis XIV, the emperor and the Empire. Charles XI was a party to the Truce, as a prince of the Empire, and could achieve none of his objectives, that the Truce recognize the Holstein-Gottorp dispute and take it under international consideration, and that his claim on Zweibrücken be recognized. He was paying the price of his refusal to send troops into Germany; the other powers were not taking Sweden seriously as a participant.[18] But behind all the turmoil over Ratisbon, there was a much more serious threat to Sweden, though it is not clear how far the king and Oxenstierna ever realized this. Louis XIV had retained an investment in the Baltic, paying a subsidy to Denmark that enabled her to maintain some military preparedness. The first French proposal was to renew the idea of Denmark and Brandenburg dismembering Brunswick-Lüneburg by a joint attack, and Denmark

---

[16] Rudelius, *Utrikespolitik*, pp. 227, 228, 230, 231, 242, 249, 256.
[17] *Ibid.*, pp. 278, 280, 282, 284, 297, 300.
[18] *Ibid.*, pp. 231–2; Landberg, *Utrikespolitikens historia*, p. 230; Fåhreus, *Sverige*, p. 209.

had moved to secure some small territories claimed by Lüneburg. The Lüneburg princes, who were still seeking a Swedish intervention, realized their peril and promptly changed sides. During the summer of 1684 they were planning to join Denmark and Brandenburg in an assault on Sweden, to seize and share out her German provinces. Sweden was saved by the same factors as operated in 1683: the mutual distrust of the predators, combined with a refusal of Louis XIV to sanction their project. He still did not want Sweden eliminated from Germany. So the proposed aggression was postponed.[19]

In reality, the summer and autumn of 1684 were the low point of Sweden's international fortunes, though a policy review in the Council in September 1684 seemed quite unaware of this. Its conclusions, confirmed by the king, were that the claim to Zweibrücken must be pursued and that monetary compensation was unacceptable. This ruled out any rapprochement with Louis XIV, and then the duke of Holstein-Gottorp must be reinstated in all his rights, by force if necessary, but for this the king would need allies. Yet he still refused to consider moving troops into Germany.[20] The king demonstrated once more that the great international issues of the day interested him only to the extent that they impacted on his own local concerns. But at this very point, Sweden was to be rescued from her dangerous isolation by contingencies beyond Sweden's control, which changed the international situation. The first sign came in October, when Frederick-William of Brandenburg, the Great Elector, signalled a change of policy in Berlin. He indicated he was considering ending his collaboration with Louis XIV and was interested in reconciliation with Sweden. In the course of 1685 the Elector did take Brandenburg out of the French camp and declared his support for upholding the integrity of the Holy Roman Empire. Then by the end of campaigning in 1684 it became apparent that the counter-attack on the Ottoman Turks was producing spectacular successes, and the position of the emperor steadily improved. It was in reaction to this that Louis XIV signalled that in spite of the Truce of Ratisbon, he had plans for further expansion at the expense of the Empire, by pressing his claims to inherit the Rhine-Palatinate on the expected early death of the current Elector. Frederick-William was only one of a number of German princes who got carried along on a wave of chauvinistic resentment, compounded among the Protestants in 1685 by Louis' religious aggressions on his Huguenot subjects. These developments gave Charles XI a quiet year in 1685. He sought to rally support in the Empire for the duke of Holstein-Gottorp, and found plenty in principle, for the duke was a prince of the Empire, and princely solidarity dictated that he should be protected from Danish aggression. But no offers of military support were forthcoming. Yet as the new international con-

---

[19] L. Stavenow, 'Sveriges politik tiden för Altona kongressen 1686–1689', *HT* 15 (1895), p. 177; Rudelius, *Utrikespolitik*, pp. 306, 323, 328, 332; Landberg, *Utrikespolitikens historia*, p. 229.

[20] Rudelius, *Utrikespolitik*, p. 335; KB, Engströmska Samlingen B. II.1.12, Handlingar rörande Karl XIs regering, KMs slutlige gottfinnande September 1684.

frontation with Louis XIV built up, it became clear that Sweden's participation was eagerly sought.

Early in 1686, Charles XI was able to conclude an alliance with Brandenburg. In January the draft treaty was discussed in the Chancery College by Oxenstierna, Lindschöld and Ehrensteen. Only the latter expressed serious doubts that the Elector really had given up his designs on Pomerania, and argued that Sweden should hold back until the Elector settled outstanding frontier disputes and committed himself to support Holstein-Gottorp. Lindschöld was very positive: 'this opportunity should not be passed up. There seems no risk involved.' He thought other German princes would follow Brandenburg's lead. The draft was presented to the Council and Oxenstierna expounded how the treaty would promote the king's strategy of reviving and extending the Guarantee Treaty alliance, and would be a blow to Denmark, while to reject it would raise doubts about Sweden's intentions. Oxenstierna asserted that the king 'had only intended to aim at how the general tranquillity and the dearly preserved peace could be maintained . . . it had been found good that the king's Majesty shall have one of the seapowers in support'. The treaty with Brandenburg was a natural continuation of this policy. There was general approbation; Christopher Gyllenstierna took it as 'a clear sign that God has blessed his Majesty's counsels, to be able to win over together those who have a common interest'. When the king asked the Council 'if we shall conclude', the unanimous response was: 'it was fortunate and nobody could be against it'. J. G. Stenbock added, 'we can expressly see that this is God's work'. Ehrensteen repeated his reservations, but did not oppose.[21] It is important to note these pious observations, which are characteristic of all political discussion within the Swedish elites. These Councillors were not secular-minded exponents of *realpolitik*, but early modern folk who inhabited a mental world which accepted that no policy could prosper unless it accorded with God's will.

This however did not exclude diplomatic subtleties, used in a righteous cause. In February 1686 the Council considered a letter from the duke of Holstein-Gottorp, proposing actions that clearly breached the peace treaty of 1679. Oxenstierna said the king could not support the duke's proposal, 'because Sweden's credibility would be much damaged by it'. The king called for a decision, should they support, yes or no? Oxenstierna said there was no need to give the Duke a definite answer and 'proposed that we can answer this way, that the king notes [the Duke's] faithful heart . . . but as far as the question is concerned, that the king leaves it to his own discretion and leaves him a free hand'. This evasion was generally approved. Another case arose in March 1686 over an appeal from the emperor for help against the Turks. No more godly cause than that could be imagined. It appealed to the piety of Charles XI and he was willing, in principle, to send 1,000 men, though they must be foreign mercenaries, not Swedes. The activists in the Council saw an

---

[21] Rudelius, *Ultrikespolitik*, p. 332; Fåhreus, *Sverige*, pp. 209, 211, 212, 215, 218; RA, Kanslikollegiets Protokoll, 1686, meeting of 2 Jan. 1686; RA Rådsprotokoll 1686, p. 1636, meeting of 7 Jan. 1686.

opening: Christopher Gyllenstierna urged the good publicity it would generate, 'it would earn the king great respect among his critics' and strengthen ties with the emperor. Gustav Oxenstierna and Göran Gyllenstierna wanted something more ambitious, a force of 4,000–5,000 men to be stationed in Germany. This was exactly what Bengt Oxenstierna had long wanted, so he said: 'when he thinks about it, he cannot see anything that will prevent a greater evil, than that we must provide to have troops on German soil'. This was immediately opposed by Wrede and Ehrensteen; the latter said all that was needed was a friendly letter to the Emperor that they would do what they could. The king perceived that the activists were trying to commit him and drew back. They must respond to the emperor's appeal, but 'to promise and not be able to perform is in vain'. This was a favourite evasive tactic of Charles XI. He pointed out the emperor was not going to pay for the troops; the emperor had written that he expected Charles XI to respond, 'out of Christian love for the preservation of Christendom'. So the king asked: 'there has to be money for what will happen, and where will we take it from?' This let them off the hook; they could tell the emperor that they would have to get a grant from the Diet, and tell him 'that we must first consult the Estates over this'. This was an interesting position for an absolute king to adopt, but it served the purpose.[22]

The matter of the contingent for the war on the Ottomans was marginal, but it showed again the king's basic refusal to commit resources, either in manpower or money, for anything that did not promote the immediate interest of his kingdom. He had no problem over renewing all his agreements with the United Provinces in January 1686, or ratifying the Brandenburg treaty in March. Then came a call from the emperor for all the Circles of the Empire to provide contingency forces in preparation for renewed aggressions by Louis XIV. It was proposed that Sweden should pledge 10,000 men to a total force of 60,000. The project advanced to the point where the emperor convened a conference at Augsburg in June. The king could see advantages for Sweden: Zweibrücken and Holstein-Gottorp could be included in the remit of the force, while to go along with the current mood of princely patriotism would build 'credibility and confidence'. But as would be expected he baulked at the figure of 10,000 men. He argued he was involved as a prince of the Empire, not as king of Sweden and proposed his traditional imperial contingent of 2,000 men as his contribution. But he added that if they included the duke of Holstein as a member, he would pay for the Holstein contingent too and raise the figure to 3,000. This was the result of a debate in the Council, where Oxenstierna had urged a bigger offer to increase confidence and good-will. The king would go no higher, though he accepted a formula that they should offer, if the Empire were attacked, 'to provide more manpower according to the condition of the times and the events, and the proportions of the danger and need'. At the conference this meant there had to be a fudge, and a form of words was accepted

---

[22] RA, Rådsprotokoll 1686, p. 1659, meeting of 1 Feb. 1686; pp. 1652–63, meeting of 17 Mar. 1686, pp. 1720–31.

that the king would contribute 'a proportionate and sufficient quantity' to satisfy his allies. Charles XI's offers clearly disappointed the German princes, but they were quite generous by his standards, and much better than the responses of William III and Frederick-William, who declined to contribute anything.[23]

The year 1686 marked a watershed in the history of Charles XI's foreign policy. The early 1680s had been a period of solid achievement based on the perception that Sweden, as a satisfied power, should seek to maintain stability. The king, after passively acquiescing in Gyllenstierna's flawed Nordic alliance policy, had come to accept Oxenstierna's assessment that in the Europe of the 1680s, it was Louis XIV who was the principal disturber of the peace. The king had steadily defended Oxenstierna against the criticisms of the pro-French traditionalists. Oxenstierna's inner thoughts remain impenetrable, being concealed behind the barrier of his official memoranda. These are a mixture of almost abject protestations of humble loyalty with exhaustive arguments expressed in dense bureaucratic prose and thickly laced with conventional pieties. But they were also crafted to satisfy the king's known inclinations: a desire to keep the peace at almost any cost, a growing distaste for all things French and the firm attachment to the Holstein-Gottorp interest. That said, Oxenstierna's persistent pressure to give more weight to his policies by establishing a stronger military presence in Germany suggests that he had a deeper and more activist perception of foreign policy than his royal master. In the early modern world, foreign policy above all demanded political skills, in which Charles XI was clearly deficient. He had a narrow, two-dimensional world view, in which there were the good people, who lived and acted in the fear of God, and the bad people, who flouted God's will. Such political discussion as there was in Sweden, in the Propositions and reports submitted to the Diets, in the rather infrequent official pamphlets and officially sanctioned news-sheets, the *Svenska Mercurius* and the *Svenska Ordinarie Post-Tijdender*, reflected the king's simplistic views. Sweden's actions were 'just' and based on divine or Natural Law, and the arguments in their favour were legalistic. Policies which succeeded clearly had God's blessing, those that did not were God's just retribution for deviating from righteousness. The king's utterances suggest that he sincerely embraced this simple moral economy. The real causes of events were rarely discussed by Charles XI, and perhaps he never properly grasped them. But if he lacked the skills, and the charismatic leadership gifts of his famous predecessors, he had one solid virtue. Though in no sense a pacifist, the king saw it as his duty to preserve his kingdom from war if he could. The Propositions to the Diets always stressed the pride he took in this, for war was the ultimate evil, God's severest punishment on sinful men. His own first-hand experience had cured him of his adolescent bellicosity. On the one occasion when Charles XI seriously intended to take up arms, in the Holstein-Gottorp crisis of 1689, he wrote to Nils Bielke that he still hoped to avoid

---

[23] Fåhreus, *Sverige*, pp. 219, 220, 223, 230, 232, 233; Malmström, ed., 'Karl XIs bref till Nils Bielke', p. 21, letter of 20 Oct. 1686; Landberg, *Utrikespolitikens historia*, p. 233.

it, 'for a war is easily begun, but the outcome depends on God'.[24] If we try to see the situation as the ordinary subjects of the king might have seen it, and bear in mind the disasters that overwhelmed Sweden under his successor, we may think there was a lot of merit in the king's sturdy simplicity.

[24] Malmström, *Nils Bielke*, p. 26.

7

The consolidation of the absolutist system

By the close of the Diet of 1683 the legal foundations of the absolute monarchy were securely established. The Danish minister, Meyer, reported this to his master in January, but added that the achievement was precarious, for it depended on the survival of the king. If anything happened to him, the old order could easily be reestablished.

Die noblesse quitiret ungern die oligarchie, und all officirer seint eingebohrne und der senatoren verwanten, und also in hofnung an solcher Regierung zu participieren; bekome alsso eine minorenitet, oder der König were ausser Reichs, durfte eine Enderung geschehen. So lange alsso die Reichstäge nicht ganz abgeshaffet, kan die eine Diaet dess vorigen Schluss annulieren.

The nobility is unwilling to give up the oligarchy, and all the officers are natives and related to the Councillors, and therefore in hopes of sharing in such a government: and if there was a minority, or the king went out of the kingdom, a change could take place. And as long as the Diet is not completely abolished, a Diet can repeal the resolution of its predecessors.

Contemporaries, like modern historians, were not even sure the king was committed to the new style of government, or whether he had acted pragmatically in response to his immediate problems. Meyer's successor, K. Stockfleth, was picking up rumours that de la Gardie might return to power as late as the summer of 1684. But the signs are that the king and his advisers were consciously set on asserting the unrestricted authority of the divinely appointed ruler. Charles XI's concern with the scandalous protocols, and the interference with his father's Testament, was deep rooted. The Estates may have supposed that their grovelling dissociation in 1682 had closed the matter. That was far from the king's mind. In October 1683 a royal letter to the Chancery reminded the officials that he wanted all the relevant documents collected, and expressed his dissatisfaction at their tardy efforts. It is clear that the king intended to use the material to instruct his subjects in what their duties to the sovereign were. This was done in the Diet of 1689, but even then the issue obsessed the king, and in 1696 he instructed the Law Commission to draft a formal statement of the powers of the sovereign and the obligation of the subject to unconditional and unquestioning obedience.[1]

---

[1] Fryxell, ed., *Handlingar*, II, p. 207, Meyer to the king 24 Jan. 1683; RA, Riksregistraturet 367, 1683, king's letter 13 Oct. 1683.

But in the 1680s the king was more occupied with demonstrating in action his style of government. There was no first minister after Gyllenstierna; the king headed the government and was served by individual ministers, each responsible for his own area of activity. But they did come together collectively when they worked on numerous special commissions which were a feature of government after 1680, and in the collegiate ministries, while the seniors met regularly in the Council, sometimes with the king present. There major questions of public policy were often debated. It has been seen how Bengt Oxenstierna directed foreign policy; the military reconstruction was overseen by the king himself, taking expert advice from men like Ascheberg, Dahlberg and Hans Wachtmeister. Finance and the budget were supervised by Claes Fleming, who stood high in the king's favour after 1680 and looked set to become the leading man in the government, but he was soon struck down by terminal illness. In January 1685, Stockfleth reported how Fleming had been working on plans to reduce the public debt over a four-year period, and 'almost every day while he is sick, the king has been down at his house and quite alone with him in his chamber'. Fleming died in 1685, deeply regretted by the king. The other key figures in government were the Secretaries of State in the Chancery, initially H. Hoghusen, J. Örnstedt and E. Lindschöld. All had been at the heart of the king's wartime government. The record shows clearly how Lindschöld became the principal Secretary. He was a prime example of a gifted commoner who had worked his way up by sheer ability. His career had been interrupted in 1679, perhaps by illness, perhaps because of disagreements with Gyllenstierna, but late in 1680 the king recalled him and he rapidly established himself at the centre of the administration. He had multiple talents as an administrator, was a gifted orator, a respectable poet and an absolutist by conviction, very well read in contemporary political thought. Lindschöld could articulate the ideas that Charles XI shared, but could not express himself. Lindschöld was eventually appointed chief tutor to the crown prince, the future Charles XII, whose career testified dramatically to the success of his teaching.[2]

In the Diet of 1682 the king had launched another of his enduring achievements, the Church Law of 1686, which remained in force until well into the nineteenth century. The process of drafting and enacting this law provides a clear demonstration of the king's style of government. Sweden had officially adopted the Lutheran religion in 1593, but the consequent revision of ecclesiastical law had never taken place. There were difficult issues to be resolved touching the relations of Church and State, and there was the mental blockage caused by the society's entrenched fear of change. It was believed that any alteration to the traditional legal texts could inadvertently subvert ancient rights and open the way to dangerous innovation. The Diet of 1668 had tried to circumvent this problem, ordering a committee to draft amendments, but so as to 'leave the actual law or Church ordinance un-

---

[2] Fryxell, ed., *Handlingar*, II, p. 283, Stockfleth to the king 21 Jan. 1685.

changed in all respects as it has been hitherto'. When the committee had completed its proposals, then the Estates, together with the king, could consider how the proposals 'can best be brought together with the original'. When a committee of royal officials was looking at revision in 1684, the same basic reluctance to change the law at all was apparent. Ehrensteen told the Council: 'as far as the Church ordinance is concerned, I have looked over the old one and find it is good enough; we have managed well with it for a hundred years'.[3]

At the Diet of 1682 the Estate of the Clergy had the Church Law on its agenda as usual, but now got an order from the king to present a final draft to the Estates. Since it was immediately clear that the other Estates had objections to the draft as presented, it was decided to submit it to a committee for revision. The king then appointed a committee of civil servants and lawyers, headed by Ehrensteen, to undertake the revision. The church leaders saw no danger in this; Spegel wrote to Lindschöld in February 1683 how the archbishop had 'emphasized his great desire that the Church ordinance may achieve completion'. He went on to enthuse about how a uniform law would eliminate all kinds of disputes, and reinvigorate clerical control of education. This was much needed, since young people were getting hold of dangerous books, like those of Spinoza, and some even worse, such 'that Caligula most approved of'. Spegel was expressing the general longing for order and assurance that traditional values would be preserved.[4]

However the committee had serious reservations about points in the clergy draft. These had built on the Lutheran doctrine of the two kingdoms, secular and spiritual, and while acknowledging that they were the king's subjects, asserted their autonomy in the spiritual sphere. They believed that a king 'must recognize a good and just separation between Church affairs and secular government', and that even kings had no power 'to legislate or command anything in a right, true Christian religion'. Neither Charles XI nor his advisers would accept such a limitation of royal authority. The Clergy had tried to realize their claim by declaring that the Estate of the Clergy was also a *Consistorium Regni*, with authority to determine all spiritual matters. The committee asserted that all ecclesiastical authority must derive from the king, 'ex concessione et commissione regis'. The king agreed and ordered his officials to revise the draft, excising all reference to a *Consistorium Regni* and asserting the king had the final authority in respect of 'religion, divine service, God's word and the sacraments'. He possessed uncontrolled patronage over all crown benefices, and in all others the incumbent must be approved by the congregation, and only then confirmed by the bishop. When the officials had

---

[3] A. Anjou, *Svenska kyrkans historia ifran Upsala möte år 1593 till slutet af sjuttande århundredet* (Stockholm, 1866), pp. 451–7, 458, 460, 463; Carlson, *Historia*, III, pp. 245–8; H. Pleijel, *Svenska kyrkans historia: femte bandet: Karolinsk kyrkofromhet, pietism och hernhutism 1680–1772* (Stockholm, 1935), pp. 15, 16.

[4] Liden, *Riksdagen 1682*, p. 267, diary of the bishop of Linköping 11 Oct. 1682; RA, R 5957, Anon. Riksdags journalen 4 Dec. 1682, peasant memorandum to the Secret Committee; RA, Kanslitjänste-mäns koncept och mittagen skrivelser, 26, Karl XIs tid, Spegel to Lindschöld 14 Feb. 1683.

completed their draft, a select group of clergy was permitted to comment on it, and according to one of them, Bishop Gezelius, they met daily until 7 in the evening to finish the job. Being realists, who now knew the king's mind, they did not press any substantial objections, so that an agreed text was passed to the Council in February 1686. The Council, with the king participating, spent three days going over it, and the tone of their discussions was firmly anti-clerical. They reinforced restrictions on the powers of the clergy to withhold absolution, order public penance or excommunicate. As de la Gardie remarked, all such powers were superfluous, 'since there is a secular authority that can punish such offences'. The clergy had wanted discretionary penalties; the king insisted on penalties fixed by law. The king also revealed his belief in equity by insisting that the rule must be the same for everyone. He opposed allowing individuals to choose where they would take communion; all must take it together in their parish church. This applied even to noblemen who were allowed chaplains: 'if there is to be a rule, then it must be the same, so that all are cleansed by the same comb', as he said. When the Council had finished, the king was still not certain that his supremacy was made sufficiently clear. Lindschöld made a final revision before printing and wrote to the king that it was unnecessary to state explicitly that the king had full episcopal authority, since no subject could presume to doubt this, and the law rested on the presumption that all authority derived from the king.[5]

The text was rushed into print and presented to the Estates in 1686 as approved by the king. The expressed wish of the Estates in 1682 that general laws should be referred to them for comment was effectively ignored. The Nobles and the Burghers accepted it as a general law without comment. The Clergy were less complacent. The archbishop tried to soften them up by stressing that the Church Law had been finalized but although 'it was somewhat altered in Chancery and in conference', there was no 'great difference' from their own proposal. This was close to a deliberate deception; most of his audience had not seen the text. A few days later he brought a message from Lindschöld that they were expected to accept it as a law. The bishop of Viborg made the reasonable objection that most of them had never seen the Law, and asked if it could be read out to them first. The archbishop answered that would be very dubious since the king had already approved it as a law. The Estate then resolved 'that we acknowledge it as a law'. There is scattered evidence of the widespread unhappiness among the clergy. The archbishop told Gezelius privately that 'when he got to see it [the final version] he did not recognize it', which was distinctly at odds with what he had told the Estate. At the extremes a few, like D. Anander, denounced the law privately as 'an unexamined Church Law, a counsel of Hamon', and called on God to reject it. Also in private, the king tried to console the archbishop about the restrictive character of the law. The king said, 'I

[5] Lindegård, *Consistorium regni*, pp. 246, 249, 253, 255, 256; Anjou, *Kyrkans historia*, pp. 463, 464, 465; RA, Rådsprotokoll 1686, pp. 1673–1702, meetings of 18, 19, 20, 22 Feb. 1686; RA, Skrivelser till konungen, Karl XIs tid, Erik Lindschölds skrivelser till KM, letter of 11 Aug. 1686.

have to look ahead. Of course I can trust you, Carlson, Spegel and others, but who knows what may happen in future, or what sort of people your successors will be?' In public he was fierce in asserting the royal supremacy. He wrote a letter to Stockholm Consistory in December 1686, because he had noted a reference by them to the '*consistorio regni*' and observed: 'We cannot actually know what you mean by *consistorio regni*, since We recognize no *Consistorium Regni*.' He then circulated his comment to all the bishops. The printed Church Law was issued to the public in February 1687, together with a royal resolution on legal proceedings before ecclesiastical tribunals, which confirmed that the right of appeal was to the secular Courts.[6]

The preamble to the Church Law recited how various kings had tried to secure such a law over the past sixty years, and how the king, conscious that God requires good order, 'observed it would be of great advantage, and necessary, and furthering of the honour of God's name . . . to frame, and without further delay have published a fixed Church Law and ordinance'. This was a model of Charles XI's absolutism in action. A long-standing problem had been speedily resolved by a ruthless assertion of the fullness of kingly power. There had been some element of consultation with those concerned, but nothing had been allowed to get in the way of the king's God-given right to order his kingdom. The method was wholly characteristic of the king. He had identified an area of confusion and uncertainty and resolved it by using his power to impose a rule book, which applied uniform regulations to all his subjects, hence the king's dislike in Council of allowing any exceptions. At the same time he prescribed sanctions to ensure it was obeyed. The king shared the view of most contemporaries that unity of religion was the main foundation of any ordered society. The Church Law, if enforced, ensured that all his subjects were following one uniform code of religious observance, and were being disciplined by a uniform code of sanctions. This forced the subject to repress his natural inclination to wickedness and to behave as God's laws required. It was precisely the kind of project for which Christian kingship had been divinely established.[7]

The calling of the Diet of 1686 was occasioned by two developments, one internal and one external. In 1680 the Chamber had reckoned the public debt as 12 million dsm. By 1685 new calculations suggested it was bigger. There were two components seen as requiring urgent action. One was 1,300,000 dsm. owing to the State Bank. The king had ordered this to be given priority for repayment in February 1685, and the thinking was revealed in a discussion in Council in May 1686, when J. G. Stenbock said: 'if the Bank is disturbed in some way to the point of collapse, the whole kingdom will collapse, or suffer a severe blow'. The other component was loans of an estimated 3 million dsm., secured on crown farms assigned to the creditors. The consequent loss of revenue, combined with the

---

[6] Grauers, *Sveriges Riksdag*, pp. 101, 102, 103; *PR*, IV, pp. 220, 257, 319; Anjou, *Kyrkans historia*, pp. 467, 468; Carlson, *Historia*, III, p. 262; Lindegård, *Consistorium regni*, pp. 257, 258.
[7] A.J. Ryden, ed., *Sveriges Kyrkolag af år 1686* (Göteborg, 1856), p. 5.

interest charges to the Bank, were crippling the budget; as Stenbock put it: 'it consumes all the king's income'. The other development was in foreign affairs. In 1686 the king of Denmark overplayed his hand by attempting to seize the free city of Hamburg. This caused a hostile reaction from the emperor and the whole Lower Saxon Circle, including Brandenburg. In August, Oxenstierna wrote that this was a chance to get restitution for the duke of Holstein-Gottorp: 'Denmark derives its greatest strength from suppressing the Duke: if he is restored, Danish power can no longer threaten Sweden.' The king agreed and told the Council on 13 September that, because Brandenburg and Brunswick-Lüneburg were prepared to use force against Denmark, 'they will hit him on the head, and then we can go over into Zealand'. The Councillors agreed; Stenbock said: 'this situation seems as if it came from God'. Therefore the king needed a grant of supply to fund possible military action.[8]

The Diet of 1686, like the Church Law, was a demonstration of absolute kingship in action. The king's wishes were explained and executed by an enlarged and rejuvenated nobility, that remained the elite group in the system. It was rejuvenated because since 1680 a core group of the magnate oligarchy had either died or left public life, and the group as a whole was economically weakened. But some of them had accepted their losses and chose to join the regime, where the king readily accepted their service. One active figure in 1686 was J. G. Stenbock, from one of the greatest magnate clans; Nils Bielke was emerging as a close personal confidant and adviser to Charles XI; the younger de la Gardies were all in service, as was J. Rosenhane who was an active financial consultant to the crown during the Diet. But they were reinforced by new-blood nobles, either promoted from Class III, or from successful commoners in public service. Both the leading business managers of 1686 were from this group. The Marshal of the Nobility, previously selected from the senior magnate families, was the blacksmith's son, Lindschöld; the chief financial spokesman was Jakob Gyllenborg, of similar plebeian background. The king's servants in the Diet showed themselves to be divided at times by personal rivalry or genuine differences over policy options, but they always dominated proceedings. The real action took place mostly in the Secret Committee and the king had made it clear that he expected the full Estates to ratify what the Committee decided. He had restructured the Committee to give it a preponderance of nobles, twenty-nine of them against twenty-three clergy and twenty burghers. This was consistent with the political marginalization of the commoner Estates after the Diet of 1682. They were no longer needed to intimidate the Riddarhus; their old political aspirations, the reduktion and ending of magnate power had been achieved, and they reverted to their traditional role of defending their own sectional interests. It is also argued that the ennoblement of Thegner, their able political manager, was part of the shift. The minutes of the Secret Committee show that the

[8] Carlson, *Historia*, III, pp. 273, 277; RA, Rådsprotokoll 1686, p. 1732, meeting of 31 May 1686; p. 1764, meeting of 25 Aug. 1686; p. 1770, meeting of Sept. 1686; Lindqvist, *Gyllenborg*, pp. 86, 91–4.

commoner delegates took little part in discussion and that the nobility had reasserted the status it had claimed earlier in the century to be the premier Estate in the Diet. The king could be confident that his programme would go through; sixteen of the twenty-nine noblemen on the Committee were career public servants. The public had noticed these developments. Stockfleth reported to the king of Denmark, and the story recurs in other sources that 'there had been found, attached and fixed to the milestones along the roads here and there in the land, notices saying, "You representatives to the Diet! Do not hurry yourselves: what is going to be done has already been decided."'[9]

The Propositions were read to the Council, in the king's presence, on 13 September, 'without any comment being made about them'. The General Propositions opened with a statement of the king's view of the role of the Estates.

Since his Majesty has, by many proofs, found and experienced what advantages the assembly of his Estates has always produced . . . it has occasioned no less satisfaction and pleasure to the king that thus he has occasion, among other things, to inform them of his continuous royal concern, vigilance and care for their welfare, tranquillity and security, and also to discuss and decide with them affairs and business, by which the king, with his heavy burden of government, has received substantial support, help and comfort from their well-intentioned advice and proceedings.

A modern observer may be inclined to dismiss this as public relations rhetoric. But that is to misunderstand the early modern world. It is likely that Charles XI sincerely meant every word. It expressed to perfection his image of a society grounded in consensus values, in which the king and his subjects were bound together in a common endeavour to discover and obey God's will for Sweden. The General Propositions then affirmed the king's hope to preserve the peace, and asked for supply to support his internal and foreign policies. They identified the debt problem as central and asked the Estates 'by what means repayment can most conveniently be brought about'. They also ask the Estates for their advice on how the economic welfare of the kingdom can be developed.[10] The Secret Propositions, which were to be disclosed to the Estates as a whole, not confined to the Secret Committee, gave a detailed account of developments in domestic and foreign policy since the previous Diet. It can be asked what was the purpose of providing so much detailed and genuine information about the work of the royal government? One intention was to show how the supply voted in the previous Diet had been used, and to give fairly precise costings of what was needed from this one. The figures showed the government could not be accused of having squandered the taxpayers' money. But it went further than this and expressed one of the strengths of the

[9] W. Carlgren, 'Kungamakt, utskott och stånd på 1680 och 1690-talen riksdagar', *HT* 41 (1921), pp. 41, 171, 172, 187, 193, 195, 196, 198, 200; Lindqvist, *Gyllenborg*, pp. 95, 97, 102; Carlson, *Historia*, III, p. 280; Fryxell, ed., *Handlingar*, II, pp. 339, 342, Stockfleth to the king 8 Sept. 1686, 13 Oct. 1686, 10 Nov. 1686.
[10] RA, Rådsprotokoll 1686, p. 1770, meeting of 13 Sept. 1686; *SRARP*, XV, p. 131.

Swedish system. Although the king claimed the authority to govern as he saw fit, he also recognized that he and his subjects were engaged in a common enterprise. In these Propositions the king was telling his subjects what he required of them, while explaining in detail why it had to be done. This made it difficult for a loyal subject to raise objections; the king's commitment to the general welfare was manifest.

The Secret Committee began with foreign policy and spent three days reviewing every aspect. Those who spoke were well informed, and the seriousness of the debate was underlined when they asked for the relevant treaties to be sent, which was done. They could see there might be war over Holstein-Gottorp and they preferred diplomatic solutions. Per Sparre took the view that Sweden was still too weak for war. In addition they were reluctant to recommend war, because they would have to finance it. On 2 October, A. Lindhielm suggested the way out: 'it is best to refer this matter to the king, who can adopt the advice the times require'. At that the Marshal agreed to ask the king if he wanted policy recommendations from the Committee. The answer he brought back was that the Propositions were meant to inform them 'how everything pointed to war, also what reasons there were for it, if the kingdom got into conflict, rather than to ask their advice. The king also said he would seek to maintain and preserve the peace to the utmost, and so far as it was possible.' It was apparent that, far from being offended that their advice was not called for, the Committee was relieved. When Sparre said 'it is much for the best to leave this to the king's pleasure and good judgement, God bless his royal Majesty's decision', there was unanimous agreement. In general, early modern Europeans were not ambitious to be involved in areas outside their competence. The Committee had no wish to take responsibility for hazardous decisions, when God had provided them with a king for that very purpose.[11]

The Riddarhus held its first meeting on 15 September and the Marshal led them straight into supply. They agreed unanimously to make a grant in principle. He warned them that in addition the debt must be tackled, but avoided debate by asking members to submit suggestions, either in writing or orally, 'so that we can choose what may be for the best. That was received by everyone with applause.' A few of the written suggestions, all unsigned, have survived but have little to offer and tend to say the Clergy and the Burghers should do more. The Riddarhus did not meet again for nine days, a sign of how decision making had moved to the Secret Committee.[12]

This began to consider domestic affairs on 16 September. They had detailed estimates of possible military expenditure and of the outstanding debt, with lists of crown properties given as security. Then Gyllenborg revealed the crown's proposals, in two parts. First they would invoke the medieval rule of *alterum tantum*, designed for the relief of poor debtors. When repayments of interest equalled the sum advanced, further interest ceased and the repayments went to liquidate the

---

[11] *SRARP*, xv, pp. 142–63; RA, R 2375, two meetings of 16 Sept. 1686, meeting of 2 Oct. 1686.
[12] *SRARP*, xv, pp. 17, 164–7.

sum owed. This rule would now be applied to the public debt. Second they proposed a general reduction of interest rates from the current 8% to 5 or 6%. The record says 'this proposal was supported by many', since it seemed a cost-free method of reducing everyone's debt burdens. The archbishop approved on moral grounds and all liked the idea of low interest rates, so there was a unanimous decision to support that proposal. They went on to discuss how to repay the Bank and every kind of tax was canvassed, while D. Cameen, for the Burghers, revived their proposal for a general property tax, based on self-assessment. There were immediate objections that 'there follow from it many inconveniences and no one would be secure in his property, but be subjected to investigations'. The delegates of the nobility then met apart to consider in detail what to offer. Gyllenborg enlarged on his proposals: to repay the Bank there should be an increase of the excise for some years, but in return the Bank should reduce its lending rate to 6%. The crown farms should be recovered by applying *alterum tantum* and cutting interest from 8 to 6%, though not retrospectively. The same general principle could be applied to the unsecured public debts, and poor creditors, mainly public servants with salary arrears, could be given some relief through a stamp tax. The war contingency should be covered by traditional subsidies. This was approved as the provisional offer from the nobility.[13]

The Clergy discussed their contribution on 20 and 22 September. The archbishop opened by telling them they must provide the sum the king had asked; it was only a question of how. Bishop Hahn seconded: 'we cannot argue over what the king demands but give it to our king'. When Professor Schültz said they must ensure that the money was rightly spent, the archbishop corrected him: 'the king shows daily his excellent management among the royal virtues: his Majesty can use it how he pleases, we simply give'. The Burghers visited them to try and promote their property tax, but the Clergy were divided on this, and told the Burghers they preferred subsidies. The Secret Committee assembled on 22 September to hear what the Estates were offering. Nobody wanted to commit their Estate; the Burghers said they needed more information; the Clergy said they would see what the Peasants were offering. A Peasant delegation was called and were asked for their proposals. They replied that if there was no war, nothing. When asked about the debt, they conceded: 'what we can do will not be lacking'. But it must be by customary methods: 'we cannot understand anything new'. A game ensued with the Marshal trying to pin the Peasants down on the grounds of the need to share the common burdens, but they remained evasive; they would consider subsidies if the other Estates did the same.[14]

On 24 September the Peasants returned to the Committee. The Marshal told

---

[13] RA, R 2375, meetings of 16, 17, 18 Sept. 1686; Carlson, *Historia*, III, pp. 287, 290; Carlgren, 'Kungamakt', pp. 188, 189; Lindqvist, *Gyllenborg*, pp. 97, 102; RA, Rådsprotokoll 1686, p. 1790, meeting of 20 Sept. 1686.

[14] *PR*, IV, pp. 225, 228, 229; RA, R 2375, meeting of 22 Sept. 1686.

them the other Estates had agreed to four annual subsidies for war contingency and expected them to give the same. In addition they proposed that the poll-tax be extended to the adult children of peasants who stayed on the farm. The Peasants were obdurate, they might consider three subsidies, but no more, and the poll-tax was out of the question: 'if we should assume such large contributions, we would promise more than we can perform'. They agreed to take the proposals to their Estate, but came back next day to say they could give nothing more. The Marshal now threatened to report them to the king, but the peasants replied: 'we know very well that the king is gracious and protects us if we humbly petition'. The spokesman excused his hard line, but he was mandated: 'nobody would believe the sort of people I have to deal with, they are not to be persuaded quickly'. To resolve the deadlock it was agreed that a delegation from the Secret Committee should go and talk to the peasants, and this worked. J. Rosenhane, who led the delegation, reported that collectively the Estate would not listen, but he spoke with each provincial deputation separately and got them to agree they would give as many subsidies as the other Estates.[15]

The Secret Committee had now settled the war contingency grant and returned to the debt. Gyllenborg repeated his proposals and provoked the most serious confrontation of the session, the last occasion that any proposal known to be supported by the king was openly resisted in the Diet. The basis of the opposition was the principle of the sanctity of contract. The secured creditors held royal letters, under the king's hand and seal, assigning them the revenues of the secured properties until the advance had been repaid. Thus to apply *alterum tantum* was a clear breach of contract and would, it was claimed, destroy public credit for all time. It is to be noted that several outspoken opponents were heavily invested in these properties, while Gyllenborg had had the foresight to sell his in 1685. The Marshal tried to argue that the application of *alterum tantum* was fair and 'consistent with the Law of God and the law of other well-governed nations'. If the creditors would consider that this was an honest attempt to repay what was possible, and 'consider the state of the kingdom . . . for that reason credit will be preserved'. On 27 September the debate continued, and the Marshal offered important clarifications. *Alterum tantum* would apply to all creditors, secured or unsecured, but it would not be retrospective, that is creditors who had already received more than *alterum tantum* on their advance could not be required to refund the excess. The trouble was that, given the known propensities of Charles XI for ruthless pursuit of the last penny of his rights, nobody was inclined to trust the assurance. This explained Lindschöld's frequent interventions in the debate to repeat: 'it has never been anyone's intention, but they are free from all retrospective accounting'. The resistance was sustained by Sparre, on grounds of sanctity of contract, and by E. Lovisin, who said bluntly that *alterum tantum* was illegal used in this way: 'there is

---

[15] RA, R 2375, meeting of 24 Sept. 1686.

no people that interprets *alterum tantum* like that'. He asserted that if legal right were violated, 'then credit will be altogether overturned'. Lichton joined in, emphasizing that these were contracts under the king's hand and seal. The Marshal was pushed into a corner and brought out the argument of last resort, when he said '*iniquis temporibus* . . . the king can interpret the law'. He probably did not realize he was saying that in Sweden, under an absolute king, there was no rule of law, because in case of necessity the king could always modify it. He reiterated the argument later in the debate when Lichton appealed to the rules of Sweden's laws, and declared: 'even if we find the actual law gives no ground, there is *necessitas publica*, which is a powerful and weighty law'. The Marshal's supporters searched for precedents, but none of them was convincing, while B. Cronskiöld suggested: 'since we get into so many difficulties in this matter, it would be well if someone could give a better proposal'. The archbishop took this up and suggested a committee: 'this is a matter of great importance . . . it would be best that a few got together and take it into consideration'. This reflected the early modern assumption that there was always a consensus to be found if they looked for it. At all costs confrontation should be avoided. It is apparent from the debate that most felt the rule of law should be upheld, but knew the will of the king could not be denied, and they were trying desperately to reconcile the two. At the end Lindschöld summed up. He started from the premiss that the existing debt could not be repaid in full, and the creditors must yield something. In these circumstances, *alterum tantum*, which had some ground in the Land Law, and gave equity between secured and unsecured creditors, 'is both Christian and just . . . when the matter is considered *secundum rationes universalis* . . . and not according to civil law', it was seen that the secured creditors had no right to more favoured treatment. The Secret Committee then separated into Estates to consider.[16]

The decision came on 27 September. The nobility had a written memorandum from Lovisin affirming that *alterum tantum* was illegal. He rubbished the supposed precedents, but then suggested an escape route. Let the secured creditors be called together and asked to surrender their properties as a free gift, once they had received *alterum tantum* and the repayment of their advance. J. Rosenhane suggested the traditional strategy for avoiding difficult decisions; he accepted the secured creditors had a legal right, but 'since in this the king's name and honour are involved, it is best to refer this to the king and do in it what seems best to his Majesty'. But most, with obvious reluctance, accepted the Marshal's argument from necessity. The Clergy said they had always supported *alterum tantum* as scriptural, and not only agreed to it, but wanted creditors whose returns exceeded it to repay the excess. The Burghers too readily accepted *alterum tantum* and this became the recommendation of the Committee. They went on to consider the additional taxation required by the king. They agreed to raise the excise by 25% for three or four years to repay the Bank. On 30

---

[16] *Ibid.*, meetings of 24, 25, 27 Sept. 1686; Lindqvist, *Gyllenborg*, pp. 106–9.

November the king reverted to the tactic, familiar from the two previous Diets, that as soon as one demand was satisfied he produced additional demands. In this case the Marshal informed the Committee that the king needed funding to redeem some small German territories that had been mortgaged to princely creditors like the bishop of Münster. At this both the archbishop and Cameen fired warning shots: their Estates had not yet confirmed the existing tax package, it was only provisional. Still the Committee considered proposals and preferred an increase of poll-tax, which would fall exclusively on the Peasants.[17]

On 1 October the Marshal took the proposals to the Council for comment and got the routine anodyne response from Oxenstierna that the Council was impressed by their labours, but 'for their own persons had no comment to make'. Then the Peasant delegation had to be called in and the Marshal put the proposals to them. They got a rough reception, though the Peasant delegation agreed to look at the poll-tax increase, but only if it applied to the other commoners as well. The Marshal argued this was a tax, not a free gift, and they must accept, but the spokesman replied: 'whatever name you want to give it, it is too burdensome for us . . . God protect us from it'. This was followed by a notable display of recalcitrance from the Peasants. Each suggestion of additional taxation from the Marshal was bluntly rejected: 'we can do no more, and hope our subsidy which we have promised will serve to repay the debt'. It showed how important it was that in Sweden the peasants were a legal Estate: they knew they could protect themselves from elite bullying and did not hesitate to do so. Their resistance was an excuse for the Burghers to announce on 2 October that they had had second thoughts about the excise. The Peasant delegation was called back, after consulting the Estate, but were as unyielding as ever; they could give nothing on the poll-tax: 'we shall never burden our brothers with that, they will kill us'. Two days later the Committee reopened the debate on the secured creditors; Axel Lillie asserted that many, like himself, faced ruin. The Marshal appealed to community spirit: 'it is better some suffer than the whole kingdom', but it was resolved to go back to the Council. There the Marshal said the nobility would welcome any alternative method, 'both to uphold credit and repay the kingdom's heavy debt'. Oxenstierna replied that he had thought the matter was settled, but agreed that the Council would consider it.[18]

While they waited, the nobility on the Committee went over the whole subject again. Lindhielm tried for evasion once more and proposed: 'we simply refer the whole matter to the king; it may be that the king can find means and methods that are salutary'. Lindschöld stamped firmly on that one; the king would not accept it. But he had realized some concession was needed and came up with a revised proposal, based on precedents he had discovered from 1615 and 1661, 'so that no one can accuse us that we have done either what is new or unjust'. Gyllenborg

[17] RA, R 2375, meetings of 27, 28, 30 Sept. 1686; *PR*, IV, p. 256.
[18] RA, R 2375, meetings of 1, 2, 4 Oct. 1686; RA, Rådsprotokoll 1686, p. 1815, meeting of 1 Oct. 1686; pp. 1826–7, meeting of 4 Oct. 1686.

joined in, conceding that perhaps his original proposal was too harsh and innovative. The Council, who had had a letter from the king instructing them to confer with the nobility, now announced they favoured *alterum tantum*, only to be told by the Marshal that the nobility had changed its mind. The whole process was an exercise in evading responsibility for unpopular decisions. The nobility in the Committee wanted the Council to share responsibility; the Council sought to evade this. The Council minute says they discussed among themselves, but it was not to be recorded on the minute. They devised another evasive response, that the Council had no doubt that the Estates were acting for the best and urged them 'to finish and complete it at their discretion'. This had to be cleared first with the king. Oxenstierna went and found him in the queen's apartments, and when the king asked what the Council was proposing, was told the Council preferred not to intervene, since, as de la Gardie had put it, 'if the Council does that, there would be no need to assemble the Estates, the king can do it with the Council'. The king appeared to accept this, so that when the Marshal came for an answer he pressed in vain for an opinion. But then someone, presumably Lindschöld, got at the king, and he wrote to the Council on 5 October that he required them to give an opinion on how the debt could be reduced. They then agreed to Lindschöld's revised proposal, combined with a general and retrospective reduction of interest rates. Their main concern was to protect the image of the king; as Wrede said, on interest rates: 'it is not the king who reduces from 8 to 5, but it is the Estates who urged the king that it should be done'. But they added that the proposals for the secured creditors should be used as an inducement to them to enter into individual settlements. The Council was warning the king not to press legal chicanery too hard. On 7 October the Committee was told the king required a decision, so they went right round the arguments again, except Lindschöld now relied on his new precedents, which had a similar effect to *alterum tantum* in that they ruled that in debt repayment, the capital was deemed to be paid off first, thus reducing the interest. The dominant worry among the delegates was retrospection; Falkenberg said: 'the Nobility have said they will not hear of any retrospective accounting', but the Marshal insisted the king had no such intention, 'so we have no need either to pursue this'. At last consensus emerged on the lines suggested by the Council. Holders of secured properties would get their contractual interest, but under the 1661 rule that capital was repaid first. If they were still entitled to possession, their interest would be cut from 8 to 5%. Unsecured creditors must also liquidate under the 1661 rule, but they should be allowed interest at 6%, which also became the general bank rate. The Committee emphasized that the secured creditors had behaved entirely legally, and urged the king to enter into private negotiations with all creditors, and 'so far as possible pay those who are poor and needy'.[19]

[19] RA, Rådsprotokoll 1686, pp. 1815–23, meeting of 1 Oct. 1686; pp. 1827–8, meeting of 4 Oct. 1686; p. 1832, meeting of 5 Oct. 1686; Lindqvist, *Gyllenborg*, pp. 106, 113, 118; Carlson, *Historia*, III, pp. 298–314; RA, R 2375, meetings of 4, 5, 7, 8, 11 Oct. 1686; *SRARP*, xv, pp. 188–207.

On 9 October the Secret Committee proposals were reported to the Riddarhus. The Marshal read them out and declared: 'now everyone is free to express his opinion'. Falkenberg asked if the secured creditors could confer privately, and this was allowed. After an hour their spokesman, Axel Sparre, said they accepted and would surrender their properties, 'of a good and free will give up their rights', to escape the indignity of having it forced on them by the commoner Estates. They hoped that the king would 'remember them graciously, so that they will not be altogether ruined'. Class I remarked that they 'beg most humbly that after this they may finally be free of all inquests and sit secure in their properties and the little they have left'. J. Rosenhane suggested that the king might apply the reduced interest rate to his own claims from the Tribunal verdicts and the reduktion, but the Marshal thought it was 'perhaps somewhat risky' to put that in writing but he would sound the king out informally. The mood of the Riddarhus was submissive and resigned, but also clearly resentful of the way their Estate had been treated and nervous about what else might come. The Estates of the Clergy and the Burghers had no problems in accepting the package.[20]

It turned out that the Riddarhus had been right to fear new demands. On 12 October the nobility on the Secret Committee were told that the king had queries about 'unpurchased rents', and the status of properties alienated before 1632. Earlier in the century the kings had raised money by offering to sell the rents on crown farms in perpetuity at a fixed price. Before 1638 this had been calculated to give a return of 3% on the purchase price, after 1638, 4.5%. These transactions, like the loans on secured properties, were formal legal contracts. The king's questions arose out of the complexities of the rental structure. Put at its simplest there were three main categories of rent on crown farms: the basic annual rent recorded in the Land Books, a category of so-called 'uncertain rents' added later, and a category of 'extraordinary rents' derived from commutations of peasant services. The purchases before 1638 had been calculated on the first category only; the later purchases included the uncertain rents. But the practice had been that the purchaser took all the rents from the farm, so it could be argued they had taken rents which they had not paid for. The king's letter implied they would be liable to refund these rents. The point about 1632 was that the reduktion resolutions of 1680 had excluded alienations earlier than that date, and the king was asking if this restriction was valid.[21]

The questions were a devastating blow; noblemen were being challenged over revenues they believed they had paid for, and faced the prospect of Chamber officials probing their finances and demanding retrospective repayments. This made it the most sensitive issue of the whole Diet. It combined a general threat to the security of property, with a specific challenge to contracts whose validity had

---

[20] *SRARP*, xv, pp. 41, 42, 44, 45, 209–10.
[21] RA, R 2375, meeting of 12 Oct. 1686; Carlson, *Historia*, iii, pp. 323, 324; Lindqvist, *Gyllenborg*, pp. 121–3, 125.

been confirmed in the Diets of 1654, 1680 and 1682. When Lindschöld broke the news on 12 October he made a remark that has puzzled historians: 'this is a matter that I do not rightly understand'. It is not credible that a man placed at the centre of government policy making could be unaware of proposals that had been discussed extensively among reduktion officials prior to 1686. But Lindschöld knew it could make trouble; as he said, this was quite different from the secured properties, 'since that concerned a few individuals, but this touches every nobleman'. The originator was probably Gyllenborg, who explained to the Secret Committee that although the contracts said 'they shall enjoy the purchased properties as their freehold', this could not be held to include the extraordinary rents. Everybody accepted the principle, stated by Cronskiöld, that 'the nobility cannot claim the rents they have not paid for'. Sparre suggested they could only petition the king that the rents had been taken in good faith and that they be exempt from accounting and repayment. Gyllenborg tried to reassure them that they could draw a line between the past and the future: 'what the nobility has enjoyed bona fide through connivance and royal benevolence' would be exempt from repayment, but 'it is best to refer this to the king's grace and justice'. This suggests the original challenge had been intimidatory, and the king had always had a compromise in mind. Rosenhane welcomed Gyllenborg's suggestion as reasonable; retrospection would be unrealistic: 'the nobility will be completely ruined and the king get no service out of them'. On the point about 1632, that restriction had been overruled by the last Diet, which had confirmed there was no limit on the right of the crown to recover properties, they could only petition for the 1632 limit to be respected, or if not for innocent purchasers to be compensated.[22]

The Committee drafted a petition to the king, begging that 'the king will not proceed to their destruction', and for the future offered to buy out the unpurchased rent, 'so that finally they may reach a conclusion'. The Marshal took this to the Council for advice, where J. G. Stenbock spoke out for the validity of the contracts. He said that when a man purchased a farm, the contract would not specify any poultry belonging to it, but it was understood they were part of the purchase; so it was with these rents. Further it would be a slur on the king's predecessors to suggest they had been negligent in these matters. The Council indicated that it approved the draft, especially as it was a petition, not an assertion of rights, and would send a similar letter of their own to the king. Next day the Marshal reported the draft of the petition to the Riddarhus. He said it was gracious of the king to have consulted them and he was confident the nobility 'would set aside all private interest and give such a response as would satisfy the king, and be just and reasonable in itself'. Gabriel Oxenstierna said they must consider the matter, but the Marshal warned that 'they look out and do not stand too much on their rights, that way they could risk being let off retrospection'. The

---

[22] Lindqvist, *Gyllenborg*, pp. 133–6, 144, 145; Carlson, *Historia*, III, p. 323; RA, R 2375, meeting of 12 Oct. 1686.

threat was clear and reinforced by Rosenhane who indicated that the king might refer the matter to the commoner Estates. All three Classes indicated their approval of the petition. While they were waiting for the response, the Secret Committee asked the Chamber for a list of the rents involved, and got the ominous reply that they were so complex, and beset with local variations that this was impossible. They also considered trying to write in to the Diet Resolution a statement that the matter was finally resolved, but decided it was not worth it; in these matters Diet resolutions were no safeguard. When the Marshal reported the king's reception of the petition he said it had been gracious, but when he ventured to ask the king if this really was the final demand, 'his Majesty did not reply specifically', which was obviously disturbing.[23]

On 26 October the king returned to the attack with a further question; some contracts had been for a 3% return, others for 4.5%: which was the correct level? This question was loaded with menace. Anyone could see that from the crown's point of view 3% was more favourable, but if that was so then those who had purchased for 4.5% had enjoyed an undeserved advantage at the public expense, and to the minds of Charles XI and the Chamber experts that meant the crown could claim compensation. The Secret Committee was very unhappy and looked for a way out of answering the question. Falkenberg asked: 'how can we say which is most just, it is not for us to judge the actions of kings, since what one does must be as valid as what another does?' They should refer the question back to the king. The irritation in the Committee was voiced by the unnamed member who interjected: 'would to God the king would give us our money back and we would willingly return the properties'. The Council had received the same query and were equally unhappy. Stenbock said 'this was a very serious matter', and the minute discreetly overlooked the discussion and stated: 'the whole Council was unanimous about this', but did not say what. The answer they sent to the king was the wrong one, that both rates had been correct and should be respected, and compounded this by dumb insolence, when they said for the future the question was academic, since 'the Council had not understood that his Majesty was intending to sell crown land'. This was probably the work of Stenbock, who was consistently opposed to using legal chicaneries which would undermine public credit. The king confronted him in the Council on 29 October, and Stenbock remarked, in reference to the secured properties issue: 'what lamentations there have been over this, since people got to know, could have been heard in Heaven', and the king conceded 'it is dangerous for credit'. But he continued to require the Council to answer his question. Gabriel de la Gardie said: 'true 3% is much better, if they had found such an idiot who was willing to give anything for that'. Yet in the end, the Council corrected its answer and affirmed that 3% was the more advantageous rate. Their independent stance

---

[23] RA, Rådsprotokoll 1686, pp. 1867–71, 1872–8, two meetings of 12 Oct 1686; *SRARP*, xv, pp. 47–53; RA, R 2375, meetings of 12, 10 Oct. 1686.

had not lasted long.[24] The Secret Committee returned to the king's question on 27 October. The Marshal produced an opinion from the Chamber that 3% was the only acceptable rate, and that purchasers had had no right to take the extraordinary rents. Falkenberg rejected this; the sales documents clearly said they could, and others agreed with him: the Chamber was wrong. Rosenhane raised the difficulty of criticizing the royal decisions: 'I always observe that [a royal decision] as equivalent to the highest law.' He deduced both rates must have been right at the time. But obviously the 3% rate was more favourable for the crown, and since that was what the king asked, 'I say no more'. Several followed Falkenberg in declining to pass judgement on a kingly resolution. So Lindschöld had to report the nobility declined to answer the question. The king then implemented the threat to consult the commoners. He told Lindschöld to require a formal answer from all the Estates. The Clergy and Burghers made no difficulty, they agreed 3% had been correct, but the Riddarhus remained obstinate. Gabriel Oxenstierna wanted to draft a petition of protest, and when the Marshal asked what the issue would be, replied: 'it is enough we shall be completely ruined by this'. The Marshal tried to soothe them by assuring them the king would receive individual petitions, 'so no one can say or complain they have not been heard', but the Riddarhus remained obstinate. The king, or his advisers, must then have decided some concession was necessary, for on the following day, a conciliatory ruling on the secured properties was announced. He modified his extreme position, the interest rate on the contracts would be reduced, but with no retrospection and the *alterum tantum* principle was dropped. The Marshal made the most of this considerable concession and told the Riddarhus the resolution was 'much more gracious than we thought'. The Secret Committee was so carried away with gratitude that it proposed to wait on the king to thank him, but the Marshal told them that the king 'does not like any extensive ceremonial', and only the Marshal, the archbishop and Cameen should come.[25]

There was still the problem of the unpurchased rents. On 2 November, Lindschöld was ill and Ståhlarm took his place. The king had sent a memorandum which he wanted all the Estates to sign. In the Secret Committee there were objections from those who insisted that the sales at 4.5% had been legal. So the memorandum went to the full Estates. The Burghers were satisfied and said they had supposed the issue had been resolved. The Clergy were initially reluctant to pronounce, despite their expressed resentment that noblemen had secured advantageous purchases, while commoners had to pay taxes. The archbishop had to get fresh instructions from the king before they agreed to accept. But in the Riddarhus there was real difficulty. Gabriel Oxenstierna, Sparre and Lichton stood out for confirmation of the 4.5% purchases, and when Ståhlarm tried to insist 'we have already

---

[24] RA R 2375, meeting of 26 Oct. 1686; RA, Rådsprotokoll 1686, p. 1901, two meetings of 24 Oct. 1686; pp. 1914–15, meeting of 27 Oct. 1686; p. 1921, meeting of 29 Oct. 1686; pp. 1944–5, meeting of 1 Nov. 1686; Lindqvist, *Gyllenborg*, pp. 139–42.

[25] Lindqvist, *Gyllenborg*, p. 114; *SRARP*, xv, pp. 67–74; RA, R 2375, meeting of 30 Oct. 1686.

decided this once', a counter memorandum was introduced, and the clerk minuted there was such a row he could not hear what was said. Ståhlarm hurried off to the king, who said that surely the Riddarhus would not contradict what had already been resolved, but when he reported this, the noise broke out again, with shouts that everyone supported the protest. Ståhlarm said he would not carry the protest to the king unless it was signed. 'We hear the king's Majesty's will: can they sign it? Until that is done I am not taking any document.' He suggested they let the Secret Committee draft a reply to the king; 'to this there was no reply' and the debate ended. The following day Lindschöld returned to preside in the Secret Committee, and after Lichton and Sparre insisted the validity of purchases at 4.5% must be upheld, though Sparre said the Riddarhus protest was not intended to be signed, the Marshal produced a draft letter to the effect that if sales at 4.5% had been approved at the time, this had been an error of judgement, because such sales had been damaging to the crown. This was a typical fudge which failed to satisfy the critics, and Lichton appealed to his fellow nobles: 'I beg you worthy gentlemen, consider what you are doing.' Lindschöld insisted a majority supported him, and turned to the Clergy and Burgher delegates, who said they supported it. The Peasant delegation was called, but they adopted a ploy they used frequently to evade unpleasant decisions and declined to give an opinion; 'these are matters we do not understand'. The reply was taken back to the Riddarhus and accepted with little further discussion. The resistance had collapsed.[26]

The outcome was surprising. The Marshal carried the approval of the Estates to the king, who having won his point on paper, then made a substantial concession. In effect he followed the view, expressed several times, that 'the preservation of the nobility must be taken into consideration'. In what the Marshal called 'a very gracious declaration and resolution', he said that despite the condemnation of purchases at 4.5%, they would not be repudiated, 'since such an alteration would have caused the ruin of many, and [he] had graciously decided to let everyone keep his purchase'. No evidence has survived of the reasoning behind the king's decision. His unyielding assertion of his will in a legally dubious claim was entirely characteristic; his subsequent retreat was not. It seems the sheer force of elite opinion, expressed in the Council, the Secret Committee and the Riddarhus, notably the outspoken views of Stenbock, and perhaps the advice from Lindschöld, had persuaded the king to back off. The relief of those who had been under threat was vocal, and the royal managers made the most of it. In the Secret Committee, Rosenhane said, 'the nobility can never praise sufficiently the king's far-reaching grace'; he had been 'graciously pleased to consider their welfare, and let them be more in his heart than his own interest'. In the Riddarhus, Lindschöld pointed the moral: 'I see that with God and Kings we achieve nothing by arguing, but with prayer.' This was the end of the legislative extension of the reduktion. For the rest

[26] *SRARP*, xv, pp. 74–8, 86, 297; *PR*, IV, pp. 262, 263, 264; RA, R 2375, meetings of 29 Oct. 1686, 3 Nov. 1686; Carlson, *Historia*, III, pp. 331–6.

of the reign the king and his agents worked within the rules they had established. The decisions of 1686 meant that for the holders of secured properties, their rate of return was cut to 5% from 1687, and the difference between this and what they actually received went to repay the capital. Most of these properties, with an annual revenue of some 250,000 dsm., were recovered by 1697. The unsecured creditors were encouraged to negotiate individual settlements, on the basis of an interest rate of 6% for cash advances, 5% for unpaid goods and services, mainly arrears of salary. Interest would stop when it amounted to *alterum tantum*. This brought about a substantial reduction in the unsecured public debt by 1697. The contracts for the purchased properties stood, but from 1687 the holders had to buy out the unpurchased rents. This was done by capitalizing them, and the crown accepting suitable landed property in settlement. This programme, devised by Gyllenborg, and driven through by the king's personal authority, had secured a useful extension of the reduktion, while narrowly avoiding a major open confrontation between the king and the elites.[27]

Instead the Diet of 1686 showed the readiness of the nobility to work with the royal government, even at the cost of sacrifices. Their main role was to make the commoners yield generous tax grants by the example of their own offerings. The Riddarhus abandoned any attempt to claim tax exemption, and virtually without debate agreed to two subsidies, with two more in case of war. Their subsidy was based on a tax of 10% on salaries, a levy on their servants that could be deducted from wages, a 25% tax on receipts from interest and a tax on second homes. In addition they would pay the new stamp tax and the increased excise. As always they attached to their grant the pious formula that 'it will not occasion any damage or detriment to our privileges, now or in time to come', an empty ritual by this time. Their programme then became the model urged on the commoners through the Secret Committee. Yet the relationship with the king was not one-sided. Their grievances, formally presented in the Diet, were considered in the Council, and the responses showed a mixture of conciliation and firmness on the king's part. He agreed on the need to regulate hired labour, so that noblemen got a fair share and the peasant farmers did not take too much. He was sympathetic to bringing in dress codes to forbid commoners to wear various kinds of finery. Their complaints at the protracted nature of the reduktion were met by the king's urging the need to get a clear and definitive outcome. The work was of a nature that took time. But the king was prepared to assure them that genuine allodial properties would be exempt. On the other hand the petition to be allowed to establish new manors was firmly rejected: 'the order that has been made cannot be infringed', while complaints about the strict enforcement of cavalry service were brushed aside: 'it is a settled matter and the king cannot permit any modifications'. Thus the king was asserting his will, but there was genuine dialogue between him and his noblemen.

[27] *SRARP*, xv, pp. 52, 84, 86; RA, R 2375, meetings of 3, 4 Nov. 1686; Lindqvist, *Gyllenborg*, pp. 120, 121, 123; Almqvist, *Frälsegodsen*, pp. 89–90.

It could not be otherwise; neither party could function effectively without the other.[28]

The Propositions of 1686 had innovated by prescribing to each Estate how much taxation the king needed. The form of voluntary grant was preserved, but the choice was not how much to grant, but how it should be levied. For the Peasant Estate this meant a prolonged round of haggling. After the early exchanges, Lindschöld tried diplomacy; he had heard that the Peasant delegation complained that, when they came to the Secret Committee, they were left to stand. He suggested to the Committee it might help if they were invited to sit, an unprecedented mark of respect, and this was done. But they still refused to offer more than four subsidies. On 15 October they did suggest they would pay poll-tax on their adult children if the Clergy and Burghers did the same for their children and servants. Their spokesman echoed the Marshal's arguments about equality of sacrifice, and like the nobility added the proviso that 'this may not draw us into a precedent'. The Marshal then had to persuade the others 'to confer together and satisfy the Peasants'. But he also continued to press them, until they complained they were being intimidated. The Marshal denied this; there was no compulsion, he sought 'only to persuade you'. The outcome was that the Clergy and Burghers accepted the poll-tax, so that on 21 October the Peasants gave in. But that was as far as they could be pushed and the obstinacy paid off; they successfully repelled all other suggestions for increasing their tax burden.[29]

The other Estates played similar games. They accepted in principle the sums demanded by the king, but complained bitterly of impending ruin before producing an offer. On 25 October the archbishop had to tell his Estate that the king 'had sent it [their offering] back again to be improved somewhat'. He then specified what was lacking and told them the proposals in the Propositions 'were to be approved as they were set down, word for word'. The Clergy submitted. There is no record of discussion among the Burghers; their bargaining counter was the increase in excise. In the Secret Committee they first claimed it would ruin them, then agreed in principle. But when they were pressed to conciliate the Peasants over poll-tax a mutiny occurred. In the Secret Committee, in the absence of Cameen, Burgomaster Robeck spoke for them and told the Marshal that if they were forced to concede the poll-tax they would reconsider the excise. The Marshal challenged him to justify this and Robeck answered curtly: 'our poverty'. The Marshal suggested that in the absence of Cameen he was not authorized to speak for the Estate, and at this his colleagues backed off and said: 'he has neither authority for this nor been asked to do it'. When Cameen reappeared, he admitted his Estate had been making difficulties, but assured the Secret Committee it would be all right: 'I hope that everything will be resolved and concluded with unity and sense.' In reality the

[28] *SRARP*, xv, pp. 263, 267, 268: RA, Rådsprotokoll 1686, pp. 1864–8, meeting of 6 Oct. 1686; pp. 1851–5, meeting of 9 Oct. 1686; pp. 1862–5, meeting of 10 Oct. 1686.
[29] RA, R 2375, meetings of 11, 15, 18, 21 Oct. 1686.

Burghers had little bargaining power. They brought their package to the king and Council on 26 October and, like the Clergy, were told it was insufficient. Cameen was told: 'if they cannot agree, then the Burgomasters must be called into the Chamber and the assessment set right there. The king will have the total completely covered.' Like the Clergy, they gave in.[30]

The sense that the traditional freedom of the Estates to authorize extraordinary taxation was being eroded caused an incident over the behaviour of a leading Chamber official, Wetterhamn. He had investigated the subsidy payments granted in the Diet of 1682 and claimed there had been serious evasion. He had then begun legal proceedings against defaulters. This angered the Secret Committee; subsidies were not royal taxes, but free gifts and the Chamber had no part in their assessment. On 5 October Wetterhamn was called into the Secret Committee, where he was quite unapologetic. He said it had been an idea worth trying: 'I only proposed this with good intentions to his Majesty's service.' The Marshal replied that 'it displeases the Estates that someone is interpreting their resolutions', but was told: 'what I did happened under the king's protection'. Wetterhamn knew he had acted in the spirit of Charles XI's resolve to extract everything that could plausibly be claimed. The Committee was outraged by Wetterhamn's insolence but had no power to act. They could only petition the king, and the Marshal, with the archbishop and Cameen, went off to find him. The Marshal got a word with the king after dinner, and reported he 'was very gracious; the Estates shall always have their liberties in their contributions, and that neither Wetterhamn nor any other shall have power to interpret a Diet Resolution, except according to the true meaning of the words and what is actually stated'. He then sanctioned a clause in the Resolution of 1686 that the grants of the Estates were to be observed to the letter.[31] But the Estates had shown their inability to enforce their rights in face of the growing arrogance of the invigorated royal administration. They could not criticize the king, whose driving will was the real cause of their grievance, so they tried to hit at his servant. That too was impossible, since Wetterhamn, as a crown servant authorized by the king, was also untouchable. All the Estates could do, like the meanest of subjects, was to make a humble petition to the king, who was the exclusive source of legitimate authority.

There were two other major policy decisions made in the Diet of 1686. The Propositions had called on the Estates to make proposals for advancing trade and manufactures. This was completely uncontroversial and the Riddarhus appointed a committee on 15 September. But with so much other business to preoccupy members they made little progress, and on 15 October, the Marshal told the Secret Committee that he had advised the king there was insufficient time during this Diet and the king agreed. The Estates would elect members to a commission to work out

[30] *PR*, IV, pp. 226, 227, 228, 257; RA, R 2375, meetings of 18 Sept. 1686, 15 Oct. 1686; RA, Rådsprotokoll 1686, p. 1903, meeting of 26 Oct. 1686.
[31] RA, R 2375, meetings of 5, 10 Oct. 1686.

proposals for future Diets. This was done and in time the commission produced a set of unremarkable mercantilist proposals. The second concerned a general revision of Swedish law. This had been under discussion for a century but was intensely sensitive. The Land Law, in print since 1608, was regarded as a foundation of the society, and treated with quasi-mystical reverence as a sacred text. It was held any tampering with this involved unpredictable dangers. Yet it had two obvious deficiences: some of the medieval terminology was incomprehensible to a seventeenth-century Swede, and juries in particular could be baffled by it, and since the last fifteenth-century revisions, there had been a corpus of royal ordinances and Diet resolutions which needed to be incorporated into a unified legal code. On 18 October, Lindschöld raised the matter in the Secret Committee; he reminded them 'of the revision of the law, how necessary it was that it be both translated into good contemporary Swedish, and improved'. He revealed that 'the king is inclined to this, so we shall do well to petition the king about it'. The government, aware how sensitive the issue was, wished the initiative to appear to come from the Estates. The Marshal had already taken soundings in the Riddarhus two days before, and at once G. Grass has warned of the perils of changing the texts. Lindschöld countered with the advantages of modernizing the language: 'I cannot see at all why the old wording should be necessary.' The Riddarhus accepted the idea. He told the Secret Committee that some of the nobility 'thought it would be dubious to change our old law, and the old Swedish', and had preferred simply to add on the recent accretions, but most had agreed it should be revised. Cameen disliked that; he was not sure the old terminology could be translated satisfactorily, and Lindschöld replied: 'I think the old law is like an old suit of clothes, the new are surely better.' The Committee agreed to petition the king, in spite of the doubts expressed. It came to the Council on 29 October, with the king present, who asked what response he should give. The Council took a conservative line, the language of the law could be modernized, 'but as for the rest, the statutes are clear that there can be no alteration of them'. The Estates were told the king would appoint a commission to review the law; he did not invite them to nominate members.[32]

The Diet of 1686 was a turning point in the history of the institution. It accepted a shift from an active to a reactive role in policy making. A crude measure of the loss of power is the brevity of the minutes, compared with earlier Diets; the full Estates no longer debated issues at any length, frequently did not debate them at all. The real discussion had moved to the Secret Committee and the Council, which had recovered a role in policy making. The causes of the change must be speculative. The growing personal authority of Charles XI was intimidatory, though no open threats were made. But the Marshal's challenges to dissidents to sign their names to their protests were made in the well-founded assurance that nobody would. He also reminded the Estates several times that implementation of the laws rested with the

---

[32] *SRARP*, xv, pp. 15, 54, 55, 163; RA, R 2375, meetings of 15, 18 Oct. 1686; RA, Rådsprotokoll 1686, p. 1925, meeting of 29 Oct. 1686.

king, and if they collaborated, the king could exercise his discretionary powers to mitigate their effects on individuals, as Charles XI commonly did. Lindschöld's aphorism that it was better to petition than to argue had force. And always, as the final resort, the king could signify that some course of action was his will. If objections were raised to this, they were invariably met by the challenge, from the Marshal, are you willing to go against his Majesty's express commandment, which had only one possible answer.

But these considerations can only be part of the explanation. It is worth considering Lindschöld's address at the closing ceremony on 9 November. He was thought one of Sweden's best orators, and if his Baroque language seems excessive to the modern taste, it was appreciated in an early modern society. Charles XI was depicted as a paragon, 'a king who does us all good', and he compared the state of the kingdom at his accession with its present condition. Remembering that he was addressing an audience, almost all of whom, apart from the Peasants, were public servants, he stressed how they 'now have their yearly salary and their secure maintenance', which was not quite true then, but substantially correct. He claimed the king's shining example of disinterested service had been transmitted to the subjects, so that selfishness was banished from the kingdom, while a later passage enthused on how public servants now 'always fear God and honour the king, hate and restrain the bad and further the good, defend the innocent and help the oppressed'. That was describing a Utopia never yet found in the real world. He claimed that 'of all the good things which God has granted and Sweden enjoys, your royal Majesty has the least part'. He illustrated this by claiming that the king took more pleasure in seeing a frontier town well fortified than in building a luxurious palace for himself. That was no fantasy, but prosaic fact. It was plausible for Lindschöld to proclaim a public service ethic: 'what the one subject grants comes immediately to the benefit of another, what the private person has lost, the public has gained'. He told the nobility: 'things are better off in the kingdom, although they were worse off in their households'. All this was idealized, but not remote from reality. And he cited the prevailing peace as a further reason why God favoured Sweden. War was 'often a sinful work, but peace is a joyful work, a work of God'. God, he affirmed, took more pleasure when 'a single subject is rescued from distress, or defended against oppression and injustice' than in the killing of thousands. Lindschöld concluded by developing the metaphor of the body politic. Just as in life head and body were bound together so were the ruler and his subjects. 'In the body politic, the harm that the subject experiences immediately reaches up to the king, who is the head and defender of them all.'[33] It was a plausible assertion, to an audience that was not highly sophisticated in political theory, that a moral economy prevailed in Sweden that upheld equity between all its different inhabitants, and they had to thank God for sending them a king who was committed to its

[33] *SRARP*, xv, pp. 288–90.

values, and had solid practical achievements to prove it. Because this seemed credible, it does as much as any coercive menace to explain why Charles XI found his subjects so biddable.

8

Completing the superstructure

It became increasingly clear after 1686 how the running of the government, under the king, was in the hands of the bureaucracy, led by their ennobled elite group, Lindschöld, Wrede, Gyllenborg and Thegner, who carried on their own power game behind the scenes to win the favour of the king. It was a sign of their growing eminence when, in 1687, six members of the elite, including Lindschöld, were made members of the Council. He was now seen as the most powerful civilian member of the administration; Stockfleth described him in 1688 as 'the strongest spirit of them all, and will easily be able to direct both people and affairs as he wills. It is said he is also poor and full of vanity.' Then in 1689 twenty-four of them were promoted to the titled nobility and moved up from Class III to Class I in the Riddarhus. Members of the magnate families like Bengt Oxenstierna, J. G. Stenbock and Nils Bielke still had an active role and exerted influence, but they were being outstripped by the meritocracy. The dispossessed grumbled to the foreign diplomats; Stockfleth sent a report about someone unnamed, who held a high position but complained: 'what oppressive conditions they now have in Sweden'. He claimed there were no prospects of secure and honourable employment, 'unless one submits to some low-born people and their principles'. Such people did not constitute an opposition; they remained passive, dreaming of some contingency that could turn the situation round.[1]

The European world was changing after it became apparent in 1688 that Louis XIV had plunged Europe back into a general war and Sweden would have to choose her role in it. Parallel with this the Holstein-Gottorp problem came to a head in 1689, as will be shown later and Charles XI was prepared to go to war to settle it. Because of this dual crisis in foreign policy, the Diet was summoned for 7 February 1689. The agenda had been carefully prepared and in the event went through without serious dissent. The real business was even more narrowly confined to the Secret Committee, which now contained eighteen career public servants, an increase on 1686. The Propositions apologized for summoning the Estates so soon after the last Diet, a reminder that to most early modern subjects, a Diet was a burden they preferred to avoid, being expensive in itself, and almost always an

---

[1] Carlson, *Historia*, IV, p. 3; Fryxell, ed., *Handlingar*, II, p. 412, Stockfleth to the king 4 Aug. 1688, same 13 Feb. 1689.

occasion for increasing taxes. But foreign developments made it necessary, since although the king's policies were aimed at 'the preservation of peace', the situation was now so threatening it was necessary 'to prepare to resist by force and ward off any violence and state of hostilities'. Therefore supply was needed urgently, and there were also important domestic matters to consider, though these were not specified. The priority to be given to foreign affairs could account for the choice of Nils Gyllenstolpe as Marshal, one of the rising meritocrats who had specialized in diplomacy and who admitted in the Riddarhus 'he had been for a considerable time distanced from internal and especially Diet affairs'. He delivered the keynote address, and, 'while his Excellency spoke, His Royal Majesty stood with bared head'. The theme was that God had blessed Sweden with a virtuous ruler, 'a living example of a right-thinking and zealous fear of God'. All the well-being that the kingdom enjoyed was due, 'after God', to his virtues, 'and the incomparable industry and attention, under which, to the utmost wonder of everyone, your Royal Majesty never tires, and in all your trouble and life's labours never varies your royal benevolence'. A cult of personality was being built up round Charles XI, but the image was far from the contemporary ideal, the Sun King, Louis XIV. The king was projected as a pious and dedicated public servant, who sacrificed his own worldly pleasures to the pursuit of public duty.[2]

Work began in the Secret Committee on 8 February, when the Council presented the Secret Propositions. They said that the king intended his Estates 'may be acquainted with both the internal and external condition of the kingdom', and offered a series of reports, some backed by documentation, on how the international crisis had developed and what the government had achieved since the last Diet, together with detailed financial accounts. These reports were solidly grounded in fact. The Committee took foreign affairs first and focussed on the Holstein problem. The Marshal invited comment, but the immediate response was to refer everything back to the king, 'since this is a business which must all be adapted to circumstances, so they recommended it all to the king's gracious decision and high prudence'. This was not what the king wanted, so next day the Marshal told the Committee that comments were invited, and he was authorized to give explanations. The archbishop asked did the king want a debate and being told he did, began probing the Holstein situation. His fear was that Sweden could find herself in a war without allies, though there were others who thought this was an opportunity to be exploited. Then Gyllenborg warned that they must think about how a war could be paid for, and the Marshal felt things were getting out of control. 'We are discussing much too extensively; to consider whether it is time to begin a war now is a matter we must refer to the king's gracious pleasure.' That closed further debate; the Committee agreed there was just cause for war and left it all to the king's discretion.[3]

---

[2] Fryxell, ed., *Handlingar*, II, p. 412, Stockfleth to the king 13 Feb. 1689; Carlgren, 'Kungamakt', pp. 199, 200; *SRARP*, xv, pp. 306, 314, 370; Loenbom, ed., *Handlingar*, III, p. 172.

[3] RA, R 2377, Secreta Uskottets Protocoll 1689, meetings of 8, 9 Feb. 1689.

The Committee began to consider the domestic Propositions on 10 February, which after surveying the whole field of public revenues and expenditure set out what the king expected the Diet to provide. In case of war, the king wanted two subsidies payable in 1689, but because he might need the cash at once, suggested that the Estates borrow the anticipated yield from the Bank and guarantee repayment with interest. He submitted detailed costings for an overseas campaign lasting five months. The increase in the excise voted in 1686 should be extended, and an urgent debt of 400,000 dsm. to the Bank should be settled. Finally the yield of the stamp tax had been disappointing, and more was needed to relieve poor creditors, who were flooding the king with petitions which increased his burdens. The minute suggests that the Marshal intended to push through the proposed cash advance without debate, for he took that point first and, 'asked if the Estates have any doubt about it'. Some among the Nobility urged immediate approval, but others said they must consider the whole package of proposals together. By now they were too familiar with the king's tactic that when one demand was settled he followed up with a new one. Falkenberg and Lovisin said they must consider alternatives to borrowing, and the Marshal backed off: 'the king will gladly relieve his subjects and does not request it all in one go'. But he brought in a Chamber official to show how the king needed 2,700,000 dsm. for a war in 1689, and had only 400,000 in hand. The commoners signalled their dislike of Bank loans, so the Estates were told to separate and consider what they would offer.[4]

Among the Nobility, Falkenberg and Lovisin pursued their objections to borrowing and no consensus appeared, but there was some support for paying the 1689 subsidy in two instalments, and then the Estates might borrow if the yield fell short. They went to ask the Council for a view, and got the standard response from Oxenstierna that the Council congratulated them on their willingness to give, and would support whatever they decided. The Marshal thanked him but said they 'wished they would express themselves more extensively on the matter'. However the Council too was divided and returned the answer that they found the proposals of the Nobility sound. In this Diet the Council firmly resisted getting involved in the supply debate; their experience in 1686 had not been encouraging. Then Gyllenborg suggested a compromise: the Estates could guarantee a loan of 200,000 or 300,000 dsm. to provide cash in hand until the subsidy receipts came in. Next day the full Committee met and the Marshal called for the offers. The Burghers emphasized that they 'must know first what the king is suggesting in total before they can say', so that their answer was provisional, 'without prejudice to our colleagues'. They then expressed strong dislike of a Bank loan and claimed however willing they were, that was impossible. The Clergy said they would, very reluctantly, consider a loan and then the whole Committee accepted Gyllenborg's proposal. The Peasants were now called, and after they were seated, the proposal was

---

[4] *SRARP*, xv, pp. 374–93; Grauers, *Sveriges Riksdag*, pp. 110, 111; RA, R 2377, meeting of 10 Feb. 1689.

explained to them. They made the ritual claim that they were already overburdened and then agreed to consider the proposal: 'we will do all that our poverty allows'.[5]

The Marshal then reminded the Committee they were still 900,000 dsm. short of the projected cost of a war, and the Nobility offered a further subsidy in 1691, which could be anticipated by borrowing under guarantee if necessary. The delegations reported back to their Estates and the Riddarhus accepted without debate. However they were clearly unhappy and took out their anger on the Bank. Axel Leijonhufvud complained bitterly how the Bank was ruthless in auctioning properties put up as security, claiming they often went for a tenth of their real worth. He personally had been ruined by this. The minute says: 'there was a great row and dissatisfaction among the Nobility over this'. But it was impotent fury; Falkenberg pointed out the Bank operated rules established by the Estates, so nothing could be done. It is known that the Clergy and the Burghers consulted to try and establish a common position, but they ended by accepting the proposals. The Clergy were sensitive about guaranteeing interest payments, and the archbishop went to lobby the king. He evaded with ease, saying 'he could not help at all, since the other Estates had agreed unanimously'. When the Peasants came back, they too rejected the loan guarantees, on the ingenious plea that they did not understand what interest was: 'it is strange to them because there are no capitalists among them . . . if those who are here agree to it, they would get trouble and hostility from their brothers at home'. They asked the other Estates to explain this to the king. The Marshal assured them it was nothing to worry about; their brothers could not object to 'what you have granted for the king's and the fatherland's service'. He then revealed that in case of war another subsidy was needed for 1690, but they went on complaining about interest until the Marshal offered to send a delegation to explain it to their Estate. They left and he pressed the Committee to complete the taxation package. The king wanted to extend the increased excise to provide for the fortresses, and Dahlberg was called in to produce drawings and estimates. The Committee agreed. To repay the 400,000 dsm. to the Bank he suggested a half-subsidy in 1691, and to relieve poor creditors, another half-subsidy in 1692. All this was agreed and reported to the Council next day, who declared their approval and it went to the full Estates. The Clergy minute suggests they accepted without debate; the Burghers agreed and the Riddarhus made no comment. It remained for the Peasant Estate to demonstrate how to play the system. First they went directly to the king, who promised they need not be involved in guaranteeing interest payments and granted them an extended period for paying their subsidies. They then claimed they could not pay a further subsidy in 1691 in case of war. They did give in on this after further haggling with the Marshal, but only after they had again gone to the king and won a new concession. The poll-tax increase on their children, conceded so reluctantly in 1686 would be

---

[5] RA, R 2377, meeting of delegation of the Nobility, 10 Feb. 1689, meeting of 11 Feb. 1689.

taken off. The Marshal told their delegates, rather unconvincingly, that although the other Estates were not as affluent as the Peasants seemed to think, they did not grudge the advantages the Peasants had won. The Peasant leaders were shrewd operators. Behind a façade of being poor, ignorant folk they had won themselves a very favourable settlement.[6]

The Estates may have thought they had now completed the financial agenda, but as usual with Charles XI there was a further turn of the screw to come. On 27 February, the Marshal reported he had taken their proposals to the king,' and the king is graciously pleased with them as long as the peace endures: but since it could happen that there is war, the king wishes the Estates to consider what may be needed in such a case since we cannot be assured of peace'. The king wanted two subsidies authorized in advance for each year the war lasted, and the authority to borrow on them in advance as needed. Nobody among the delegates of the Nobility objected; they followed Falkenberg who said they were ready for any sacrifice: 'rather than the king's interests, glory and reputation, and the safety of the kingdom should suffer'. It was better to make provision now, so that in case of war the king need not wait for a Diet. The delegations separated and the Nobility agreed to the whole proposal, but the commoners were unhappy and said they must consult their Estates. The king seems to have realized he was pressing too hard, and let the Marshal know that if there were no war in 1689, he would not take the second subsidy already approved for that year. This opened the way for a consensus proposal, for which the Burghers, who had already indicated they saw the multiplication of subsidies as going too far, were responsible. In case of war, there would be a subsidy in 1690 and each year thereafter as long as war lasted. If this proved insufficient, the king could borrow as much more as was needed and the 'Estates agree about repayment. If we now promise so many subsidies yearly, then we could not keep it.' The Secret Committee modified this slightly by stipulating the king could borrow the equivalent of a second subsidy, and the Estates would repay it after the war. The Peasants were called and made their usual response; they could not consider any further grants. The Marshal, presumably wearying of the game, told them to tell that directly to the king. It still had to go to the Estates for approval, and the king made a further concession: he would not take the offer of an immediate 200,000 dsm. cash advance from the Bank. The Riddarhus adopted the proposal unanimously; only one speaker, Baron Ekeblad, showed awareness of the constitutional issue involved. While the proposal implied that even in wartime, only the Estates could authorize extraordinary taxes, they were proposing to forgo this right for an indefinite period. Ekeblad asked 'if we could not set a specific time for the grant?' The Marshal dismissed this: 'who can know how long a war may last?' Nobody seconded Ekeblad, so presumably they felt that such abstract principles mattered little in face of the king's will. The commoners were more

---

[6] *Ibid.*, meetings of 11, 13, 14, 15, 19, 20 Feb. 1689; *SRARP*, xv, 1689, pp. 320–3; *PR*, IV, p. 334.

concerned. The archbishop had challenged the Marshal who said: 'the Estates will scarcely go against the king's will without pressing cause'. The archbishop then asked was this proposal commanded by the king? The Marshal did not want to say this: 'I never said it was the king's command, only that the king recommends it.' The archbishop gave up: 'if it is so acceptable to the king, then it must be done'. But the Clergy Estate was less complacent; the proposal was attacked as 'very hard and harmful', so they consulted the Burghers, but in the end could find no acceptable way to decline. The archbishop told his Estate: 'we must regard the king in this case as a father, and he deals with us in it as children, and in no way seeking to harm us'. It is apparent how contemporary beliefs about authority derived from God trapped them in a mental hold. It was the same with the Peasants. After the protest of impossibility, and further claims they could not understand it, they gave in. Their spokesman declared: 'we say nothing against it; we will happily do everything the king requires of us, that is our duty'. The Clergy did carry one amendment. Instead of specifying the king could borrow the equivalent of a second subsidy, they left at his discretion how much he borrowed; the Estates would repay all. This apparently alarming loosening of restraints was meant to reduce the burden; they hoped the king would not need as much as a full second subsidy amounted to. Yet the combined Estates knew what was happening, and how their powers were being subverted. For in the Resolution they added, after the grant: 'we live in the most humble confidence in his Majesty's grace, that this grant of ours will not be any damage or detriment to us in our privileges now or in time to come'. They reinforced this pious hope by stipulating that the grant was only to be applied according to the literal meaning of the words. The wording then specified that the grant was applicable only to the current war contingency. But nobody could have had had any illusions at this stage that this formula could secure anything if 'necessity' should arise.[7]

A modern observer must decide for himself why the Swedish Estates failed to resist repeated royal initiatives that were eroding in fact, though they did not deny in theory, the right of the Estates to be consulted and to consent. They were aware of what was happening but seem to have chosen rather to concentrate on bargaining for their sectional interests. They could do this best through the grievances presented at the Diet. The Clergy in 1689 had serious complaints about the working of the Church Law. They submitted fourteen critical observations and got a full reply to each one. Some the king accepted, others he promised to consider and some he refused, letting his short temper show through, as when he told them in reply to one point they clearly had not read the law properly: 'they should be familiar enough with the Church Law, so that they do not bother the king with what has already been resolved and agreed in it'. Still they could put their case to the king and receive a considered response. And on matters of faith they could be

---

[7] RA, R 2377, meetings of 27, 28 Feb. 1689, 1, 2, 4, 5 March 1689; Carlson, *Historia*, III, pp. 379–85; *SRARP*, XV, pp. 334–7, 339, 421; *PR*, IV, pp. 349, 350, 351.

adamant in face of the king's will. In 1689 the king wanted a change in the baptism service; he disliked the reference to the new-born infant as 'in the power of Satan'. He was simply told by the Clergy that it was scriptural and must stand, and accepted this. The Nobility too presented their complaints, mostly about the application of the reduktion. They added a special petition to the king, couched in the most respectful terms as 'father of the country and appointed by Almighty God' against the several special commissions operating, claiming their activities were creating 'many subjects who are powerless and incapable of your Majesty's service'. They begged for them to be moderated or wound up. The royal reply asserted the overriding need to restore the kingdom's finances and discover their full extent. Individuals who felt aggrieved should petition privately and 'the king will consider what grace can be applied, in one measure or another, according to each one's deserts'. The king's narrow legalism was immovable, but he signalled that individual petitioning, not public protest, was the way to get relief. This was further emphasized by another attempt to further an unsigned petition in the Riddarhus about communion fees charged by clergy under the Church Law. The Marshal and a Riddarhus committee refused to accept it; not only was it unsigned but 'it does not show that respect for the king that it should'. The Riddarhus voted that it was unrepresentative and mischievous. The content implied that the king had been misinformed and made a wrong ruling, and further said it was unsigned because 'no one could be surprised who knows anything about conditions in the Riddarhus', plainly insinuating there was intimidation. It also claimed that putting names to petitions in the Riddarhus was an innovation and should be rejected, and the petition was justified because it was true. This admittedly marginal episode does show, nevertheless, that the absolutist pressures on the Diet were resented by some.

The dominance the king had acquired over the minds of his subjects was demonstrated in the other main business of the Diet of 1689, a formal public denunciation by the Estates of the offensive protocols. It has been noted that Charles XI had not been satisifed with the renunciation of 1682 and in 1689 embarked on an exercise in political education. For some reason it was managed so as to make it appear that the initiative came from the Estates. On 22 February 1689, in the Secret Committee, Lovisin said he had heard of the existence of obnoxious protocols and he thought the Estates ought to see them. The Marshal professed to know nothing of this, but agreed it should be investigated, 'in order to confirm the love between the king and the Estates'. Only two members expressed reservations; one was Axel Wachtmeister, who wanted the business kept confidential, and suggested anyone interested could look at them privately, and the other was G. Sparre, who thought 'it might be best to do it privately . . . and if there are some scandalous protocols to be found they could be quietly annulled'. It is unclear why these two wanted to avoid the publicity, which was the whole point of the exercise. The Committee agreed to ask the king for permission to read the protocols, and the stage management was exposed when it was revealed that everything had been set up in readiness. The next day Secretary S. Leijonmarck began reading extracts, mostly from the period 1633 to 1680, and taken from the minutes of the Council of State, though there was material from Diet debates as well. There were two principal subject areas, statements claiming that there were limits on the king's sovereignty, that he was bound by the Form of Government, that he could not make appointments without consulting the Council, that he could not legislate by himself, or review cases from the Courts, or interpret law; and specific claims of powers belonging to the Council of State, that its advice was binding on the king, that it was a mediator between the king and the subjects, that it had sought to rule that the reduktion was unlawful. It took two days to complete the reading of the material, after which the Marshal asked the Committee for appropriate action, and Falkenberg proposed that they should be formally annulled. Sparre insisted all these issues had now been settled: 'would it not be best that they be annulled quietly?' The Marshal replied it must be public, otherwise people would think they were doing something wrong. The Estates delegations separated to consider, and returned to agree that there should be a formal public Act, and that any of those responsible who survived must apologize. The king agreed and asked the Estates to draft an Act to be confirmed by the Estates and the Council.[8]

In the first Secret Committee discussion on 28 February, the Marshal stated that the aim was to reinforce social ties. 'What we are doing is to create harmony between king and subjects; it is necessary that every subject knows his duty and the king's power.' He returned to this theme on 6 March: 'we see many disturbances in the world proceed because subjects do not understand their duty to the sovereign'. The archbishop agreed: 'the nature of authority is sacred and indivisible, and nobody can have a share in sovereignty'. The draft Act was read out and Axel Wachtmeister again argued for privacy, since it was sedition to utter these thoughts. 'It does no good that one and all become familiar with them', and he said that in time to come, people would be astonished that 'we have come to argue about the king's sovereignty, which should be sacred to everyone. It is hazardous for posterity.' But others pointed out they could not condemn the errors if it was not specified what they were. The draft was approved and the Peasants called, but as usual said 'we are simple people' and would go along with whatever the others decided. The draft was taken to the Council, where Oxenstierna said they were appalled by what they heard and commended what the Estates had done. It was the king who noticed that one offensive speech had been uttered by Oxenstierna himself, and wrote: 'in view of the great services of that gentleman, these words should be left out'.[9]

---

[8] *PR*, IV, pp. 331, 345, 347, 349, 421; *SRARP*, XV, pp. 328, 329, 332, 396–404, 405–7, 408; Carlson, *Historia*, III, pp. 386–97; RA, R 2377, meetings of 22, 23, 25 Feb. 1689; *Handlingar rörande Skandinaviens historia*, XXVIII (1847), pp. 257, 261–8, 270.

[9] *Handlingar rörande Skandinaviens historia*, XXVIII, pp. 271–4, 275–6, 280–5; RA, R 2377, meetings of 28 Feb. 1689, 6, 7, 13 Mar. 1689.

The draft came to the full Estates, and after the Marshal explained in the Riddarhus the purpose was to ensure that subjects 'have a correct idea about the king's sovereignty and their humble duty', the draft was accepted without discussion. When the archbishop explained it to the Clergy they showed no interest at all; they were preoccupied with drafting a complaint that the king's subjects were attending deviant religious services in foreign embassies. In all the discussions nobody is recorded as saying a single word approving of any of the condemned ideas, and it does appear that the absolutist ideology was acceptable to most, at least as their public stance. It is known there were dissenters, but it would have been futile and dangerous for them to identify themselves. The Danish minister noted a further factor that explained the public attitude. The process was a condemnation of the former oligarchy, and an affirmation of the new system of advancement on merit. He wrote to his king:

it still weighs on the hearts of many, of all Estates, that there have always been a few known families who think themselves as worthy as the royal family, and assumed to themselves a precedence and prerogative over everyone and in everything: they did not let anyone to high office and dignity except their children, friends and family; other legal grants and facilities also had to come through their hands, and in this there was no merit, but a servile dependence on them and theirs.

The modern observer must remember that the alternative to the absolutism was not a more open or liberal regime, but an equally repressive system controlled by an oligarchy. To some absolutism was a liberation, to others no worse than what had gone before.[10]

The Diet Resolution of 1689 was a summary of the king's achievements to date. In foreign affairs it ascribed the ten years of peace as due, after God, to the king, 'who has in all his counsels and actions as his first aim, the preservation of peace'. The Estates then solemnly promised to uphold his domestic reforms for ever.

The kingdom's welfare and security depends on what has been set out, as a sure foundation for a well-ordered government, being kept in effect inviolably and for all time, we declare . . . that he who directly or indirectly presumes to attempt anything against what the king has done so well, and so graciously performed and commanded, shall be held as disloyal to the king and hostile to the Fatherland.

Charles XI meant his work to last for ever, so that even to discuss the possibility of change amounted to treason. This was reinforced by including the Act repudiating the protocols in the Diet Resolution. This did not wipe them from the record, as suggested at first, but listed and condemned their pernicious ideas, and reminded all subjects that they had no right to express opinions critical of what their

---

[10] *SRARP*, xv, pp. 341–3; *PR*, iv, pp. 352–3; Fryxell, ed., *Handlingar*, ii, p. 425, Stockfleth to the king 13 Mar. 1689.

sovereign chose to do. 'He who shall in any way undertake to speak or act against this, secretly or openly, shall be considered a breaker of oaths, and forgetful of the duty and responsibility to God, the king and the Fatherland that lies upon him.' The Marshal closed the Diet with a eulogy on hereditary monarchy. 'It was a special Providence of God that the royal throne, established by God as an hereditary right . . . became through your Majesty's most happy birth, as though once more strengthened and fortified by a new assurance.' The subjects acknowledged that their present welfare derived wholly from the tireless labours of the king. They also knew 'that God himself directs the sceptre in your Majesty's hand and strengthens his arm to guide and protect the kingdom'. The social consensus was now firmly reestablished and it is no wonder that the king expressed his private satisfaction to Lindschöld, in a letter in his own hand: 'the Diet is proceeding really well, God be eternally thanked and praised, and I have never seen my faithful Estates so willing to contribute as now'.[11]

The next Diet of the reign, and the last, was called in 1693 because of the death of the queen, Ulrika Eleonora, on 26 July 1693, when she was, as the king noted, with his characteristic fascination with detail, thirty-six years, ten months and fifteen days old. The Diet was summoned for 2 November so that the Estates could participate with the king in the funeral ceremonies and exemplify a society united in its grief. Those attending wore mourning clothes throughout. The historian can say little about the royal marriage, for evidence is thin: no letters between the royal couple seem to survive; a few carefully guarded letters of the queen to her brother the king of Denmark and diplomatic reports from Stockholm constitute the hard evidence; the remaining material is unverifiable gossip and rumour. It was an arranged marriage in the fullest sense; the couple never set eyes on one another until the wedding night, yet it seemed to work well. Both shared the sense of duty derived from a common Lutheran piety, and looked for no reward in this world. In 1685 when the couple lost three infant boys, the queen wrote to Pontus de la Gardie: 'nature urges me to grieve when sickness strikes my children, but my reason tells me that the most fortunate thing that could happen to them, or me, would be to be able to leave this life, before they can witness the setbacks and misfortunes which will certainly occur'. In her later years, the suburban residence of Karlberg was the queen's favourite. She commissioned a painting by the Court painter, Ehrenstrahl, of herself gazing at her four dead sons in Heaven, with the text: 'Thy Will be done.' The king shared her tastes. The walls of his favourite country retreat, Kungsör, were decorated with biblical texts. The king appears to have been well satisfied with his wife; her financial settlement was generous and her solemn entry and coronation in 1680 lavishly staged. The queen in turn set about endearing herself to the Swedish public; she quickly

---

[11] *SRARP*, xv, pp. 416–21; Loenbom, ed., *Handlingar*, II, collections; III, pp. 175–8; RA, Lagkommissionen 1686–1736, protokol, extracts from 1689 riksdags beslut; RA, Kongliga concept, Karl XI, egenhandiga bref, king to Lindschöld 20 Feb. 1689.

The royal family in 1683, by D. K. Ehrenstrahl. From left to right: the king, his mother,
his aunt, the infant Prince Charles, Princess Hedvig Sofia and the queen.
A portrait of his father Charles X Gustav hangs on the wall.

replaced her Danish entourage with Swedes, and was from the first a major public
benefactor from her own endowments. She financed an orphanage for poor
children in Stockholm, and when she got Karlberg, set up a tapestry weaving
factory in the grounds, again for poor children. Her pension list for 1686 contained 1,700 persons, including victims of the reduktion and the Tribunal, like the
de la Gardie family. She would accept nothing in her settlement that derived from
the reduktion, because of the injustices she believed it involved; and the king

respected her wishes. There is good evidence that Ulrika Eleonora became very popular in Sweden.[12]

One factor that could have wrecked the marriage was the queen-mother. The cause was partly political; she was of the Holstein-Gottorp family and rootedly anti-Danish, and strove at all times to assert her influence with the king in that sense. She also insisted on her precedence over the queen, something in which Charles XI always supported his mother. This could have poisoned relations but it did not, because the queen decided to humour her mother-in-law, despite endless provocations. She wrote, in 1688: 'je n'ai pas besoin des honneurs, mais qu'il me faut du repos' ('I do not need honours but I must have rest'). The relations became particularly strained in 1689, during the war crisis; the queen regarded the queen-mother as a warmonger, but again she conciliated, even stopped writing to her brother for a time. The intimate relations of husband and wife can only be guessed; on one level they worked: the queen was eight times pregnant in her first eight years, after which her health began to fail. Sadly only three of the children survived into adulthood, the crown-prince Charles and two of his sisters. But there were problems of temperament that divided the couple. The queen was an educated woman of an artistic temperament, said to be a competent painter and in spite of her piety a sociable and outgoing person. She would have liked a socially active Court, with music and dancing and theatricals. The king, though ready to participate in unavoidable official ceremonial, hated what he regarded as expensive and frivolous socializing. It is true that during his travels round the kingdom he would join in village festivals and weddings, but at his own Court he tried to avoid involvement. Charles XI did indulge in social drinking according to the custom of the society, but there are no accounts of his being drunk in public. The Danish minister reported the christening festivities for his first-born in 1681, with the king calling the toasts, and remarked: 'no one can remember such a massive debauch here in Stockholm', but that was not the queen's taste. In 1682 he wrote to his king: 'I am not leaving a Court, but a wasteland and great palaces with no one in them. To tell truth it is wretched to see so many honourable people so unhappy at one time.' In 1683 the queen tried to arrange a party to celebrate the king's return to Stockholm, but he repeatedly put her off; the minister reported: 'if there is some kind of pleasure that the king is inclined to, it is not in this kind of entertainment'. Though at Christmas 1683, the king did agree to the staging at Court of Racine's play *Iphigenia*, which the queen had promoted.[13]

There were signs of relaxation later in the reign. In the winter of 1687–8, Prince Frederick of Holstein-Gottorp paid an extended visit, and there was music and dancing at Court. The Danish minister reported: 'it is something infrequent and unusual here and has not often happened these last five years'. He noted that the

---

[12] Hildebrand, ed., *Almanacksanteckningar*, p. 269; Malmström, *Ulrika Eleonora*, pp. 22, 36, 49, 65, 67, 87, 99, 103, 108; Åberg, *Karl XI*, pp. 169, 175, 177; Nilsson, ed., *Svenska historien*, pp. 92–7.

[13] Malmström, *Ulrika Eleonora*, pp. 69, 89, 112, 115, 119; Åberg, *Karl XI*, p. 165.

king frequently retired to Kungsör to escape it. In 1690 the *Almanack* recorded that the king had been to a wedding, 'and this is the first wedding my wife has been at'. 1692 brought another Holstein family visit, and he wrote of going to a masquerade dressed as a peasant. If the marriage relationship succeeded it owed much to the intelligence of the queen, and a calculated measure of submission on her part. There were some other significant disagreements; the queen strongly opposed appointing Lindschöld as tutor for the prince, partly on political grounds: he was a partisan of the queen-mother and the Holstein faction. The minister reported: 'it seems as though her Majesty now no longer conceals that it is greatly against her advice and will'. But despite such open dissent, and her criticism of the reduktion it seems she held the personal regard of her husband. On the birth of their first child the king put off a journey of inspection to be with her and 'had shown a great tenderness towards her Majesty'. When she became terminally ill, in June 1693, the king astonished everyone by moving into Karlberg and nursing her himself. The *Almanack*, on the day of her death, recorded: 'I have lost a God-fearing, virtuous and dear queen and wife to my great misfortune and grief.' At the end of 1693 he reflected: 'God comfort me, a poor sinner, in my great grief and trouble and give me, when it is his pleasure, a blessed ending from this trouble-some world. I beg this of you God, for the sake of the precious and bitter suffering of Your son, Jesus Christ. Oh Lord, hear my prayer.' The queen-mother said once that her son was never again 'really at ease' after the death of the queen. Although he was only thirty-eight, the idea of remarriage never seems to have crossed his mind.[14]

There was no substantive business for a Diet; the foreign situation was excellent, and no initiatives were needed in domestic policies. Somewhere in the government it was decided to use the session for a coordinated publicity exercise to drive home to subjects the legitimacy of absolute, Christian monarchy, and give it credibility by reciting the achievements of the reign, and show that after years of sacrifice for the common good, the rewards were beginning to materialize. In the process the Diet did produce two significant developments: a permanent arrangement for wartime taxation, and a further affirmation of royal sovereignty. But essentially it was a feast of self-congratulation for the ruling elite of the regenerated political order. The tone was set from the start. The Marshal was Jakob Gyllenborg, an archetypal new man. He told the Estates how, despite the unspeakable grief caused by the queen's death, the king 'had not allowed the business and activity of government to stop, but keeps them on their right course, basing all his actions on our and the kingdom's welfare. It is through her Majesty's, as well as our king's God-fearing-ness that we enjoy the glorious peace and all prosperity.' The Clergy spokesman announced another theme of the Diet: gratitude to the king for his condescension in calling the Estates and giving an account of his policies, 'which his Majesty, as a

[14] Nilsson, ed., *Svenska historien*, p. 97; Hildebrand, ed., *Almanacksanteckningar*, pp. 181, 222, 280; Malmström, *Ulrika Eleonora*, pp. 110, 117, 138.

sovereign king who commands according to his pleasure, without being limited or bound, had no need to do'. This resolute, absolutist rhetoric dominated the whole Diet, with the Clergy as its leading exponents.[15]

The Secret Committee met to consider the Secret Propositions on 6 November, and the Marshal drove home the message that the Propositions showed 'what a great and incomparable care and provision the king has shown for his subjects' welfare'. It was a major condescension that he deigned to explain in full what he had been doing since the last Diet. As the material was read out, the Marshal kept up a running commentary on it. In foreign affairs, due to the king's untiring endeavours he was now being courted by all the belligerents, while trade was growing as never before. The Committee agreed that thanks were due, 'but they could never sufficiently thank his Majesty for all that'. Burgomaster M. Törne agreed about trade, but suggested the king could seek compensation from Britain and France for the shipping they had seized. This was the only comment on foreign affairs. In domestic affairs the first item was the king's complaint that not all of the subsidies voted in 1689 had been fully paid over. The Committee agreed this was unacceptable, and forgetting these were supposed to be free gifts from the Estates, authorized the king to collect the arrears by any way he pleased. When they reached trade and industry, Törne had some ideas on developing reexport trades and import substitution by developing new manufactures in Sweden. When all the reports had been read, the Marshal stressed two points: '1, that the Estates will be willing henceforth to grant supply when it is needed. 2, that the arrears on the previous grant of supply be paid up.' He then said the king would communicate the Secret Propositions to the full Estates, not so that they could be debated there but so that 'in this way we realize how well, graciously and justly the king has ordered everything, and prescribed and carried on the work of government and the domestic economy'. He further revealed how this Diet was for image making, not the transaction of business, by suggesting the Estates do not bother the king 'with all too many grievances'. Finally the Marshal suggested the Secret Committee choose a small drafting committee to draw up their answers to the Propositions, and that its remit should be 'so to proceed that they repeat what stands in the Propositions, and humbly thank his Majesty for his unbounded care, diligence and trouble . . . so that everything is so well regulated and brought into good order'. This was agreed without debate, and the Marshal, with six reliable crown servants, chosen to do the drafting.[16] It might seem that Charles XI had reached that legendary position where he could tell his subjects: 'when I want to hear your opinions I will tell you what they are'.

The drafting committee worked very fast, and sent their report to the Secret Committee on 9 November. The foreign affairs section was read and 'the Committee as a whole declared they were satisfied with the proposed response and that they

[15] *SRARP*, xv, pp. 1, 10.
[16] RA, R 2378, meetings of 4, 7 Nov. 1693

had no comment to make about it'. The Marshal prefaced the domestic section by reminding them that: 'We have come to thank God and his Majesty, who have put the kingdom in such a fortunate condition, so that the budget is balanced and all state servants are properly paid and everything else that concerns the security, defence and the rest of its welfare is being dealt with.' The Marshal compared this with the bad old times, and actually apologized in the king's name for the hardships imposed on individuals by the reduktion, but it had all been for the common good, and the king personally had derived no benefit from it. So it was scandalous that some people still expressed dissent from what had been done. Then the responses were read, 'and were approved, except it was pointed out that they should insert the provision, that the Estates undertake to provide, when it is needed, the contingency supply granted in 1689, which was immediately added and read'. In this casual fashion the Estates suspended their last surviving power, that of consenting to extraordinary taxation in time of war. The king now had an open-ended authority, throughout a war, to levy two subsidies a year and borrow as much more as he needed, and the Estates would repay it.[17]

The Secret Committee of 1693 finished its work in five days and made no input of its own. The declaration of sovereignty which was inserted into the response had never been discussed at all. It remained for the king to present his revised Testament to the Committee and the Peasants. This had had to be changed because of the queen's death, but it followed closely his father's Testament of 1660. It provided that a regency government would still be answerable to the Estates, so they were not being written out of the kingdom's constitution. Given the compliance of the Estates in 1693 there was no reason why they should be. Yet it is probable that to the king's traditionalist thinking, to deny the Estates a role, however notional, was neither necessary nor acceptable. When the Testament had been read, the Estates agreed with the Marshal that 'as honest and faithful subjects they hold inviolate this, his Majesty's will'.[18]

The Committee's report then had to be adopted by the Estates. The Clergy minute for 1693 is thin; the clerk appended a note that because of the amount of committee work, his record is incomplete and not all important business is included. It shows the Clergy spending most of their time on professional concerns and when the Secret Committee report was read out, there is no record of any discussion, nor was there on 18 November when the final Diet Resolution was read. The archbishop simply declared: 'the Clergy approve and acknowledge it with the deepest respect and humility'. On the war contingency provision they said: 'for the rest what your royal Majesty is pleased now, or in the future graciously to command us, his faithful subjects, we shall continuously accept with unswerving obedience and respect and carry out to our uttermost ability'. It was consistent with their position that the clergy did not present any grievances, so as to spare the king

---

[17] *Ibid.*, meeting of 9 Nov. 1693.
[18] *Ibid.*, meeting of 11 Nov. 1693.

in his time of mourning.[19] It was read in the Riddarhus on 10 and 11 November, with the Marshal making comments that became a monologue; there were few interventions from the floor. The Marshal had sweeteners to offer; he said that the king hoped to finalize the reduktion within a year, and emphasized how no further extraordinary taxation was needed. He lectured them on the superiority of hereditary monarchy and asserted: 'the more we increase the king's power and authority, the happier we ourselves and the kingdom's inhabitants in general are'. He added a further tax concession; the king would remit the poll-tax on the servants of the nobility. Finally the Marshal asked the Riddarhus if it had any comments to make: 'to this few responded except a few individuals, who said there was nothing in it to comment upon'. Thus the sovereignty declaration was not discussed at all. Later when the Diet Resolution was presented, 'all three Classes declared they were satisfied with it'. The Nobility did present grievances, several related to the harsh conduct of the royal officers, who were alleged to be breaking the rules laid down by the king himself. This only irritated the king, who said, through the Marshal, that they had improperly included private cases in the grievances, and that his officials were a fine and honest body of men. The Marshal added a warning they must 'take care that they do not in any way infringe on the king's sovereignty and the crown's rights'.[20]

The Propositions of 1693 described in close detail the whole range of the government's activities. They naturally presented these in a favourable light, but they are filled with genuine and accurate information. In foreign policy they explained the king's aim to avoid involvement in the European war, 'valuing the enjoyment of peace and neutrality as best able to promote the service and prosperity of his kingdom and subjects'. They stated the five principles that the king intended to follow. All the domestic programmes were described in minute detail, as was the financial situation. This amounts to what is called in modern terminology, transparency. There is an apparent contradiction between the repeated assertions that the king is answerable to no one but God, and his willingness to tell his subjects what his policies were. It seems to express the underlying sense of social cohesion, that the king and his subjects were a commonwealth, engaged on a joint enterprise. The Propositions had concluded by the promise of the rewards that were now materializing. The king could have asked for further supply, for example to defray the funeral expenses, but had decided not to:

the king will provide that he, through good housekeeping, may be able to keep the work going with the ordinary revenues of the kingdom, in so far as this is practicable, since the king is very reluctant to burden his faithful subjects and Estates with any heavy burdens, but is graciously inclined to protect them so long as the situation and eventualities allow it.

---

[19] *PR*, IV, pp. 421, 422, 433, 440, 445.
[20] *SRARP*, XVI, pp. 15, 16, 17, 18, 20, 22, 26, 27, 79–81.

This meant not only that there would be no additional taxes, but they would begin to decline as previous extraordinary grants expired.[21]

The so-called declaration of sovereignty of 1693 was not a formal declaration of the law, like the recognition Acts of 10 December 1680 and 16 November 1682. It was a passage in the Secret Committee answer to the Propositions, repeated in the Riddarhus response and thus incorporated in the Resolution of the Diet. The passage says that on the basis of the right of hereditary succession, the Declarations of 1680 and 1682, and the law of God and of Nations, as 'an absolute and sovereign king, who is responsible for his actions to no one on earth, but has authority and power, according to his pleasure, and as a Christian ruler, to guide and direct his kingdom', it was an extraordinary act of grace that the king had condescended to give this account to his subjects. Modern historians debate whether this is just a passing comment, a seventeenth-century platitude, or whether it does constitute a significant extension of the royal power. The passage was certainly not inserted by chance; the drafting committee of senior crown servants would have chosen the words carefully, and indeed the formula recurs on other occasions in the 1693 proceedings. It has also been noted that in 1693 the whole Riddarhus were told the king required them to sign and set their seals to the Diet Resolution, 'as an Act that shall be signed'. A few days later the Marshal reminded them and 'asked that no one who is here will neglect that: if they do they may be fined'. But since the passage is only a part of the Resolution, the insistence could equally be grounded on the need to recognize the sanctity of the royal Testament. It is also pointed out that the 1693 formula left out the phrase in the Act of 1680 that the king rules 'according to law and legal rules'. Yet since it confirms the 1680 Act, this proviso was clearly still in force. Also in 1693 the king did not highlight the passage, or specifically confirm it, so Charles XI may have seen it as a platitude. The French diplomat, d'Avaux, thought so at the time. Further the total compliance of the Diet of 1693 and the absence of any motive for seeking to extend royal power support the view that this was not meant to assert an additional authority. Finally the style and practice of the royal government after 1693 in no way differed from what went before. It may be that some modern commentators have identified an issue here which contemporaries would not have recognized.[22]

The absence of any critical comment in the Diet of 1693 did not mean that there was no one in Sweden who was unhappy about the developments. Indeed the various conciliatory gestures by the royal government, the halt on extraordinary taxation, the undertaking to wind up the reduktion quickly, the half-apology for the hardships it had entailed, the hints of more prosperous times to come, all signify a

[21] RA, R 2378, text of the Secret Propositions.
[22] *Ibid.*; Carlson, *Historia*, IV, pp. 244–6; L. Thanner, 'Suveränitetsförklaring år 1693. Tillkomst och innebörd', *KFÅ* (1954), pp. 7, 10–11, 24–9; *SRARP*, XVI, pp. 24, 25; H. A. Olsson, 'Karl XI och lagen: några synpunkter mot bakgrunden av 1693 års suveränitetsförklaring', *KFÅ* (1969), pp. 83–108.

regime aware that it may have been pushing too hard. But the discontents were not politicized; they did not translate into active resistance to royal policy. This was partly because the hardships were offset by real advantages; the avoidance of war, the regular payment of salaries, a degree of careers open to merit were genuine gains. But the basic reason why resistance could not develop, apart from the obvious fear of repression, was that the critics had no viable alternative to offer. Surviving evidence in private papers, and a few printed pamphlets, testify that there was opposition, and they are presumably the tip of an iceberg. Yet the only serious critical analyst remains Claes Rålamb. He thought politically and could recognize how, for example, debate in the Diet had been stifled by confining discussion to a hand-picked Secret Committee. It is hard to fault his comment that 'this way, through the Diet itself, its most essential function was suppressed, and only a shadow of it, as an appearance of liberty, left for the simple folk'. Thus he could argue that the Diet Resolution of 1693 was null and void. But Rålamb also argued this because he did not see a Diet as a sovereign legislature. He thought that like all other institutions it was bound by Sweden's fundamental laws. He asserted that a people can no more 'cut off from themselves and their descendants, immemorial rights and liberties legally belonging to them, than a king has the right to give away his throne to whom he will'. He did not believe in the sovereignty of the people, any more than of kings; in fact he did not believe in sovereignty, except of God, at all. Rålamb's crippling weakness showed when he talked of what might be done. He ruled out disobedience to a lawful prince, so fell back on the traditional 'evil councillor' concept; subjects could remonstrate humbly, 'not against the king, but against Göran Persson [the king's favoured and loyal spokesman of the Peasant Estate] and similar godless councillors and disturbers of the peace'. Beyond that, the subject could pray God to open the king's eyes to what was happening. It goes without saying that Rålamb never published his thoughts, though they seem to have circulated in manuscript within a narrow circle. In any case these academic reasonings were not the stuff from which resistance is generated.[23]

On the Sunday preceding the queen's funeral, all the churches in Stockholm had a sermon on the text from Samuel I, chapter 8, where he tells the Israelites the power of a king, opening with: 'ye shall be his slaves'. It attracted notice as an obvious part of a government propaganda campaign, and there are manuscripts protesting at it. One, from an anonymous clergyman, argued it was an abuse of Scripture. All right-thinking theologians knew that God's prescription for a king was in Deuteronomy, where Moses laid down rules of a much more restrictive character, and in the Prophets, when they denounced wicked rulers. Samuel was describing a tyrant, as warning to the Israelites of how God might punish them if they did not repent their sins. But his solution was the same as Rålamb's: they must

---

[23] KB, Rålambska Manuskriptsamlingen: Fol. Nr. 5: Book III, 'Angående några särskilta Å.80 Åhrs Rickzd. Generaliter', chapters 14 and 15.

pray to God, 'that He will graciously strengthen Sweden's king to goodness and mercy, love and justice against such temptation'. There was a sterner clerical dissenter, Jacob Boethius of Mora, who had been critical of the Church Law and was provoked by the sermons of 1693 to a frontal attack on absolutism. His biography says he believed it was 'contrary to God's honour and Holy Word'. He discussed his doubts with fellow clergymen, but they insisted he was wrong, and should keep quiet. On the death of Charles XI, Boethius wrote a memorandum to Charles XII setting out his criticisms. He was promptly tried for sedition and sentenced to death, though this was commuted to confinement in a fortress for life. He had told the king that Scripture does not teach that 'God put kings and rulers in His place on earth'. Boethius is almost unique in declaring his dissent, and his fate cannot have encouraged others. Most critical material is crude polemic against individuals, like a tract purporting to defend 'that old Swedish fundamental, the king should have his superiority, the Council its authority, the Estates their liberty'. But this too, evidently addressed to the new king in 1697, recommended as remedy: 'let us turn to our young king. God grant a happy entry into the government.' Always the hope for change rests with God and the king; there are no other channels open to the subject. As Rålamb put it: 'every honest Swedish man . . . has the right to assert and justify his liberty by lawful means, which do not consist in seditious conspiracy to damage and scorn the ruler, but in faithful supportive quietness and respectful remonstrance'. Before 1680 this had been the privilege of the Council of State; now it was up to the individual, and Boethius showed how dangerous that could be.[24] Besides there is also material suggesting that the absolutism did have popular support. There are manuscript polemics in a populist style, usually in crude doggerel verse, and these demotic jingles could have been far more representative of what ordinary folk thought than Rålamb's intellectual analyses. One such, *A dialogue between a foreigner and an honest Swede*, started with the foreigner asking: 'does not your king wish to rule absolutely?', and the reply comes: 'that could well happen if he is given enough time'. The foreigner then says: 'it will be difficult for him to accomplish that', and is told: 'every honest Swedish man will help him'. It continues: 'what is the reason they would do that? Where there are too many cooks, the kitchen is badly run.' The foreigner asks if there are not dangers in absolutism, but is told: 'when Sweden's kings decide, they will always be gracious'. The theme is simple; only a strong king can protect the common folk from exploitation by the elites, among whom the new nobility are the worst. 'A newly promoted nobleman is like a beast' for he must get rich off the peasants; 'where there are many goats, the pasture must suffer'. This is the voice of the common people, and is echoed in peasant wisdom all over Europe: 'better one

---

[24] *Ibid.*, chapter 15; KB, Rålambska Manuskriptsamlingen: Fol. Nr. 71, 'Politiska pasquiller': anonymous critique of the sermons of 1693; '*Severii Alethei . . . Epistola Familiaria*': Loenbom, ed., *Anecdoter*, section IV: 'Om Jacob Boethius', pp. 5, 6, 7, 8–9; *PR*, IV, p. 437.

master than a hundred'. With this kind of popular support, the monarchy had little to fear from Rålamb and the aristocratic malcontents.[25]

The Diet of 1693 marked the apotheosis of Charles XI and moved to its climax in the magnificent state funeral of the queen on 28 November. The four Estates attended the royal family and the Council, in a massive demonstration of the unity and integrity of the Swedish body politic under its God-given ruler. The participants got a commemorative medal, and the king dined afterwards with the Nobility, Clergy and Burghers, while a separate festivity, no doubt well lubricated with spirits, was put on for the Peasants. In the proceedings of 1693, although the Estates had given up their last real constitutional power over taxation, there was no thought of dispensing with them. The king's Testament showed they still had a role, and so interestingly did the draft royal law produced by the Law Commission in 1696, which envisages a place for them in government. Only now they would revert to their primitive function, as extraordinary gatherings to deal with extraordinary contingencies. For the regular business of government, they were no longer needed.

[25] KB, Rålambska Manuskriptsamlingen: Fol. Nr. 71: 'Ett samtahl emellan en utlandsk och en uprichtig Svensk . . .'; 'Pasquinius till Svea Ständer om riksens nuwarde tillståndh.'

9

The royal government at work

The king was the driving force of the system of government; all public acts from the greatest to the smallest were in his name, and authority for them rested on a paper carrying the king's signature. A general decree for the whole community was issued as a law, or an ordinance or a proclamation, and would usually be printed and then read out in the churches, law courts or at other public assemblies. Decisions concerning a particular group or an individual were issued as a royal letter, authorized by the royal signature, counter-signed by two secretaries in Chancery and entered in the official register, the *Riksregistratur*. Thus the same royal signature that validated the Church Law of 1686 also validated the letter authorizing the peasant Nils Olsson to marry his niece, 'since this was not expressly forbidden in the Word of God', and that allowing the widow of the Postmaster of Falun to take on his appointment, providing she hired a competent assistant. This personal omnicompetence of the king was clearly a fiction. No individual could have processed that volume of business, not even Charles XI, who regularly started his day at 4 a.m., and apart from the times reserved for prayers and Bible reading, worked on through his waking hours, and kept no routine for retiring to eat or sleep. The king was to some extent programmed by his advisers and servants.[1]

His conception of the kingly duty was expressed in a holograph letter to Nils Bielke. While he waited for his blessed release from this vale of tears, he sought 'at the same time to put the kingdom in such condition, that my successors and faithful subjects may enjoy advantage and security from it'. The king, in another letter, indicated how this was to be achieved: 'the general government of a kingdom should not be based on, or hindered by, private rights of exemption, charters of liberties and privileges, but it is both the right and duty of a king to order and bring to pass what is necessary for the welfare of the whole people'. The realization of this Utopian but authoritarian ideal depended on the agents the king had to work with. The personality of Charles XI left him vulnerable to manipulation. He had a limited intellectual capacity, compounded by a defective education and his difficulties with reading, writing and fluency of expression. He avoided public speaking entirely, was awkward in private discourse and the surviving personal papers and

---

[1] RA, Kongliga concept: vol. 287, Sept–Nov. 1682, king's resolution on Olsson 2 Nov. 1682; king's letter to Burgomaster of Falun 6 Nov. 1682.

annotations expose his limited powers of expression. In a system which depended heavily on the written word, these were serious handicaps. Apart from the Bible and works of piety, he seems to have read nothing. Yet he had an enquiring mind, as his *Almanack*, with its obsession over statistical details, or his fondness for tourist attractions as he travelled the kingdom, like the great copper mine at Falun, or an abortive attempt to view the midnight sun at Torneå, witness. He could absorb information; though he had no legal training he took part in Council sessions that resolved legal appeals, and the minutes show how he came to grasp basic legal concepts, and could intervene effectively in discussion. What Charles XI lacked was the capacity for analytical thought. He lacked imagination and probably never entertained an original or novel idea in his life. His expressed opinions are platitudes and his actions rooted in precedent. His mental world seems to be two-dimensional, black and white without intermediate shades. There was right conduct, in accordance with God's will, which was to be fostered and rewarded, and there was the rest of human behaviour, tainted by the sin of Adam, which was to be avoided and repressed. The certainties that this generated were an obvious source of strength; the inflexibility, almost tunnel vision, was a weakness. In the real world he worked with men who had more supple minds, were better educated and informed and were often skilled communicators. Such men had the capacity to manipulate the king and promote their personal or collective ambitions.

There was no chief minister after Gyllenstierna. But some royal advisers carried more weight than others. There are shadowy figures who have left little evidence, like Jakob Hastfer, commander of the Life Guard, who by virtue of his post was always near the king, and Christopher Gyllenstierna, governor of Stockholm, a fierce absolutist and also well placed to advise. One influential adviser was Field Marshal Rutger von Ascheberg, the foreign mercenary who had impressed the young king during the war, and became a father figure. The king had to communicate in his rather shaky German, and wrote in 1680: 'alt das ovrige da ich in dieser kriger gelerent habe, habe ich den HFM vor som danken' ('for all the rest I have learnt in these wars I have to thank the Herr Field Marshal'). He enlarged on this a few years later to Bielke: 'I can assure the Councillor [Bielke] that I love him [Ascheberg] as if he were my father, for all the little I have learned about soldiering I have him to thank for.' But Ascheberg stayed on the periphery as Governor General of Skåne and was rarely in Stockholm, though much consulted on military matters, and one of the few individuals the king trusted. He wrote in 1684 how he wished 'dass alle mein ministri so treu waren und so wohl mit mir meinten wie der Herr Feldmarschall' ('that all my ministers were as faithful and well-intentioned towards me as the Herr Field Marshal'). Another man with the potential to become a personal confidant was Nils Bielke. This relationship too grew out of the war, and after it ended, Bielke was allowed to enter imperial service and distinguished himself against the Ottomans. The king was a natural chauvinist, and gloried in Bielke's reputation; he wrote after the battle of Mohacs: 'the Councillor has made an imperishable reputation before the whole world, which is a great honour to the whole Swedish nation'. But Bielke, unlike Ascheberg, had his own political agenda; he led the pro-French faction, took a pension from Louis XIV and did his best to unseat Oxenstierna. For a time he looked like succeeding, but in 1692 overplayed his hand by negotiating with foreign courts without the king's permission. He got a letter from the king cancelling all previous assurances of favour, though he kept his post as Councillor and Governor of Pomerania. It took him two years drudgery, pushing the *reduktion* in Pomerania before the king restored him to favour, and then the old confidence was lost. In 1695 the king told Bielke he had received a letter denouncing him as a traitor, describing it as 'that wicked letter which a scoundrel has written about the Councillor'. He assured Bielke of his continuing favour, but warned he must keep 'God before his eyes', and pursue the good of the kingdom impartially, 'then no one in the world is capable of putting the Councillor in the wrong with me'. The one other minister who became close to the king was Lindschöld. He had been recognized as preeminent among the secretaries since 1680, but from 1687 to his death in 1690 he rose to membership of the Council, tutor to the prince, president of the Law Commission and membership of Class I of the nobility. When Lindschöld died, the king told Bielke: 'I can never sufficiently lament him, I have lost in him a faithful, honest and dear friend, who meant well to me, my son and the whole kingdom . . . I grieve for him with all my heart.' Yet the king had known of his marked pro-French preferences, and probably of his deserved reputation for taking gratuities. So when he was appointed tutor to the prince in 1687, he and his colleagues were warned. The king wrote,

so I will give them notice to remain firm in the alliances which I have made, which I find are best and safest for Sweden's interest. Because France has deceived me once, so I have been burned and shall not go there any more. I warn you herewith to avoid intrigues and factions, but be purely Swedish and pursue my dear son's and the Fatherland's true interest and continuance.

The king exposed his simplistic views of foreign policy, but also a realistic appreciation of the unreliability of advisers; he does not seem to see Lindschöld as an exception.[2]

Because of the absence of a chief minister or favourite, Swedish government, to an extent unusual in early modern Europe, actually worked through the official channels. The highest level, under the king, was the Council. The common belief that after the downgrading of the Council of State, the new King's Council was confined to hearing legal appeals, and thus marginalized, is wrong. A proclamation

---

[2] Malmström, ed., 'Karl XIs bref till Nils Bielke', p. 24, king to Bielke 13 June 1687; p. 26, same 5 Nov. 1687; p. 68, same 14 May 1690; p. 70, same 11 June 1690; Sjögren, *Karl den elfte*, p. 460; Carlson, *Historia*, IV, pp. 3, 27; UUB, E472, Kongl. brev till Fältmarskalken Rutger von Ascheberg, king to Ascheberg 30 Mar. 1680; Malmström, *Nils Bielke*, pp. 137, 138, 173, 176, 181, 182; RA, Kanslitjänstemäns koncept, 26, Karl XIs tid, king to Lindschöld 19 Oct. 1688; KB, Engströmska samlingen B.II.1.12, Handlingar rörande Karl XIs regering, king's letter to the tutors 1 Feb. 1687.

of 1686 reminded all the king's subjects that the new King's Councillors enjoyed the same respect and precedence as the former Councillors of State. It remained constant in size at around nineteen members, though at any one time as many as half were absent from Stockholm on official duty. Records suggest a degree of specialization was developing; some members concentrated on judicial business, others on aspects of administration, so that when there was a mixed agenda, some would leave when their area of business was concluded. Specialization suggests the Council had serious work to do, but that the former concept of the Council as an omnicompetent corporate body was being superseded. Some policy was still determined by debate in Council. In May 1695 it spent two days discussing coinage policy. J. G. Stenbock can be seen in the minute trying to explain the issues to a puzzled Charles XI, who after a long debate on the second day said: 'we have talked about this enough, let everyone give his opinion', and they voted. This was an issue where the king clearly had no opinion of his own. Most real decision making in Council was administrative; the one area of political debate was foreign policy, about which the government was genuinely divided, with the king and Oxenstierna adhering to their anti-French line, while a majority seem to have preferred the traditional French alliance. The Council continued to hold an annual foreign policy review, usually in October, and also considered all major developments. Oxenstierna set out the general practice in a memorandum of 1688: 'over the main policy, and when something happens of such importance that it involves the basis of policy . . . the method has always been followed up to now that discussion about it is held in Council'. For these debates, Oxenstierna and his subordinates would circulate long memoranda on the arguments for and against, and these were the agenda. Some commentators dismiss the debates as empty rituals, because the king's view was already known. This was not always the case; in March 1686 there was a real discussion over whether to send troops into Germany, with the king and Oxenstierna on different sides, but generally Oxenstierna's line, often a minority view, was adopted because the king declared for it. The King's Council, after 1682, had a continuous role in government, partly ceremonial, mostly practical administrative work. But it was not the centre of policy making: this lay in the Chancery, a combined foreign ministry, ministry of the interior and government secretariat, and Chamber, which was the ministry of finance.[3]

The Chancery was directed by Bengt Oxenstierna, with the title of President of Chancery, not the former title of State Chancellor. He was assisted by a fluctuating group of Chancery Councillors, of whom the most important was the 'Court

---

[3] Loenbom, ed., *Handlingar*, II, collection V, p. 166; VIII, p. 222; A.-B. Lövgren, *Handläggning och inflytande: beredning föredragning och kontrasignering under Karl XIs envälde* (Lund, 1980), pp. 117–27, 128, 136, 137; RA, Rådsprotokoll 1694–5, vol. 91a, Bergenhielm, Protokoll hållna i KMts. kammar, meetings of 8, 9 May 1695; Munthe, *Utrikesförvaltningen*, pp. 158–9; RA, Rådsprotokoll 1686, pp. 1720–31, meeting of 17 Mar. 1686.

Chancellor', referred to as 'the king's principal representative'. Under them the secretaries of state were the officers responsible for secretarial services, for drafting business for the king's consideration, and putting his resolutions into appropriate royal letters. Since it was a rule that all royal letters were issued by the Chancery, these men had the pivotal position. Chancery was still notionally a collegiate ministry, but this had broken down after 1680; as Oxenstierna told the king in 1694: 'what happens is the whole College rarely meets'. This had a simple cause: gross overloading of its officers; the economy-minded king would not pay for extra staff. An example from 1688 was an appeal to the king, because the Chancery messengers were kept so busy that 'the Council chamber, and the Chancery door and office remain unguarded'. When group meetings did revive in the 1690s, they were reserved for foreign policy. Recent research has shown how Chancery functioned. Each day the contents of the incoming post were distributed according to the nature of the business. Some was handled by the secretaries within Chancery, more specialized business was sent to relevant experts for a report. The actual presentation of a report and recommendation to the king took place informally on any convenient occasion, and there are no records of these transactions. It is therefore difficult to discern who made any particular decision. Some business, like army appointments and promotions, was reserved for the king; there was no report and the Chancery was simply instructed to draft the necessary documentation. But most decisions rested on the report of the secretary, or the expert consultant, and comparison of secretaries' drafts and the final royal letters shows that usually the king accepted the advice he was given. So some 80% of the decisions embodied in royal letters were made by the secretaries. They could further influence the outcome by their control of the flow of presentation to the king, through which they could advance or retard the processing of business. So it was generally true that Sweden was ruled by its bureaucrats. The subjects knew this, because Chancery records are filled with the letters of interested parties, asking the secretaries to promote their requests. Lindschöld got letters from the powerful Claes Fleming in 1681, thanking him for help to secure his promotion to the Council, and enclosing a modest donation to help Lindschöld with his gambling debts. At the other end of the scale, Per Höök, promised a property to keep him and his wife in old age, asked Lindschöld whether, 'he would be of assistance to a poor, elderly servant of the crown, so that I can get his Majesty's letter for this'. He knew that a secretary could convert a royal promise into an actual grant. It was universally understood that these services to the public were not free. In 1680 Hoghusen received various tactful promises from suitors: one expressed extreme gratitude and added: 'and for a small token to begin with, the Chancery Councillor's stable here in Stockholm shall be supplied with a load of oats'. Another promised a reward 'shall be paid unfailingly to the Chancery Councillor's dear wife, when I hear that the gracious resolution has passed on it'. Ebba Ulfeldt told Hoghusen she would see to it 'that I get something in hand, with which I can show the thanks that I owe'. No one in the early modern world would have expected anything different.[4]

The foreign ministry function of Chancery was personally dominated by Oxenstierna. He rationalized this in an undated memorandum, claiming that everyone else was too busy, so that only Thomas Polus, a new secretary specializing in foreign affairs, and the veteran secretary S. Åkerhielm could help him. He also argued that it was in the nature of foreign policy, which demanded secrecy and swift action, that collective decision making was impractical. But the king's economy drive meant even this team was overloaded. Åkerhielm wrote in February 1697 how posts were left vacant:

> Polus has to tutor the prince and also deal promptly with the business that belongs to the foreign secretaryship. The German secretaryship, which Polus held before, stands vacant and the salary is saved. If something happens, Polus has to deal with it . . . so far as my post goes, I have to put up with sometimes one kind of work, sometimes another, and can certainly feel I am needed. But I am getting old and tired.

The king's input was not all negative. From 1679 the foreign embassies were given fixed allowances, and these were assigned on secure revenue sources, and equipment allowances were granted. Then in 1687 the king created an additional salaried post of Commission Secretary in each embassy. The basic duty was to handle the correspondence, and establish an archive, besides assisting the minister. It was explained these were training posts for aspiring diplomats, and those who did well could expect subsequent preferment. This investment in professionalism was paralleled in the Chancery, when the foreign policy archive was separated from the domestic records in 1684. There is no doubt that the king's search for efficiency savings could upset the efficient functioning of the Chancery, but he tried to compensate for this by maintaining close personal supervision. In 1687 Chancery was ordered to set up a new Diary in two columns, one recording instructions received, the other the action taken on them. The king's many annotations on this are evidence of how he tried to maintain control.[5]

It can be argued that the core of Charles XI's government was the Chamber, in 1680 a collegiate ministry, under the Treasurer, the magnate Sten Bielke, with comprehensive responsibility for public finance. The king's policy here was to devolve functions to special Commissions. There was the Great Commission which

---

[4] Lövgren, *Handläggning*, pp. 11–12, 88, 90, 138–46, 165, 169–70; A. Munthe, *Kungl. Maj: ts kanslis historia*, I: *Kansliet under det karolinska tidevarvet* (Uppsala, 1935), pp. 136, 138, 141, 142; RA, Skrivelser till konungen, Karl XIs tid., Bengt Oxenstiernas skrivelser till KM, Oxenstierna to king 25 Nov. 1694; same 2 May 1688; Munthe, *Utrikesförvaltningen*, pp. 162, 165; RA, Kanslikollegium till KM: I, 1656–95, Chancery to king 1 June 1688; S. Norrhem, *Uppkomlingarna: Kanslitjänstemännen i 1600-talets Sverige och Europa* (Umeå, 1993), pp. 9, 23, 112–15, 116–18, 121, 123.

[5] RA, Skrivelser till konungen, Karl XIs tid, Bengt Oxenstiernas skrivelser till KM, Oxenstierna to the king 2 May 1688; Munthe, *Kansliet*, p. 143; Munthe, *Utrikesförvaltningen*, pp. 161, 163, 164, 171–4; A. B. Carlsson, *Den svenska centralförvaltningen 1521–1809: en historiskt översikt* (Stockholm, 1913), pp. 98–100.

condemned the regency, the Reduktion Commission, the Liquidation Commission for the debt, the Execution Commission for prosecuting crown claims and the Deputation of 1687 for winding up the Tribunal and reduktion processes. There were a series of small Commissions to implement the indelningsverk and the knektehåll. These Commissions operated in areas normally covered by the Chamber, but then they were largely staffed by Chamber officials, and depended on Chamber process for the legal enforcement of their decisions. The advantage for the king was that he could more easily participate in and supervise the Commissions, which throughout the reign were one of the main theatres for his personal intervention. The Commissions were all temporary, *ad hoc* institutions. The king's lasting achievement was the Budget Office, which still exists. The order for this was issued on 11 December 1680, with a remit to two men, the Treasurer and a Budget Commissioner, to act as the executive of a new department, answerable directly to the king. It would have 'disposition and assignment of all the king's and the kingdom's revenues, both within and without the kingdom, whatever title or nature they may have, without exception, which shall come directly under their administration'.

There would be an annual budget, authorized by the king and legally binding. 'The king himself will annually set up a budget and organize all the kingdom's resources and income into a fixed disposition, how they shall be used and paid out, which the king will sign . . . the signed budget and disposition may in no way be exceeded by anyone, but shall be observed as a fixed foundation and guideline.' If the king himself inadvertently controverted the budget, the Treasurer would not comply, but bring it to the king's attention. The purpose was defined as the achievement of a permanent, balanced budget.[6]

In 1684 Bielke died, and Claes Fleming succeeded with the title of President of the Chamber, and *ex officio* of the Budget Office. He wrote a memorandum recommending changes. The present rules did not establish a clear chain of command, necessary for good order. It was wrong to assign disposition of the revenues to the Budget Office, 'because for that, only the king alone has authority'. Nor was it realistic to say the Budget Office answered only to the king, 'because to pretend that the king should take on the auditing of the administration of the Budget Office would be to put on the king a burden which the king may well pass up, since the king is sufficiently weighed down by other pressures of government'. Fleming acknowledged that his proposals 'can be seen as if I, in many ways, was tying my hands', but he was telling the king that unlimited powers belonged to kings alone, and could not be devolved to subjects. Fleming's amendments were adopted by royal order of September 1685, and stood unchanged until 1720. The routine was soon established: the Budget Office got the revenue returns in September and set

[6] Eden, *Kammarkollegiets historia*, pp. 132–5, 137–8; J. Kleberg, *Kammarkollegium 1634–1718: svenska ämbetsverk*, VI.1 (Norrköping, 1937), pp. 15, 16; L. M. Bååth and A. Munthe, *Kungliga statskontoret 1680–1930* (Stockholm, 1930), pp. 19–23; Styffe, ed., *Civila förvaltningen*, pp. 124–8.

about drafting a budget, feeding in any expenditure instructions from the king. There was then a conference in the Budget Office, when the king 'is graciously pleased to take the trouble to come down into the Budget Office and himself go over the draft budget and also graciously declare himself over each entry in particular'. The minute of this conference was the basis for the final budget, usually issued in January. In this way the king assured to himself the ultimate power of the purse, and was rewarded in 1686 with a balanced budget, and after 1693 with significant annual surpluses, which remained entirely at his personal disposition.[7]

The Chamber had plenty of work left to it; it was the audit and record-keeping department, and still controlled directly the special budgets for the Church, educational institutions and hospitals, and the budgets of each corporate town, whose revenues came from crown assignments. Its structure was revised in a Chamber Ordinance of May 1694, when it was confirmed as a collegiate ministry under the President and four Councillors, each with his own remit, but collectively responsible for the department. There remained one further reform. Since 1687 the king has been expressing dissatisfaction with its audit and prosecuting functions, and in a letter of September 1695 announced the separating out of the audit functions because these were not being executed 'so promptly and precisely as Our service and vital interest demand'. A separate audit department, with its own secretariat and records, was established, linked to the Chamber only through its President, who remained a member of the College. It was required to meet daily, giving its mornings to prosecutions, and afternoons to auditing. The king proved more willing to invest in financial administration. The Budget Office got substantial increases of staff in 1682, and so did other Chamber departments, while there was a general upgrading of salaries. The Treasurer had received 7,500 dsm. annually, but by 1691, Wrede, as President of the Chamber got 11,250 dsm. By 1697 the reorganization of financial administration was complete, and the budget of 1696 became the reference point for public finances through the eighteenth century.[8]

The king's approach to his bureaucracy overall was pragmatic, driven by two imperatives: to ensure his personal control and to save expense by driving his servants to their limits, in the same way as he drove himself. He almost made a joke about this to Nils Bielke when he regretted he could not afford generous remuneration: 'the will is good, but the means are weak', and continued: 'my servants do not become happy with me, nor do they get rich'. His officials were frequent victims of his notorious temper. When Axel de la Gardie, Governor of Estland, ventured to query a royal proclamation, he was rebuked like an office boy: 'do not argue, but simply and immediately publish the proclamation'. When Posse, a provincial

[7] Styffe, ed., *Civila förvaltningen*, pp. 129–42; Bååth and Munthe, *Statskontoret*, pp. 25–6, 97; Lagerroth, *Statsreglering*, pp. 113–17.
[8] Lagerroth, *Statsreglering*, pp. 94–6; Eden, *Kammarkollegiets historia*, pp. 142, 149, 152–5; Carlsson, *Centralförvaltningen*, p. 95; Kleberg, *Kammarkollegium*, pp. 18–19; Cavallie, *Fred till krig*, p. 40.

governor, was detected misusing funds, and pleaded a royal letter praising his past services, the king was infuriated. He wrote: 'concerning that letter, it was sent to him by Us when We were not so aware of his deceitfulness . . . for he is a completely deceitful person, that is absolutely certain'. A provincial book-keeper who failed to produce his accounts in the stipulated twelve months was immediately arrested and brought before the Chamber. The Chamber College itself got a letter in 1684: 'I warn you by this, that you do not again resort to intrigue, or I shall certainly give you a sound beating and teach you to know what you ought to do.' When the commerce department recommended a man with a criminal record for an appointment, the king told them: 'you have acted directly against your sworn duty, and I shall not hereafter pay much attention to your recommendations, nor give credibility to your letters: if you come again with such a recommendation, the Prosecutor will be ordered speedily to come after you'. It is an open question whether the king's bullying and intimidation were the best way to motivate his servants, or maintain an efficient administration. But it reflected his belief that all men are by nature corrupt, and will follow their evil inclinations, unless checked by fear of punishment.[9]

Charles XI saw his administrators as falling short of the ideal; historians have judged that he was served by the most effective bureaucracy of its day. They stress particularly its professionalism and meritocratic character. It was professional in the sense that it offered a successful entrant a career for life, with guaranteed remuneration, and a promotion ladder that could end in ennoblement. The Table of Ranks set out a framework, and affirmed that status in society was based on official function, not birth. The bureaucrats were also professionally trained. Under Gustav II Adolf it had become policy to train public servants in university, though the intention was partially blocked by the conservatism of the clergy, who controlled higher education, and resisted putting modern subjects like law and politics into the syllabus. Even so most civil servants were university graduates in law or politics, though further vocational training had to be added. There were various schemes for this, but basically a graduate was attached to an institution, and either paid a small remuneration, or left to support himself by casual earnings from the public or his superiors. Thus he gained experience and enjoyed an insider position from which to apply for permanent employment. The Chancery and the Chamber offered a few paid apprenticeships, but the most productive training scheme was the attachment of unpaid student learners to the two High Courts, the *Svea hovrätt* and the *Göta hovrätt* as *auscultanter*. They were then considered for recruitment into all branches of the administration, and in the hundred years before 1720 produced 850 trainees. This helped to satisfy the considerable enlargement of the

[9] Malmström, 'Karl XIs bref till Nils Bielke', p. 32, king to Bielke 29 Nov. 1687; Carlson, *Historia*, III, pp. 159, 162, 163, 177; Hildebrand and Grimberg, *Källorna*, p. 218, king to the commerce Deputation 22 Apr. 1684.

bureaucracy which by the mid-eighteenth century was 45% bigger than in 1650, with most of the increase coming after 1680.[10]

The element of meritocracy must, however, be seen in an early modern context; it was one element in appointment. Sons of noblemen started with advantages: they could better afford to take unpaid apprenticeships, they had connections, they could wait for the better postings and could more easily opt for military service. But there were never above 25% of noblemen among the entrants. Once in service, a commoner had a 20% chance of becoming ennobled, though it could take twenty to thirty years service. Once inside the service, competence was a major consideration for advancement. When the Chamber official, P. Kalling, was threatened with redundancy, the Chamber wrote to the king that they could not afford to lose such an experienced and competent administrator, and they knew that 'your Majesty is always accustomed to consider graciously those who serve well, and for that reason ask for his assistance'. But merit alone was never enough; men advanced by the mixture of merit, patronage, nepotism and purchase that prevailed all over Europe. The ideal was a meritocratic public service, but the reality fell short. Any appointment or advancement needed recommendations of a patron; this was so well known that model letter-writing books used in schools included examples of how to approach a patron. It could be done in stages; Samuel Stekeus wrote to another commoner, Anders Graan, to write to the magnate Bengt Rosenhane for a recommendation. Graan wrote: 'I assure you that your graciousness would promote a Christian act, since otherwise he has none to recommend him who would make an effort for him.' Even at the top, recommendation was needed; Ulf Bonde sought appointment as a provincial governor and wrote to Rosenhane to ask 'how and what way and through whom you think I shall apply for it'. In the end there was money. Bonde offered Secretary Rehnskiöld 200 ducats if he got the appointment. Adam Lewenhaupt complained he could get no advancement, 'since I have neither patrons nor money to employ in it'. In the 1690s it was common talk that Secretary C. Piper, then rising in the king's favour, expected clients shall 'put something heavy in his hand'. What can be affirmed is that in Sweden, merit and competence did weigh heavily in appointments; there was no sale of offices on the French pattern, and Charles XI was ruthless in eliminating sinecures. The majority of appointees to the civil and legal bureaucracies were born commoners, or came from families very recently ennobled, and men like Lindschöld, Gyllenborg or Piper could get right to the top of the hierarchy. The old magnate families could still serve, but were swamped by self-made men advanced on merit. It was then inevitable that the new men in turn began to form an oligarchy of birth. Even when the new men were ennobled, they were not accepted by the old families as social equals; there was little intermarriage. So the new nobles married among themselves and sent their offspring into the public service. The trend can be seen at secretary

[10] Norrhem, *Uppkomlingarna*, pp. 14, 36, 53, 55, 56; D. Gaunt, *Utbildning till statens tjänst: en kollektivbiografi av stormaktstidens hovrättsauskultanter* (Uppsala, 1975), pp. 39, 52–5, 86, 91.

level: after 1650 more than half the appointees were related to the existing incumbents. Throughout the system, it was always a career advantage to be related to an insider. Under Charles XI, three-quarters of new entrants were commoners, but at the top a group of new official families was consolidating its predominance.[11]

The image of Charles XI's central government in action may be rounded off by returning to the diary of Henrik Horn's visit to Stockholm in 1684–5. Horn was no ordinary subject; he came from a top family, was a count, member of the Council of State, a field marshal after a creditable military career and currently Governor General of Bremen-Verden. He had problems with the *reduktion* to settle, but his real problem was Georg Guthrie, a successful Stockholm merchant of Scottish origin who had gone into Chamber service, been ennobled and appointed Director of Chamber administration in Bremen-Verden. A naturally aggressive character and a protégé of Lindschöld, Guthrie clashed fiercely with Horn, criticized his accounting and sought to undermine him. When Guthrie returned to Stockholm to report in 1684, Horn followed, determined to sort Guthrie out. It should have been no contest between the aristocratic soldier and a foreign plebeian upstart, but it proved otherwise. Horn arrived at Court in January 1684 and was warmly received by the king and the queen-mother. He opened his campaign; the routine was to go early to the Castle and catch the king at breakfast for a talk, since otherwise it was difficult to find the hyperactive monarch, who was always going somewhere. Horn tried accompanying the king to the opera, where his mother had dragged him, but the king left early and at 2 a.m., had departed for Gävle, so Horn had wasted his time. The problem, when the king was there, was to get his attention. One day Horn went to the Castle at 5 p.m. to hand over a petition, 'but since it dragged on until 7 o'clock and the king still had not come out, I went home again'. In conversation it was necessary to be careful, for the king was touchy. While he lobbied the king about one of his lawsuits, the king got the impression Horn had been obstructive, 'whereat the king got very angry, so that I got very uncomfortable'. Horn had to talk his way out and 'when I most humbly asked the king not to take it ungraciously and told him that I submitted completely to his gracious ruling in the principal matter', then the king calmed down. Horn's weakness was that the king was susceptible to lobbying. In June 1684, Horn got 'a stern letter from the king concerning Wismar garrison [there were alleged financial irregularities] from which I could see that Guthrie brought it about'. He rushed to the Castle to ask the king what Guthrie had said and got the discouraging response that the issue would be referred to a Chamber tribunal.[12]

Although Horn had open social access to the royal family, he kept dubious political company. He associated with collaborationist magnates, Sten Bielke, J. G.

---

[11] Gaunt, *Utbildning*, pp. 117–18, 138, 182; F. Persson, 'En hjälpande hand: principiella aspekter på patronage i förhållande till nepotism och meritokrati under stormaktstiden', *Scandia* 59 (1993), pp. 54, 58; Norrhem, *Uppkomlingarna*, pp. 61, 67–71.

[12] Munthe, 'Ett stycke karolinsk vardag', pp. 113, 120–4, 125, 127, 128, 138, 143.

Stenbock and Claes Fleming, and his legal adviser was Anders Lilliehöök, who had been in such trouble in the 1682 Diet. This group dined frequently and drank 'more than normally' and agreed together about public affairs. But that put Horn in opposition to Lindschöld and the plebeian absolutists who were supporting Guthrie. Horn tried to bribe Lindschöld: 'I sent my secretary to Mr Chancery Councillor Lindschöld with a present of 200 ducats, but it was not accepted'. The secretary's superior access to government nullified Horn's social advantage. He handed a petition to the king on one occasion, but 'the king went into another room, and took Lindschöld with him'. Horn, Bengt Oxenstierna and Bielke, all magnates, were left waiting outside, until informed the king would be occupied for some hours, so they drifted off to eat. Lindschöld was not openly hostile to Horn, that was not his style, but his letters 'more afflict than console me'. Horn won in the end by persuading Charles XI that Guthrie's conduct was undermining the whole structure of authority in Horn's province. He got Fleming and the Budget Office to endorse a statement and travelled out to Ulriksdal, where the king was, and showed it to him, 'which the king himself read with great displeasure at the Inspector's insolent proceedings. I stayed until after dinner with the king and queen and then followed the king to Stockholm.' Guthrie was dismissed, his post abolished and replaced with a Chamber official of much lower rank. Horn's narrative shows first that the king was indeed the centre of the government; when he was incapacitated by illness for a time in 1685, the machinery of government ground to a halt. It also illustrates how the plebeian bureaucrats were succeeding in establishing their predominance over the surviving magnate officers. Charles XI appears as an irresolute and suggestible figure, open to lobbying and uncertain which tendency to support. But in the end a Governor General was a representative of royal authority and had to be upheld. The king listened to Horn, whom he respected as a fighting soldier, but he also listened to Lindschöld pointing out that men like Guthrie did a vital service watching the activities of former oligarchs like Horn. The outcome was that an experienced and competent official, like Horn, who had been serving well for fifteen years, had to spend a year and half away from his post to mend his fences in Stockholm. It was not an ideal formula for efficient administration.[13]

A different level of government was where it interacted with the ordinary subject. The key figure of royal authority here was the provincial governor. The office was regularized after 1634 and the kingdom divided into twenty-four provinces, seventeen in Sweden and seven in Finland. The governor sat 'in the king's place and position, to uphold and administer the royal government in his Majesty's absence . . . the chief and head man of the province'. Provincial governors were noblemen who were career public servants, and rarely from the province. They were not intended to stay in one place too long; the appointment came towards the end of a career, though a governor could go on to become President of a Court or a

---

[13] *Ibid.*, pp. 126, 136, 140, 145.

department, or perhaps a Councillor. He had two statutory subordinates, a province Secretary, to handle correspondence and records, and an Accountant, responsible for all the accounts of the province. Charles XI had no plans to modify a system which most opinion agrees worked very effectively. He tended to increase the governor's functions and tried to tighten his supervision of their work. The annual report of Jakob Gyllenborg, as governor of Uppland in 1696, suggests the range of activity. He had reviewed and settled the finances of the Church locally, inventorying its properties and checking on rights to patronage. He had supervised the Courts, sitting in on many sessions and ensuring no irregularities occurred, and supervising the execution of their decisions. He claimed: 'it is a great satisfaction that no one has had occasion to complain about me to your royal Majesty'. He had completed the assignments for the military indelningsverk in the province, and was now doing the same for its civil administration, and had instituted an annual census. His main problem was always law enforcement: 'this vexatious, distasteful activity over executions, with which I am daily and all too much overloaded and pestered over'. The king would set priorities for his governors. In 1685, Fabian Wrede, an earlier governor of Uppland, gave pride of place in his report to the suppression of illegal manors and stopping the enclosure of peasant farms for pasture. He prided himself on his exemplary record keeping. Charles XI was not easily satisfied. He displayed his distrust in October 1681 when several governors were called to account for 'certain abuses and arbitrary actions in their offices'. The letter books are rich in vitriolic letters from the king when he has caught them out in some misconduct. This distrust decided the king to draw up a rule book for the office. The governors were circularized in November 1685 and told to send in reports on their functions, with documentation, with a view to establishing standard regulations. These appeared in 1687 as 'Instructions according to which the king's subject and governor over N . . ., both he who is at present in post and those who come into service after him, must conform themselves'. It was made clear that the province Secretary and Accountant, though nominated by the governor, got their commission from the king and were answerable to him. A new officer, the Treasurer, had responsibility for collecting all the crown revenues and making all the out-payments, rendering a monthly account to the governor. The provincial governors were the key men in local administration; they enforced all the king's internal reforms, and were the main channels for transmitting and executing the king's commands in the localities, but also controlling traffic in the other direction, receiving petitions and grievances, and after filtering the unacceptable, passing them to the king.[14]

The authority of the governor also extended to the urban sector, if such a term

[14] O. Sörndal, *Den svenska länsstyrelsen: uppkomst, organisation och allmänna maktställning* (Lund, 1937), pp. 35–8, 48–52, 56–60, 61, 63; *Handlingar rörande skandinaviens historia*, XXVIII (1847), part 32, pp. 320–7; part 33, pp. 306–19; Carlson, *Historia*, II, p. 351; UUB, E491, Handlingar till Sveriges politiska historia 1680–6, king's letter to the governors 17 Nov. 1685.

applies to seventeenth-century Sweden. Even by contemporary standards, there was only one major city, Stockholm, which passed the 50,000 mark under Charles XI. Forty towns were represented in the Estate of Burghers, but most were large villages, sustained by privileges derived from the crown. A handful of places, Uppsala, Gothenburg, Kalmar, Åbo in Finland, were genuine urban communities. And Gothenburg at this time was largely run by Dutch and Scottish merchants. The dependence of the towns on endowment by the crown made them vulnerable under the reduktion. In 1680 the Nobility, when surrendering their donations, asked why the towns should not do the same, and returned to the attack in 1682, asserting that 'all the revenue, which the towns of the kingdom enjoy, are undeniably public revenues, which are at the king's disposition'. The point is the towns were acutely aware of how vulnerable they were and how much they needed the king's support, hence they were no way inclined to make problems by resisting the royal government. The whole concept of municipal autonomy was unacceptable to Charles XI; the urban sector was one where the absolutist style of government had free play.[15]

Stockholm, by its size, its near monopoly of overseas trade, and being the sole source of large cash advances to the royal government, had real economic clout. It was governed, like most towns, by a magistracy consisting of a Burgomaster and a Council. But although the old tradition of general citizens' assemblies had died out, it had an elected assembly of Elders, with power to agree and collect the local taxes. In the war, Stockholm had been encouraged by an undertaking of the king to Thegner, that in future it could elect its Councillors and Burgomasters. In March 1680 further royal letters granted the right to audit their own accounts, to retain a portion of the excise they collected and for the magistracy to assume full control of the town budget. These assurances were worthless; Charles XI did not accept a town council could have any rights that would diminish his personal authority. In 1681 the Chamber challenged Stockholm's right to audit its own accounts. The dispute went to the king, who ruled that everyone must account to the Chamber. When the magistracy produced the royal letter exempting them, he ruled it was invalid, 'because it takes from Us Our rights, and frees them from their duty'. He added that if the magistracy persisted they would have 'strong reasons to repent'; the magistracy gave in. A further reason why municipal governments could not resist the royal authority was that they did not represent their community. Throughout the kingdom, Burgomasters and Councillors were royal officials, appointed and paid by the king. In substantial towns they were graduate civil servants, trained in law. The magistracy comprised three elements: bureaucrats on passage to higher office; men like Gyllenborg, Lovisin, Carl Piper were natives of Stockholm, from the wealthiest burgher families. Next were the career local bureaucrats, and then a handful of lay Councillors, men like the two Törne

---

[15] C.-F. Corin, *Självstyre och kunglig maktpolitik inom Stockholms stadsförvaltning 1668–1697* (Stockholm, 1958), pp. 18–20, 220, 223–5, 284.

brothers, or Mårten Bunge, who were merchants, but usually heavily involved in public service enterprises. The children of such men rarely continued in trade. The magistracy usually tried to defend municipal interests; after all they lived in the community, and had to win its cooperation, but in Stockholm they were dominated by the town Governor, Christopher Gyllenstierna, a fierce absolutist, with power to determine the town budget and the salaries of its officers. A revised budget for Stockholm was worked out in the Chamber and confirmed by the king in July 1682. In 1693 the king decided to revise Stockholm's budget; he thought the current one too loose, and wanted something like the national budget with each item of ordinary revenue and expenditure specified. The king's real motive was economy; Gyllenstierna told the magistracy 'that some savings shall be made on the existing budget'. Savings, including reductions in salary, were forced on the reluctant magistracy and the budget signed by the king in November 1693. Gyllenstierna warned the magistrates to observe it exactly, 'if they value avoidance of the summons and trouble which will follow'. This was not an empty threat: in 1695 Gyllenstierna found illegal payments in the accounts, and told the magistrates it was 'intolerable to play around with the town's revenues against the king's orders'. He went on: 'do not believe we have some kind of republic here, but all are subjects and servants, bound to obey orders'. The magistracy grovelled: 'God keep us from such thoughts, or that they could ever come to that forgetfulness of their humble duty to their most gracious superior, that they either have or could have such reprehensible thoughts.' This led to a long paper war, typical of the bureaucracy at work; in December 1695 Gyllenstierna submitted a 194 page memorandum to the Chamber on the failings of the magistracy, and a legal tribunal was threatened. Yet when it all got to the king, he ruled against any proceedings. Presumably the threat was only a warning. There was often an inconsistency between the stern language of the royal letters and the actual consequences.[16]

Further it was possible for the community to negotiate with the government. Stockholm was by long usage obliged to billet the royal Guards regiment. But after 1680 that had increased in size and the magistracy pressed for relief. In this case, while the king would not yield on the principle of the obligation, he was in fact ready to negotiate and an agreement was reached. The financing of the billeting was transferred to the magistracy, who set up a committee of Councillors and business-men to run it, and this worked to the satisfaction of both sides. Another issue was tax assessments, handled by the Council of Elders. Although after the late 1680s the Elders were coopted, not elected, they were still representative, and the assessment meetings were occasions of genuine public debate. Gyllenstierna often attended and uttered warnings 'to remember their humble obedience and allegiance, to which they are obliged by their sworn oath to their king'. There could be no question of challenging the sum demanded, but since the Elders usually did

[16] *Ibid.*, pp. 23, 28, 210, 217, 228, 230, 284–7, 289, 293, 427–8, 438–9, 478, 482–4, 486, 500, 520.

produce it, they were given discretion over how it was assessed and allowed to collect it themselves. The government's need for smooth administration and social cohesion meant that some degree of self-government survived.[17]

The urban sector was an exotic part of seventeenth-century Swedish society; most of the king's subjects lived in rural communities. Here the central government had to work with an old tradition of populist self-government. The basic institution was the *häradsting*, the district Court, and it was a popular institution, at which the whole community would gather on Court days. Originally an elected judge, the district chief, had presided and verdicts were given by the jury of twelve men. In addition to crime, the Court resolved most community problems, and property transactions had to be formally registered at the Court. Studies of the Courts in the seventeenth century suggest they were in a transition phase. In some, oath-helping was still used until it was officially abolished in 1695. The records show that decisions might be made by the jury and the attendant public, though usually the jury determined verdict and sentence. The common formula, 'it was judged by the twelve men', suggests the judge was only an expert adviser, but in some Courts the jury gave the verdict and the judge determined the sentence; then the formula was 'it was said by the Court', meaning the jury and the judge acted jointly. Down to mid-century the predominant impression is that the judge had little training or social status, and was elected. The aim of the Court was not to dispense formal justice, but to promote conciliation and community peace, so that most offences were settled by fines. Thereafter changes were evident: the printing of the Land Law in 1608 provided a national rule book, and new classes of offences were coming in to supplement it. It was traditional that deficiencies in the Land Law could be made good by reference to the law of God set out in Scripture, which often demanded fixed, severe penalties for offences like adultery and blasphemy. Disregard of royal orders also figures more widely; non-payment of dues, non-performance of services, illegal trading were being prosecuted, and this was facilitated by the appointment of an executive officer, whose first duty was to see the crown's orders were published. He could inspect the records to check if they were being enforced. Also it is apparent that formal justice became the aim; the concept of evidence and proof, rather than local opinion, was becoming the basis of verdicts. There was a clear trend; the district Courts were being adapted to become instruments of central control and social discipline, but at the same time their activities were extending to matters like roads and transportation, forest and settlement laws, and the agents in charge of these activities were usually elected by the Court, and while this system prevailed there was a broad scope for real local self-government.[18]

---

[17] *Ibid.*, pp. 257–9, 262, 375–82, 385–91.
[18] K. G. Westman, *Häradsnämnd och häradsrätt under 1600-talet och början av 1700-talet: en studie med särskilt hänsyn till upplandska domböcker* (Uppsala, 1927), pp. 3–6; M. T. Sjöberg, 'Staten och tinget under 1600-talet', *HT* 110 (1990), pp. 162–5, 174, 175, 180–1; Ingers, *Bonden*, pp. 318–22.

The most powerful tool for imposing central control was the High Court, the *Svea hovrätt*, instituted by Gustav II Adolf. It was modelled on a traditional Court, with a President and twelve assessors. The key factor in its development was professionalization: as the Law Faculty at Uppsala began to produce trained jurists, and the *auscultanter* system developed, qualified manpower became available. The High Court spread its influence first through its status as the highest appeal Court. It set precedents, standardized sentencing, demanded that lower Courts submit records for inspection, ruled that all capital sentences be referred to the High Court for confirmation. Parallel to this the High Court became a channel for a growing legal patronage. Early in the century the post of district Court judge was becoming a crown appointment. However, it also became a sinecure for magnates, who sent young law students to officiate at minimum salaries. Such men lacked the experience or status to control the juries. It was one of the earliest reforms of Charles XI to end this system. In 1680 W. Klerk, a legally experienced nobleman, was appointed a district Court President in Västerbotten. His letters of appointment specified he was to control sentencing in the Court, and keep a duplicate record of its proceedings, sending one copy to the High Court. Finally he was to be personally resident: 'he shall himself, in his own person, preside over the Court, hear the cases and judge and answer for it . . . constantly hear and relieve the complaints of the community and not, as has mostly happened hitherto, carry this out through any kind of substitute'. The system was then generalized, supported by the Diet Resolution of 1680, 'that the district Court President shall reside in his place, perform the office himself and for a fixed salary'. Subsequently letters of appointment were standardized, and in April 1683 the king ordered the President be provided 'a good and substantial residence in the district which is under his jurisdiction'. These changes soon reduced the jury to its basic role of delivering verdicts. Some evidence might suggest the jury was being eliminated altogether, but this was not the practice. A dedicated absolutist bureaucrat, Gyldenstolpe, told the Law Commission in 1688 that it was necessary: 'the jury at the District Court retains its function according to law, as it has previously been the custom to observe and apply, namely to examine the facts, since they who know the district can do it more easily, as well in criminal as in civil disputes'.[19]

It was the peculiar strength of Swedish absolutism that it did not eliminate the institutions of popular involvement in government, but used them to impose its own programme. In this area, the Court records show how the bulk of the increased activity of the Courts arose from the enforcement of royal regulations, with an accompanying sharpening of sanctions, a trend towards more punitive sentencing.

[19] S. Petren, S. Jägerskiöld and T. O. Nordberg, *Svea hovrätt: studier till 350-årsminnet* (Stockholm, 1964); S. Jägerskiöld, *Hovrätten under den karolinska tiden och till 1734 års lag: Svea Hovrätt: studier till 350-årsminnet* (Stockholm, 1964), pp. 121, 131–48, 236–8; Gaunt, *Utbildning*, pp. 179, 193; KB, Engströmska samlingen B.II.1.12, king's letter to W. Klerck 20 Dec. 1680; king's circular letter 26 Apr. 1683; *SRARP*, XIII, pp. 52–5; Westman, *Häradsrätt*, pp. 38–41, 44.

For example, corporal punishments were rare in the early seventeenth century, common for the poorest defendants by the end. The same was true of the death penalty: one typical Court passed seven death sentences between 1600 and 1672 and all of them were commuted. From 1673 to 1691, there were six, none of them commuted to a fine, though some were reduced to life imprisonment in a fortress. The freedom of the jury to determine local tax assessments and exemptions was brought under strict control. But popular input at the district level survived. The peasants could protect their rights through grievances presented by the Peasant Estate; the relationship of the jury to the crown officers had to be negotiated, for in the end the jury could practise passive resistance. It was one thing to get an order at the Court, quite another to get it enforced. One exasperated district official wrote of his jury: 'they do not show that obedience and compliance that they should, but neglect it, even though the bailiff wrote to them in strict terms'. If the crown officials worked amiably with the jury, they could secure reasonable levels of compliance, otherwise their working lives became an endless struggle with local recalcitrance. It was worth a few concessions to local demands to buy cooperation.[20]

Charles XI always rejected any idea that there was a contract between a king and his subjects. But he did acknowledge his duty to God, and one central part of that was to administer justice impartially to everyone. The records are filled with reprimands from the king to officials who failed in this, and he was personally active in judicial business in Council, and maintained close supervision of the High Court. His style was illustrated in a circular to the High Courts in July 1682 about the imminent vacation. It began by reminding them they now got regular salaries and he expected effective delivery of services in return. He had already told them

that you should not separate before all unresolved cases, and especially criminal cases are settled. None the less We have to note with displeasure, from various grievances and lamentations received, that cases are still unresolved, to the great harm of faithful subjects, and especially many sit in prisons in various places to their double torment, and great annoyance to Us. Therefore it is Our gracious will and command to you that you convene your absent members, that they immediately return and do not break up before everything is properly settled . . . so that once and for all you have a clean desk.

There was another very characteristic letter to the High Court in 1687; 'since it is sufficiently known how strong Our desire is that the work may be carried forward to the satisfaction of those seeking justice, so they can be quickly relieved', he pointed out their orders specified that business should begin at 8 a.m. He told them that this did not mean 'the Court shall assemble after 8', but that business should start promptly at 8 a.m. He required a weekly report that this was being done. In this instance the Prosecutor, who was to make the report, told his colleagues, but not

---

[20] Sjöberg, 'Staten och tinget under 1600-talet', pp. 167–9, 175, 176, 184, 185, 187; Villstrand, ed., *Kustbygd*, pp. 196, 197; E. Österberg, 'Folklig mentalitet och statlig makt: perspetiv på 1500- och 1600-talens Sverige', *Scandia* 58 (1992), pp. 95–6; E. Österberg, 'Bönder och centralmakt i det tidigsmoderna Sverige', *Scandia* 55 (1989), pp. 76–7, 81–5.

the king, that most delays were the king's fault: 'as we sit and work on a case, then comes the king's order that we give an opinion . . ., that we shall go up to the Council, that this or that Assessor shall be on a commission'. The problem of overload, imposed by the king, clearly affected the Courts as well, yet there were impressive improvements made. From 1661 to 1682, the *Svea hovrätt* processed 2,531 cases. In the five years 1682–7 it settled 1,077 cases, suggesting a massive efficiency gain.[21]

One basis of the popularity of the absolutism must be the king's vigorous enforcement of impartial justice and a rule of law, even though he never compromised for a moment on his prerogative to override the law in case of necessity. 'The right and superiority belonging to Us alone to annul a judgement' was precisely to enable him to relieve the subject. He was obsessive about equity between subjects. He fully supported the President of the *Svea hovrätt* in 1687, when he insisted that a King's Councillor enjoyed no precedence before the Court. He intervened repeatedly to punish army officers convicted of withholding pay from their soldiers, or demanding unwarranted services from them. He never hesitated to prosecute: for example, an order to the provincial governors in 1683 regulated the rights of a nobleman over his tenants. They were entitled to labour services,

but after reason and moderation, so that he shall see that the peasant can bear it, and in no way to exhaust him through toil and labour that he is driven into the ground . . . Because it also concerns Us to see that nobody may so abuse his property, to the prejudice of himself or others, much less oppress the common people, that they fall into total ruin and the land into desolation, since they do not cease to be Our subjects, although they are peasants of the nobility, and deserve Our protection and defence in all reasonable matters, the same as anyone else.

It can be seen how this generally uncharismatic man became a legend among the common folk, 'old grey cloak', who rode anonymously about the kingdom, to appear unexpectedly to put down the mighty and protect the humble.[22]

The other universal interface between authority and the ordinary subject was the Lutheran Church. Its importance cannot be exaggerated; it was fundamental to the working of the system. It is axiomatic that stable government depends not on coercive force, but on its legitimacy in the eyes of the governed, so that its rulings are obeyed not out of fear, but as a moral obligation lying on all. All over Christian Europe it was a duty of the Church to provide the necessary indoctrination and therefore it was almost universally agreed that religious dissent was a mortal danger to any society. Svedberg visited England in 1674, and admired almost everything he saw, except the religious dissent, which appalled him. 'Disunity is of the Devil, who promotes it and derives the greatest satisfaction from it, especially in the

---

[21] Jägerskiöld, *Hovrätten*, pp. 123, 124, 247, 262; Hildebrand and Grimberg, *Källorna*, p. 217, king's circular letter 22 July 1682.

[22] Jägerskiöld, *Hovrätten*, pp. 310, 320; Ingers, *Bonden*, pp. 313, 314.

teachers of the congregation.' There was no Catholic threat in Sweden; old practices survived in the countryside, but organized Catholicism did not. The Church was neurotic about the menace of Calvinism, and the king shared its anxiety, and supported all measures to exclude it. Foreign Calvinists resident in the kingdom could practise their faith in private, but if they settled must bring up their children as Lutheran. Thus Sweden enjoyed the rare distinction of being a community without significant religious dissent. Only in the distant frontier provinces of Kexholm and Ingermanland was there a Greek Orthodox population. The regime tried persecution and forced conversion, but the Tsar protested, and the peasants threatened to migrate into Russia, so in the end an uneasy coexistence prevailed. But that was no danger to metropolitan Sweden and Finland.[23]

The Church was essential to government, but it could also be a possible competitor with royal government for authority. That was why the Clergy draft of the Church Law had been rewritten to stress royal supremacy. When Lindschöld drafted the ordinance on ecclesiastical tribunals in 1687, he considered inserting a statement that the king was *summus episcopus*, but decided not to. To claim it for the king, 'now, for the first time as something new to assign to yourself', would be a mistake, since 'that same right is always attached to the sovereign's office, and they are both alike given to your Majesty by God, and both come by inheritance'. The king agreed; in a letter to Axel de la Gardie in 1691, he told him he must 'explicitly understand that We shall exercise the episcopal power, as a right belonging to Us alone', and the king added in his own hand: 'another time you must keep a better look-out and observe Our supreme power, otherwise we shall not remain friends'. Therefore the king asserted his absolute power to regulate the Church, and in doing so asserted lay superiority over it. The Church Law made that clear enough; for example in choosing a bishop, the Chapter could put forward names to the king, who would select one, 'or else someone other whom We judge to be worthy'. The instructions for provincial governors made it clear they were to supervise the work of the Church, check on local preaching and intervene to suppress dissent. If the governor discovered 'something improper and unfortunate is going on, so he shall inform the bishop and Chapter and urge them to punish, prevent and eliminate it'. There is also the record of the king's resolute rejection of the very idea of a Church Consistory, implying a degree of autonomy. When the royalist bishop Carlson had an unusual fit of independence in 1696, and ventured to argue with the king about an appointment, he provoked an outburst of royal anger. The king demanded if he was playing a game, 'do you want to show posterity that you undertook to argue with Us whether Our or your will shall prevail?' The king hinted that perhaps Carlson was finding the office of bishop too much for him and ended: 'We conclude herewith, wishing graciously to warn you to correct your behaviour.' The king did not lack respect for the legitimate function of the clergy. The Church Law ordered

---

[23] Wetterberg, ed., *Svedbergs*, pp. 70–8.

them to preach and their language 'must be clear and plain and grounded in the Holy Scripture'. If they did, then the king could accept even public criticism of himself. The bishop of Gothenburg, a favourite of the queen, preached at Court against the injustices of the reduktion. The king reproved him: 'you are preaching sedition in the hearts of my subjects', but the bishop's reply, 'no, such was far from my intention, but my aim has been to preach insurrection in your Majesty's heart', was accepted. The best known anecdote is from Svedberg, who said courtiers complained about his radical preaching. The king asked if the sermons had been grounded in God's Word, and when it was conceded they had, said: 'when a priest has God's Word on his side and expounds it honestly, then kings have nothing to say about it'. There is an instance too of the king's respect of the rights of parishioners. In 1679 he proposed to nominate J. Iser to a living in Gothenburg. The parishioners petitioned that they had the traditional right to choose their pastor. The king agreed and 'graciously resolved that they shall be free to choose the parish priest themselves' and wrote to Iser that if they wanted someone else, then he would find Iser an alternative preferment.[24]

The clergy appeared to be wholly submissive under the royal authority, but were capable of opposing the king where their professional interests were at stake. Tensions arose because the king had reformist impulses, when almost all his clergy were steeped in tradition and fearful of change. One of the most basic educational tools was the catechism, which all subjects were required to learn by heart. The Swedish Church had never had one uniform catechism, though Luther's *Small Catechism* was accepted as the model. The king, with his passion for order and uniformity, set up a committee under Spegel to draft a catechism and present it to the Diet of 1686. The king approved Spegel's draft, and confidently had 6,000 copies printed in readiness. But when it was presented to the Clergy Estate, the Uppsala conservative, Professor Schültz, denounced Spegel's work as full of error, and the archbishop could not control the protests. Yet it was the king who conceded; Spegel left the Diet, denounced by his colleagues as incompetent or worse, the printed copies were pulped, and a revision of the draft promised. A new committee, excluding Spegel, was appointed by the king, and presented an acceptable draft to the Diet of 1689. Something similar happened over the revision of the *Psalmbok*, the hymnal which ranked with the catechism as a means of teaching the common folk basic religious ideas. A committee which included both Spegel and Svedberg was instructed to revise it. A draft appeared for the Diet of 1693, but it too caused controversy in the Estate. The king wrote to the archbishop that he wanted a text ready for publication as soon as possible, and one was printed in 1695. Svedberg has described the uproar which followed among the clergy. The king had

[24] Pleijel, *Kyrkans historia*, pp. 20, 71, 73–4, 127; Normann, *Prästerskapet*, pp. 300, 321; Anjou, *Kyrkans historia*, pp. 465, 471, 515; Ryden, ed., *Kyrkolag*, pp. 27, 236, 272; Hildebrand and Grimberg, *Källorna*, p. 221, king's letter to Carlson 10 Feb. 1696; Wetterberg, ed., *Svedbergs*, p. 136; Carlson, *Historia*, IV, p. 275; Loenbom, ed., *Historiskt archivum*, p. 34.

told him that this time he would wait for the reactions and 'see what weight there might be in what one or another may have to comment on it'. That was wise, 'the *Psalmbok* had hardly appeared . . . before disfavour, anger and jealousy, and their promoter Satan, came forth'. The critics said 'the king and Svedberg will make a new religion'. The trouble was that the editors had sought out and translated new German hymns, which were alleged to be infected with Pietist heresies. The king backed off and referred the problem to the bishops, who excised nearly all the new material, and produced a slightly modified version of a *Psalmbok* of 1645; only fourteen of the seventy-eight new hymns were retained. The king's last project, to make a new translation of the Bible, was blocked completely. The king approved the idea in 1686, and it met instant rejection; the very idea of altering the received text was abhorrent. So although Svedberg was encouraged by the king to go ahead, he recounted subsequently how 'the other bishops, either from jealousy, that they had not been consulted in it, or for other reasons which God knows (Satan gave much assistance), were happy to see the work stopped'. It was, despite letters from the king, urging continuation. A consistory of clergy in 1695 confirmed the objections to retranslation; at most a new version with marginal annotations might be considered. Even then it was ten years after Charles XI died before a new Bible in that format was published. The limits of the king's power over the Church were clear: he could promote and encourage men like Spegel and Svedberg, but the resistance of the Church establishment could negate their reforming endeavours.[25]

What worried men like Svedberg was the stifling formalism of established religion. He wrote: 'I sighed and sigh still . . . how badly most Lutherans understand Luther's doctrine . . . If men go to church and take communion at the appointed time in the year, while at the same time are living with all kinds of sinful, fleshly practices . . . no one will say they are other than good Lutherans.' His opponents knew that the suppression of stimulation was the price they must pay to preserve the religious cohesion they enjoyed. So all novelty was blocked out. The king wholly approved of that; a censorship law of 1684 required pre-publication censorship of all printed material, either by the universities, or by Chancery. A few thought this went too far; Bishop J. Rudbeck commented: 'no honest man can now write anything useful in public, and I would be a delinquent if I did'. Thought control and conditioning was the main business of the Church. It was given total control of education, and all teachers were members of the Estate of the Clergy. The education Ordinance of 1693, largely the work of Spegel and Lindschöld, confirmed this. There was to be a gymnasium in every diocese, and a system of Trivial Schools to feed them. A national curriculum was prescribed, of a strongly conservative, Aristotelian character. It was the king's intention that all his subjects

[25] J. Helander, *Haqvin Spegel: hans lif och gärning intill år 1693* (Uppsala, 1899), pp. 64–9, 71, 73, 74, 77, 96; *PR*, IV, pp. 238, 249, 251, 253–4, 255, 264, 266, 445; Pleijel, *Kyrkans historia*, p. 80; Anjou, *Kyrkans historia*, pp. 501, 509, 510; Wetterberg, ed., *Svedbergs*, pp. 148–51, 177, 181–3, 184, 186; RA, Kanslikollegiets Protokoll 1686, meetings of 8, 15 Feb. 1686.

educate their children in the system, writing to the governors in 1693 that they must see the nobility sent their offspring to the gymnasia. He also demonstrated his seriousness of purpose by establishing an education budget, with national pay scales for teachers, which had been revised upwards, and a detailed budget for each individual school. The king's enthusiasm for a national education system, run by the clergy, was based on the certainty that they would instil into his subjects correct political ideas.[26]

The basic textbook on politics, used by the Swedish Church, was the *Loci theologici* of the sixteenth-century German scholar, M. Haffenreffer. This defined a ruler as 'a person established by God to be . . . a faithful guardian of both tables of the Decalogue and other good and useful laws agreeable with this. Therefore it is customary in Scripture to call rulers gods, because they exercise an office conferred by God.' This basic idea was endlessly repeated and embroidered by successive generations of Swedish academics. A typical example of this was Olaf Moberg, a professor at Dorpat, who set out his views in 1691. He asserted that since the Creation, people had lived under patriarchal authority, and then cited the Old Testament to show how God had instituted monarchy. It was self-evident that the people could not confer power on their rulers, for God had never given them any to confer. So even if a king was elected, his powers were conferred by God. The laws of Nature demonstrate how men are naturally social beings and need government, but on his argument this could only come from God. Svedberg, for all his interest in reform, agreed wholly with Moberg's views. He described how, as a professor at Uppsala, he had to preside over a dissertation presentation in the presence of the king. The subject was the Roman leader, Fabius Maximus, but as the argument developed, Svedberg was alarmed that 'there was somewhat incautious discussion by the opponent about political authority and its power: whether it should be of God or man to choose and call up a ruler'. He stopped the debate as improper, 'when the ruler himself was present, to listen about his authority and have it put in dispute if it were of God'. This reflected the general assumption that such delicate questions should not be discussed at all. Charles XI had warned Uppsala in 1689 that all teaching must be in accord with accepted doctrine, and academic discussion must accept this limitation.[27]

The basis for most of the teaching and preaching in the churches were the collections of printed sermon notes; some parishes possessed several, and these uniformly assume that monarchy is the best form of government, and that unconditional obedience is due, even to tyrants, 'since because they are God's executive officers, obey them like the Lord God himself'. Some did express reservations about the interpretation of I Samuel 8, suggesting God only approved such extreme

---

[26] Pleijel, *Kyrkans historia*, pp. 153, 164; Anjou, *Kyrkans historia*, pp. 383–4, 386; Carlson, *Historia*, IV, pp. 240–84, 302; Helander, *Spegel*, pp. 80, 82, 84, 86; Lagerroth, *Statsreglering*, pp. 94–6.

[27] Normann, *Prästerskapet*, pp. 13–16, 49, 50–67, 70, 143; Wetterberg, ed., *Svedbergs*, pp. 174–6; Ryden, ed., *Kyrkolag*, pp. 430, 433.

conduct in extreme cases; as a popular commentary by J. Hülsemann put it: 'urgente reipublicae necessitate'. But most accepted it as God's ruling, as Bishop Gezelius did in a sermon in 1688: 'so Luther himself and most of the pure Evangelical theologians agree, that in that place it is not just some right of usurpation or some assumed right, but a legitimate right granted by God that is declared, . . . which therefore a king rightly and with good conscience may exercise'. When Spegel was bishop of Linköping, one of his theological students wrote a thesis which argued that this text was a description of a tyrant. Spegel felt he must report this to the king, who proved tolerant and assumed the student knew no better. He left it to the bishop to put him right. A questioning attitude was no part of clerical training. A study of papers presented at the clergy conferences, which the Church Law required each diocese to hold annually, shows the topics were chosen and presented in a deliberately non-controversial way. They were handled in very general terms; examples from Swedish historical experience were avoided. Since they were Aristotelian, they had to accept that he had recognized three forms of government as valid, and that God had not actually ruled which He preferred. But they studiously avoided discussing the relative merits of each form, and the papers simply assume that monarchy is the norm. If the discussion strayed onto dangerous ground of what the ancient philosophers had said, the bishop could always call it to order by reminding them: 'we follow Holy Scripture, not the philosophers'.[28]

Orthodox belief was transmitted by the universities and schools, and through the professional training of the clergy down into the homes of the people. The Church Law, following well-established practice, prescribed that the priest must maintain a full list, house by house, of all his parishioners and visit them systematically. He was to ensure that all, including wives, children and servants, could read in a book, 'and so see with their own eyes what God in his Holy Word commands and orders'. There were three levels of competence in reading: to read Luther's *Small Catechism*, to read Luther's *Preface* to the catechism and finally to 'learn the language of Scripture on which our faith rests, and also with their own simple words to say whether they understand its true meaning'. This was backed up by the compulsory catechism school every Sunday afternoon, and the work of the parish clerk, who should be literate, and had the duty of teaching basic religious knowledge. There was a powerful sanction: attainment of first-level reading proficiency was a requirement for confirmation and marriage. The experts will continue to dispute how effective this was; first-level competence could be gained by learning the text by heart, the level of literacy of many parish clerks is questionable and the incentive for humble folk to master the skills of reading was lacking. The king had no doubts; he applied the literacy requirements to his soldiers, as Spegel testified from his experience as chaplain to the Life Guard. Spegel paid for copies of the *Catechism*,

---

[28] Normann, *Prästerskapet*, pp. 101–46, 149–55, 232, 248, 265; Carlson, *Historia*, IV, p. 302.

and offered prizes for reading, but also sent the king a list of recalcitrants. The king promptly ordered them set in the stocks to encourage them; 'after that they became obedient and pious'. It seems established that literacy in early modern Sweden was high by European standards, and the *Catechism* ensured that all the king's subjects knew the basic Scripture texts on authority, particularly Romans 13: 'there is no authority but from God. The ruler who is in place is established by God. But they that set themselves against him set themselves against God's decree. And they that set themselves against, they shall receive damnation.'[29]

The services which the Church supplied to the royal government went far beyond this. The Church Law placed on the clergy broad duties of record keeping. Beyond the basic register of births, marriages and deaths, they maintained a census of their parish and its dwellings, an inventory of its communal resources, a parish history noting all unusual happenings and a register of catechism hearings. Potentially the Swedish crown had access to records beyond the dreams of most early modern governments. Beyond this the parish provided public services in addition to these educational and recording activities, being the basic level where authority interacted with the subject. In medieval times the parish in Sweden had a range of functions, which it carried out by the priest working with a parish assembly, which chose an executive group, analogous to the jury in the district Court, though it usually had six men. The Reformation, by stripping the parishes of most of their assets, had left little business to be done. But in the 1590s, reforming bishops like Laurentius Gothus and John Rudbeck realized that if the Church was to regain some of its autonomy, it needed a popular base. Hence the parish assembly was revived and resumed responsibility for local ecclesiastical discipline and community affairs. The regulation issued in 1619, being authoritarian, assumed the jury, or Parish Council, would be the active agent, but it seems parish priests learned they could work better with the general assembly, which generated real participatory democracy, where even women had a voice. The only basis in law was the Clergy Privileges of 1651, which stated that the priest has power 'to hold parish assemblies in the parish hall and the sacristy'. Their remit covered finance, discipline and 'other needs and activities pertinent to the congregation'. Meetings worked by consensus, majority votes were indicative only, and until a Diet resolution of 1697, it was unclear whether decisions were binding on absentees.[30]

The parish managed poor relief, raised funds, sometimes maintained a poor house, more often billeted paupers on households in return for labour, or issued begging licences. They might support education, paying for a school or giving the parish clerk a fee for his teaching work. They administered the common lands, organized wolf hunts, regulated new farms, licensed tradesmen and controlled their

---

[29] Ryden, ed., *Kyrkolag*, p. 45; Pleijel, *Kyrkans historia*, pp. 100, 103, 106; Wetterberg, ed., *Svedbergs*, pp. 123–4; Normann, *Prästerskapet*, p. 10.
[30] Pleijel, *Kyrkans historia*, pp. 90, 336, 338–42; Ingers, *Bonden*, pp. 328–31.

prices. Then they exercised discipline; it is clear they tried to keep their discipline problems within the parish, and avoid involving the bishop or the district Court. In the assembly the jury presented offences, though they could also be presented from the floor, and the assembly resolved cases, with the traditional aim of conciliation rather than punishment. But serious offences like blaspheming or oath breaking could lead to fines or setting in the pillory. It is apparent that many offences that should have gone to the district Court were resolved in the parish.[31]

Charles XI was content to see parish self-government integrated in the general machinery of social control. The proclamation against swearing and sabbath breaking, of October 1687, provided the first offences were dealt with in the parish. It was only after a third offence that the accused were referred to the district Court, where penalties could be much harder. Though the king, on occasion, provided back-up to the system. In 1688 he ordered that on Sundays in Stockholm, half the Life Guard would attend church, the other half would be on patrol to hunt out absentees during service time. But the king's appreciation of the advantages of popular participation came out most clearly in his attitude to election of parish priests. In most of early modern Europe, where the graduate, professional clergy-man was becoming a figure of authority, detached from his parishioners and part of the ruling elite, the election of the priest by the common folk would have flouted the structure of authority coming down from above. In Sweden the position had been ambivalent; there was no established right to elect in crown parishes, or where a nobleman held the patronage. Elsewhere the bishops had asserted a right to suggest candidates and veto unsuitable choices. The Church Law, on the contrary, reinforces free choice for the parishioners. On a vacancy they had six months to choose a successor, with the bishop simply supervising the process, and even in crown livings, the parishioners could petition for the right to elect. It was common for hard-headed peasants to make it condition of appointment that the incomer marry the widow of the previous incumbent, thus saving expense, or chose his son to succeed the deceased, for the same end. The Church Law did not forbid this, only insisted that parish livings 'are nobody's hereditary right, but a free and orderly choice, which with good reason should fall on those who are best qualified or most deserving'. When the archbishop complained to the king, in 1687, that parishes were choosing candidates from outside their diocese, breaking a long-standing rule to the contrary, the king defended free choice. 'Since priests get most of their income from the parishioners, so it is very damaging to force some priest on them, against the will and pleasure of the congregation.' He then added how important it was to maintain 'the love which should exist between the pastor and his flock, which can be promoted most readily and easily if the congregation is left to its free choice'. The king was accepting that common people do have rights to a voice in some of the decisions which affect them, and that it was in the public interest to

[31] Ingers, *Bonden*, pp. 332–4, 336, 338–42; Pleijel, *Kyrkans historia*, pp. 92–6.

encourage a relationship of reciprocal dependency between the priest and his parishioners.[32]

The Swedish Lutheran Church had a very important place in the machinery of government, which arose from its being a church of the people. It was virtually all-inclusive, and it was run by commoners; children of the nobility almost never entered the clerical career. The Church recruited from two sources, bright sons of peasants who managed to get an education, and increasingly the sons of the clergy themselves. Studies of university graduates show that those of peasant origin nearly always made their careers in the Church, not in the royal service. But in both cases, the priests came from the same social level as their parishioners. This meant that the parish clergy, not just the priests but also their assistants and chaplains, could play a pivotal role in administration. The clergy transmitted the government's orders, and explained and justified them, and gave the government invaluable statistical information. But the clergy were not only government agents, they also spoke for the community to the government. The priest's position as chairman of the parish assembly was crucial. It was the clergy who drafted the petitions and letters from the peasant communities to the authorities, and acted as mediators. A recent study of popular discontent in Kexholm province has shown how the local clergy wrote documents, used parish funds to finance deputations to Stockholm, wrote the necessary travel passes for the peasant delegates. In the end the Governor complained to the bishop, who intervened to restrain his clergy.

Kexholm was not typical, and in this case special factors were involved, but there is evidence from the whole kingdom that the peasant communities expected the priest to be on their side. It was, of course, within the powers of the parish assembly to make the lives of their priests easier or more difficult. They could determine the stipend. Charles XI, in his usual search for standardization, proposed uniform remuneration for parish clergy. He was met by peasant protest; they wished 'to keep their customary agreements with their pastors, as something that they find more acceptable'. The king gave way, conceding there was a case for flexibility and instructed bishops and governors to ensure that the contracts were reasonable. It is clear the peasants realized the advantage of a negotiated customer–supplier relationship.[33]

The Church was a vital component of the absolutist system of government. It propagated its values, proclaimed its legitimacy and rendered important administrative services. But it also provided that within the system, which was an authoritarian hierarchy, the common people at the bottom, who were the vast majority, were not just passive objects of government by the elites, but had their own input

[32] A. A. von Stiernman, ed., *Samling utaf kongl. Bref, Stadgar, och Förordningar angående Sveriges Rikes commerce, politie och oeconomie*, IV (Stockholm, 1760), p. 991; Anjou, *Kyrkans historia*, pp. 528, 529, 531; Ryden, ed., *Kyrkolag*, pp. 242–6; Pleijel, *Kyrkans historia*, p. 82; Loenbom, ed., *Handlingar*, II, collection, V, p. 168, king to the archibishop 1687.

[33] K. Katajala, *Nälkäkapina, veronvuokraus ja talonpoikainen vastarinta Karjalassa 1683–1697* (Helsinki, 1994), pp. 279, 281, 282, 286, 288, 291; Pleijel, *Kyrkans historia*, p. 84.

into the processes of government. It is then clear that Charles XI, more than some of his bureaucrats and soldiers, thought that that was how it should be. Whether consciously or unconsciously he had grasped that an element of consultation and negotiation at the grass roots level would strengthen, rather than weaken, the authoritarian structure.

10

The external territories under the absolutism

By 1660 the king of Sweden was also lord of a string of peripheral territories, mostly acquired by conquest over the preceding hundred years, in addition to his core kingdom of Sweden–Finland. The acquisitions had not been the result of any coherent design, although some contemporary leaders, and many later historians, have sought to invent a rationalization of the process. Each territory had been taken for what seemed, at the time, compelling reasons, but collectively the 'empire' remained a miscellany of unconnected parts. They all presented the metropolitan government with two permanent problems: how to retain possession of the territories, and how to make them financially self-supporting, for they had always been a drain on the Swedish budget. These lands can be classified into distinct categories, of which the first were the frontier provinces taken from Denmark after the two wars of aggression of 1643–5 and 1657–60. The various Swedish regimes had always had a clear programme for these territories, full incorporation into the kingdom and assimilation of their inhabitants. There was a basis for this: their Norwegian and Danish inhabitants spoke distinct languages, which were yet sufficiently close to Swedish as to present no serious obstacle. The same kind of similarity applied to their legal and administrative systems and their social structures, while most important of all, they shared the Lutheran religion, with regional variations of practice. On the other hand, the differences were written into the successive peace treaties which transferred the territories. The treaty of Roskilde of 1658, confirmed in 1660 and 1679, guaranteed the inhabitants security of property, together with 'their customary rights, laws and ancient privileges and liberties, undisturbed and unhindered, so far as these do not extend or conflict with the fundamental laws of the Swedish crown, with which these ceded lands and provinces shall be incorporated in perpetuity'. But the treaties also assured them they could 'enjoy, together with the native Swedes, the same access to offices and titles'. It goes without saying that no Swedish government had any intention of giving them all the rights of Swedish subjects while they also retained their distinctive laws and institutions.[1]

Swedish policies had always aimed at total assimilation. The two Norwegian

[1] J. Rosen, 'Statsledning och provinspolitik under Sveriges stormaktstid: en forfattningshistorisk's kiss', *Scandia* 17 (1946), p. 224.

frontier provinces of Härjedalen and Jämtland and the Danish island of Gotland gave no serious problems. They were poor peasant communities, without resident noblemen or other elite groups capable of articulating protest. With the passage of time, and the phasing out of the original Norwegian/Danish clergy, who were gradually replaced by Swedes, the peasants did the only sensible thing and yielded to the powers that be. Matters were different in the Danish lands round the southern tip of the Scandinavian peninsula, Skåne, Halland, Bohuslän and Blekinge. The latter two were easier, since they also had few resident nobles, but most of Skåne and Halland belonged to the great European plain, where conditions had favoured large-scale demesne farming, concentrated on raising cattle for export. A tight group of some forty noble families made up a ruling oligarchy; in Skåne they owned 54% of the peasant farms, and possessed over a hundred extensive manors, and over these they enjoyed tax exemptions, and rights to labour services, more favourable than in Sweden, and in addition they enjoyed legal jurisdiction over their tenants and extensive church patronage.

The regency government after 1660 was not looking for confrontation, and magnates also acquired properties in Skåne by crown donation or purchase, on which they had the same rights as Danish noblemen, and so had no incentive to try to eliminate their traditional privileges. The Swedish government therefore confined its efforts to encouraging a larger Swedish presence by facilitating voluntary sales. In 1664 they suspended the transfer tax of one sixth, levied on money transferred out of the kingdom. The aim was 'to ease selling for the Danes by remitting the tax, so that the province may be peopled with Swedish subjects on whom we rely'. The result was disappointing; by 1673 some 28% of nobles' farms had been sold to Swedes, but most of these were absentee landlords, so that the administration of the properties remained in local hands. Other Swedes showed no enthusiasm for migrating to Skåne, so that on the eve of war only one priest in sixteen was Swedish, and it has been estimated that if the soldiers and administrators are counted, there were about 2,000 incomers in a community of 200,000. The Danish nobles took their places in the Riddarhus in 1664, but few entered crown service, while the university at Lund, established to encourage assimilation, was small and struggling.[2]

During the war Charles XI acquired first-hand experience of conditions in Skåne. The population welcomed the Danish invasion; significant numbers of clergy, burghers and officials openly resumed their Danish allegiance, while in the villages a dangerous guerilla movement developed, encouraged by the Danish king, with an escalating series of ambushes, attacks on couriers and supply trains, met by

[2] Ingers, *Bonden*, pp. 278–81; Nilsson, ed., *Svenska historien*, pp. 57–62; A. A. von Stiernman, ed., *Bihang utaf åtskillige allmena Handlingar ifrån år 1529 intil år 1698* (Stockholm, 1743), p. 408; J. Rosen, 'Sjättepenningen och den svenska godspolitiken i Skåne på 1600-talet', *Scandia* 15 (1943), pp. 41–6; K. Fabricius, *Skaanes overgang fra Danmark til Sverige: studier over nationalitetsskiftet i de Skaanske landskaber i de naermeste slaegtled efter Brömsebro og Roskildefriedene* (Copenhagen, 1952), III pp. 12–20.

punitive repression, summary executions, burning of villages, collective punishments. In this, though the king was following the rules of war, he showed considerable restraint. In agreement with Gyllenstierna, even after a year of bitter conflict, the king offered an amnesty and protection to all inhabitants willing to take an oath of loyalty. But experience convinced the king of the basic disaffection of the local population, and with Gyllenstierna plans were made for a post-war policy based on enforced assimilation. After the peace treaty, which again guaranteed the legal rights of the inhabitants, had been concluded, Gyllenstierna was appointed Governor General over the Danish provinces, and his instructions referred to 'the king's formed intention on this, and he should therefore so act in future, that the inhabitants themselves will desire a uniformity in this matter with the king's subjects in Sweden'. Shortly after Knut Hahn was installed as bishop of Lund with a prepared programme for integrating the Church. After the war, about a third of farms in Skåne were empty, in badly affected areas up to 70%, and this was worsened since the peace allowed a period of twelve months, during which any inhabitant was free to leave, and the Danish king encouraged them to go, so that around 10,000 collaborators and suspects left for Denmark. Swedish incomers were offered generous tax concessions to take the vacant farms.[3]

The unexpected demise of Gyllenstierna led the king to appoint Ascheberg as Governor General, a post he held until his death in 1693, so that the post-war reconstruction in Skåne was largely his work, and he immediately protested to the king at plans which amounted to ethnic cleansing. Ascheberg, of course, was not a native Swede which may have affected his approach, but he wrote at once to the king that although 'Johan Gyllenstierna had notably begun to put his hand to the work, and shown he was a good patriot and king's man . . . he also left posterity in suspense how far his proposals were practicable and could be carried out to a good effect'. It was Ascheberg's great strength that he enjoyed the entire confidence of the king, and could modify, or even disregard, instructions he disapproved of and get away with it. From the start the king assured him he had not intended 'that you should be obliged to carry out the plans, which the late Gyllenstierna had in hand down there for one thing or another, but rather modify what is in them'. Ascheberg wanted to use conciliation rather than coercion; he consistently recommended employing locals who showed loyalty and encouraged intermarriage with Swedes. His approach was expressed in a letter of 1687, praising the work of Bishop Hahn, 'who achieved much more with his gentleness than could have been brought about with force'.[4]

Hahn's instruction in July 1680 told him to start organizing his bishopric in the

[3] Fabricius, *Skaanes overgang*, III, pp. 33, 37, 44, 77, 96, 100, 107, 152, 186; Nilsson, ed., *Svenska historien*, pp. 125, 132, 137; M. Weibull, *Samlingar till Skånes historia, förkunskap och beskrifning: Tidskrift utgifven af Förening för Skånes Fornminnen och Historia genom M. Weibull*, 3 vols. (Lund, 1868–71), I, pp. 29, 35, 39; Pleijel, *Kyrkans historia*, pp. 47–50.
[4] J. Rosen, 'Rutger von Aschebergs ämbetsberättelse 1693', *Scandia* 17 (1946), pp. 13–15, 26; Åberg, *Karl XI*, pp. 136–7; Rosen, 'Sjättepenningen', p. 49.

Swedish manner, but discreetly, so 'it can appear that the province has not been forced, but accepted it with their good-will and agreement'. Hahn employed collaborationist local clergy to urge the parishes to petition the king for uniformity, reminding them to stress to the parishioners 'with what an unbreakable bond they are bound to their lawful ruler', and that 'he who sets himself against the ruler, sets himself against God'. The petitions soon started to come, 'that we may hereafter be regarded as an equal and uniform people with your royal Majesty's subjects in Sweden'. Thus Hahn's campaign prepared the ground for a meeting of clergy in Malmö in May 1681. Ascheberg welcomed them and declared how the king was pleased 'with the desire they themselves have expressed to incorporate themselves with our beloved Fatherland'. He promised financial assistance and warned them to look out for rumour mongers and dissidents. The meeting affirmed its loyalty and asked Hahn to petition the king for incorporation. The king graciously agreed, and in August visited Skåne and was able to reward Hahn's collaborators, and announce he was ending the investigation of wartime disloyalty and would pardon all but four of the clergy who had gone over to the Danes. It was a model operation; the clergy seem to have realized that Swedish rule was irreversible and, as was pointed out to them, they would enjoy a better status under Swedish law; the Danish law 'reeks of the Danish nobility's envy against the spiritual Estate'.[5]

After this strategic breakthrough, Hahn went on to attack the patronage rights of nobles, 'which can in no way deny or diminish the king's right of superiority in the Church', and the right of urban corporations to appoint school teachers, 'a great occasion to obstruct the king's intentions and plans gradually to accustom youth to the reading and use of the Swedish language'. But the key figure was the parish clerk, who was responsible for teaching basic literacy. Hahn was authorized to put out unsuitable clerks and override patronage rights to prevent unsuitable appointments, 'and especially those who do not urge and advise assimilation'. In 1684 all clerks were tested on their knowledge of Swedish, and those who were deficient could be compelled to retrain. The king backed this with the order to every parish to acquire Swedish Bibles and hymnals, and he had 2,000 Swedish ABC-books specially printed for Skåne. They had to work on the young, the entrenched conservatism of the old was unshakeable; as late as 1694 the provincial governor of Bohuslän complained that Danish usages still lingered there. In an optimistic report of 1684, Hahn claimed the policies were working.

There are many thousand children who know the Swedish catechism . . . and a large part of them read and write, which is stranger and more pleasing here for ordinary people, since it was previously very rare that a peasant was able to read in a book or write. I truly hope that this may be a means which tames and disciplines the people . . . At first almost all were discontented, since they had the impression from the other side, and from opponents here in

---

[5] Pleijel, *Kyrkans historia*, pp. 50–2; Weibull, *Skånes historia*, I, pp. 48, 50, 52, 55, 59; III, pp. 97, 114, 116, 127; Anjou, *Kyrkans historia*, pp. 373–4.

the province, that it was a foreign language and a new religion they were being burdened with: but now they see that the young children read and understand the Swedish catechism without any difficulty, and that we above all down here are trying to advance them in their Christian belief, they are well satisfied.

Hahn was basically right; the test came with the next attempted Danish invasion in 1710, when Skåne remained loyal to the crown. Once the clergy had demonstrated that collaboration paid, the burghers followed their example and petitioned for incorporation into the kingdom, and there is some evidence of meetings of peasants to do the same. Thus all the commoners had renounced their treaty rights to preserve their Danish customs and institutions.[6]

Dealings with the Skåne nobility were complicated by the king's resolve to apply the full reduktion to the province, by the complication of the transfer tax and by the position of Ascheberg. He did not disguise his dislike of aspects of reduktion policies, though he did apply them in his province. But he was in the same situation as Horn in Bremen-Verden; he was watched by a commoner-bureaucrat from the Chamber, G. Adlersten, who consistently criticized his financial administration. Ascheberg complained to Charles XI in 1684 that Adlersten continually insinuated that 'I made little or no effort over the king's service, or withheld my assistance, when someone needed it for your royal Majesty's service'. Adlersten had spotted an opening when he suggested to the king, during his visit in 1681, that money could be made from the transfer tax. The king could declare the suspension of the tax during his minority had been unlawful, and then claim repayment with interest, which in some cases would produce a demand equal to the value of the property, which could then be resumed. This outrageous legal chicanery was too much, even for a hardened absolutist like Gyllenborg, who argued in the Chamber 'it was harmful if they be charged with the levy of one sixth, if they purchased the property simply and openly when the regency's letter came out, since then it was a law'. But it was a character defect of Charles XI that he was prone to pursue immediate fiscal advantage, regardless of any collateral damage it might do. So the king resolved to prosecute his claims; as a royal letter put it: 'the nobility in Skåne, by unlawful advice, procured for themselves a resolution in Our minority', which was therefore invalid. The threat came at the time when Ascheberg was working to induce the Skåne nobility to petition for incorporation. He succeeded in holding back implementation of the scheme, and even won a concession from the king that the nobility could retain their advantageous manorial rights, 'partly because of the nature of the province and its traditional agriculture, partly because of the wholly different nature of its manorial farms'. Helped by this, Ascheberg was able to persuade the nobility to petition for incorporation in 1683. It was granted and the legal foundations for

---

[6] Anjou, *Kyrkans historia*, p. 374; Pleijel, *Kyrkans historia*, pp. 53–9; Weibull, *Skånes historia*, I, p. 60; Åberg, *Karl XI*, p. 138; Rosen, 'Statsledning och provinspolitik', pp. 266, 268.

the assimilation process had been secured by consent. Immediately the king acted in the characteristic style of his fiscal regime, and having got the incorporation, ordered Ascheberg to proceed with the full reduktion programme, and to recover the transfer tax. Ascheberg fought, with some success, to modify the policies, pursuing the rational aim of encouraging Danish landowners to sell to Swedes. It took six years to persuade a reluctant king, first to allow Ascheberg discretion whether to apply the tax to future purchases, then, even more reluctantly, to agree not to seek refunding on past purchases, where the sale had been made to a Swede. The crown did manage to extort 320,000 dsm., mainly from Danish landowners in the province. The end result was that by 1700 there were only six surviving Danish nobles in Skåne, and the old nobility, the most dangerous obstacle to successful assimilation, had been neutered.[7]

The aim of the fiscal policies was to raise enough revenue from Skåne to support its military establishment. In this they succeeded; in Ascheberg's last official report in 1693, he claimed that there was now a surplus on the ordinary budget, so that everyone was being paid in full and 'the provinces are not only capable of sustaining their own budget, but also are placing a good deal in reserve'. But the full indelningsverk could not be implemented in Skåne; the local cavalry regiment was put into the scheme, but the king insisted that the manpower should be native-born Swedes. Ascheberg pleaded to the end to experiment with local recruits; it would be effective in developing mutual confidence, and 'your Majesty's royal splendour, power and glory would be better known down here among the peasants'. But the king's rooted distrust was persistent; he rejected a petition from the tenants of the cavalry farms to be allowed to recruit locally: 'no other than Swedes born up here shall be accepted and employed in the regiment'. There was no attempt to introduce the knektehåll in Skåne, or to raise an infantry regiment, but Ascheberg used the possibility of conscription to induce peasants to win exemption by taking on tenancies of vacant crown farms. History records that the assimilation of conquered populations is a process with a very high failure rate. The successful assimilation of Skåne, which has endured to the present day, was one of the major successes of Charles XI's reign. In 1680 Ascheberg had reported on the 'secret aversion and concealed hatred between the Swedes and the inhabitants of these provinces . . . and with it an inner desire to be reunited with Denmark'. Some of the credit is the king's, for deciding after 1679 not to exact retribution from the disloyal provinces, and for his tolerance of Ascheberg's moderating activities. But if he, and the bureaucrats in Stockholm, had had their way, a harsher and more coercive regime would have been enforced. The credit belongs to Ascheberg and Hahn, whose judicious mixture of persuasion and manipulation, combined with the good luck that Ascheberg survived in control until 1693, and that the loyalty of the

---

[7] Nilsson, ed., *Svenska historien*, pp. 140, 200; Rosen, 'Aschebergs ämbetsberättelse', p. 9; Rosen, 'Sjättepenningen', pp. 46, 51–3, 59, 60, 61, 67, 69, 71, 76, 77, 84; RA, Kongliga concept: vol. 287, 1682, king's resolution 26 Oct. 1682; Ingers, *Bonden*, p. 280.

population was not tested again for thirty years after 1679, undermined the old Danish elites and steadily conditioned the new generation of Skånians to accept Swedish rule.[8]

The second category of external territories were the German duchies of Bremen-Verden, the enclave of Wismar and the duchy of Pomerania west of the Oder. These were all acquired during the Thirty Years War and confirmed to Sweden by the Peace of Westphalia. Legally they were no part of the kingdom of Sweden and could not become so, because they were territories of the Holy Roman Empire, only the ruler happened to be king of Sweden. Their legal and constitutional status was guaranteed by the treaties, and in each case shared authority between the ruler and the Estates, which had right of appeal against their ruler to the imperial Courts and the emperor. The king had a limited exemption from appeals from subjects individually, but had been obliged to establish a separate appeals Court, the Tribunal at Wismar, to which he nominated the President and Vice-President, but the six Assessors were appointed and paid by the Estates. The Tribunal would nearly always uphold provincial privilege against Swedish encroachment. Swedish law could not be introduced in the provinces, and they had only a small corps of Swedish officials, the Governors General and their staffs, since imperial law and local privilege reserved local offices for natives, and this included patronage in the Lutheran Church. In Charles XI's day no one seriously asked whether these territories were worth keeping, though a strong pragmatic argument could be made that they were not. It was accepted that possession was a major factor upholding Sweden's international position. Militarily they were a potential threat to Denmark from the south, but more importantly they symbolized Sweden's status as a power in Germany and a guarantor of the Westphalia settlements. The king of Sweden was a member of the Imperial Diet, and of the Upper and Lower Saxon Circles in the Empire. The problem they presented for the king was how to finance their defences. There was a case, put several times in the Council, for keeping a small field army in Germany, but the king always rejected this as too costly, and besides would be seen as a provocation by neighbouring rulers. So the policy was to maintain and garrison fortresses, manned by locally recruited mercenaries, supported by the modest local contingents the provinces were obliged to maintain for imperial service. These stood at 862 men from Bremen-Verden and 236 from Pomerania, but larger contingents could be called for when the Empire was at war. Charles XI was generally conscientious, for reasons of status, in fulfilling his obligations to the Empire.[9]

Charles XI's main preoccupation after that was to ensure that the provinces

---

[8] Rosen, 'Aschebergs ämbetsberättelse', pp. 18, 39, 42–4, 45, 49–50; Gahm-Persson, *Stadgar*, II, p. 5, king's resolution on the Skåne cavalry 17 Jan. 1686; B. Fredriksson, 'Krig och bönder', in Revera and Torstendahl, eds., *Börder*, pp. 163–73.

[9] W. Buchholz, 'Schwedische-Pommern als Territorium des deutsches Reichs 1648–1806', *Zeitschrift für neuere Rechtsgeschichte* (1990), pp. 16, 26–7, 28, 30.

covered their own expenses. He told Nils Bielke, Governor General of Pomerania from 1687, he must see the Pomeranian Estates met this requirement: 'you must say to them the budget requires so much, and you must contribute in accord with it, share it out among you the best you can'. But Pomerania had suffered severe war damage. Bielke reported on taking over that no official salaries had been paid for 1685 and only half-pay for 1686. In the capital, Stettin, there were 300–400 empty properties; in the countryside a third of the farms were untenanted. So the Swedish budget had been forced to subsidize Pomerania, and the king determined this must stop. He wrote: 'they must do what all my other provinces do, which have been in the war, and have since carried the burden alone, without getting any help from the kingdom'. He repeated this to Bielke later, revealing his tendency to identify strongly with Sweden, when he insisted the Pomeranian Estates 'must not imagine that my dear and faithful Swedish subjects shall be their servants'. Bielke offered a suggestion that they should copy other rulers, like the Elector of Brandenburg, and invite French Huguenot refugees to settle and boost the local economy. The king refused, ostensibly, as he wrote, because 'it may be found in the peace treaties that no other religion shall be allowed in Pomerania than the pure Lutheran evangelical doctrine'. From what is known of the king's thinking, it is more likely he agreed with his clergy that Calvinists were as bad as, or worse than, papists, and he was not going to pollute his province with their presence for mere material gain. So policy concentrated first on inducing the Pomeranian Estates to pay up. This was difficult, as Bielke reminded the king in 1687, because imperial law applied and must be observed. On the other hand the Estates had undertaken, in the Recess of 1681, to balance the budget by 1689. The king suggested that if they tackled tax evasion, and extended the excise, it could be done, but the Estates proved unreceptive, and sheltered behind their legal rights. Charles XI, who had no experience of such recalcitrance from the Swedish Diet, was baffled; he wrote Bielke that they were forgetting their duty, 'as if they were not our subjects at all, but a separate republic with which we must formally negotiate'. Their duty was 'to receive law and regulations, but are in no way authorized to make or prescribe them'. The king told Bielke to proceed without consent because the Estates 'are obliged to the ruler ordained by God'. The Estates then opened negotiations, and the king noted: 'the Pomeranians are beginning to behave like Christians. But as far as their proposed conditions go, I regard them as very hazardous to accept, for I note well that they always want to bind my hands.' The latter was absolutely ruled out in absolutist thinking, as incompatible with God's ruling on the relationship between a king and his subjects. The king, fully conscious of his own integrity, just could not understand: 'I would like to hear from them if the interests of myself and the country are not all one, not distinct. For I ask nothing more of them than they keep up a militia there which can be a defence to the country.' Gustav de la Gardie, who was sent over to reinforce Bielke, had to report the Estates were immovable, they would give no reasoned replies, 'but only say like the Poles, Nie pas volo'. The German style of political bargaining between Estates and rulers was quite alien to the Swedish elites.[10]

In 1690 the king raised the stakes. He put forward an offer: he would guarantee to keep military expenditure fixed, if the Estates would fund it, and if any surplus developed on the budget, the Estates could dispose of it. But he also demanded the acceptance of reduktion for Pomerania. The Estates replied that if reduktion were applied, they must be allowed to administer it. The king refused that, and after further negotiation, in March 1692, simply ordered that reduktion be enforced; those who cooperated would be offered the chance to lease back their donated properties, those who did not would be sequestered and taken to the Tribunal at Wismar. The king then met obstruction from Bielke, who was opposed both to enforcing reduktion, and to the whole current line of the king's foreign policy. Bielke first asked for a transfer, preferably to a military command, and when told to stay on and carry out the policy, asked that the Estates be allowed to participate, knowing this would hold up the process. The king told him the Estates had no competence: 'the decision has been made by the sovereign authority'. Bielke then urged he was unqualified in such matters; the king replied: 'the business is not so complex that your capacities, which cope easily with everything else, cannot handle it'. Both Bielke and the Pomeranian Estates were miscalculating: the former was presuming on his intimacy with the king to the point of defying his orders; the latter supposed they could offset any revenue regained by reduktion against their tax obligations. Charles XI did not play that kind of game with subjects; he told them what their duty was and expected them to find ways of complying. Bielke was told by the king he was in disfavour; he tried to plead his record of service, but was informed in March 1693 it was the duty of a king to correct erring subjects. A king, he wrote, 'is an echo that gives a pleasing response when a pleasing call comes in, but on the contrary gives a discouraging response, when something objectionable is shouted'. The king made Gustav de la Gardie President of the Reduktion Comission for Pomerania, and told Bielke he must cooperate. He had no choice, though he complained bitterly to friends of how disadvantaged he was, stuck in Pomerania, while his enemies had the ear of the king in Stockholm. He could do nothing but comply and work his way back into favour by loyal service.[11]

The Pomeranian reduktion was a model of Charles XI's style of government. He personally drove it forward, disregarding all protests. In May 1694 all the local administrators were told to work on it daily from 8 to 12 in the morning, and send him monthly progress reports. De la Gardie was literally killed by his labours on it.

---

[10] Malmström, 'Karl XIs bref till Nils Bielke', p. 30, king to Bielke 26 Nov. 1687; p. 50, same 23 Oct. 1688; p. 60, same 1 May 1689; p. 64, same 17 Oct. 1689; p. 67, same 23 Nov. 1689; Malmström, *Nils Bielke*, pp. 4, 5, 7, 9, 14, 37, 40, 47, 49; RA, Skrivelser till konungen, Karl XIs tid, D, G.A. de la Gardie to the king 13 Apr. 1689.

[11] Malmström, *Nils Bielke*, pp. 101, 104, 123, 128, 129, 132, 133, 136–8, 142, 143, 147; Carlson, *Historia*, IV, pp. 151–6; Malmström, 'Karl XIs bref till Nils Bielke', p. 78, king to Bielke 16 Nov. 1690; p. 81, same 17 Dec. 1696.

Bielke survived and got his reward, he was restored to favour in 1694, when the king wrote: 'you can be assured that We recognize with special gracious approval, the zeal with which you promote the reduktion process; you have done Us a true service, and We shall not fail to acknowledge it on all occasions'. The Estates too yielded to the royal will; they denied they had ever opposed reduktion in principle, they had merely wanted to be consulted, and they then conceded a satisfactory settlement of the Pomeranian budget. The fruits of the king's effort were however disappointing; the revenues recovered in the Pomeranian reduktion amounted to only 66,500 dsm., the smallest yield of all the external territories. The need to respect imperial law limited the possibilities; for example some recipients of donations had taken the precaution of getting them confirmed by the emperor, and the king accepted it would be impolitic to challenge them, just as he was careful not to pursue his argument with the Estates to the point where they might appeal for imperial intervention. On the other hand, by 1696 Pomerania was financially self-supporting, and its military establishment and fortifications had been modestly improved. The other German territories gave no trouble; Wismar was an enclave containing a major fortress; it had no possibility of covering its costs, but Bremen-Verden was a more affluent region, little damaged in the war, where the Swedish administration under Horn had a comfortable working relationship with the Estates. Its budget showed a surplus, which was used to support Wismar, so that by the 1690s the German provinces presented no financial problem. Further Bremen-Verden consisted of two secularized bishoprics and the king applied reduktion by reclaiming the former episcopal estates, which caused little trouble there, and brought in an additional revenue of 223,000 dsm., almost four times the yield in Pomerania.[12]

The final group of peripheral territories was clustered round the eastern Baltic shore. It had three components. First were the two frontier provinces of Kexholm and Ingermanland, ceded by Russia in the peace of Stolbova in 1617. Second was Estland, a part of the former lands of the Teutonic Knights, which in 1563 had sought the protection of the king of Sweden. This had been a voluntary transfer of allegiance and the treaty included all the usual binding assurances that the rights and liberties of the province would be preserved. Third was the much more substantial province of Livland, another section of the lands of the Teutonic Knights, and its status was debatable. In the 1560s it had accepted the overlordship of the king of Poland, on the usual terms. But it had unquestionably been conquered by Gustav II Adolf and then ceded by Poland to Sweden. So it could either be regarded as a conquered province, in which the case the king of Sweden had a free hand, or the acquisition could be seen as a transfer of overlordship from the king of Poland, in which case the guarantees he had given were still in force. This distinction became an important issue under Charles XI. Finally there was the

---

[12] Malmström, *Nils Bielke*, pp. 135, 146, 148, 149, 150; Carlson, *Historia*, II, p. 286.

island of Ösel, a last fragment of Danish empire in the eastern Baltic, ceded to Sweden in 1645. It was geographically and ethnically part of Estland, but ranked as a separate province.[13]

Kexholm and Ingermanland were undeveloped frontier wilderness; the expectation that trade with the Russian interior would pass through to the Baltic was not realized. Further a large part of the original population of Orthodox Karelians, Ingrians and Russians had chosen to move back into Russia, anticipating correctly they would be persecuted by the Lutheran administration. There was some immigration of Finnish peasant settlers, but official efforts to attract migrants and forced settlement of criminals and undesirables from Sweden–Finland had only a marginal effect. The crown tried to deal with the area by making large donations to Swedish counts and barons, who, as absentee landlords, left the administration to local bailiffs and stewards, who frequently doubled as crown officials, under a Governor General in Narva, and subordinate Governors for Kexholm and Ingermanland. Swedish law and administrative structures were introduced, and it would have been reasonable to attach the area to Finland. But although the *hovrätt* at Åbo was the appeal Court, and the Finnish bishop of Viborg shared ecclesiastical administration with the Superintendant of Narva, the provinces were not incorporated and not represented in the Diet. Charles XI had two concerns in this remote frontier area: one was defence and there were plans to fortify Narva and other strategic points, but since the Russians were quiescent after 1660 these had low priority and little was done. The other was reduktion, since the donations fell in under the legislation of 1680. Protests from the donatees were brushed aside and that left the problem how to administer them. Initially the king intended to follow the advice of Governor General Hindrich Piper to retain the properties and put them into an indelningsverk to cover the costs of local administration. In 1683 a new Governor General, Göran Sperling, said direct administration was costly; it was very difficult to use revenues in kind in such a remote region, and in April 1684 recommended fixing the peasant taxes, and then leasing the properties to contractors for a fixed rent. The contractor could collect the taxes, and would be entitled to reasonable labour services to work the demesne, and take his profit from the proceeds of demesne farming, which would be tax free. This had the further implication that all crown properties must be included, since any that remained under crown administration would be seen as offering the tenants more favourable conditions, and peasants would seek to move into them, and the contractors have difficulties taking their profit.[14]

The king accepted the advice because it promised to reduce costs, and the effect was to establish a colonial settler regime. The contracts were taken by the old estate

---

[13] M. Roberts, *The Swedish imperial experience 1560–1718* (Cambridge, 1979), pp. 87–94; S. Lundkvist, 'The experience of empire', in M. Roberts, ed., *Sweden's age of greatness* (London, 1973), pp. 39–45; Nilsson, ed., *Svenska historien*, pp. 200–3.

[14] Carlson, *Historia*, ii, p. 277; Katajala, *Nälkäkapina*, pp. 72, 73, 76, 89, 91–3, 95–6, 99, 102, 120.

administrators, local garrison officers and even some NCOs, and other crown officials. These constituted a settler elite seeking to exploit the peasantry, and working together in the colonial administration in support of one another. The peasants were not helpless victims; they had the right of all the king's subjects to petition, and showed considerable organizing ability in drafting complaints and sending delegations to Stockholm. They got their hearing, but usually the case was referred back for settlement by the local Courts. Evidence from Kexholm suggests that the settlers managed to control the district Court juries, so that a high proportion of complaints were dismissed as groundless. Occasionally, peasant discontent got out of hand, and there was rioting, in which case the local garrison was always at the service of the settlers to restore order. Thus Kexholm and Ingermanland continued as colonial backwaters, and the opportunity offered after 1680 to bring them under direct crown administration and incorporate them into the kingdom was passed over as too demanding of resources.[15]

Estland and Livland were also colonial settler societies but of a quite different character. The ruling elites, the landlords, garrison officers, urban corporations, which included two towns, Riga and Reval, which were major centres of Baltic commerce, and the clergy were the heirs of medieval German colonists, except that in Livland the crown had made major donations to Swedish nobles, who, mainly as absentee landlords, held nearly half the farms. The language, laws and culture of the society were German, as were its institutions of self-government. There was a Diet, the *Landtag*, representing the landlords and the Corporation of Riga, which elected its own Marshal, and a standing executive committee, the *Landrat*, as their collective representative to the ruler. Estland had its own comparable Diet. The countryside was controlled by the landlords, with powers of feudal jurisdiction over the peasantry and full control of clerical patronage. The Estonian or Lettish peasantry, descendants of the aboriginal inhabitants conquered by the Teutonic Knights, were serfs, brutally exploited, with no defensible legal rights, alienated by language and tradition from the German elites. The region was notorious as one of the most oppressive feudal regimes in Europe. The Swedish landlords, despite the example of the Oxenstiernas, among whom Axel Oxenstierna had prided himself on seeing his peasants as human, and entitled to reasonable treatment, quickly adopted the local values. In the first flush of conquest, the Swedish government had contemplated a policy of assimilation, but it had not been pursued and there was little enthusiasm on either side. If anything the Swedish policies developed local autonomy. There was a Swedish Governor General in Riga, assisted by a Swedish Secretary, a German Secretary and a Treasurer. The Governor General was vested with the full powers of the king. There were provincial governors for each of the Circles into which the provinces were divided. The Swedish administration had tended to upgrade the role of the Diet. In Livland, in 1648, the size of the *Landrat*

---

[15] Katajala, *Nälkäkapina*, pp. 122, 123, 125–30, 135–8, 159, 226–30.

was doubled to twelve members, half Swedish, half German, and four of them sat as Assessors in the appeal Court, the *hovrätt*, at Dorpat. The nobility had the duty of maintaining a militia, which they officered themselves.[16]

The events in Livland are interesting for an understanding of the absolutist regime, because they represented the only occasion on which a determined body of the king's subjects openly opposed his policies, and sought to use their legal rights and privileges against the king's assertion of his sovereign power. It is, however, necessary to bear in mind that although the Livlanders were legally the king's subjects, in the king's mind, the relation between them and their ruler was qualitatively different from that between the king and his Swedish–Finnish subjects. The big issue between Charles XI and his subjects in Livland and Estland was the application of the reduktion in the provinces. One problem was how far the legislation of a Swedish Diet, in which these provinces were not represented, was binding on them. Another, much more important, was the fact that given their history, as societies formed by colonial conquest, it could be argued that almost all land titles derived from donation by the crown, or its legal predecessors, and could be recalled. It is estimated that in Livland, in 1680, 84% of properties were donations, and in the whole province, only 1.25% of properties were still in the possession of the crown. The potential impact of a full reduktion was enormous, though complicated by the fact that in 1680, half the donated property was held by Swedes.[17]

The threat had been posed first by the reduktion law of 1655, which left it to the crown's discretion how far it applied to the non-Swedish provinces, in the light of the laws and customs of each. Nothing had been done to implement this, but the Livland nobility were sufficiently concerned to draw up a statement of their rights in the Diet, and send a deputation to present it to the king in 1678. The king's reply assured them that any reduktion would be negotiated with the Diet and that 'the nobility shall in no way be disturbed in its established properties'. But it added at the end a standard reservation: 'Our and the kingdom's superiority and right is reserved in everything'. The Livland nobility thought they had a firm assurance that there would be no reduktion without their consent; the king thought otherwise, for after the Diet of 1680 he appointed a Reduktion Commission for Livland under Robert Lichton, with the remit that all donations made since the Swedish conquest were liable to resumption, but they could be offered back on lease to the existing holders. The nobility were assured by the Governor General that nothing would be implemented without consultation, but Lichton's instruction belies this; the assurance was cosmetic, to create 'a favourable impression in the world'. The king would base his actions on his sovereign right to recover all former public property. When the Diet met in 1681 it naturally stood on the assurance of 1678, but was told this could not affect the king's right to use his sovereign power for the

[16] E. Dunsdorfs, *The Livonian estates of Axel Oxenstierna* (Stockholm, 1981), pp. 3, 4, 5.
[17] A. Isberg, *Karl XI och den livländska adeln 1684–1695: studier rörande karolinska enväldets införande i Livland* (Lund, 1953), pp. 3, 8, 11, 14.

common good. The issue was determined. When the Estland nobility pleaded to be exempted, they too were told that no part of the king's dominions could be excused from contributing to the general welfare.[18]

In practice the regime moved cautiously; the limitation to donations made since the Swedish conquest meant that most of those affected would be Swedes, and for the Germans, this would eliminate the Swedish presence from the Diet and the *Landrat* and restore German hegemony. The donations to Germans, which represented 40% of all property at risk, mostly dated from before the conquest. Further the Germans, where they were involved, were to be offered a perpetual lease of their family estates, so did not face dispossession, although the rental would constitute a standing tax on properties that had previously been tax exempt. In August 1685 the main Reduktion Commission in Stockholm reviewed the Livland situation. Wrede, as President, argued the Diet Resolutions of 1680 and 1682 had removed all limitations, so the process could also extend to the pre-conquest donations. Anders Lindhielm made a lawyer's objection that this would violate the Livland privileges, but the king supported the hard line. The Diet Resolutions overrode all privilege and nullified the letter of 1678. But for tactical reasons they decided to take the post-conquest properties first. To clear the way there was a change of control in Riga. The Governor General was the magnate Krister Horn, appointed in 1674, and the two commoner bureaucrats sent to prepare the ground, J. Schneckenschöld and M. Strokirch, found him unenthusiastic. It was probably they who prompted the king to write to Horn, in November 1685, that he heard Horn wished to retire. Horn replied the reports were untrue, though he would retire if suitably compensated. Schneckenschöld then moved to speed him on his way by bringing charges before the Chamber that there were irregularities in Horn's accounts. Horn appealed to Charles XI to protect him, and the king offered to withdraw the case, but only if Horn retired unconditionally, and without compensation; he must surrender 'his outstanding claims of whatever kind they may be'. This was an offer Horn could not refuse, even though evidence suggests he had been framed by Schneckenschöld. It was a good example of the devious ruthlessness and bureaucratic infighting in Charles XI's administration. The king went along with it, because he got rid of Horn cheaply and without a public confrontation. In February 1686 he appointed a new Governor General, Jakob Hastfer. He was by birth a Baltic-German, a successful soldier ennobled in 1678, and intimate with the king as commander of the Life Guard. He went on to become a member of the Council and a field marshal. Hastfer was a brutal and ruthless man, and his remit was to break resistance by the Livland nobility to an unrestricted reduktion. But he also knew the local circumstances, and as a practical administrator, often argued for restraint.[19]

When the Livland nobles were refused a Diet to discuss the extension of the reduktion, they began to organize their resistance. They sent a letter of protest to

[18] *Ibid.*, pp. 6, 13, 15, 16–18; Carlson, *Historia*, II, pp. 283, 284.
[19] Isberg, *Livländska adeln*, pp. 28, 33, 44, 46–8.

the king, stating that resolutions of the Swedish Diet were of no effect in Livland: 'kein Reichstags-beschluss EKM Wort und Hand ändern, noch uns vom EKM Gnade und Erbarming abtrennen' ('no Diet Resolution [can] alter your royal Majesty's word and hand, or deprive us of your royal Majesty's grace and compassion'). They conceded nearly all Livland property was donation and asserted they faced total ruin. The king rejected the protest, but agreed to call the Diet in January 1686. The Marshal, Gustav von Mengden, issued a call to fight: 'Man vom Schlaf der Sicherheit aufwachen, und, da nunmehr fast wenige ja keiner versichert wäre, dass ihn die Reduktion nicht treffen und gefahren dürf, nach Mitteln sich umsehen möchte, welche Gestalt das vorstehende Übel vom Lande abgekehrt werden könnte' ('We must awaken from the sleep of security, and now ever fewer and fewer are assured that a reduktion would not involve and end them, we must cast around for measures whose content will be able to avert from the Land the impending evils'). The Diet sent a formal protest to the king at the violation of the undertaking of 1678 and asserted only treason could justify confiscation of property. There was only one dissentient, a former Marshal, Otto Albedyl. Hastfer seized on this: in his response he said the reduktion was a regrettable necessity and the king could not compromise the public welfare of his dominions, but he noted the protest was not unanimous and demanded a list of names for and against. This was blatant intimidation, but based on the broad early modern commitment to seeking unanimity and consensus in decision making. Any mere majority decision could be challenged, and Albedyl, who had been close to Charles XI, had created the opening. Hastfer was also trying to conciliate; a letter assured the nobility that individual grievances could be considered by the king and stressed the offer of lease-back, but the request for a further Diet to consider this reply was refused. Hastfer said it would only provoke 'ein Haufen neue Lamentationer und Querellen' ('a heap of new complaints and disputes'). He then returned to Stockholm for the Diet of 1686 and did not return to Riga until July 1687.[20]

In February 1686 the Council had discussed the terms for the proposed leases, should they be perpetual, should cavalry service be included in the rentals. The king said the principle of lease-back was settled, 'since that the nobility shall get leases, that is promised them'. J. G. Stenbock said the rental must leave them a fair livelihood, but if the leases were perpetual they must first deal with the evils of serfdom, 'to abolish the darkness and tyranny over the peasants'. With the act of resumption, the peasants became the king's tenants, and this opening should be exploited to protect them: 'he thinks no nobleman hereafter shall have as much say over them as now'. Wrede had doubts whether the properties were viable without labour service, but he recommended favouring the small landowner; it was dangerous to create large estates. The king agreed; small landowners could have perpetual leases, but the leases for the big estates would be renewable. In all cases, however,

---

[20] *Ibid.*, pp. 38, 41, 42, 51, 52, 56, 57.

cavalry service must be extra. He too was concerned about serfdom, 'that the nobility may not tyrannize over the peasants as they wish'. The attitude of the king and his advisers to serfdom needs explaining: they were not sentimental men where the lower orders were concerned. But Swedes had tended to make a virtue of the fact that in Sweden the peasant was a free man and to claim this as evidence of the superiority of their society. The record suggests the king's attitude was both moral and pragmatic. He did in fact mitigate conditions of service on all properties that fell to the crown, and told the nobility that serfdom was 'against Christian love, hinders mutual trust between master and servant, and undermines all incentive to migrate into the province'. He told them no protests shall 'hinder Us from abolishing slavery on the properties that fall in to the crown'. It seems fair to credit Charles XI with genuine compassion for these unfortunates, who were after all his subjects, and fellow Christians it was his duty to protect. His actual measures were pragmatic, conditions were improved on the minority of property held by the crown and the new leases had provisions curtailing the more extreme forms of exploitation, and provided the peasants with access to legal redress. But he could not ignore Wrede's point that to abolish serfdom would wreck the local economy.[21]

When Hastfer returned to Riga in 1687 he called the Diet. There is no record of the debates on the king's replies, but they clearly revoked their protests, and Hastfer gave up his demand to see the voting lists of the previous Diet. The Diet expressed its gratitude for the lease-back scheme, merely expressing the humble expectation that 'die Gnaden Tur noch weiter öffnen und dero hochheiligen Wortes sich gnadigst erinnern' ('the door to grace will open ever wider and he will most graciously remember his most sacred word'). There followed a public ceremony at which the Estates took the formal oath of allegiance to Charles XI. Superintendent J. Fischer preached on the duties of subjects, and Hastfer reported he 'justifierte die Reduktionen mit herrlichen Gründen und bewegte einen jeden mit durchbringenden Worten zu ihrer schüldigen Plichte und Treue' ('justified the reduktion with sublime arguments and moved everyone, with penetrating language, to the duty and allegiance that they owe'). But in the Recess of the Diet, the Livlanders slipped in the petition that the king 'als ein sorghabenden Vater, ihrer allerhertigsten Bebrieffungen von 1678 eingedenk sei' ('as a caring father, will recall his most esteemed letters of 1678'). They were still trying to assert that the king's letter of 1678 had been valid. When Hastfer sent the Recess to Stockholm, he urged the king to overlook the implied criticism as an empty gesture. But he failed to understand the king's character; Charles XI took deep offence at the reference to 1678, and rebuked the Livlanders for their ingratitude and said if they persisted he would withdraw the lease-back arrangements. Hastfer felt he too was being criticized by the king, and urged the *Landrat* to strike the offensive reference from the Recess. The *Landrat*, now wholly German, refused and Hastfer declared the

---

[21] RA, Rådsprotokoll 1686, pp. 1663–71, meeting of 15 Feb. 1686; Carlson, *Historia*, II, pp. 279–81.

Recess unacceptable and void. The king then carried out his threat over lease-back by hardening the terms. Before leases were given, all properties would be revalued, naturally upwards so that the rents would be higher. And the large estates, defined as those worth more than 1,500 rd. a year, would be put on twelve-year leases to be auctioned to the highest bidder. This would exclude most of the German nobility from getting the leases.[22]

The king now drove his officials to maximize the returns and at the same time teach the Livland nobility a lesson in obedience. They began to call in the donations granted before the Swedish conquest. The first legal obstacle was the clause in the treaty of Oliva of 1660, which formally confirmed the transfer of Livland to Sweden, and guaranteed the nobility possession of the lands they held at the date of transfer. The king issued a ruling in 1688 that the Diet Resolution of 1682 had nullified this. He reinforced this by getting an opinion from an Estland judge, Gustav von Lode, that the pre-conquest donations had never been on allodial terms, they had been 'ein inngeschrenktes und conditioniertes Erblähn – oder Erbrecht, nicht aber ein Allodialrecht' ('a limited and conditional hereditary grant – or inheritable title, but not as an allodial right'). The Diet was reconvened in 1690 and resolved to send a delegation to Stockholm to plead their privileges, and the two men chosen were J. R. von Patkul and Leonhard von Budberg. Patkul's emergence as a leading figure in 1690 is a mystery; he was an obscure garrison officer with no previous political record. But he took the lead in a series of meetings in Stockholm, including personal interviews with Charles XI. No concessions were offered; the bureaucrats insisted on the king's sovereign right to resolve all contentious issues. This was endorsed by the Council. When they returned they were not allowed to report to a Diet, but the king authorized a *Konvent*, a meeting of the nobility only to settle the affairs of their Estate. This heard a report from Patkul, reaffirmed its stance on all the disputed issues and elected a standing Commission to act in their name, and guard against 'die Erhalt und Belästigung des Vaterlandes Immunitäten, Freiheiten und Priviligien' ('the preservation and infringements of the Fatherland's exemptions, liberties and privileges'). The members were the Marshal, Streiff von Lauenstein, Wolmar von Schlippenbach, von Mengden, Patkul and some lesser supporters of his. They drafted a protest to the king in May 1692.[23]

This document represents the only occasion on which Charles XI was openly challenged and told by his subjects that he had done wrong. He was told that Livland was desperate, that he had been misled by evil Councillors, that the terms for the reduktion were impossible and would ruin them all, that both nobles and peasants were being driven to emigrate and, as a parting shot, that if they had to choose between the present oppression and the miseries of a war, they might well prefer a war. This was signed by the Marshal and five other members of the Commission. Hastfer decided to punish Patkul first, and since he was a captain in

[22] Isberg, *Livländska adeln*, pp. 56–62, 63–74.
[23] *Ibid.*, pp. 76, 81–3, 101–6, 112, 119, 121, 125, 129–34, 148, 161–70, 175, 176.

the Riga garrison, court-martial him for mutiny. Patkul fled to Kurland to avoid an obviously rigged trial. Hastfer was sure he was the chief trouble-maker; he wrote to the king that Patkul 'diese Konstitution concipiert und ohne Zweifel auch autor derselben sei' ('drafted this document and without doubt is also the author of it'). It was decided to summon the signatories to Stockholm and put them on trial. The Diet was also convened and was challenged to say whether it approved the protest. They split, but a majority declared that they did, that they meant no offence to the king, but it was their duty to inform him of the truth. They were dismissed, but an encouraging number of individuals came to Hastfer to repudiate the protest; the resistance was cracking. The king decided to proceed with the prosecution of the signatories and they were called to Stockholm. In March 1694, the Council met to discuss how to handle the matter. The protest was read and denounced as scandalous; Wallenstedt said: 'these are serious and absolutely unfit expressions'. Hastfer said the complaints were groundless; Wrede said it was seditious: 'they are subjects and should obey their superior's command, and his will should be a law for them'. Falkenberg said if they did not repudiate it, 'it must be regarded as rebellion'. Bengt Oxenstierna was fiercest of all; the Diet had 'acted in everything like a Polish Diet'. The whole legal position of Livland should be reviewed: 'let their so-called privileges and all illegality and misconduct be abolished . . . then the king at his pleasure . . . sets law and order in the province in a better state and security, like a sovereign'. Most speakers disagreed with the king's suggestion that if the accused repented publicly they might be pardoned. It was decided to prosecute, and a Tribunal appointed, with Oxenstierna as President, and eleven other Councillors and officials as members.[24]

The trial opened in April, and Patkul was induced to appear under a formal safe-conduct. All the accused except Patkul pleaded that the content of the protest was the collective act of the nobility, though they offered to apologize for signing it and ask pardon; Patkul did not, he claimed he had merely been the secretary, not the author. It is to the credit of the Tribunal that it quickly realized it had a poor case in law. It could not be proved that Patkul had written it (though in fact he had), nor could they disprove the claim that it was the collective act of the nobility. The accused did not confess; key documents had been lost or could not be authenticated and the trial reached an impasse. In November it was Charles XI who insisted they proceed to judgement and sentence, at which point Patkul wisely left Stockholm. In December the Council met to consider the conclusions of the Tribunal. One accused had been acquitted, and Patkul was picked out as the chief criminal. He was sentenced to lose his right hand for having written it, and then to be executed. Three others were condemned to death. The king indicated he wanted no executions, and suggested three years' imprisonment as a commutation, but except for Hastfer, who had to think of his future in Livland, the Council insisted on harsher

[24] *Ibid.*, pp. 171–4, 186, 188, 190–2, 197, 201, 202, 212, 214, 216, 217, 221–5.

penalties, and they settled for six years' imprisonment. It had been a purely political exercise, designed to intimidate and demonstrate to all subjects that the actions of kings were not to be challenged.[25] The demonstration was followed by remedial action. A Commission in Stockholm considered the future of Livland: Hastfer argued strongly for incorporation in Sweden; Oxenstierna led the others in opposing this and it was resolved to reform the Livland Diet. It would be reduced in membership, and a committee like the Swedish Secret Committee instituted, to be nominated by the king. The *Landrat* and the office of Marshal were abolished; the king would nominate the presiding officer. Its powers were reduced to consenting to extraordinary taxation and presenting grievances. In August 1695, Hastfer returned to Riga and summoned a Diet under the new rules. The outcome of the Tribunal was formally communicated, and a sermon preached on 'Fear God, honour the king.' Hastfer addressed them. He reproached the Livlanders since, despite Charles XI's loving care of the province, 'einige unruhige und verirrete Köpte aus der Ritterschaft solche hohe Gnade nicht erkändt, sondern ihr untertänige Schuldigkeit gar vergessen' ('some restless and deceived heads among the nobility did not acknowledge his preeminent grace, but almost forgot their duty as subjects'). The king was merciful and gracious to all those not actually involved, but insisted on changes in the constitution. In the outcome, the only point debated was the abolition of the *Landrat*, but the presiding officer insisted the new nominated committee was much better; it would eliminate all the 'Misshelligheit, Streit und Jalousie' ('disagreement, conflict and jealousies') associated with elected committees. At the end Hastfer could report to the king that the result was excellent: the nobility were contrite and cooperative. So the one open challenge to the authority of Charles XI's regime ended in abject defeat. The absolute monarchy had steamrollered the opposition and asserted the fullness of royal power. In these monolithic political systems, there was no room for any concept of loyal opposition. All opposition to the will of the king was both blasphemy and sedition.[26]

The king's political victory in Livland paid big dividends. The full enforcement of the reduktion recovered revenues worth 5,500,000 dsm. in Livland. The nobility in Estland, who read the signals better and submitted in time, and could exploit their status as an acquired not a conquered province, got off lightly with 85,000 dsm. recovered, and their privileges and institutions intact. The result was that not only were these provinces self-sustaining financially, they were paying a subsidy of nearly 10% of the metropolitan budget. The salaries of the Council were paid from Livland revenue, so was a substantial part of the salaries of ambassadors, while the Admiralty got a generous subvention. Further, once the lease-back system operated, the crown received major receipts in kind, mainly grain, which were used to

---

[25] *Ibid.*, pp. 226–42, 244–8, 256, 261–70; RA, Rådsprotokoll, vol. 91a, meeting of 13 Dec. 1694.
[26] RA, Rådsprotokoll, vol. 91a, meetings of 20 Dec. 1694, 26 Jan. 1695; Isberg, *Livländska adeln*, pp. 275–89, 290, 293, 294.

stock up the fortresses and build up the reserve magazines which were being developed for relief of harvest failure. But it remained true that Charles XI had no vision of an imperial policy beyond achieving budgetary self-sufficiency, and improving the defences. There were developments that pointed to closer integration. Trade between Riga and Stockholm grew in the 1690s, mainly in grain, but this may be the fortuitous consequence of taking rents in kind. It became an enduring economic link that survived the loss of Livland after 1721, but it was no part of any planned policy. The most interesting development, which was deliberate to some extent, was to strengthen the Swedish presence in Livland and Estland. Gustav II Adolf had established the High Court at Dorpat, and the University in the same town. The High Court was influenced by Swedish law and in the 1690s there seems to be an intention to extend this. At least Lindschöld wrote to the king in 1690 about filling a vacancy, and how it was necessary for his service 'to have some good, honest Swedish man, when the new law and Swedish legal process are to be established among the subjects here in the province'. The city of Riga decided to change to Swedish law, and in the constitutional reform of 1695 a new crown law officer, the Circle Bailiff was introduced, and in 1699 the Swedish system of district Courts was ordered to be set up. The German nobility had largely boycotted the University of Dorpat as a Swedish institution, but then found a rule introduced that all candidates for office in Livland must qualify by two years' study there.[27]

The project nearest to the interests of Charles XI, and most threatening to the hegemony of the Baltic Germans, was his attempt to upgrade Church life in Estland and Livland. The Lutheran clergy there were German, and had little interest in crossing the language barrier to communicate with the Estonian and Lettish peasantry. This was unacceptable to Charles XI as a Christian prince, and he launched a policy of active intervention, overruling local claims of autonomy. He told the Governor of Estland in 1691 that 'We will exercise *jus episcopale*, as a right belonging solely to Us, there as everywhere else in Our kingdom and its subordinate provinces.' He enforced acceptance of the Church Law of 1686, and encouraged the training of Estonian and Lettish students at Dorpat, where the University was, for the first time, taking a serious interest in the local languages. The nobility were alarmed to see steps taken to translate the Bible into Estonian and Lettish, and by a royal order that there be no labour services demanded on Saturday afternoon or Sunday, so that the peasants could attend church, and a start was made to introduce parish schools for the peasants. Further the reduktion brought most Church patronage into crown control, opening the way to break the German grip on the parish ministry. This could indicate that there was an official project to bring about major social change in the provinces; it is not possible to judge, since the reforms only began in 1690 and were aborted by the war after 1700. But it could

---

[27] Cavallie, *Fred till Krig*, pp. 23, 26; RA, Skrivelser till konung, Karl XIs tid, Erik Lindschölds skrivelser till KM, Lindschöld to the king 23 Feb. 1690; Isberg, *Livländska adeln*, pp. 182, 289; RA, Rådsprotokoll, vol. 91a, meeting of 29 Mar. 1694.

have been that the king's genuine piety and the appetite of all bureaucratic machines to extend their power at the expense of local immunities were working in parallel. It certainly stands to the credit of Charles XI and his officials that they were the first rulers in the two provinces who took seriously the idea that the native Estonians and Letts were fellow Christians and entitled to be treated as such. On the other hand the possibilities of amelioration were restricted by the realities of early modern society. Estland and Livland could not be governed at all without the cooperation of the German Baltic nobles, burghers and clergy. In theory the king could have used the reduktion to break their power and emancipate the serfs; in fact, as the lease-back policy testified, he could not. Charles XI demonstrated in Livland the awesome power of an absolute king, but seventeenth-century reality imposed limits that could not be overridden.[28]

The story of Charles XI and the Baltic-German nobility leaves a glow of satisfaction. The Baltic-German nobles were as unpleasant a gang of robber barons as ever darkened the pages of European history. That they were defeated by a royal absolutist, as predatory in his will to power as they were themselves, has a certain moral fitness. It all showed the raw power of the absolutist idea. This nobility had possessed their lands, many of them for generations, and were accustomed to freedom to exploit their possessions without restriction. Yet they submitted to being stripped of them without violence. No one was killed in the process, though Patkul undoubtedly would have been had he not fled in time. Their submission looks like that of the Swedish nobility, but there was a difference. In Sweden–Finland the reduktion was solidly grounded on a plausible interpretation of the Land Law, and approved by the Diet. But the Swedish Diet Resolutions themselves expressed uncertainty how far they could apply to the external territories. The reduktion in Livland and Estland had been an act of pure power; as regards donation made by Swedish rulers after taking over, it rested on the claim that a reigning king, as sovereign, and acting for the public good, is not bound by the acts of his predecessors, or even by his own, as the king's disregard of his letter of 1678 showed. As for properties donated before the Swedish conquest, in Livland these were guaranteed in the treaty of Oliva, and in any case had, *de facto*, long been recognized as allodial. The legal case for extending reduktion to these properties was dubious, but since they comprised 40% of the properties available, the king was determined to have them. The nobility had tried all lawful means, through the Diet, the *Landrat* and by petitioning to enjoy their lawful privileges, and had been treated as rebels and intimidated by a blatantly unfair, pseudo-legal process. They were lucky that Charles XI was not a bloodthirsty or vengeful man, or some would have paid with their lives for challenging the express will of a lawful, Christian king. But physical force had played almost no part. The Livland nobility was trapped in the mental world of early modern Christian Europe. In face of a

[28] Normann, *Prästerskapet*, pp. 321–2; Carlson, *Historia*, III, pp. 176, 177; Roberts, *Imperial experience*, pp. 112–14.

legitimate, hereditary king there was no way a subject could legally defy his will. He could plead law, custom, privilege and liberties, but kings were empowered to override all of these in case of necessity, of which they were the sole judge. There was no way out of this circle except the unthinkable – a direct challenge to the decrees of divine providence.

The maturing of Charles XI's foreign policies

It has been remarked earlier that Charles XI did not feel able personally to direct his kingdom's foreign policy, but consulted routinely with the Council and his circle of advisers. The procedure for consulting the Council was described in a royal resolution in September 1684, which stated how Chancery had prepared a paper setting out the options, which the king had graciously received. 'And after the king permitted these matters to be examined in his Council and in his high royal presence, having graciously considered the speeches made by each of his royal Councillors, their opinions and humble reflections, so the king's Majesty has declared his royal will and resolutions as follows.' This was the routine for strategic planning: the day-to-day operation of foreign policy was handled in Chancery, where it was directed by Bengt Oxenstierna. In the second half of the reign the senior officers of the Chancery did revive collegiate consideration of day-to-day issues, but it was inevitable that much of the immediate business was decided by Oxenstierna himself, as he had explained in a long exculpatory memorandum of 1688. He asserted that he would have preferred collegiate working, 'since I can say without boasting that I love order', but this was not possible, 'therefore I am compelled now, as previously, to move forward and despatch everything that is important and will suffer no delay'. Thus Oxenstierna justified his role as senior policy adviser to the king for the whole period after his appointment in 1680. The critics at Court and in the bureaucracy, who sought to undermine his hegemony, were faced over the years with solid evidence that his policies were successful. In his memorandum he was able to appeal confidently to the king to recognize 'in what a difficult condition the main work stood, when your Majesty was pleased to give me direction of affairs'. His remit had been to keep the peace if that were possible and this, he claimed, with the help of God's Providence he had achieved.[1]

The king's resolution in 1684 set out the parameters for Swedish foreign policy. They accepted the Truce of Ratisbon, because Sweden wanted to keep the general peace, and the king had no fundamental quarrel with Louis XIV. He was prepared

[1] KB, Engströmska samlingen, B.II.1.12: Handlingar rörande konung Karl XIs regering, KMs slutlige gottfinnande Sept. 1684; RA, Kanslikollegiets Protokoll, 1686, meetings of 18, 19 May 1686; RA, Kanslikollegiets Protokoll, A.II a. 7, 1687–9, meetings of 29 Jan. 1689, 4, 8, 14 Feb. 1689, 1 Apr. 1689; RA, Skrivelser till konungen, Karl XIs tid, Bengt Oxenstiernas skrivelser till KM, letter of 2 May 1688.

to have normal relations with the French crown, though he reserved his position on Zweibrücken, which the Truce left under French control. But the king had grave doubts about the durability of the Truce, and would therefore maintain Sweden's commitment to the anti-French coalition. He would not 'separate himself from the friends and partners, with whom the king had formal alliance, but it would be best to uphold them'. Therefore the king was willing to discuss a commitment to military support of the coalition in case of war. The priority issue, however, was Holstein-Gottorp, and specifically Denmark's sequestration of the duke's possessions. This action of the king of Denmark,

the king cannot see otherwise than as an open violation of the Nordic treaties and since Denmark . . . does not wish to admit the king's good offices . . . but will rather bring things to a head than restore the duke, so there can be no doubt that his Majesty is justified in taking up arms against such insolence, and that his Majesty's own interest and security in maintaining peace in the North is close friendship and a strong alliance with the duke, and his own great concern that Denmark shall not keep such an accession of strength [from dispossessing the duke].

The reasons were elaborated in a memorandum for the Council of 1688. If Denmark

through the acquisition of Slesvig can get to round out its borders and be a united power, where formerly it was divided, then Denmark will become a more difficult neighbour than before to Sweden, and will not stop at Slesvig, but then go further on one side or the other, and therefore Sweden's interest demands, even if it were not that of the duke of Holstein, that Denmark shall always be kept preoccupied with the Holstein dispute.

From this it is apparent that Sweden did not want a peaceful resolution of the Holstein-Gottorp dispute, but was intending to keep it permanently unresolved, as a threat to Denmark.[2]

International developments in 1685–6 moved in Sweden's favour. Louis XIV demonstrated he had no intention of honouring the Truce, which resulted in the formation of the League of Augsburg in 1686 to restrain him. This coincided with the change of policy in Brandenburg, whose Elector gave up, temporarily, his claims on Pomerania in order to join the defence of the Rhine. Hence his alliance with Sweden in 1686. Charles XI built on this by joining the League of Augsburg in July 1686, as a prince of the Empire, and promised a contingent of 3,000 men for the proposed imperial army. He went further and reinforced his alliance with the United Provinces by undertaking, in case of war, to hire 6,000 men and twelve warships for Dutch service. This meant that the emperor, William of Orange and the German princes all had an interest in preventing a war developing over Holstein-Gottorp, which would help Louis XIV by distracting his opponents.

---

[2] KB, Engströmska samlingen, B.II. 1. 12: Handlingar; Stavenow, 'Sveriges politik tiden', p. 279.

Finally the king of Denmark miscalculated in 1686 by a sudden attempt on the Free City of Hamburg. This alarmed the princes of the Lower Saxon Circle, led by the brothers George William of Celle and Ernest Augustus of Lüneburg-Hanover, who had no wish to see Denmark strengthened in north-west Germany, and were supported by Brandenburg in threatening armed intervention. Denmark was forced to back down, and Charles XI tried to persuade the Lüneburg princes and Brandenburg to follow up by forcing the restoration of the duke of Holstein-Gottorp. The king's instructions for Wellingk, his agent with the Lüneberg princes, stressed 'we must connect the Hamburg and Holstein affairs so that they are not separated in the decision, but follow one another, step by step'. In this he failed, since once Denmark gave way on Hamburg, Brandenburg lost interest in using force on Denmark, and instead supported the emperor's initiative to establish a conference of ambassadors of the German princes concerned, to negotiate a settlement of the Holstein-Gottorp dispute. This conference established itself at Altona. All the king could secure was an undertaking from Lüneburg that if the diplomacy failed, they would join Sweden in forcing a settlement on Denmark.[3]

By the summer of 1688 it was clear that the Altona diplomacy was deadlocked. The Council discussed the situation in July and decided in favour of a military solution in alliance with Lüneburg. The international situation favoured this; a new European war was now inevitable, and the emperor and William of Orange, anxious to keep Charles XI in their camp, indicated they would not oppose a quick military solution. As Oxenstierna told the king, the international crisis was an opportunity, 'and if it is used correctly, an advantage may develop to your Majesty's interest, and considerably assist the restitution of his Highness, the duke of Holstein'. The king ordered open military preparations to begin, and assured Bielke, who worried that Denmark might launch a preemptive strike, and urged that Sweden should get her own blow in first, that 'God will be in support of us if Denmark is so immoral as to start something'. It took until February 1689 to conclude a treaty with Lüneburg for a joint operation. Sweden would attack from Skåne, and into Norway, while the Lüneburg forces came up from the south. Swedish mobilization, sanctioned by the Diet of 1689, began in earnest, though the king still hoped to avoid war. In a Chancery discussion Lindschöld urged restraint, 'as long as the country here remains in great poverty, worse than we may think. So that if the duke gets his satisfaction, then we could resolve the other matters amicably.' Oxenstierna agreed: 'God forbid that we strive after war: these war preparations have already brought the Danes to this offer of restitution, which is a sign they cannot sustain a war.' Pressure was stepped up in June, when Wachtmeister was ordered to take the fleet to sea, and engage the Danish fleet if he encountered it. The king of Denmark was strongly advised by Louis XIV to climb down, and on 20 June formally offered the full restitution of the duke of Holstein to all his lands. This settlement was

---

[3] Landberg, *Utrikespolitikens historia, I. 3*, pp. 231, 233–4; Stavenow, 'Sveriges politik tiden,' pp. 178–83, 186, 188, 189–91.

confirmed by the Altona powers and by William of Orange, now also king of England.[4]

This was the high point of Charles XI's achievement in foreign policy. By cautious exploitation of favourable conjunctures, arising from the developing European crisis, the Holstein-Gottorp dispute was resolved in Sweden's favour without any fighting. This left Sweden in a most advantageous position. As the only considerable military power not involved in the general war, none of the combatants could risk offending Charles XI and driving him into their opponents' camp; on the contrary they all had an incentive to try to enlist Sweden on their side. Charles XI naturally gave the credit to God. On 26 June 1689 he entered a rare reference to foreign affairs in his *Almanack*:

when I came to town I found a courier, Christopher Cronhielm, for me, who was sent from Colonel Mauritz Wellingk and had the good news with him that they had come to a conclusion of the Holstein affair. God be eternally thanked and praised, who has let this matter come to a happy end and blessed us all with a noble peace.

He wrote to Bielke of his satisfaction 'without a sword stroke to have achieved the desired outcome and conclusion. If the Almighty were pleased to increase the blessing already extended to Us, with the continuance of this achievement, so is Our comfort in it so much greater.'[5]

Yet Sweden's position after 1689 was always precarious, and complicated by an internal power struggle to undermine Oxenstierna and influence the king. Nils Bielke led the attack, advocating an alternative policy of covert collusion with Louis XIV, that Bielke believed might result in further territorial gains for Sweden in Germany. There were two urgent problems to be resolved: one was the development of relations with Denmark; the other problems raised for Swedish commerce by the Anglo-Dutch blockade of French ports. These were linked because Danish trade also suffered from the blockade. The Danish king, having lost the Holstein dispute, immediately proposed renewing the Nordic alliance and pursuing joint action against the blockade. He wrote to his sister, the queen, of his sacrifice for peace, but 'so consoliert mich doch hingegen, dass damit der bisherige stein des anstosses unserer heuser gehoben und zu einer guten vereinigung dass fundament wieder geleget worden' ('I comfort myself that in consequence, the previous stumbling block between our Houses is removed and the foundation established once more for a good agreement'). In reply, Ulrika Eleonora warned her brother against over optimism and with good reason. No sooner had the duke of Holstein recovered his lands, than he responded to urgings from Wellingk and Bielke to build a new fortress at Toning to secure them, and hire Swedish troops to garrison

---

[4] Stavenow, 'Sveriges politik tiden', pp. 262, 271, 279, 286, 289–90, 291, 298; Malmström, *Nils Bielke*, pp. 10, 24, 26, 32–6; Landberg, *Utrikespolitikens historia, I. 3*, p. 238; RA,Kanslikollegiets Protokoll, A.II a. 7, 1687–9, meetings of 1, 4, 16 Feb. 1689, 1 Apr. 1689.

[5] Landberg, *Utrikespolitikens historia, I. 3*, pp. 239–40; Hildebrand, ed. *Almanacksanteckiningar*, p. 162; Malmström, *Nils Bielke*, p. 36.

it. Bielke followed this by urging Charles XI to reinforce the alliance with the duke by marrying his daughter, Hedvig Sofia, to the duke's heir, Prince Frederick. The king liked the idea, but to his credit declined to commit his daughter before she was old enough to consent. The significance of these moves was to demonstrate how the Swedish leadership had no thought of conciliating Denmark, and would continue to use the duke of Holstein as a weapon against her. The alliance of Denmark and Sweden was formally renewed in March 1690, but in a truncated form, and the Council had already resolved to reject Danish proposals for joint action against the blockade.[6]

Sweden's position in relation to this was complicated. Charles XI, as king of Sweden, was neutral in the European war, and hoped to develop profitable trade with all the belligerents. But as a prince of the Empire he was part of the Augsburg coalition, and supplied troops for its struggle with France. It was then further compounded by the king's resentment of the enhanced status of William of Orange as king of Great Britain. He was committed to hiring warships to the United Provinces, though these were hardly needed by William in his new position. The king decided to hold his ships back, telling Oxenstierna that for his royal ships to serve under a republic was 'an offence against Our royal dignity', and on another occasion asserted: 'however great the friendship we have for him [William], Our dignity does not allow any concession to the king of England'. It was this cast of mind that gave Bielke and his allies openings to win the king over. Louis XIV sent an unofficial agent to Stockholm in 1689, who offered annuities to Swedish ministers, which Bielke accepted, and hinted that if Sweden only withheld her contingents to the alliance, French subsidies might be paid. Even Oxenstierna was influenced, for in March 1690 he read a long memorandum to the king. He argued that Sweden's supreme interest was to uphold a balance of power in Europe. The king, by pursuing this aim, could secure 'a considerable increase of his own glory and earn substantial merit in the whole Christian world, with many associated advantages and considerable profit'. Oxenstierna's case was that currently the balance had swung too far against Louis XIV, who was admittedly the original disturber of the peace. But the emperor had won striking victories over the Ottomans, and the House of Austria, 'after previous examples of such great and unexpected success, through the encouragement and instigation of the Jesuits . . . gradually and in time [will] return to its old maxims of oppressing Germany and its neighbours and especially the total extermination of the Protestants'. If, in addition, William of Orange overcame Louis XIV, he would 'grow to an all too extensive power'. So he recommended that while Sweden should hire the 6,000 men to the United Provinces, she could withhold the warships. Then they should negotiate with Lüneburg to build up a joint third force of 30,000 men in Germany,

---

[6] Malmström, *Ulrika Eleonora*, p. 119; Å. Stille, *Studier över Bengt Oxenstiernas politiska system och Sveriges förbindelser med Danmark och Holstein-Gottorp 1689–1692* (Uppsala, 1947), pp. 53, 55, 59, 90; Malmström, ed., 'Karl XIs bref till Nils Bielke', p. 62, letter of 17 Aug. 1689.

and propose armed mediation. The king could later recoup his expenses, and probably recover Zweibrücken.[7]

This memorandum from Oxenstierna, who had been consistently pro-imperialist and anti-French since his appointment, and always more enthusiastic for the Augsburg alliance than the king, exposes limitations in Swedish thinking about international affairs. Oxenstierna was stuck in the time warp of the Thirty Years War, imagining a triumphant emperor launching a new Edict of Restitution. Nor was his assessment of the current situation well founded, since 1690 was one of the best years of the war for Louis XIV, so that Oxenstierna, in September, appended a note to his memorandum, that since France had not collapsed it needed rethinking, 'according to the present state of things and as we can work out what is to come, but still so that the balance remains the basis of all policy making at all times'. It is indeed possible that in 1690, aware that Bielke's influence was rising, Oxenstierna was manoeuvring defensively. Bielke had a good year in 1690: he handled the duke of Holstein successfully, but also was brilliantly successful in managing Sweden's contingent for the Empire. He readily persuaded Charles XI to hold back sending the troops, urging they were needed for security against Denmark. The king hoped to avoid letting them go at all, but if that was impossible, 'the Councillor must so arrange that I get my troops back in the autumn'. So when Bielke skilfully exploited difficulties in negotiating transit for the contingent, so that it arrived too late to do any serious fighting, and then brought it back intact in October, the king was delighted. He wrote: 'with what joy I learned yesterday . . . that my troops are on the return march, I cannot describe. Thanking God with all my heart, who directs all, so strangely against human expectation. This is certainly God's work alone.' That was unfair to Bielke who had fixed the whole thing, but it also exposes a defect in the king's grasp of international affairs. All the king saw in 1690 was that Sweden was under no immediate threat, so why should his soldiers be wasted fighting other peoples' battles? It is one of the king's more attractive features that he genuinely disliked spilling his subjects' blood, an unusual attitude in a monarch of that time. He wrote to Bielke: 'Our people are too good to be led to the slaughter house.' In another letter he said: 'Our troops are too dear to Us and too expensive, that We should let them be thrown away like that and perish through scarcities.' The battle of Fleurus, in 1690, where the Swedish troops hired by William of Orange were nearly destroyed, only strengthened the king's attitude. It was the more professional Oxenstierna who argued in vain that such sacrifices were a necessary investment to sustain the king's international credibility.[8]

Through 1690, Oxenstierna appeared to be losing. Bielke had the support of

[7] Landberg, *Utrikespolitikens historia, I. 3*, p. 243; Carlson, *Historia*, IV, pp. 27, 32–6; Stille, *Studier*, pp. 115, 126, 133, 140; Å. Stille, 'Bengt Oxenstiernas memorial våren 1690', *Historiska studier tillägnade Nils Ahnlund 23.8.49* (Stockholm, 1949), pp. 205–14.

[8] Stille, 'Bengt Oxenstiernas Memorial', p. 214; Malmström, *Nils Bielke*, pp. 64–8, 74, 77, 78, 80, 81, 82, 84; Malmström, ed., 'Karl XIs bref till Nils Bielke', p. 72, letter of 27 July 1690; p. 74, letter of 16 Oct. 1690; Carlson, *Historia*, IV, pp. 24, 27, 28.

Lindschöld, until he died in June, and of Wrede and Gyllenstolpe. When William of Orange sent an envoy to offer subsidies and concession on the blockade, in return for stronger Swedish commitment to the alliance, only Oxenstierna argued for acceptance, and the Council rejected the offer. Bielke was now pushing the idea of third-force mediation, and negotiating actively on his own initiative to promote it. Oxenstierna could not block Danish proposals for cooperation against the blockade; in June 1691, the Danish king thought he was making headway on that, and wrote to the queen 'wie gott lob nun wore zwische Uns und Schweden ein gahr gutes vertrauen gestifftet worden und haben die Künste und intriguen, so Einige dagegen formiret solches nicht hindern können' ('how, God be praised, a firm confidence between Us and Sweden has been established and the tricks and intrigues, if some people should advance them against it, cannot hold it back'). He was mistaken; Oxenstierna, seconded by the imperial minister in Stockholm, was convincing the king that Bielke was engaging in unauthorized negotiations with foreign princes. When Bielke returned to Stockholm in 1691, he was confronted by Oxenstierna in Council and defeated, and the plan for an armed, third-party mediation rejected. The king told Bielke: 'it is best that I keep my hands free and arrange that nobody else but me offers mediation'. Oxenstierna prevented joint action on the blockade; instead he succeeded in getting worthwhile concessions for Swedish shipping by bilateral negotiation with William of Orange. The process of his recovery of influence was completed in 1692, when Bielke fell out of favour with the king, and in that year the agreed Swedish contingents for the allies were sent in good time, and incidentally suffered heavy losses.[9]

An indicator that Oxenstierna was recovering his grip was an order by the king to the Council in May 1692, to consider whether the last war had been caused by the French alliance. Oxenstierna prepared a long memorandum, which ran to thirty closely packed pages. This argued that Sweden had indeed been deceived and manipulated by the cunning of Feuquières into entering the war, 'although it was directly against Sweden's true interests'. The emperor had been willing to reward Sweden for staying neutral, so the war had been wholly avoidable. Oxenstierna asserted that a basic principle of Swedish policy must be 'that we allied ourselves with those powers whose interests were consistent with ours' and 'at all times to keep one maritime power in hand'. In the debate he rejected third-force mediation: 'I could not, without hurt to my conscience approve that proposal.' It was a plot to detach Sweden from the allies and embroil her with the emperor. The lesson of the last war was that France was useless as an ally, and the king should adhere to current policy, retain the confidence of the allies and pursue policies of neutrality and mediation. He concluded: 'if the current situation is used rightly, your Majesty can sit here at home and in the provinces in great security, and make himself so considerable with all the powers, that on all occasions they will seek your Majesty's

---

[9] Landberg, *Ultrikespolitikens historia, I. 3*, pp. 245–8; Malmström, ed., 'Karl XIs bref till Nils Bielke', p. 83, letter of 24 Jan. 1691; Malmström, *Ultrika Eleonora*, p. 126; Malström, *Nils Bielke*, pp. 128–9.

friendship and alliance'. It is not difficult to see why Oxenstierna won the argument. Bielke's policy offered wholly speculative gains of territory in Germany, of doubtful use to Sweden. Oxenstierna was realistic; with the support of the maritime powers and the emperor, Sweden was invulnerable to attack, except by Russia, which was not then a serious threat. The king could follow his resolve to avoid armed conflict, was saved spending extra money that would ruin his budget reforms, and left him free to perfect his internal changes in peace. When a new French minister, the comte d'Avaux, came to Stockholm in March 1693, he confirmed this assessment. 'Je trouve le crédit de M. le comte d'Oxenstierne si bien établi, qu'il y a peu d'apparence de le détruire, ainsi je ferai tout mon possible pour me mettre dans ses bons grâces' ('I find M. Oxenstierna's credit so well established that here is little likelihood of destroying it, so I shall do everything I can to win his good opinion'). In a later despatch he identified the reason for Oxenstierna's strength: 'qu'il n'entrât dans aucun engagement que lui pût attirer la guerre. Rien n'est plus selon l'humeur avaricieuse du roi de Suède, qui passe ses jours entières à travailler avec ce qu'on appelle les reductions' ('that he does not enter into any commitment that could draw him into war. Nothing is more in agreement with the avaricious disposition of the king of Sweden who spends entire days with what they call the reduction').[10]

Oxenstierna scored a further success late in 1692, when the emperor renewed his treaty of alliance, and excused Charles XI from providing further troop contingents, so that he was free to pursue mediation. This eased relations with the allies, and left the vexing problem of the treatment of Swedish shipping. A report from Chancery in 1692 was very harsh in its condemnation of Anglo-Dutch conduct. 'Your Majesty's navigation and trade have been suppressed, seamen maltreated and barbarously handled, and neither passes, public certificates or witness statements have any effect.' Oxenstierna had to fight to prevent the king agreeing to join Denmark in a policy of reprisals. In 1693 there was a further disturbance, when the Lüneburg princes were bought off by the emperor with the title of Elector of Hanover. Charles XI, as a prince of the Empire, had reservations; an electorate was a very prestigious dignity, and he worried over the prospect it could prejudice the chances that he, or his heir, might inherit the Palatinate electorate. Oxenstierna warmly welcomed this development; it was a setback to the Danish king, and his ambitions in Germany, and killed the third-force option. Bielke, out of favour and confined to Pomerania, seized on reports that Oxenstierna was in disgrace. In May 1693 he wrote hopefully to one correspondent: 'Oxenstern a eu un reprimande terrible, et le Roi de Suède est parti, sans lui avoir donné le main, après l'avoir traité terriblement mal sur l'affaire d'Hannover' ('Oxenstierna has got a terrifying reprimand and the king of Sweden has left without offering him his hand, after having

---

[10] RA, Skrivelser till konungen, Karl XIs tid, Bengt Oxenstiernas skrivelser till KM, memorandum of 17 May 1692; Correspondance diplomatique: vol. 73, d'Avaux: 1693 pt 1, p. 67, d'Avaux to Louis XIV 11 Mar. 1693; p. 100, same 25 Mar. 1693.

treated him terribly over the Hanover affair'). It seems this was wishful thinking based on rumour. Oxenstierna remained in control; he again frustrated the faction in Council that wanted to join Denmark in breaking the blockade by force, and once more brought off a successful bilateral agreement with the United Provinces, granting concessions to Swedish shipping. Oxenstierna's rooted hostility to Denmark was one of his strengths, for the king shared it. In 1694, the duke of Holstein alarmed them by showing signs of seeking conciliation with the Danish king, and sent home the Swedish garrison from Toning. It was fortunate for Charles XI that the old duke died at this point. His successor, Prince Frederick, was more deeply committed to accepting Swedish protection, and keen to assert his claim to keep independent armed forces. The Danish king withheld investiture, Sweden protested and a new confrontation was under way. It is evidence of the king's limited ability to think through his foreign policy and grasp the interconnections between events that he seems unaware how the standing threat of conflict with Denmark over Holstein-Gottorp, which may have weakened Denmark, seriously affected his relations with the emperor and Brandenburg, and indeed all the north German princes, whose support was vital to upholding the legal status of the duke, and who did not want further conflict.[11]

The king gave a comprehensive review of foreign policy to the Diet of 1693, which closely followed the views of Oxenstierna. It took credit for having avoided war in 1689 and said that relations with Denmark were now satisfactory. It was claimed that Sweden had fulfilled her obligations to the allies, and noted with satisfaction that the renewed alliance with the emperor accepted that Charles XI, as king of Sweden, was 'in neutrality and friendship' with the king of France. The king intended to stay out of the European conflict, 'reckoning the enjoyment of peace and neutrality as what can best bring service and profit to his kingdom and subjects'. The king defended a policy of mediation as a Swedish interest, because as long as the war continued, 'we are always in danger of becoming involved in it, often against our will and desire'. The report emphasized the principle of pursuing a balance of power: 'the major interest the king has in the general situation [is] that no one power or another shall get such a preponderance, that the kingdom of Sweden, as well as others, shall suffer for it'. This was a well-reasoned programme, and it was more or less adhered to for the rest of the reign. There was the danger that if it became too obvious that Sweden would never take part in the war, the belligerents might decide she could be disregarded. But as long as the king was known to have a substantial army and navy in a high state of readiness, that was unlikely to occur. The weak link in the policy was the king's narrow focus on Sweden's immediate interests, an attitude that can appear parochial, and his inability to grasp wider European perspectives. His unusual reluctance to sacrifice his subjects' lives in the service of other powers suggests he was not much

[11] RA, Kanslikollegium till KM: I, 1656–95, letter of 5 Sept. 1692; Landberg, *Utrikespolitikens historia,* I. 3, pp. 247, 248, 250–2; Stille, *Studier,* pp. 214, 248; Malmström, *Nils Bielke,* p. 176.

concerned with the world beyond Sweden's borders. The one exception to this was his concern over his status as a guarantor of the treaties of Westphalia. But even here he was not prepared to do very much, and like most of his advisers was caught in a time warp. When the alliance with Brandenburg was renewed in 1696, it had a secret clause providing for cooperation in upholding the 1648 religious settlement in the Empire. When the Council debated the subject, the king declared: 'it would be very good to try to preserve the Protestant League against the Catholics', and reminded them how Westphalia obliged the king of Sweden to uphold the religious liberties of Protestants. In the world of the 1690s, when the elites of Europe were slowly secularizing their thinking, these ideas were becoming outmoded. Charles XI was still fighting the Thirty Years War, though it is to be noted that he added that these obligations must not result in Sweden, 'becoming too deeply involved'. The king wanted to have a major role in the international relations game, but sometimes he balked at paying the entry fees.[12]

Through 1694 the king pursued his mediation effort, and resisted offers of Louis XIV for the full restitution of Zweibrücken, in return for collaborating with France and Denmark to pursue joint grievances against William of Orange. For the moment no basis for mediation was found which was acceptable to all parties. But the year did see the rehabilitation of Nils Bielke. He had been commissioned to take up an offer from the Elector of Brandenburg to settle a series of minor disputes with Sweden, and made a great success of the negotiation. The king was impressed and wrote to Bielke in July 1694 that his services would not be forgotten. In February 1695, Bielke was allowed to return to Stockholm, and stayed for more than a year, taking a full part in Council discussions. It is apparent from a letter which the king wrote to Bielke in May 1696 that a fairly emotional reconciliation had taken place between the two men. Bielke naturally resumed the leadership of the faction struggle to undermine Oxenstierna. During the last phase of the European war, the allies were pressing Sweden to renew her military commitment to the cause. In January 1695 the emperor called on the princes to enter formal alliances to support the Elector Palatine against French threats. J. G. Stenbock, in a Council debate on this, took the line that this would be dangerous, but could not be refused outright. The king agreed it was dangerous, 'since the emperor wants that We shall immediately declare Ourselves and take up arms against the king of France'. Oxenstierna did not dispute the risk, but insisted they must make some positive response. It was agreed to try to postpone a definite answer until after the conclusion of a general peace, and then put in a counter-proposal. As the year went on, and the new Holstein-Gottorp dispute sharpened, Charles XI pressed the emperor and William of Orange to reaffirm their support of the Altona settlement, but they naturally bargained for a return, demanded that Sweden should resume sending her military contingents to the alliance. Bielke strongly urged the king to evade any commit-

[12] RA, R 2378, Secret Propositions read 4 Nov. 1693; RA, Rådsprotokoll 1696, 91b, meeting of 22 Sept. 1696.

ment, and argued his case in the Council, which had the question of whether to send contingents for 1696 under intermittent review until February 1696. At first Bielke seemed to prevail. In November, Wrede had told the Council that the French minister was telling people how pleased Louis XIV was that Sweden would withhold her contingents. He said: 'it is strange that France knows about the sending of assistance before any discussion on this has taken place here'. Bielke had obviously been feeding d'Avaux with encouraging reports. Yet in the end Oxenstierna prevailed; in the February meeting of the Council, it was agreed in principle to send the contingents for 1696, because of the need for imperial support over Holstein-Gottorp.[13]

During the last eighteen months of Charles XI's life, he continued to waver in face of pressures from Bielke. At times his irritation with William of Orange over the blockade, and a minor dispute he had with the emperor over the succession to the territory of Güstrow-Schwerin, where a relative of his mother was a claimant, led him to lose sight of the principles set out in 1693. But in the end, despite flattering hints conveyed through d'Avaux, he held to Oxenstierna's line. In May 1696, when the mediation was stalled, and the king was using blatant obstruction to avoid sending his contingents, as he had agreed to do in principle, he also announced publicly that any settlement mediated by him would be based on a strict interpretation of the settlements of 1648 and 1678. This would compel Louis XIV to return the considerable gains he had made since 1679. It was a demonstration of which side he favoured, though the reality was that Charles XI's wishes did not carry much weight in the eventual peace settlement. His mediation was a charade, because the real agreements were all worked out by bilateral negotiations between the belligerents. Only when they had come to terms did they find it convenient to ask the king to convene a general peace conference at Rijswick, a message conveyed to Charles XI on 7 February 1697. On 5 April the king died, and thus did not live to enjoy the prestige and acclamation that would have accrued to him, even though Sweden's mediation had been essentially cosmetic. It would have sustained the illusion that Sweden was still a European power of the first rank.[14]

It is no discredit to the king and Oxenstierna that they sought to uphold his status. Cold analysis would suggest that Sweden's pretensions to a place among the leading powers were unrealistic. But this is to misunderstand the vicious power game that constituted international relations in the seventeenth century. The participants could not choose to detach themselves from it. If Charles XI had given the least sign that he accepted that Sweden no longer had the will or the capacity to sustain her position, relative to the other powers, the predators would have fallen

[13] Landberg, *Utrikespolitikens historia, I. 3*, pp. 251, 253–4; Malmström, *Nils Bielke*, pp. 149, 152, 153, 170, 181, 182; Carlson, *Historia*, IV, pp. 379, 389; RA, Rådsprotokoll vol. 91a, meetings of 8, 15, 23, 28 Jan. 1695, 29 Nov. 1695, 17, 22, 30 Jan. 1696.
[14] Landberg, *Utrikespolitikens historia, I. 3*, pp. 254, 256–8; Malmström, *Nils Bielke*, pp. 154–8; Carlson, *Historia*, IV, pp. 396, 400, 404.

on her and dismembered her, as they had planned to do in 1675, and partially succeeded in doing through the great Northern War after 1700. Charles XI and Oxenstierna had pulled Sweden back from the brink of disaster after 1680, and given the kingdom eighteen years of admittedly precarious peace. The king also left his kingdom with a system of alliances, and a military machine that gave as much security as could be attained in that brutal and violent world, and this at a cost commensurate with the society's resources. This was certainly no slight achievement.

12

The last years of the reign

The year 1693 can be taken as a notional watershed in the history of the reign, marked by the death of the queen in July, and the meeting of the last Diet of the reign in November. It has been noted how the strength of the king's emotional attachment to Ulrika Eleonora, however out of character it seems, was clearly demonstrated and was one reason why he never contemplated remarriage. But there were also good pragmatic grounds for remaining a widower. He had performed his dynastic duty; his three surviving children, the crown-prince Charles, and his two sisters, Hedvig Sofia and Ulrika Eleonora, were past the worst perils of childhood and grew to healthy adulthood. His foreign relations were sound and there was no obvious, advantageous dynastic marriage he could make. For domestic comfort, to which he never attached much importance, there was the court of the queen-mother, to whom he always showed the respect required by Scripture towards a parent. The crown-prince, unlike his father, was being carefully educated for his role, and proved a diligent and promising pupil. It was too soon for the emergence of the antagonisms that were so common between kings and their heirs; father and son seem to have enjoyed a close and friendly relationship. Charles XI had fulfilled his duties as head of the family, and trustee for his dynasty and could rest satisfied. This was displayed publicly at the Diet of 1693, with its detailed reviews of the achievements of the reign and pointers to the expected further developments. The programme outlined for foreign and domestic policy indicated that all the major policy projects had now been initiated, and that some were coming to maturity, while others needed more time to complete. But in either case, the king's intention was to supervise and consolidate his achievements for the kingdom, and guard against any backsliding. There were no new policies in the 1690s; the king had set his course and pursued it doggedly to the end.

It has been shown earlier how there was critical material circulating among the elite, generated by the dispossessed survivors of the old regime, and their heirs, and by the losers under the current system. Foreign ministers at Stockholm, like Stockfleth in 1689, or d'Avaux in 1693, reported rumours that the regime was so insecure that, for example, the king dare not engage in war, for if he led his army out of the kingdom, he was unlikely to return, so intense was the disaffection of the whole community. It must be said that this seems to be fantasy; there is no convincing evidence that widespread alienation from the regime existed. The most persuasive and well-reasoned critique of the reign is in the writings of Claes Rålamb, which were discussed above, in particular his *Proceedings of the 1680 Diet*, which does make valid points about the crude tactics and bullying, and the disregard for legal niceties displayed in the establishment of the regime. It was natural for a lawyer to criticize the violations of the principles of the law of contract and property, and claim that the regime had built on maxims worthy of Machiavelli, 'which cannot be studied in any other academy but one where Lucifer was the senior professor'. Rålamb's besetting weakness was that he had no solution to offer, as a convincing alternative way of dealing with the very real problems facing Sweden in 1679. Nor could he really explain why a 'reasonable inhabitant of Sweden would freely, and in cold blood, without preparation or coercion, have wanted to throw himself and his heirs into slavery and serfdom'. He could only advance conspiracy theory, based on the age-old myth of the evil Councillors who manipulated a virtuous ruler, citing the traditional hate figures from Scripture, Saul and Rehoboam and above all Achitophel.[1]

The other surviving material is less impressive than Rålamb's writings, and could have been found in any contemporary European society, where the elites were literate. It consists of crude polemic, conspiracy theories, personal denigration and scandal, contempt for low-born, mercenary advisers and laments for the good old days. In truth, very similar material is to be found in the contemporary media of the twentieth century. There is no way of even guessing what the effect of this material was on those who were acquainted with it; it is safe to assume that the human appetite for scurrilous gossip and scandal has been a constant through the ages. It can simply be affirmed that there is no convincing evidence of any active opposition to the operations of Charles XI's government, or any real challenge to its legitimacy or authority. There was principled criticism of the absolutist agenda, like a long pamphlet attacking the organized preaching at the Diet of 1693. The author, probably an anti-clerical nobleman, analysed the sermons, trading Scripture texts, mixed with attacks on the clergy interfering in politics, seeking to prove that, 'the preachers . . . leave aside the rule for all kings that God has given, through Moses, and instead seek to recommend them this kind of government, abominable to God'.[2]

There is evidence that the government was sensitive to this criticism, over and above its harsh retaliation against any individual foolish enough to identify himself, and the rigid censorship regime. On the king's death, Jakob Gyllenborg drew up a memorial, which he says was commissioned by Charles XI, to refute the criticisms that were circulating. It is obviously partisan, but it does state a reasoned case for the regime. It is built around the financial reconstruction, describing the desperate

---

[1] Fryxell, ed., *Handlingar*, II, p. 412, Stockfleth to the king of Denmark 3 Feb. 1689: Correspondance diplomatique: vol. 73, d'Avaux: 1693 pt 1, p. 100, d'Avaux to Louis XIV; KB, Rålambska Manuskriptsamlingen: Fol. Nr. 5: 1680 års riksdagsärenden: chapter 15.
[2] KB, Rålambska Manuskriptsamlingen: Fol. Nr. 71: Politiska Pasquiller, Anon. tract.

situation in 1672, when the effective reign began. It was typical of the early modern mind that Gyllenborg presented the king's policies as a restoration, a recovery of revenues rightly belonging to the crown. The reader was told that 'the revenues which the king used are not any new discoveries and proposals, but such as Sweden's earlier kings, the King's Council and the Estates, have unanimously proven, ordained and decided were both necessary and profitable and legal'. Gyllenborg then claimed, against all the evidence, that Charles XI had been reluctant to embark upon the reduktion policies. He recognized that the holders of donations had acquired them legitimately as rewards for public services, but, 'since the kingdom was in the greatest extremity, and the Estates saw no other way out . . . the king had to pursue the proposal'. But if this interpretation strains credulity, Gyllenborg's analysis of the king's intentions is well grounded. They were 'to set up such a budget . . . that both the king's magnificence, the protection and defence of the country can be maintained, and spiritual and secular, civil and military servants have been able to secure their yearly salary and maintenance'. He then listed the results that flowed from budgetary reform, adequate defence forces, improved fortifications, new codes of conduct for all government departments, avoidance of new indebtedness and settlement of old obligations, and finally the accumulation of substantial financial reserves. He asserted that,

from all of this, the king has gained nothing but a great reputation, sleepless nights, troubles and labours, and a worn-out body, since the king himself must be in every place to advance the work, and abolish rooted indiscipline and self-seeking, and along with this the only real pleasure that the king experienced, through God's blessing, and his own labours, [was] that his faithful subjects have for eighteen years been able to live in a peaceful and secure condition.

Gyllenborg was putting the most favourable interpretation possible on the achievements of the reign, but it remains much closer to reality than the wild assertions of the critics.[3]

Charles XI expected that God would judge him on how he had exercised his stewardship of 'my kingdom granted by God to rule'. The historian should do the same, and review where the king had got to in his various endeavours when he was cut down in 1697, at an age when he could reasonably have expected to reign another twenty years. He would have accepted that, if Providence had so decreed, but with resignation, not enthusiasm. A cult of personality was developing around the king in the 1690s. A pamphlet of 1692 referred to ancient runic prophecies of how the kingdom would enjoy felicity under a great king. The king's father, Charles X Gustav, had been such a ruler, but in his son, the kingdom had acquired 'a great king's only Phoenix, and our matchless Hercules of the Nordic world, our present most gracious reigning king [who] has so far ruled his fortunate hereditary kingdom with such mild, courageous and prudent hands . . . with every royal grace,

---

[3] Loenbom, ed., *Handlingar*, III, collection, IX, pp. 11, 28, 75, 107, 149, 153.

honour and mercy . . . our most gracious Father and King of the land, Charles the Great'. The anonymous author went a bit far, perhaps, even by the Baroque standards of the seventeenth century, but Bengt Oxenstierna, in an address at Uppsala University in 1693, in the presence of the king, was not far behind. Oxenstierna described how in Charles XI, Sweden enjoyed 'a great and powerful king and lord, whose sacred countenance we now have here, to regard and honour with deep veneration. We have a king, I say, who should be as highly and widely exalted, as a royal title and glory may ever, with reason, be conceived and recalled.' After dwelling on what a blessing and a paragon of kingship he had been to his fortunate kingdom, Oxenstierna declared that all that remained to wish for was that this felicity should continue. Fortunately God had seen to that as well; they had a crown-prince 'so like and so honourable as his great father, not only in name, but also in Christian and lawful virtues, so that the merits of the one can in a manner be seen and read in the eyes of the other'. This public rhetoric was certainly extravagant; we cannot know what Charles XI thought of it, except to note that his repeated private reference to himself as a poor sinner suggests that he took a more measured view of his achievement.[4]

The first duty of a king was to uphold true religion, by setting an example of godliness himself and ensuring that his subjects followed it. Charles XI took this very seriously, for after all, the penalties that God might inflict on the kingdom if he did not were dire. Wachtmeister wrote to the king from Karlskrona about a case where, by the slackness of the local magistrates, a murderer had escaped punishment. Wachtmeister appealed to the king to intervene, 'so that God may not be angered at the country and its people by such a gross outrage, in which two lives are lost without the offenders answering to authority and being punished'. The king immediately ordered the case to be reopened. In the Diet of 1689, the Clergy Estate petitioned that in small towns, where there was often only one clergyman, the requirement of the Church Law to preach two sermons on a Sunday be relaxed. The king was not persuaded: 'the king's Majesty wishes to know what kind of towns there are, which have only one priest'. He would look into the matter, but in the meantime the Church Law must be enforced to the letter. Skara diocese was exposed in 1685 for ordaining unfit candidates for the priesthood. The king wrote of one such, P. Asuerus: 'so ignorant in his Christian knowledge that he could not answer various questions, fit for children'. But what infuriated the king was the excuse put up by the dean, 'that this Asuerus was as good as many others ordained at various times in the diocese: since the responsibility and zeal which God has set on Us, through Our kingly office, demands that We in every possible way prevent, that God's Word and the office of preacher should be so abused, and Our subjects' salvation put in danger'. The king ordered an immediate examination of all the

---

[4] Malmström, ed., 'Karl XIs bref till Nils Bielke', p. 59, letter of April 1689; Loenbom, ed., *Handlingar*, III, collection VII, p. 193; UUB, E491, Handlingar till Sveriges politiska historia, Oxenstierna's oration as Chancellor of Uppsala University 3 Mar. 1693.

clergy of the diocese, with those found incompetent to be dismissed and replaced. It is easy to sympathize with the dean, no doubt a practical administrator, who knew that if the Church was too fastidious about whom it ordained, it would soon be severely understaffed. But with Charles XI such pragmatic considerations carried no weight at all.[5]

The king was unyielding in his assertion of his superiority over his Church as an Evangelical prince. He told Bishop D. Wallerius in 1682 that ultimately all patronage belonged to the king: 'the sovereign in his country and kingdom is the first and pre-eminent Patron and Nurse of the Church, both by the laws of God and the world'. But he used his position to protect what he recognized as the rights properly belonging to the Church. He would uphold the authority of its bishops; when the archbishop wrote to complain of difficulties in getting the parish clergy to attend the statutory diocesan synods for training, no doubt because they saw them as a tedious and burdensome imposition, the king ordered a fine of 2 dsm. an hour on absentees. Equally the king required obedience and respect from the laity. It was revealed in the Riddarhus debates of 1682 how the nobility nurtured plans for further ecclesiastical asset-stripping, and an assertion of their rights of patronage. The king made it clear he would allow neither. On the contrary he consistently stressed that nobles must attend their parish churches like any other parishioner, and have their children educated in the public schools. Perhaps the most striking assertion was the king's attitude to doing public penance in church. Most European societies had a system for the public exposure of sinners, but it was universally understood that members of the elites could buy themselves out of performing it. It was not so in Charles XI's Sweden; the king insisted on real performance by all. The king also showed his personal respect for religious obligation. He studied his Bible every day, and would interrupt public business to attend church services regularly. It has been seen how he pressed the clergy to revise the catechism, the hymnal and the translation of the Bible, but in each case he accepted the delays imposed by the protests of the conservatives at anything they regarded as innovation. The king pressed hard for the creation of uniform, revised texts, but conceded that their actual content was a professional matter for the clergy to decide. At the same time he was strict in policing clerical misconduct towards the laity, mostly over fees and other dues. The king urged the drafting of legal contracts in parishes to define exactly what the mutual obligations of clergymen and parishioners were, and was severe on cases of priests trying to levy unauthorized charges.[6]

It remained true of Sweden, as of all human societies, that there is no wholly effective way to stop the possessors of wealth, power or privilege from exploiting

---

[5] RA, Skrivelser till konungen, Karl XIs tid, Hans Wachtmeisters skrivelser till Kongl. Mt. 1677–90, letter of 17 Oct. 1685; *PR*, IV, p. 386; KB, Engströmska samlingen: B.II. 1.12: Handlingar rörande Karl XIs regering, king to Skara Consistory 15 June 1685.

[6] RA, Riksregistraturet 357, 1682, p. 483, king to Bishop Wallerius 5 Apr. 1682; Carlson, *Historia*, IV, p. 271.

the common people who have none of these attributes, and constitute the majority of the population. But the king knew he had a duty to make the attempt, and he tried to fulfil it. It was characteristic of his stinging rebukes to those in authority that he would order they must be read out in church. There was probably a price to be paid for the king's integration of the Church into the machinery of government, under his own direct supervision. It was smothering spiritual life by reducing religion to the mechanical performance of the prescribed rituals and duties. The ideas of German Pietism, which were filtering into Sweden at the end of the century, were in part a protest against a formalistic faith, and the Church under Charles XI made no room for such deviations. The ordinary churchgoer, on the other hand, may well have appreciated this formality. He knew that if he followed the rules, he would be left alone. The Swedish Church did not seek to make windows into men's souls.

After the upholding of true religion, the next most important duty of a king was to dispense impartial justice to all his subjects. In the early modern world, this emphatically did not mean treating them all alike, regardless of status. It would have been an absurdity, defying God's law, to treat a nobleman in the same way as his farm servant, and the servants themselves would have been disoriented by a ruler who tried to do so. God had created the hierarchical order in society and ordained that some should rule and others should be ruled. The very existence of the body politic depended on the ability of the head to direct the members. Charles XI was very conscious of the importance of hierarchical order. This lay behind his order of 1686 that although the title of the Council had changed, the respect and precedence due to its members had not; they were still the highest ranking of the king's subjects to be addressed as 'Excellency'. This occasioned the king's angry rebuke to Axel de la Gardie, who was a Councillor and a Governor General, who would put his signature on documents on the same level as a provincial governor, and failed to assert his precedence when attending a wedding. Such conduct was 'directly against Our royal respect and preeminence, and the status and authority which We have graciously assigned to the office of King's Councillor'. Such negligence was intolerable, and the king's letter expressed 'the displeasure which We therefore have cause to conceive at your conduct'. The same considerations brought a furious reprimand from the king to the judges who had handled a case of defamation against Fabian Wrede, a royal Councillor and senior crown official. Wrede was accused by three men – a district Court judge, a bailiff and a peasant – of abusing his office by defrauding the king, oppressing the subjects and taking bribes. He had shown the Court a letter from the king that he was convinced of Wrede's innocence, and reminding it what a grave offence it was to slander a king's Councillor. The court had judged there were mitigating circumstances. In the king's view, the bailiff, 'was so gross, and so highly and nearly takes away Royal Councillor Wrede's reputation and honour, that there was every reason . . . to condemn him to death'. Instead, all the satisfaction Wrede got from him was 'a forty daler fine'. On the district Court judge, they had ruled that 'he had not intended to insult and disparage the Royal Councillor', and he went unpunished. 'Should this man, or any other, write what he wants with impunity . . . and be able to deny that he intended anything bad by it? That would become a dangerous and deplorable example.' Yet, as often happened with the king's outbursts of wrath, the end result was an anti-climax. After declaring that the conduct of the Court had been 'almost criminal', the king told them he would be keeping his eye on them, and expected improvement. But it did show the king's sensitivity to any perceived challenge to hierarchical authority.[7]

What the king demanded was not equality, but equity, which to him meant the unfettered access of all his subjects to the royal justice. When the king reformed the district Court judges' appointments in 1680, their remit was to judge 'without respect of persons according to Swedish law', and to be available at all times to hear the grievances of the peasantry. The circular to provincial governors in 1682 ordered them to be assiduous in hearing the complaints of the people and helping them to justice. A similar circular of 1683 on abuses arising from the indelningsverk, told the governors the king would not tolerate such malpractices, and was determined that 'Our poor peasantry be secured in their property and protected from all violence and injustice.' This circular was to be read out in all the churches. Governors too could be guilty of abuse. In 1682 Henrik von Wiken, Governor of Älfvsborg, had been interfering in the district Courts. The king wrote that he had 'assumed to yourself, through a groundless comparison, such a right or authority . . . as a Colonel [has] over his regiment . . . which by no means, and in no case belongs to you, since the lower judges stand under Our High Court, and not under Our provincial governors'. In the Diet of 1682, the nobility petitioned that in future half of the district Court juries should be tenants of the nobility. The thinking behind this was transparent and the king rejected it.[8]

The king was not sentimental about the peasants. Those whom the reduktion transferred from the nobility to the crown did not find that their obligations were reduced by the change. It is indeed likely that the rising efficiency of the bureaucratic machinery meant that the enforcement of rents, taxes and services was more effective than it had been. But the king does seem to have acted on the principle, and this was not common in early modern Europe, that peasants too were subjects with legal rights, as were the elites, and that it was a function of kingship to see those rights upheld. This was apparent in the official responses to the grievances of the Peasant Estate at the Diets, which were generally positive. In response to the third article of the grievances of 1680, that the king's orders were not being applied

---

[7] Loenbom, ed., *Handlingar*, III, collection VIII, p. 22, king to Axel de la Gardie 10 Oct. 1691; KB, Engströmska samlingen: B.II.1.12, king's letter 21 Nov. 1687.
[8] KB, Engströmska samlingen: B.II.1.12, king's letter to W. Klerck 20 Dec. 1680; Hildebrand and Grimberg, *Källorna*, p. 222, circular to provincial governors 12 Apr. 1682, king's letter to H. von Viken 8 June 1682; p. 223, circular to provincial governors 10 Sept. 1683; Westman, *Häradsrätt*, p. 8.

by the royal officials and the Courts, the king replied that all the governors 'are strictly commanded that they hold a strong hand over the execution of the king's decisions and instructions, so that the peasantry shall not be deprived of them, to their great hurt and expense, as they complain'. At the end the king ordered that a copy of the Diet Resolution and the answer to the grievances be preserved in the community chest, and officials were strictly forbidden to conceal knowledge of their content. The king added: 'for the rest, the king's Majesty always remains favourably disposed to his faithful subjects of the kingdom's peasantry, with royal favour and grace'. In the absence of enough detailed research, it is not possible to know how effective the king's good intentions were in practice, but it can be affirmed that the peasants did freely exercise their rights to appeal to the royal justice, and petitions did get an official answer, though if they were judged frivolous or disrespectful to lawful authority it could bring retribution down on the petitioners. And it is a historical fact that the relatively free Swedish rural society did survive, with its rights intact, into the modern era.[9]

In the closing years of the reign, the king's budget project was brought to near completion. The Diet of 1693 was told that the programme outlined in 1680 had now been effected, and that the state budget was balanced, and beginning to yield a surplus. The first move to utilize the surplus had been taken in 1692, when the king ordered that accumulated funds to the value of 145,000 dsm. be kept in a reserve treasury in the main fortresses of the kingdom. During the following year, the king began to accumulate the surplus, as a secret reserve fund, in the Elephant vault under Stockholm Castle. This reserve was secret and did not appear in the Chamber accounts, and could be used only on the personal order of the king. Fortunately a report from the Budget Office to the Diet of 1697, after the king died, describes the development. Wrede presented the report and began in 1686, when he took over the presidency of the Budget Office. In 1686, the budgeted expenditures were 4,389, 193 dsm. and there was a surplus of 347,110 dsm. In 1697 the corresponding figures were 6,356, 539 dsm. and 529,586 dsm. But by then there were large accumulated reserves, the 145,000 dsm. in the fortresses, 526,919 dsm. in the various military reserve funds, and 1,849,413 dsm. stored in the Elephant vault, and these accumulated reserves equalled roughly a third of one year's crown revenue. In addition the king had funded the mobilization of 1689, the contingents sent to the Allies, the queen's funeral expenses and a large rebuilding programme for Stockholm Castle out of the surplus. On top of this there had been a substantial reduction of crown debts, partly through the repudiations sanctioned in the Diet of 1686, partly through the willingness of creditors to settle for half their claims, and partly from a further 3.5 million dsm. paid out of the surpluses. Then financial administration had been reorganized by the Chamber Ordinance of 1694, entitled 'the king's orders how the activities of the Chamber College shall be divided among

---

[9] Stiernman, ed., *Beslut*, II, p. 1826, Resolutions on the grievances of the Estate of Peasants 22 Nov. 1680.

the members for the prompt despatch of business'. It was a typical rule-book of the period, such as the king was trying to draw up for all branches of the administration. The organization was rounded off by setting up the autonomous Audit Department in 1696. It was then possible to declare the budget of 1696 as the definitive model for all time to come.[10]

The financial reorganization was one of Charles XI's monumental achievements, and very much reflected his style of government. There was nothing original in anything he did, but he took concepts and practices, long familiar in the kingdom, and built them into a coherent structure. The king's personal input had been considerable, as Wrede reported it: 'the king was pleased to take the trouble to come down into the Budget Office and look through everything himself, at the same time graciously declaring on each and every specific item'. While the *Riksregistratur* alone is massive evidence of the king's involvement in every aspect of financial administration. Modern commentators have tended to describe the king's financial structures as obsolete even when they were set up, and even retrogressive. They treat the kingdom like a private estate, within which the king lives of his own. They seem to compartmentalize each category of expenditure and to impose an inflexible structure on the public finances. The critics also note the significant proportion of the revenue still collected in produce, and describe it as a relic of an outdated system. This kind of critique does less than justice to the rationale of the king's achievement. The persistence of revenues paid in kind was a fact of life in seventeenth-century Sweden, in an economy that was not yet fully market oriented, or monetarized. The indelningsverk allowed these revenues to be taken and used at source by the public employees, freeing the crown from the problem of trying to convert them into cash, while the recipient was spared the expense of trying to secure payment of his salary from a central treasury in Stockholm. It was in fact an economical and rational method for making the best use of a revenue source that could not easily be changed. The system was also more flexible than it might seem, in that although most of the annual revenue was permanently assigned to specific items of expenditure, the surpluses in the different branches were aggregated at the end of the year, and used as required to meet contingencies, or pay off debt, or be placed in reserve. It seems strange to modern eyes that the kingdom's surplus cash was locked up in the castle vaults, but it is not easy to see what else the king could have done with it. The only bank in Sweden was the Kingdom's Estates' Bank, an autonomous institution protected by law, which the king was scrupulous in respecting, and managed by a committee elected by the Estates. The Bank in the 1690s was flush with money, and actually refused to accept any further interest-bearing deposits. The Bank had the same problem as the king, that in the circumstances there were no safe outlets for profit-making investment of surplus cash. In order to appreciate Charles XI's financial achievement, it is necessary to

[10] Cavallie, *Fred till krig*, pp. 40, 42; Loenbom, ed., *Handlingar*, V, pp. 10, 13, 14, 16, 19, 29, 30, 35, 39, 40, 48; Eden, *Kammarkollegiets historia*, pp. 151–3; Lagerroth, *Statsreglering*, pp. 141–4.

put aside anachronistic modern ideas about public finance, and compare Sweden's public finances with those of most contemporary European states. Sweden was not in the same economic league as the United Provinces or Great Britain, and comparisons with them are meaningless. But it can be asked, where else in contemporary Europe was there a monarchy with a comprehensive national budget that reliably sustained the running costs of its civil and military establishment, with low administrative overheads, a shrinking national debt and a regular surplus that was building up into a substantial and very liquid reserve fund, capable of covering the immediate demands of any likely contingency?

It is the other main component of the king's financial policies that is open to reasonable criticism. The continuing pursuit of the reduktion proceedings, and the parallel drive to recover as much as possible from the heirs of those condemned by the Regency Tribunal, continued relentlessly to the end of the reign, and in this matter it was the king's will that was the main driving force. Here there is a good case to be made that, after realizing the gains made possible by the extension of reduktion to purchased and mortgaged properties, and the partial application of *alterum tantum* to some of the debt, which had been legalized by the Diet of 1686, it would have been politic to close the process down. The argument would be that the remaining potential for augmenting the revenue did not compensate for the resentments which the process generated among the nobility, and the collateral economic damage done by the continuing uncertainty over titles to property, and the undermining of public credit. The case was put, in the most respectful language, in a petition presented to the new king, Charles XII by the Riddarhus. They started from the assertion that the nobility had been brought to ruin by the reduktion process, 'so that not only a great part must languish in deplorable poverty within the kingdom, but one after the other, God grant without danger to their souls, are forced by the most compelling need to seek their bread in foreign lands'. They acknowledged that the king was entitled to his rights, but hoped that just as God does not enforce his full rights over sinners, so 'your royal Majesty, as a God on earth and the gentle father of the country [they were addressing a fifteen-year-old youth!] will not deal with us as his supreme right may demand'. They made the point that an impoverished nobility would be unable to give the king the support he would need in time of trouble, and then went to the economic heart of their case, the uncertainties created by the reduktion process, 'the uncertainty and insecurity which exists over the nobility's property, holds back all trade, confidence and credit'. They pointed to the volume of litigation that was generated by the reduktion and implied that the whole economy was grinding to a halt, and would not recover until 'everyone is made secure in his property'.[11]

The petition certainly exaggerated the economic distress of the nobility; some

---

[11] KB, Engströmska samlingen: B.II.1.12, petition of the Riddarhus 10 Dec. 1697.

families had been hard hit, but most managed to adapt and survive, retaining a tolerable style of life. But it did make a crucial point in insisting how destructive it was to the whole economy that there was general uncertainty over the ownership of property. Reduktion presented an open-ended threat to all kinds of property, and because property was the main basis of credit in that kind of society was a real braking force on economic development. Further, as the petition showed, it created fear and resentment among the nobility, a social group in a key position of power, whose good-will was necessary for the orderly functioning of the society. Charles XI exposed his personal and intellectual limitations by his consistent failure to see the reduktion process in its broader social context. All he could see was that the crown, and the public good, were entitled to recover these revenue sources, and it was his duty to see that this was done. He had explained his position to the Livland nobility in a letter of 1686, in which he acknowledged 'the inconvenience which one or another may experience because of it', but pleaded that there was overriding necessity and the public good was 'both ground and occasion for such a reduktion, which first and foremost is intended so that the kingdom can be in a condition and on a firm foundation, so that not only Our and the subjects' own advantage, but also the long desired safety and certainty' can be secured.[12]

The king did state repeatedly that it was the intention to bring the process to a speedy conclusion. The Propositions to the Diet of 1693 promised this would be done, and a definitive register of property titles established. The Marshal had told the Riddarhus that 'the king expects to bring an end to the reduktion process within a year'. Yet the Propositions themselves had revealed how unlikely this was, when they described a list of twenty different categories of property, whose liability to reduktion was yet to be determined. It was further stated that the whole property of the nobility must be examined, to see if it had ever belonged to the crown, and so the Reduktion Commission must search the records 'back into the earliest times', adding superfluously that this would occasion a lot of work. The king wrote a letter in his own hand, to the Reduktion Commission in 1688, which illustrates how he was the driving force behind the process. He suspected them of trying to cut short the proceedings, and warned them:

if any of you, against all expectation, shall presume to moderate, or adapt other principles than are contained in the actual Diet Resolutions, the reduktion ordinances, the royal resolutions and letters, We reserve to Ourselves and Our successors, now and for all time [the right] to call you to answer for it: since *jus Majestatis* has no limit of time, but stands open for ever.

This gives a direct insight into the king's thinking, and the implication is that the reduktion process could never be closed. Further evidence of this was the way in which, whenever the officials discovered a new legal category, the king would order that all existing settlements be reviewed in the light of it, 'so that all may receive like

[12] *Ibid.*, king's letter to the Livland nobility 1 Apr. 1686.

justice'. There was no legal protection of any avail to owners of landed property against the unlimited sovereign power vested in the king by God.[13]

The king's justification was that while he insisted that the reduktion must be pursued to its uttermost limits, he could and did use his sovereign power to mitigate the effects for unfortunate and deserving suitors. Rålamb was right to say that the procedures were pursued 'without regard to deserts, without any end, without any legal proof', and that this was an exercise of arbitrary power. But the allegation that, in consequence, noble families were literally reduced to beggary, forced 'to look for sustenance from good folk by begging and many had to turn to their former tenants for a mouthful of bread', has never been substantiated, and is in the highest degree improbable. The king shared the inherent sense of social proprieties, and the necessity of hierarchy that permeated the society, which made such an outcome unacceptable. Rålamb himself, who could be described as es-pecially hard hit by the process, because of his known opposition to it, continued to live well above the poverty line. What the king did do was to insist that the rules must be applied in full, and then he would consider relief. The experience of Bengt Oxenstierna, who was heavily involved, both in consequence of the Regency Tribunal and the reduktion, grew so desperate by 1686 that he threatened to retire from public life. The king wrote in January 1687 that the case against him must be prosecuted, 'for the sake of example', but that 'whatever the accounting shows as being due to Us, We will relinquish to him, and he shall never be troubled for it'. Such a total remission was very unusual and it should be noted that if the king had subsequently changed his mind, the letter would have afforded no protection at all. In general, lesser men could look for some relief, if they petitioned with suitable humility, though the relief given was rarely generous.[14]

It was therefore Charles XI who drove the process forward, regardless of the animosities aroused and the diminishing financial returns. In consequence some reduktion officials were making a career out of it, endlessly looking for new categories for investigation. From 1687, the power-house of the reduktion was the new Deputation, of which Jakob Gyllenborg was President. Its full title was, 'The Deputation for the conclusion of the reduktion.' It rested on an assumption that the process was almost finished; the documents setting up the Deputation stated: 'for the most part it seems to depend only on the Chamber officers' verifications'. The remit of the Deputation was to assist the Chamber by handing down definitive rulings on doubtful cases. Gyllenborg was one of the officers who had shown enthusiasm, but not without some reservations, for extending the reduktion to its limits. It was Gyllenborg who had identified an interesting category of grants made in satisfaction of unpaid salaries. The point he discovered was that the claimant was entitled to no more than his salary arrears, so that if the yield of the granted

---

[13] *SRARP*, XVI, pp. 17, 97, 106, 107; RA, Riksregistraturet 1688, p. 241, king's letter to the Reduktion Commissioners 24 Jan. 1688; Carlson, *Historia*, IV, pp. 112–16, 119, 120, 137.
[14] RA, Rålambska Manuskriptsamlingen: Fol. Nr. 5, chapter 6; Carlson, *Historia*, IV, p. 144.

property had exceeded that, the excess could be reclaimed from him. But then suppose the claimant for salary arrears was given cash, and then he had immediately used it to purchase crown property. Was he entitled to the full revenue from his property, as a bona fide purchaser, or was it in effect a settlement of salary arrears, with any excess coming back to the crown? This was one of several cases which caused long argument in the Deputation, with the king usually in support of Gyllenborg's hard line. In June 1688, Gyllenborg procured the publication of a series of royal resolutions, which tightened the rules on a number of issues.[15]

The ruthlessness of the officials involved, generally with the support of the king, can be illustrated from many examples. The Copper Company had been set up in the 1620s to farm the crown's copper revenues. It stood accused of defrauding the crown of over 1 million dsm. The evidence for this was disputable and two Chamber officers, Lars Skragge and Sven Leijonmarck were ordered to report on it. Both made the error of reporting that in fact the crown had made a substantial profit from the contract, thus destroying the case against the Company. Both men were called to answer for their reports to the Deputation. Skragge grovelled and repudiated his report, Leijonmarck was stubborn and defended his, and was for a time imprisoned and his conduct investigated on the order of the king. He must either have submitted like Skragge, or succeeded in establishing his innocence, since he was released and in December 1689 appointed to the Law Commission. But the episode does suggest that independent thinking was not encouraged in the royal officials. The king accepted that there were limits to the methods that could be used. It was Leijonmarck who exposed a colleague, J. Schiller, who in his search for documentary evidence that certain grants of Gustav Vasa were subject to reduktion, actually tampered with the documents. When this was exposed, the king took it very badly; Schiller was tried and condemned to death, though the sentence was commuted. The king drew the line at forgery, but he could be very flexible in setting rules. In 1686 there was a debate on the definition of a 'forbidden area', in which no crown property could ever be alienated. The king ruled, in effect, that he could retrospectively define such areas, since 'it had never been the king's intention to tie his hands, but rather to reserve to himself the right and liberty which, in this as in other cases, is vested in and belongs to the king'. He could be persuaded sometimes it was unprofitable to pursue claims in full, as when Gyllenborg demonstrated that to process one category of claims would take a Chamber official a fortnight's work on each one, and at the end of it the person involved might prove to be bankrupt. The king reluctantly agreed not to proceed in such cases. But this was unusual. In 1689 the Deputation discovered a category of purchases of crown properties, made in the 1620s before an official sale price had been determined. Most of these purchasers had paid less than the price subsequently set. There was a case that the purchaser, who had taken the full rents from the property, had not

---

[15] Sjögren, *Karl den elfte*, p. 455; Lindqvist, *Gyllenborg*, pp. 166, 167–71, 176.

paid for all of them and could be required to refund the unpurchased rents with interest. The Deputation considered that this would be going too far, and the unpurchased rent should be written off. The king's reaction to this advice, in a letter of June 1689, was one of outrage. He told the Deputation he was astonished that they suggested he might forgo his legal claims, and demanded to know which members of the Deputation had recommended this. In the end he took no retributive action, but it was his interpretation that was adopted. The quest for new categories went on as long as the king lived; the Council was often involved in 1695 and 1696 in ratifying new rulings handed down by the Deputation. In some of these the Council divided and even went to a vote, but if the king were present, and his view was known, it usually prevailed. In January 1695 there was such a case: it concerned a purchaser of a crown property, who subsequently put additional tenants on it and took their rents. It was argued he had not paid for this extra income and should refund it, with interest naturally. This was the king's view, and when he asked the Council for comment, there was none. So the king pronounced: 'it cannot be found otherwise than that his ruling, in all its parts, is just and reasonable, and therefore We confirm it and approve it'. Cases like this suggest that the supply of exploitable property within the nobility was drying up, and there is evidence the king's attention was turning to the assets of the commoners. The Commission set up to define the bounds of the royal forests was encroaching on the traditional rights of common enjoyed by peasants and townsmen. The Estate of Burghers was hit after 1693 by allegations of systematic evasion or underpayment of subsidies, and the payment of all the alleged arrears was demanded, and in 1695 there was a general review of the entitlements of the clergy, with the intention of clawing back some parts of them. It does seem that for the king, the increase of his revenues was becoming an end in itself, and was being intensified at the very time that his earlier success had balanced the budget, and the need for additional revenue was no longer obvious.[16]

It is clear that the officials engaged in the reduktion process were acquiring a vested interest in keeping it going. There has been little investigation of the extent of corruption among the Chamber officials involved, but there were very widespread allegations that they took bribes and exploited the rules for personal gain. There are a few examples where malpractice can be documented. Joel Gripenstierna was one of the most spectacular victims of the process. He had been a speculator, financier, revenue farmer and crown official. But he was eventually ordered to repay the crown over 1 million dsm. Gripenstierna was unusual in that he fought to the end, never admitted liability, and so did not qualify for possible royal mitigation. He resisted so successfully that he delayed final sequestration until 1694. His defence was that he was being framed by his enemies in the

---

[16] Lindqvist, *Gyllenborg*, pp. 177–80, 181–7, 188, 190, 195, 199–202, 204–9; Sjögren, *Karl den elfte*, pp. 456–7, 459–60; RA, Rådsprotokoll 1694–5, vol. 91a, meetings of 26 Jan. 1695, 4 May 1695, 2, 17 Jan. 1696; Carlson, *Historia*, IV, p. 200.

Chamber, of whom he had many. At one point he wrote to the king that 'the whole world looks in amazement at what Christian plots are played out against me, there are scarcely worse practised in Turkey itself'. However, when a liquidator who was a former colleague was appointed for his case, Gripenstierna immediately wrote to him, expressing his confidence that now at last he would get justice. As a token of his confidence, he offered the liquidator a property worth 1,500 dsm. a year, a substantial sum, with the assurance that the gift would remain secret, 'although it is nothing criminal, but clean and honourable'. There is no evidence on whether the gift was accepted; it certainly did not mitigate the rigour of the liquidator's final account. What is significant is that it was offered in the clear expectation that it would be accepted. It is also of interest to discover that when the reduktion recovered a group of properties in Färentuna district, among the list of the new landlords was Gyllenborg, with five farms, his colleague, Peter Franc, with two, and Erik Lovisin and Elias Adelstierna, both Chamber officials, with one each. This is unlikely to be coincidence, or an isolated instance, yet this kind of evidence can only be indicative. At present there is no basis in research for estimating how widespread the practice of reduktion officials using the process for their own private advantage was. Charles XI, through his narrow, legalistic pursuit of what he conceived to be his and the kingdom's rights, had set in motion a process that became self-sustaining, and which he lacked the perception or the will to halt. By the time of the king's death, what had been a rational policy which met a national need was degenerating into practices that sometimes bordered on extortion. The king and his officials were trapped in a maze of their own making, and reduktion was becoming an end in itself rather than a means, however harsh, for achieving financial stability for the kingdom.[17]

At the same time, the king's second most important enterprise, the reform of the kingdom's defence capability, was being brought to a successful maturity. An essential part of the process was the unremitting personal oversight and intervention of the king. Every summer, and occasionally in winter, the king undertook tours of inspection in the provinces, in which the main activity was the inspection of the local military establishments. In his last years, Charles XI went to Norrland, Gothenburg and Bohuslän in 1694, Västergötland in 1695, Västerås and Uppsala in 1696. When he was in Stockholm he gave close attention to all military decisions, especially questions of promotion and appointment, but also to apparently marginal details as well. The king inspected a consignment of cavalry horses, which Bielke had purchased and despatched. He complained to Bielke that they were 'altogether too thin', because of the negligence of the official in charge of them. He was sent a stern reprimand in a letter from the king. Whether this kind of personal intervention was a profitable use of the king's time and energy is open to debate. But it was part of Charles XI's character that he had difficulty in distinguishing the trivial

---

[17] A. Munthe, *Joel Gripenstierna: en storfinansiär från Karl XIs tid* (Stockholm, 1941), pp. 220–2, 246–51, 263.

from the important, and he wanted in principle to know everything and to be omnicompetent. Beyond that, all things military, and horses in particular, were his special concerns.[18]

Military appointments were taken very seriously by the king. Nils Bielke was one of the few senior commanders to whom the king was willing to delegate some powers of appointment, but even then, the king imposed his own agenda. The king persistently pressed for the replacement of foreign mercenaries in the officer corps with native subjects, and told Bielke in 1688 of his wish 'to be rid of them [the aliens] and to appoint Swedish officers instead'. The king revealed the care with which he checked on appointments when he wrote to Bielke in 1696, rejecting his proposal to appoint a Major Claeson, 'since I have seen the report which is here on the service record of all officers, and see from it that Major Claeson has not been in my military service, except as stable-master to the late Field Marshal Königsmarck, but has since served other masters, so it seems best to me that the Councillor take a Swede for it'. He then emphasized his point: 'the Councillor shall hereafter always try to get Swedish officers in his regiment, since I would rather have my own subjects in regiments which are Swedish'. Another feature of the king's appointment policies which emerges is that he was restricting privileged entry into service for the relatives and clients of magnates, and at the higher levels, the rank of major and above, he was imposing a career structure based on seniority. Before 1680, it was common for a client of a magnate to become a colonel by the time he was thirty. After 1680, almost nobody, not even the children of King's Councillors, enjoyed such a privileged fast-track in army service. The age for appointment to senior rank was rising steadily. Below the rank of major, on the other hand, it is apparent how the regime's own military and civil servants were monopolizing entry into army careers for their offspring. This was a further factor in the process by which the old social structure was being modified, and the former oligarchy of magnate families was being pushed aside by the new hereditary service class, for whom full-time royal service was becoming the normal way of life.[19]

By the year 1690, the main elements of the reformed military establishment were in place. It gave the kingdom a standing army of just over 60,000 men, 37,000 of them based in Sweden–Finland in territorial cavalry, infantry and dragoon regiments, supported by the indelningsverk and the knektehåll. The remaining 24,000 men were mercenaries, mostly stationed in fortresses and provincial garrisons. The core field force consisted of native troops, adequately and reliably funded, provided with uniform clothing and equipment, all of which was manufactured within the kingdom. They were subjected to a systematic training programme based on one uniform instruction manual, and lived with the constant possibility of royal

---

[18] Sjögren, *Karl den elfte*, p. 461; Malmström, ed., 'Karl XIs bref till Nils Bielke', p. 91, letter of 30 Mar. 1694.

[19] Malmström, ed. 'Karl XIs bref till Nils Bielke', p. 44, letter of 24 Mar. 1688; p. 97, letter of 9 Dec. 1696; p. 99, letter of 9 Dec. 1696; Asker, *Officerarna*, pp. 114–16, 117, 118.

inspection and reprimand. Because of the level of professionalism that this achieved, it was probably the best fighting force in the Europe of its day. The main unfinished business in the 1690s arose from the king having realized that the original indelningsverk for the cavalry was inadequate. So the whole system had been restructured and new resources, largely procured from the widened reduktion approved in 1686, were provided. The king reported to the Diet of 1693 that this process was almost complete. The Propositions said: 'the king allows himself the firm hope that the cavalry indelningsverk will soon reach a satisfactory and definitive conclusion'. The king had also become aware of the problem that some tenants of cavalry farms were not very competent farmers, and could get into difficulty meeting their obligations. To remedy this each cavalry regiment had to establish a contingency fund, to which each tenant paid 6 dsm. a year, and this was then put in the Bank. By 1697, these contingency funds for the cavalry, assigned to maintaining equipment and meeting mobilization costs, amounted to 526,627 dsm. And there was a further levy to build a fund for hiring extra cavalry NCOs in time of war. By 1693, most of the infantry regiments were on the combined indelningsverk and knektehåll system, except in parts of Finland, notably Österbotten, which chose to keep conscription. The 1693 report to the Diet said that most of the formal knektehåll agreements had now been completed and sealed. The king also imposed a contingency levy for the infantry regiments, which by 1697 amounted to 367,627 dsm. The reports to the Diet in 1693 stressed how the king had personally scrutinized all the details of the agreements. The Marshal dwelt on the achievement, and invited the Estates to recall 'how wretched and miserable a soldier was in this country before the late war, but now God be praised, his condition is wholly different. Over the years we shall feel the advantage more and more, so that no faithful subject can fail to recognize with acclamation the king's great labours in this.' It was asserted that the king had examined the accounts of every cavalry farm himself, 'finally assigning to each as high a charge as the king, after careful enquiry, found was appropriate to the condition of the farm'. Given the king's known appetite for work, this is quite credible.[20]

A further improvement reported in 1693 was the new mobilization scheme set out in the king's military transit ordinance. This was based on the levy of a small property tax on the whole kingdom to cover the costs of troops on the move, especially in the case of a general mobilization. The actual routes and timetables for this had all been set out, and depots and billeting arrangements made in advance, while for all troop movements, the fund would pay cash to the localities for the expenses incurred. Over all of early modern Europe, the transit of soldiers was something to be feared by the communities through which they passed. The Marshal could boast that now, in Sweden, this was no longer the case: 'this is as salutary and useful a system as any in the world . . . in case a war breaks out, the king

---

[20] Cavallie, *Fred till krig*, p. 34, 42; *SRARP*, XVI, pp. 15, 88–9; Loenbom, ed., *Handlingar*, V, collection XIV, pp. 168, 170, 172.

will know precisely every day how the marches are going, and where the regiments and companies stand each day'. The Propositions of 1693 claimed that as a result of the ordinance, 'not only have all complaints in this matter ceased, because all now carry the same burden, but all transport and accommodation, together with carriage of equipment are paid for with ready money'. Under the old order all these burdens fell disproportionately on the communities which lay along the main roads. The 1690s also reflected growing budgetary stability by increases of pay for junior officers and the programme for providing standard service housing for the army. A building programme was launched to make this available for the personnel of the territorial regiments. The final aspect of the reform of the land forces was the continuing investment in the frontier fortresses, as capital became available, following the comprehensive plans drawn up by Dahlberg. Priority was still being given to the Danish–Norwegian frontier, and Germany, and the frontier with Russia was left to a later phase. This turned out to be a mistake, but a wholly natural one; the Russians had given no serious trouble for forty years, and their government seemed to be in considerable disarray. It is understandable that the Russian danger was not being taken seriously.[21]

The navy in the 1690s seemed to become more and more the personal empire of Hans Wachtmeister. The central feature was the development of the base at Karlskrona into a proper fortified town, populated with Admiralty officials, dockyard workers and seamen, with their families. The Admiralty report to the Diet of 1697 was confident and self-satisfied; the fighting fleet had been largely rebuilt and had thirty-eight ships of the line, in contrast with the twenty-seven that had done so badly in the late war. But the main problem had been providing manpower. Karlskrona, in the former Danish province of Blekinge, was far from the coastal parishes of the Gulf of Bothnia, from which the navy used to levy most of its men. To compensate for this, the scheme outlined in the Propositions of 1693 had been implemented, of negotiating with the former recruiting communities to commute their obligation into a cash payment. The money was then used to hire a cadre of professional seamen to serve in Karlskrona. This was being done, but there were difficulties; some communities preferred to provide conscripts rather than cash. So there was a further scheme to attract professional sailors and their families to settle in Blekinge permanently, which had the added advantage of diluting the Danish population, still politically suspect, with loyal Swedes and Finns. The king had shown a stubborn reluctance to change from the old system of recruiting conscripts. A report from Wachtmeister and his fellow admirals in 1686 set out clearly the advantages of having a smaller number of professional seamen, paid a retainer to settle in Blekinge, over a larger number of conscripts who would have to be transported long distances to Karlskrona. In any case paid, experienced seamen were much more efficient than conscripts and cheaper in the long run. The king

---

[21] Cavallie, *Fred till krig*, p. 36; Loenbom, ed., *Handlingar*, v, collection xiv, pp. 176, 178; *SRARP*, xvi, pp. 91–2.

was opposing Wachtmeister's proposal as late as 1691, but the Admiral wore him down and it was announced as a settled policy at the Diet of 1693. Wachtmeister pointed out in his report that he needed 'a few thousand men on hand, so that if a squadron must be got away in haste, they will always suffice for crewing it'. By 1697, about 1,350 seamen and their families had been brought into Blekinge, who did indeed dilute the original Danish population of about 10,000. In case there was a general mobilization of the fleet, then conscripts would have to be brought in to supplement them. When the time came in 1700, the navy performed well, and most of the credit is Wachtmeister's for standing up for his professional opinions against the king. He was helped by his expertise in an area where the king had none, and by Karlskrona being too far from Stockholm for the king to visit it very often. The establishment of Karlskrona as the principal base for the Swedish navy is another of the regime's achievements that has survived to the present day.[22]

In early modern Europe, all governments had traditionally aspired to regulate and control economic activity. This gave rise to a spectrum of strategies to which historians long gave the name of mercantilism, though they have been arguing ever since over what, if anything, the content of this concept should be. If mercantilism existed, then Charles XI and his advisers were mercantilists, for they pursued the same economic objectives, by the same means as every other European kingdom. Discussion of this subject is hampered by the lack of firm evidence about what the practical result of the policies on the kingdom's economy was, although the negative impacts are easier to discern from the loud protests of those affected by them. The utter conventionality of Swedish thinking about economic policy is revealed in the report to the Diet of 1697 from the Commerce College. This College, originally independent, had been merged into the Chamber in 1680, but was quickly reestablished as an autonomous sub-department under Claes Fleming, who was President of the Chamber and of its commerce department. The report of 1697 defined the intention and method of the policy, as it reviewed the numerous

royal ordinances and statutes, which have mainly been designed so that the country can best be provided for, the king may properly receive the rights that belong to him, and trade and industry be adapted to the general welfare, according to the characteristics of each region, as well as the special privileges lawfully granted and assigned to one and all, which the College in accordance with the king's trade and other ordinances . . . has striven after.

The strengthening of the domestic economy was the unifying purpose of all its activity, 'whereby everyone, of whatever estate or calling he may be, who pursues his work and profession with the necessary prudence and diligence, and does not ruin himself through idleness, slackness and extravagance, may enjoy his share'.[23]

This rhetorical introduction summed up the economic consensus of early mod-

---

[22] Loenbom, ed., *Handlingar*, IV, collection XI, pp. 113–26; Villstrand, *Kustbygd*, pp. 390, 391, 393, 394, 396, 398, 400, 404, 408–12.
[23] Loenbom, ed., *Handlingar*, II, collection III, pp. 5–63.

ern Europe. It was axiomatic that government should regulate economic activity in the interests of the community as a whole. Usually this involved encouraging economic expansion, but not in disregard of other considerations. The sort of contradictions that could arise were revealed in the Diet of 1693 when the Marshal suggested that the Estates should petition the king for a code of dress, prescribing what the different social groupings might wear. The aim was to preserve respect for social hierarchy, and suppress needless luxury. A regulation would be the means 'whereby the disorder and extravagance which spoils and ruins many folk could be abolished'. The benevolent paternalism of this kind of regulation, however, ran up against the hard facts of economic life. Those who understood the working of the contemporary economy knew that it was the luxury trades that were the principle motor of economic expansion, because only the relatively affluent elites had any surplus spending power. In the 1693 debate, which in this field was free and open, speakers showed awareness of how the luxury trades expanded employment for the poor. Wellingk, for one, argued for caution. They must consider that 'it could be very useful, if such a dress regulation did not hold back manufacturing'. The desire to regulate and protect could clash with the aim of expanding the economy. L. Creutz, a provincial governor, stressed how in his provincial capital, Åbo in Finland, the poor were eager to supplement their income by weaving at home, but were prevented by existing guild regulations. If allowed, such cottage industry enabled 'poor folk in the towns and the peasants in the countryside opportunity to earn themselves some money by this means'. But there were also moral aspects to consider: the Stockholm magistrate, M. Törne, deplored the idea that valuable metals, like copper and iron, were exported to earn foreign exchange for buying 'silk cloth and other such vanities'. On the whole public discussion of economic issues was conducted in terms of such traditional values, and nothing original emerged from it.[24]

It is difficult to demonstrate how far the orthodox policies followed by Charles XI and his officials were effective. The report of 1697 noted the encouragement of native shipping by preferential tariff exemptions, the expansion of shipbuilding, in particular the development of a major new shipyard in Stockholm and official encouragement and assistance in the development of new techniques. There was one undoubtedly successful new industry that had been supported: the manufacture of tar in the backwoods of northern Sweden and Finland, wherever there were navigable rivers to take it to the coast. It was in this period that 'Stockholm tar', so called because Stockholm was the compulsory staple port for exporting it, was developing into one of Europe's most valued naval stores. The report celebrated this, and claimed that during the king's reign, 'through the blessing of almighty God and sound advice it has achieved such growth that the common peasants, the burghers and the merchants have prospered substantially more from it than ever

---

[24] RA, R 2378, meeting of 7 Nov. 1693.

before'. The report also noted there had been revision of guild regulations, to open the way for new developments, and how the king had encouraged import substitution by developing native manufactures, using import prohibitions and protective tariffs. It was claimed that the resulting economic growth easily compensated for any short-term loss of customs revenue, and asserted that since 1687, the receipts from the customs had risen by 1,900,000 dsm. They listed the expanding textile trades, the establishment of domestic tobacco growing, the development of native salt manufacture, though it was conceded that imported salt was still cheaper. They had not overlooked agriculture, as some contemporaries fixated on manufactures and exports tended to do, though there was not a lot to show, except introducing the cultivation of hops in Sweden. The king's personal drive to improve the breeding of horses, which was canvassed in most of the Diets of the reign, was politely blocked by the Estates who showed no enthusiasm for sharing in the costs.[25]

Charles XI was enthusiastic, if rather ill-informed, about economic policies, having no doubt that it was both right and effective for him to exercise his royal authority in a command economy. In this, as in other areas, he exhibited his dour integrity. One of the forbidden imports was linen, to protect a struggling native manufacture. It was put to him that he should use imported linen for the royal Court, but he refused: 'since the import of linen is forbidden, We ourselves will not breach that prohibition'. There were not many monarchs in contemporary Europe who would have been so scrupulous. The king's economic enthusiasms bore particularly hard on the citizens of Stockholm, who since they were acutely aware how their municipal privileges depended on retaining the good-will of the king were hardly in a position to refuse cooperation. Though it is to be noted that the Stockholm magistracy, who were mostly career bureaucrats, largely detached from trade and industry, were more compliant than the real trading community in the city. They had expressed their view at the Diet of 1680, when they protested at the protection of domestic manufactures, since they represented consumer and commercial interests. But most contemporary wisdom was better represented by a Scottish entrepreneur, D. Young, later ennobled as Leijonanckar, who claimed that subsidizing and protecting native manufacture was always for the general good. He was petitioning for a contract to set up a textile manufacture at Barnängen, near Stockholm. He said that 'everything that you load on to foreign wares, above what is levied so far, apart from salt and wine, does us no harm, but everything that we lay on our own produce . . . damages us seriously'. He claimed that all manufacturing brought profit both for the community and the king. In 1685, the Stockholm magistracy echoed his views: all manufacturing was advantageous, and should enjoy tariff protection, since it helped reduce 'begging and other devices', and was 'of service to the ruler and to the prosperity and strength of society'.[26]

The king was an easy prospect for such sales talk and expected Stockholm to

---

[25] Loenbom, ed., *Handlingar*, II, collection III, pp. 14, 16, 22, 26, 34, 41, 45, 59.
[26] Carlson, *Historia*, IV, pp. 85, 97, 98, 100; Corin, *Stockholms stadsförvaltning*, pp. 30, 328, 334, 339.

fund his enthusiasms. Thus the municipality had to put up the money to launch the new shipyard in Stockholm that proved economically viable; even so the city was pressing for its transfer to private ownership by 1691. In 1687 the king was enthused by a projector, P. Starbus, with a proposal to start domestic manufacture of the new flintlock muskets that were coming into service all over Europe. It was a project near the king's heart, so he ordered the magistracy to fund it out of city funds. They were unenthusiastic, but they complied. Their worst experience came over the attempt to start up a domestic silk manufacture. A group of merchants, allegedly Armenian, came to Stockholm in 1687 with a stock of raw silk, and the king pressed a reluctant Stockholm magistracy to buy it. They had to borrow 40,000 dsm. to fund the purchase. The king then instructed them to start a manufacture, offering to impose a prohibition on the import of silk goods. The merchant community knew it would be an economic disaster, but the king insisted. In 1690 Stockholm petitioned to be allowed to cut its losses and pull out of the project, but this was refused, and when the magistracy discussed the king's response nobody was ready to propose a protest against the king's order. So they ploughed on, piling up losses each year. In 1691 the king assured them that the enterprise was 'a notable success for the public and a general benefit and advantage for the country's inhabitants'. In the end the power of absolute monarchy met consumer resistance. One protesting Stockholm shopkeeper, who had to stock the silk goods, claimed: 'as soon as some female came into his shop and saw them, she recognized them as made in the town and for that reason would not buy'. When the municipality was at last permitted to withdraw from the project in 1694, it had lost 80,000 dsm. and 60% of its stock of silk goods remained unsold. It had been a classic example of the hazards of economic planning under an absolute king.[27]

Economic development had been on the agenda of the Diet of 1686, and as a result a Commission was established to consider ways and means. Their report came up with a string of economic clichés: they deplored the export of unprocessed metals, the decay of sail-making, the import of superfluous luxury goods, which they alleged, improbably, cost the kingdom 2 million dsm. a year. They recommended tariff protection for domestic manufactures, especially linen, and that in general the use of domestic products be required, while the mining industry must earn its privileges by processing its output before export. When the Commission report was put to the Riddarhus, it was accepted without question. 'The nobility were altogether satisfied with what the Commission had done.' It was decided to maintain it as a standing Committee on trade and manufactures. It is well established that there was significant economic development in Sweden in the 1690s; the economy was diversifying and some improvement in living standards was taking place. Much of the development arose from shipping, and the growing Swedish involvement in oceanic trade, basically in commodities like salt and wine from

[27] Corin, *Stockholms stadsförvaltning*, pp. 344–56, 368–70.

southern Europe. Swedish ships also had a share in the European carrying trade; some penetrated into the Mediterranean, but part of this depended on their status as neutral shipping during the general war, and was clearly vulnerable to a change in circumstances. Some of the manufacturing developments proved solid, the tar manufacture for one, and the processing of copper and iron for another; it was in this period that Sweden became the world's biggest supplier of bar iron. But it is impossible to evaluate how much of the development was promoted or furthered by government policy, or would have taken place in any case. The developments certainly reinforced the belief of the king and his bureaucrats that they had the ability to direct economic development.

An interesting project, in which Charles XI was closely involved, was a system-atic effort to combat the menace of famine. Until the nineteenth century, all the countries of Europe, with the exception of the United Provinces and England, with their relatively advanced systems of farming for the market, were at risk of famine and its attendant epidemics in years of bad harvest. Contemporaries lived with this stoically, as a fact of life, and rationalized it as God's retribution, visited on communities where the level of defiance of God's laws reached unacceptable levels. The prescribed remedies were repentance and prayer. The king and the Swedish Church wholeheartedly subscribed to this scenario, yet, rather inconsistently, the king tried to evade the divine scourge by accumulating grain stocks in years of abundance to relieve shortages when the harvests failed. The stocks were financed by the king, and in time of need were not distributed free, but either sold at a low fixed price, or loaned to the producers, in which case they were due to be repaid with interest when conditions improved. Charles XI's government was unusual in its willingness to invest for this purpose. There was no sentimentality involved; it was a pragmatic policy, discussed and approved in the Diet of 1689, when resources began to be available, and reported on in the Diet of 1693. It was told that the king 'partly had, partly intended to establish, magazines and stores for grain'. Already some local disaster areas had been relieved, 'where after crop failure they had neither bread to eat, nor seed to sow'. There was a strictly practical motive for the policy, since famine resulted in deserted farms, 'to the great damage and loss of the king in his revenues'.[28]

In the autumn of 1695 the report from the governors indicated that the harvest had failed over much of northern Sweden and Finland. There was now a new resource available to the king, the reduktion revenues in cash and kind from Livland. The king ordered shipments from Riga of 6,000 tons of grain to Öster-botten, of which a fifth was lost by shipwreck, and 5,000 tons to Västerbotten. The governor was in charge of distribution, making lists of the neediest farms and rationing the sales at a low fixed price. Only the farmers could purchase, the labourers could not buy even if they had money. They would have to get relief

---

[28] RA, R 2375, meeting of 15 Sept. 1686; *SRARP*, xv, pp. 34–6; RA, R 2378, meeting of 4 Nov. 1693.

through the employers. If the number of vacant farms in 1696 is a reliable indicator, the worst consequences were averted. But in the summer of 1696 it was clear the crops had failed again and the local price of grain soared to record levels. So the king ordered a second round of relief supplies, and also ordered any local grain given in payment of taxes should be retained in the area. Even so the famine effect was cumulative, because in the last winter of the king's life, mortality rose sharply and mass migration of starving people began from the affected area. The result was that in 1697, 6% of the farms in the two worst hit provinces were vacant. In his last weeks of life the king was ordering preparations for a further relief operation for 1697–8, but as it happened the worst was over, and conditions returned to normal in 1698. The famine of 1695–7 was a real test of the ability of the absolute monarchy to be an effective guardian of the public welfare. The success of the relief programmes was clearly limited, and hampered by the difficulties and hazards of distributing bulk supplies with early modern transport facilities. But it remains a very creditable operation; few other contemporary governments would have had the resources, the will or the administrative capacity to have achieved as much.[29]

The last great project of the reign of Charles XI was the revision of the Land Law, raised in the Diet of 1686, ostensibly as an initiative from the Estates. In response the king appointed the Law Commission to undertake the work, and it functioned for the rest of the reign, and long afterwards, until in 1734 it produced a codification of the law, which remained the basis of the Swedish legal system into modern times. It has been noted earlier that the case for revision was based on the archaic language of the Land Law, as printed in 1608, and the fact that the sixteenth- and seventeenth-century legislation by Diet Resolution, royal ordinances and statutes, and the considerable body of rulings from the new High Courts and the Council, through appeals procedure, had not been incorporated into the Land Law. Two factors stood in the way of revising or editing the laws. One was the consequent investment of the time and energies of skilled manpower in such a complex task, at the expense of other government activities. The other was the rooted conservatism of the whole society. The Land Law was regarded as a sacred text, one of the very foundations of society, which bound the community together by defining the duties and privileges of its members. It was not seen as open to change; at most it could be interpreted and extended to meet developing needs. In a culture which equated change with decay and degeneration, there was an almost paranoid reluctance to contemplate any tampering with the traditional texts. It was a feeling analogous to that of the clergy, when faced with calls to revise the catechism, or retranslate the Bible. Once the bare possibility of change was admitted, who could tell where the process might stop. There was a further particular problem with the Land Law. The section entitled the *Konunga Balk*, the

---

[29] I. Mäntylä, 'Kronan och undersåtarnes svält', *KFÅ* (1988), pp. 51–3, 54–8, 60–3.

Royal Chapter which was virtually the kingdom's constitution, had been drafted for an elective monarchy and never revised after the adoption of hereditary kingship in 1544.[30]

It can be argued that prior to 1672 the magnate elite, which repeatedly discussed revision in Council and Diet, had no interest in implementing it. They controlled the High Courts and the Council, and could use appeals procedures to interpret the laws as best suited them. But they too were against change on principle. Rålamb laid down, in 1664, that 'it is dangerous that the law should be changed, but that it be revised is useful'. The Justiciar, Per Brahe expressed a further reason against change in 1668: 'it is very dangerous to change or disturb anything in the law, which for so many hundred years has stood undisturbed, and been a guideline for all Sweden's inhabitants'. But he added a warning to the Council that talk of changing the law always foreshadowed an attack on the privileges of the nobility. 'We can be sure and certain that by that means, our privileges will experience some damage and diminution.' It remains clear, however, that the conservatism extended over the whole social spectrum. No Estate was more vigorously opposed to law reform than the Estate of the Peasants. And when it was discussed, words implying change were studiously avoided. The acceptable word was *revidera*, implying examination, adjustment, perhaps revision. The use of sovereign power to legislate, to change the law at will, as exemplified in Roman Law, and justified in that period in the works of Thomas Hobbes, was unacceptable in Sweden. It might seem that the Diet Resolution of 1682, which recognized that the king had an unrestricted power to issue ordinances that were legally binding, meant that the king could alter and remake the law at will. It is certain that no one at the time, certainly not the king, would have interpreted it in that sense. When the king did issue an ordinance, it was always submitted to the legal authorities for comment, and their traditionalist views were constant. Thus in 1686, Charles XI issued a major statute on wills and testaments, which went through the usual consultative procedure before it was issued. At a discussion in the Law Commission in 1690, this was taken as a precedent. 'When the ordinance about wills was issued, the king's most gracious will was only to interpret the law, and in no way to make a new law, but to declare as permanent what his Majesty found was closest to the sense of the law.' It was a classic articulation of the traditional consensus view that law developed through evolution from an unalterable base line.[31]

It cannot be proved that the decision of 1686 was not an authentic initiative by the Estates to which the king responded. But it is highly unlikely, for the driving force was Lindschöld, then the king's chief adviser in internal affairs, who is a

---

[30] H. A. Olsson, 'Laguppfattningen i Sverige under 1600- och tidiga 1700-talet: en huvudlinja', *KFÅ* (1968), pp. 8, 9, 12, 13–14, 19; H. Ylikangas, *Suomalaisen Sven Leijonmarckin osuus vuoden 1734 lain naimiskaaren laadinnassa: kaaren tärkeimpien säännöstöjen muokkautuminen 1689–1694* (Helsinki, 1967), pp. 230–1.

[31] Olsson, 'Laguppfattningen', pp. 14, 16, 18; Olsson, 'Karl XI', p. 98.

known enthusiast for modernizing the laws so that they were better suited to an absolute monarchy. The agreement of the king was wholly consistent with his passion for codifying all aspects of government, and his lifelong concern with the effective administration of justice. It has been suggested that even if it was a royal initiative, it did not at first include a revision of the King's Chapter. If that were so, the king quickly changed his mind, since within a few months Lindschöld had been instructed to revise the Chapter. Indeed it is almost certain there was a political agenda, since the reduktion could be carried through more effectively if property laws on matters like the rights of widows, the laws on marriage contracts, and other issues involved in any transfer of landed property were clarified. It has been shown how the proposal did meet with conservative suspicion in the Diet, and the actual petition from the Estates was cautious. It welcomed 'your Majesty's most gracious pleasure to order that the law be looked over, improved and brought into good order, and into our current Swedish language'. The emphasis was on editing and translating, but it went on to agree that redundant elements could be eliminated, and in their place royal ordinances and statutes, Resolutions of the Diets and modifications sanctioned by long-established custom could be inserted in the appropriate divisions. This emphatically did not envisage an Enlightenment style project for a rewriting of the Law from first principles.[32]

The king responded by appointing the Law Commission of twelve experts, all royal servants and known enthusiasts for the absolute monarchy, of whom three were burghers, including Cameen, and they were given the urban and commercial law to consider. Lindschöld was appointed President, and when he died in 1690, was succeeded by Nils Gyldenstolpe, an equally enthusiastic absolutist. The method of working was to divide the laws up under twelve headings, and each member took one of them. When a member had a report ready, it was debated in the Commission and an agreed text was evolved. If the king approved this, it was circulated to the Council and the judges of the High Court, the provincial governors, and the judiciary of each province for comment. The Commission would consider these, and draw up the definitive text, which, if approved by the king, would be printed and issued as the law. It must be noted that the provision of the Diet Resolution of 1682, that if the king issued a general law, it should be referred to the Estates for their opinion, was ignored. When the procedure was explained to the Secret Committee in 1693, there was no comment on this point, which might indicate how much the authority of the king had grown in ten years, or might simply mean that the consultative process which was to be followed was adequate. There is no evidence that there had been a deliberate decision to exclude the Estates; the order which established the commission in 1686 referred to it as being in response to 'the humble request of Our Estates at the last Diet', but there has been discussion about whether the remit set out differed significantly from the

---

[32] *SRARP*, xv, pp. 241–2; RA, Lagkommissionen 1686–1736: ÄK 15:25, inkomna skrivelser från Kongl. Mjt., letter of 16 Dec. 1687.

objectives in the Estates' petition. The king's instruction to the Commission defined their task as

to look over the Law and put it into good, up to date and useable Swedish, and at the same time leave out what is now out of use, and put in its place what We and Our royal predecessors . . . through lawful statutes and ordinances have commanded from time to time, also various Resolutions made at the Diets and long received custom, so that all may be brought into good order and condition.

That seems very close to the wording of the petition, and indicates a process of rationalization, which would leave the traditional body of the Law unchanged, except in respect of the language used. A further remit to the Commissioners described their task as 'humbly to present what they find necessary for the perfection and improvement of the Law in one case or another'.[33]

If the actual work of the Commissioners is examined it can be seen that there were some more radical individuals on the Commission who wanted to make changes. The general trend, as far as this can be discerned, was to widen the scope of the law at the expense of individual rights. One example was the law on the marriage of females, which fell to Sven Leijonmarck. He observed in his report how 'the world is turned upside down, that God's law is disregarded and thus the civil law, which is for good order, takes in all matters that come under it'. He was thus a social conservative and proposed a change to the law, that an unmarried servant girl should have her employer as legal guardian, if there was no relative available. His proposal was: 'if a woman has no father, mother, male relative or guardian, then he in whose household she is dwelling must be approached and spoken to for her marriage'. This was to strengthen the principle that everyone in society was subject to patriarchal authority, and especially that all unmarried females had a responsible male guardian until marriage. When this came to the Commission in 1690 it was fiercely debated. Gyldenstolpe was enthusiastic, it would reinforce the hierarchical structure, but others felt this was carrying the authoritarian principle too far. This episode was typical of what happened when individual members brought radical proposals: in the debate in the Commission, which as always was looking for consensus, they would be weakened, and this even before they were exposed to the views of the external judiciary. A memorial to Lindschöld, always one of the most radical, reminded him that the Commission was not supposed to change the old Law, but where absolutely necessary, they could add marginal notes by way of explanation. A comment from a member of Göta High Court appealed to the terms of their remit: 'I cannot honestly see that his royal Majesty's most gracious will is that some new Law Code shall be made, but that the Law Code be examined.' He added a practical consideration to support his view. The common folk could not in any case fully understand the

---

[33] RA, Lagkommissionen: protokol, meeting of 16 Dec. 1686; Ylikangas, *Sven Leijonmarckin*, p. 28; RA, R 2378, meeting of 6 Nov. 1693; Olsson, 'Karl XI', p. 99.

written law; many were illiterate and others who could read would find even the modernized language too difficult. The common folk had absorbed a body of basic legal concepts by tradition, and would be baffled and confused if these were changed. And since in Sweden, the common juror had a vital function in the system this was a serious consideration. At the end this spirit of pragmatic caution prevailed, the Code of 1734 was a classification and rationalization of the traditional laws, not a reconstruction on novel principles, and this is what must have been intended. To the early modern mind, the idea of changing traditional structures was alien; everything rested on the laws of God at root, and everyone knew that God's laws were immutable and the same for all ages.[34]

In the end, the Law Commission laboured for forty-eight years and finished its task thirty-seven years after Charles XI had died. This was not at all what the king had envisaged, a further indication that he saw the task of the Commission as editing and translating. At first he was angered and baffled by the lack of progress. When the Commission met in November 1687, Lindschöld called for progress reports, 'since his royal Majesty is wondering about it'. One by one the Commissioners confessed they had been so occupied with their other duties they had got very little done. Lindschöld told them, correctly, that this would not please the king: 'he had the king's command to enquire whether everyone is ready with their work . . . it would be good if, before Christmas something could be shown . . . it is now close to a year and a day since the Commission was ordered'. The king was indeed displeased and told the Commissioners he would wait until January, and after that 'the king graciously wills to be informed monthly how things are in this so urgent business'. The minute books show that the Commission met infrequently in 1688 and 1689, followed by a pause until the summer of 1690, when they were very active. In this phase they were concentrating on land and property law. Two blank years followed, after which the Commission was active in 1693 and 1694, followed by another hiatus until the last year of the king's life. The records have little to say about the king's personal role in the work of the Commission. He certainly had the naive expectation that it could finish its work in three or four years, but reality did break in, and in 1688 he agreed to try and lighten the work load of some members, though he also complained to Lindschöld that the work they did submit was too verbose: 'his royal Majesty is looking for the utmost brevity'. It seems probable that he came to realize that no amount of pressure from him would speed things up, accepted that it would be a long-term project, and lost interest. This can be deduced from his order to the Commission in 1690 'that it is his royal Majesty's most gracious will that the Commission should prepare one Chapter after the other, and specifically in the order they should and can follow'. On the other hand he made the Commission's work more difficult, when some critical issue came to the High Courts or the Council, by referring it to the Law Commission for an instant

[34] Ylikangas, *Sven Leijonmarckin*, pp. 80–1, 233.

opinion. It can be observed that in the report to the Diet of 1693, there was no suggestion that the Commission's work would be finished soon.[35]

In 1696 there was a change of policy on the Law Commission, originating with the king. Charles XI had always shown himself very conscious of the need to define and protect his royal prerogatives. Although he was deficient in academic training, and showed no interest in abstract ideas as such, he had very clear notions of his position as king by the grace of God. None of these was original; as with his religious beliefs, he took his ideas ready formed from the prevailing orthodoxies. The king knew that he was, literally, God's Deputy on earth, with unlimited authority to order his hereditary kingdom at his will, and that he was accountable for his actions to God alone. The subjects were bound, as a religious duty, to yield unquestioning obedience to the king's commands, which to them were equivalent to God's commands. The king had no problem about the basis of his authority, it was grounded on the clear Word of God in Scripture. The king's views had been fixed at an early stage and did not change or develop over time. Yet despite his confidence in his rights, he always showed himself acutely sensitive to any perceived challenge to his sovereignty.[36]

In June 1681, the king had rebuked the Council for presuming to reopen a case which he had already resolved. Final judgement in any legal case was a power reserved 'to Our supreme sovereignty by Sweden's fundamental law'. Next year the *Svea hovrätt* made the same mistake, and was told to 'be content to carry out your office towards those who seek their rights from you'. In 1685 he wrote to his royal cousin, Duke Adolf Johan, a prince of the Empire, and a rather choleric character, about his assertion that his properties in Sweden were exempt from reduktion, because of his princely status. The king told Adolf Johan he was mistaken. His claim 'in no small way concerns Our royal rights and preeminence and Sweden's fundamental laws: also *jura communia gentium et regnorum*, which does not permit *status in statu*, but binds all, high and low together under its jurisdiction'. The duke had further offended by writing directly to the *Göta hovrätt*, asserting his claim. He was told: 'it is not fitting for Us to allow anyone to argue about, or contest Our royal rights and jurisdiction within Our kingdom'. The king was telling the duke that he was not just absolute, but that his position was beyond discussion, and put him down by saying he could expect the same justice in Sweden as anyone else in the kingdom. The king made much the same points, this time in a friendly letter to the directors of the Bank, who were appointed by, and answerable to, the Estates. The royal Liquidation Commissioners had objected to the Bank charging compound interest on advances it made to the crown. The Bank

---

[35] RA, Lagkommissionen: protokol, meeting of 15 Nov. 1687, and meeting n.d. to consider the king's letter of 16 Dec. 1687 and meeting of 15 Mar., 6 Apr., 24 July, 12, 14, 19, 22 Dec. 1688; meetings of 12 Sept. 13, 19, 26 Nov, 3, 4, 6, 13, 17 Dec. 1689; meeting of 11 Feb. 1690; RA, R 2378, meeting of 6 Nov. 1693.

[36] Grauers, *Sveriges Riksdag*, pp. 118, 119, 120.

had replied that this was based on the king's undertaking of 1675 to observe the rules laid down by the Estates. In his letter to the Bank, the king graciously confirmed his promise of 1675, but pointed out that no orders issued by the Estates, or the Bank, had any force until the king had confirmed them, 'since power and authority in Our kingdom is bestowed on and belongs to Us alone, and everything that is done in any way, without Our gracious will, knowledge and confirmation, is itself without force and altogether invalid'. He told the Bank to submit copies of all its relevant rules for confirmation. At the Diet of 1689, the Bank directors wrote to the king, admitting their error in issuing orders on their own authority, and humbly submitted all their proposed regulations to the king because they 'have their first origins from your royal Majesty's most gracious consent and confirmation and all their strength and content depend only upon your royal Majesty's most gracious protection'. That pleased the king who wrote back that he confirmed all their regulations. He still took the opportunity of reminding them that even if their regulations had been confirmed by his predecessors, if they were prejudicial to the royal sovereignty, they were void and 'shall not have any continuance, but be regarded as if they had never been made, since no king has power to give away any part of the royal sovereignty and rights from his royal successor or descendants, since the *jura majestatis* are inalienable from the kingly powers'. Charles XI grasped the paradoxical position that although the royal authority had no limits, nothing done under it could infringe the rights of a succeeding king, thus emphasizing how personal the royal sovereignty was. That was the basis of the reduktion law of 1682, which asserted that the all-powerful king could not alienate permanently any part of the crown estates, because his successor could always revoke the grant. The king was eager to stress to his subjects the personal character of kingship, in his assertions that no distinction could be made between the person of the king and his kingdom. When the title of the Council was changed in 1682, the king explained that 'between Us and the kingdom there is no separate or special interest, but there is a unity which in itself is completely inseparable and can in no way be divided or distinguished'.[37]

The king's confident assertions of his royal sovereignty do conceal a problem with the concept. The early modern mind was never totally comfortable with the doctrine of absolute sovereignty. Hobbes, who expounded it in its modern form, was generally denounced by those in authority wherever he was read. The problem was how, with such a doctrine, could an absolute king be distinguished from a tyrant? Everyone understood that Charles XI was an absolute king, but the Ottoman Sultan, who had the same powers, was a tyrant. The difference was, of

---

[37] RA, Lagkommissionen 1686–1736: ÄK 15:8, king's letter to the Council 25 June 1681 (also in Riksregistraturet 1681, p. 798, king's letter to the *Svea hovrätt* 15 Sept. 1682, king's letter to the Duke (also in Riksregistraturet 1685, p. 346), king's letter to the Directors of the Bank 30 Apr. 1689, king's letter to the bishops 11 Mar. 1682; S. Brisman, *Den palmstruckska banken och riksens ständers bank under den karolinska tiden* (Stockholm, 1918), pp. 97–100; Olsson, 'Karl XI', p. 104.

course, that Charles XI was a Christian king, and thus subject to the Law of God, which was why when a priest expounded God's Word, kings had nothing to say. The point had come up in the Law Commission in 1690, when it was discussing blasphemy and whether the king could pardon an offender, when Scripture clearly said that the penalty for blasphemy was death. Lindschöld, for all his unyielding absolutist views said:

it seems to me that a king should be able to dispense when there is an offence against all that concerns the king himself, his sovereignty, rights, etc. But where God's sovereignty is involved and there is a clear command from God on the offence and its punishment, in that case it seems to me neither the king, nor anyone else has the least power to dispense.

Swedish Courts had long accepted the priority of God's laws, and hence implicitly recognized a restriction on the king's authority, though Lindschöld did not discuss the consequences if a king did flout God's laws. It is almost certain he would not have thought a subject could protest.[38]

For an absolutist like Lindschöld the problem was insoluble, and it would have been for Charles XI, if he had ever conceived the possibility of his acting against the Law of God. Potentially there was another constraint on royal sovereignty. The declaration of the Estates of 1680 had said that the kings of Sweden were absolute Christian kings, who ruled their kingdom 'according to law and lawful custom', and although that phrase was left out of the sovereignty declaration of 1693, it can be held to be implicitly confirmed by it. This raised the question of what sort of a constraint this was, and it was the king himself who tried to give an answer, in a letter to General Schültz about litigation in which the general was involved, in March 1682. The king wrote:

We can be said, in a case, to be above the law, to the extent that We have power and the right, with mature and deliberate advice, to change, or proclaim, or modify the Law when some evident reason, or unavoidable necessity demands and permits. But, without due legal cause and in the ordinary processes authorized by Us, to make an alteration, or esteem Ourself so above the law, that We will not allow Our subjects to enjoy and profit from it for their security and defence, that is absolutely foreign to Our royal office, and incompatible with Our subjects' security which We have promised and sworn to them in return for their duty of faith and obedience.

This letter shows that the king was himself confused. His sincere wish that the subjects should enjoy a rule of law was obvious. He referred frequently to his duty to see that all had free access to impartial justice. Yet he had a higher duty to God to preserve intact the sovereignty that God had conferred on him. Charles XI had no solution to this problem, which arises in any political system built around the sovereignty of the state. Logically, under any system of absolute state sovereignty, there can be no meaningful rule of law. The king's last sentence exposed further

---

[38] RA, Lagkommissionen: protokol, meeting of 11 Feb. 1690.

mental confusion, for it clearly implies a contract between the king and his subjects embodied in the coronation oath. Yet Charles XI would have been the first to dismiss such an idea as absurd, if anyone had put it to him. A king answered only to God.[39]

It was a feature of the active reign of Charles XI that the king and his advisers had given high priority to educating the subjects in their duty to their God-given ruler. The basic message was repeatedly conveyed to them. The formal declarations in the Diets of 1680, 1682 and 1693 had spelled out the basic concepts of what was due to an absolute Christian king. The whole business of denouncing and repudiating the offensive protocols had been educational, to eliminate erroneous ideas about the relations of kings and their subjects. This purpose was made clear when the king sent a circular to the heads of all educational institutions in April 1689, following the Diet proceedings.

We send you what is set down by the Diet in point 2.a of the Resolution about Our hereditary power and authority and the subjects' office and duty of obedience, that you may communicate the same to all the professors and teachers, that they may follow an appropriate conformity in teaching the youth and remove all previously asserted false opinions on these matters: so that subjects from the first beginnings may get to understand and know their duty as subjects, and thus be more encouraged to conduct themselves in accordance, and with an obedient devotion to Us and Our royal house, seek to earn for themselves Our royal grace and favour.

This indicated that the long campaign over the protocols had been more than a dutiful attempt to remove public slights on the reputation of the king's father. These public declarations were then reinforced by the king's control of his Church, which ensured that through its catechizing and preaching, correct ideas about the duties of subjects were regularly instilled in every parish in the kingdom.[40]

The king's inner reasons for this emphasis on political education must remain speculative. It certainly did not arise from any real challenge to his authority from within the kingdom, since there was none. The fact that in his last year he revived the campaign could have arisen because he was conscious of declining health, and the possibility of another regency, and felt it necessary to spell out yet again the nature of royal authority. In March 1696 the king wrote to the Law Commission, changing their instructions. He required them to speed up their rate of work by more frequent and regular meetings, and to concentrate on rewriting the *Konunga Balk* of the Land Law. 'His Majesty has graciously resolved to have introduced and read what is the core of the Laws, namely the Royal Chapter, to display through it his gracious intention to enable subjects to see and know what is included in his Majesty's rights.' From that point, until the king's death, the revision of the Royal Chapter became the main preoccupation of the Commission. Lindschöld had

---

[39] RA, Lagkommissionen: ÄK 15:8, king's letter to Schültz (also in RA, Riksregistraturet 357, 1682, p. 98); Olsson, 'Karl XI', p. 102.   [40] Carlson, *Historia*, IV, p. 302.

written a revised draft which was shown to the Commission in May 1687, and referred to by the king in a letter of December 1687, where he told Lindschöld that 'We graciously remember that you told Us last summer what you had drafted for a Royal Chapter.' But no copy of Lindschold's draft has been found, only it is known that it was used as a basis of the draft introduced by Gyldenstolpe in March 1696. The only light thrown in the brief discussion of 1687 was that the Commision thought the draft contained too many latinisms, which should be replaced with Swedish words. There had been a further brief debate on terminology in April 1688, when Lindschöld had reminded them that terms like 'Council of State' and 'Consistorium regni' were unacceptable, and suggested that throughout, the term 'king' be used instead of 'crown'. The Commission had agreed; Gyldenstolpe said that 'it strengthens further the mutual love between king and subject if the word king is used in place of crown, for the word king is more appropriate for an hereditary monarchy, and an hereditary kingdom is a gift of God'. It is clear that Gyldenstolpe's draft of 1696 was shorter, since it left out some material that Lindschöld had included, and was in twelve sub-sections, where the original Chapter in the Land Law had had twenty-four. Gyldenstolpe explained his thinking on this: 'there should only be included in the Law what concerns the subjects' duties and the penalties on those who offend against the king's rights, and then only a summary of the supreme royal sovereignty, and that briefly, since we cannot reckon up and include all of them'.[41]

The first section of Gyldenstolpe's draft declared that Sweden was an hereditary kingdom, to descend in the male and female line for all time. A separate Succession Ordinance was drafted to specify the rules of descent. Anyone who sought to challenge the succession was guilty of treason, and it was open to the king to extend the penalties to the offender's children and family. This was to emphasize the sanctity of the hereditary principle. The second section set out the royal powers under seventeen heads. The first was quite unambiguous: 'the king's power and command over the whole of his hereditary kingdom is completely unlimited since the king does not owe any account, in any respect, but to God alone, through Whose almighty power the royal government is guided and supported'. It followed that the king could issue ordinances and statutes at will in spiritual and secular matters, appoint all public officers, grant titles, approve and confirm all privileges, declare war and peace, and control public finance, 'and in every case of emergency imposes taxes on his subjects'. There was no hint that any process of consent was involved. The king had the final disposal of all the crown's assets and could recall or revoke all grants at will. The last heading attempted to sum it all up, 'therefore the supreme power and authority belongs to the king alone to act, alter, command and order over all his kingdom and subjects,

---

[41] RA, Lagkommissionen: protokol II, meetings of 9 May 1687, 6 Apr. 1688, 3 Mar. 1696; G. Hasselberg, 'Det karolinska kungabalksförslagen och konungars makt över beskattningen', *KFÅ* 1943, pp. 56–8, 59,60–3.

both in secular and spiritual and ecclesiastical affairs, without any exception'. Gyldenstolpe had made a clean sweep: the idea of consent to taxation, contained in the Land Law, and observed in practice by Charles XI, had disappeared, so had the idea of community consent to changes in the laws. In fact the whole idea of constitutional limitation or constraint collapsed in face of the assertion that the king's authority was a trust conferred by God, and could not be shared or devolved without a breach of that trust.[42]

The next five sections concerned the coronation, royal marriages, the queen's dowry, the support of the royal children and royal funerals, making the point in each case that the subjects were obliged to contribute to the costs of each of these. And then came a point close to the king's heart, the inviolability of the Royal Testament; it would be sedition in a subject to seek to alter its provisions. There followed a section on the duties of the subject. The subject was bound to loyalty and obedience. Loyalty involved that he or she, 'in good time, and to his full extent seek to support the king and the royal House and the royal government's advantage, profit and benefit, and reveal all harm in time and with his uttermost strength help protect it'. Obedience involved 'an indefatigable zeal to do and effect the king's order and instruction, whether it be the organization of work or other special purposes: also to carry out all the king's commands and orders, whether they issue from the king himself, or in his name by his officials and commissioners'. It was treason to oppose the king's will through actions, conspiracy, writing or word of mouth. If taken literally, this implied that a subject could assert no right or privilege against a royal command, or even remonstrate, however respectfully. There was provision for the Council, whose members were to advise the king when asked, but also to inform him of anything to his advantage and warn him of any dangers they became aware of. In this limited sense, the traditional right of the Council to advise the king unasked was retained. It would be a capital offence deliberately to slander or libel a King's Councillor. The explicit requirement of the Land Law that Councillors must be native born was left out. A further section concerned the king's officers, who were also protected against malicious libel, and the final sub-section affirmed the inalienability of the crown's rights and properties.[43]

Gyldenstolpe also drafted a coronation oath. It could be argued that this was inconsistent and empty of meaning in the light of what went before, since if the king chose to disregard the oath, the subject had no means of securing redress, or even voicing a complaint, except directly to God through prayer. Charles XII was being consistent when he declined to take a coronation oath; it was a contradiction in terms if taken by an absolute king. What is interesting about it is that the coronation oath was used to suggest that some of the constraints on government in the Land Law would remain in effect under an absolute king. There were six clauses in the oath, and the first was a promise to uphold true religion, as set out in the Confession

---

[42] RA, Lagkommissionen: protokol II, meeting of 3 Mar. 1696; RA, Lagkommissionen: ÄK 15:8, Konungabalken, 1696 års förslag.   [43] *Ibid.*

of Augsburg and Uppsala meeting of 1593. The second was a promise to uphold justice and truth and repress all wrongdoing by use of the kingly power. The third promised the equal protection of the royal justice to all the king's subjects, rich or poor, for their lawful rights and possessions. None should be deprived of life, limb or property except by due process of law, and the king would respect all rights and privileges 'which do not conflict with the kingly rights and authority'. The fourth promised to rule with the advice of his Council, and to appoint only native-born Protestants as Councillors. The fifth was a promise never to alienate the royal properties and revenues, and the sixth was a promise concerning taxation. The king would levy no taxation, except such as was necessary for war, defence and the upkeep of royal castles, properties and fortresses, or for other, 'unavoidable occasions and necessities, then I shall either myself ordain what is needed and required, reasonably and justly between my loving subjects: or ask their opinion how the taxes may best and most bearably be equalized and shared out, so that the service of my kingdom . . . may without delay . . . be adequately provided for'. This draft coronation oath certainly softened the impression created by the Royal Chapter itself, that the regime would be an arbitrary royal dictatorship, exercised without limits. The coronation oath, by reinstating concepts from the Land Law, acknowledging that subjects had rights, even implying the possibility of consultations with the Diet over taxation, sought to reassure the subjects, without giving away any of the fullness of power granted by God, that under the absolute monarchy there would still be a rule of law.[44]

The Law Commission discussed the draft Royal Chapter at their session on 3 March 1696, and two days later they approved it for circulation to the provincial governors and the judiciaries. The one issue that had caused serious discussion in the Commission was the penalties for treason and whether they should extend to the whole family of anyone convicted. One rather junior member, Abraham Hylten, argued that it went too far: 'what is said about the children seems quite right . . . but about family who did not have anything to do with it, it seems they could be excluded'. Nobody supported him; a burgher member, Gustaf Holmström, asserted that 'in the king's safety our safety certainly depends, and this is directed at that'. The issue was clinched when Gyldenstolpe pointed out that the provision simply adopted the Mosaic law, which says explicitly that the whole family of a traitor should be eliminated, whether or not they were guilty. Assessor Bromen agreed: 'here is nothing other than to secure the ruler in the supreme government conferred by God', and it was an offence of such enormity that justified the most draconian penalties. Besides, if anyone could prove his innocence, the king would surely spare him. Of course, if this was a case of the law of God in Scripture, it was not clear that the king was authorized to do that. Gyldenstolpe said that in any case it did not matter: 'it is better in the last resort that an innocent

---

[44] RA, Lagkommissionen: ÄK 15:8, dokumenter angående det Konungliga Wäldet och därtill höriga höga Jura och Rättigheter, Konungens Försäkring.

shall be left and put at risk, if it should be necessary for the ruler's safety'. So the Commission left the provision unchanged.[45]

The draft was sent to the Chancery to check 'what is in conformity with Resolutions, statutes and ordinances'. It was discussed in the College and came back with the assurance that everything in the draft was in accordance with existing laws. The working papers associated with the draft show that considerable care had been taken to reconcile it with the previous legislation. The Diet Resolutions since 1680 were one strong support, so were the contingency tax provisions of 1689 and 1693. It is of interest, and consistent with what had gone before, that although the draft Royal Chapter was deduced from the general principles of kingship by direct grant from God, its framers wanted to show that it was also based on the traditional laws and custom.

During the remainder of 1696, the draft circulated round the provinces and comments trickled in. They were sparse, though there was some support for Hylten's position on the penalties for treason. There were commentators who recognized the inherent contradiction involved in defining the powers of an absolute king. Any definition implied a limitation, and that was absurd and contradictory. The Kopparberg judiciary took that view, so did Södermanland. Gotland said the description of the king's legislative powers was deficient, and suggested instead

the king, as the living and supreme and immutable fundamental law of his hereditary kingdom, is sole legislator . . . the king alone has the supreme power at his own discretion to make law for his whole hereditary kingdom, . . . to command or alter, diminish or repeal laws issued by himself or his forefathers, also to exempt from the law whom or what he himself pleases.

Gotland clearly preferred plain speaking. One seriously critical comment came from Vadstena, and concerned the possibility that the succession might come to a foreign prince, who was unfamiliar with Swedish law and custom. To secure the subject from that danger, they suggested reactivating the provision in the Estates' declaration of 1682, that Estates should be given an opportunity to comment on changes in the law. They went further and queried the unrestricted power to make war being vested in the king. 'Defensive war is natural and excusable, but all offensive war is hazardous.' They linked this to the danger from a foreign successor to suggest that after the death of Charles XI, 'when an offensive war is to be launched, that the Estates be summoned as a Great Council'.[46]

It must seem strange to the modern observer that a draft with such far reaching implications for the future government of the kingdom elicited so little response. One reason may be simple prudence among those consulted. They were all career

[45] RA, Lagkommissionen: protokol II, meeting of 3 Mar. 1696.
[46] Hasselberg, 'Det karolinska kungabalksförslagen', pp. 70–1; RA, Lagkommissionen 1686–1737: ÄK 15:9, 10, Påminnelser till Konungabalken, 1696, 1697.

public servants. The draft was presumed to carry the king's approval; they may well have felt that it would be both ill-advised and pointless to voice criticism. There are some responses that do seem to indicate a desire not to get involved. Falkenberg, the Governor of Åbo, replied that the king's rights and authority 'were so well described and set forth in it, and the said Chapter otherwise so perfectly set up in all its parts, so that I have no humble observations to make on it'. Hans Wachtmeister, in his capacity as Governor of Blekinge, may have felt he had quite enough on his hands with the navy, and replied that his opinion 'had not been any other than to applaud what has been so thoughtfully discussed and decided'. However it may be over simple to ascribe the response entirely to fear or prudence. After all some who thought the treason penalties excessive said so, and the Vadstena judiciary had identified a real problem following a foreign succession, which was by no means a remote possibility, and they stated their views. It has to be considered that the lack of critical comment was due to most of those consulted being in favour of the absolutist agenda, because in their experience of it, under Charles XI, it operated in an acceptable manner, and seemed at least as good as any conceivable alternative. It is possible to detect that some of them had not wholly internalized the logic of the system. The Vadstena judiciary should have known that if there were a foreign succession, that was because God had chosen it, and it was really no business of theirs to question the consequences. They were, though almost certainly did not realize it, being critical of divine Providence. They could only see a practical problem and they suggested a pragmatic solution in calling in the Estates, as in some sense partners in the exercise of sovereignty. Real absolutists would not have made that mistake. Gyldenstolpe had commented on the possible function of the Estates to the Law Commission, and put them right on the issue: 'here in an hereditary kingdom, the Estates are to be regarded quite differently than before, here the Estates can do nothing other or further than the king gives them permission and instructions and then confirms it, otherwise the proceedings and resolutions of the Estates are of no effect'. It is plausible to argue that the Swedish elites, who broadly gave their support to the absolutist agenda, did so because they accepted the premiss that it was founded on divine Providence, and in their experience it worked. It can be noted that some of these same men, who were active absolutists in the 1690s and later, had discovered by 1718, through bitter experience, that sometimes absolutism did not work in an acceptable fashion. Then they cheerfully scrapped whole project, and set up and participated in a completely different system of government.[47]

By February 1697 the responses to the draft Royal Chapter had been collated and sent on to the Council for comment, and in March the Commission went through them. They rejected the objection that the formulation of the fullness of the royal powers was inadequately expressed, on the grounds that additional specification

---

[47] RA, Lagkommissionen 1686–1737: ÄK 15:9, 10, Påminnelser till Konungabalken, 1696, 1697; RA, Lagkommissionen: protokol II, meeting of 3 Mar. 1696.

would be embodied in other Chapters of the Law, 'so here it is only in general terms, and is more specific in other Chapters'. They noted concerns raised over the problems of a female succession and referred these back to the king. On the question of penalties for treason, Gyldenstolpe repeated that they could assume the king would pardon a truly innocent family member, and this was an adequate safeguard. The Vadstena concerns about a foreign succession were dismissed as unnecessary. So the original draft Chapter was approved by the Law Commission, almost unaltered, and they ordered that a clean copy be prepared, 'the text prepared for his Majesty to examine'. Several drafts of this final text exist, but no complete copy of it has been discovered. If they had thought more deeply about their project to write a rule-book for an absolute monarchy, they would have seen that it was a logical contradiction, and not worth proceeding with. For that was the conclusion the Law Commission did come to in 1715, when they returned to the question. Now they did perceive the contradiction, and noted 'it was found best to pass by discussion of a Royal Chapter, since nothing could be prescribed in it for the king, since he is the supreme authority'. A few weeks later they made a further comment that, 'as far as the king is concerned, since his royal Majesty has an unlimited power and authority, it should not be discussed, but the subjects always put themselves in humble obedience to king's gracious will'. That was really all that needed to be said about the constitution of a Christian, absolute kingdom.[48]

But the immediate reason in 1697 why the proposed Royal Chapter was not completed and issued as a law was the intervention of divine Providence. By March of that year, Charles XI was terminally ill, with cancer of the stomach, and had to take to his bed. He made a good end, as would be expected of a pious Christian, and bore his sufferings with exemplary patience and stoicism, and died on 5 April 1697. A contemporary diarist has left an account of the end, and recorded that the king died 'saying shortly before, that now he was glad to meet his God and his departed queen and children, in an eternity of bliss'. This seems so consistent with what is known of the king's personal view of the world, that it is probably true.[49]

[48] RA, Lagkommissionen: protokol II, meetings of 17 Sept. 1696, 23, 30 Mar. 1697; Hasselberg, 'Det karolinska kungabalksförslagen', pp. 78–82, 88, 89.
[49] Arfwidsson, *Mecks dagbok*, p. 120.

13

The absolutism of Charles XI

It is difficult for the twentieth-century mind to to make a realistic appraisal of the successful consolidation of the system of royal absolutism in Sweden under Charles XI. For the modern observer derives his values from the Enlightenment and the French Revolution, and most of us have internalized the very dubious assumption that the only valid form of government for human societies is one based on representative democracy and respect for the rights of the individual. Most of our early modern ancestors would have considered such ideas mad, or bad or both, and utterly destructive of any ordered society, and also a blasphemous contradiction of the Word of God. It is natural for the modern enquirer to pose the question how could a society like that of early modern Sweden, with a centuries' old tradition of the rule of law, and the practice of extensive community self-government, submit itself to an authoritarian, centralizing monarchy, without any serious attempt at resistance? The obvious answer that springs to the modern mind is that the absolutism was forced on a reluctant society by a ruthless, power-hungry king and his collaborators, using all the coercive means that lay to hand to stifle protest or opposition.

It was indeed a generally accepted rule of the European culture of the seventeenth century that a subject had no right to voice critical opinions about his own, or any other government, and those who ventured to do so were subject to draconian penalties. The censorship ordinance issued under under the regency government in 1665 denounced 'malicious people who, out of a vicious recklessness presume to concoct' all kinds of publications, 'and through them scandalously outrage rulers and states'. The censorship ordinance of 1684 dismissed as absurd the notion that printers who issued 'a quantity of abuse about individual people, or their conduct', should be permitted 'to publish whatever new matter they please'. Dutiful subjects, like the Clergy Estate in 1680, readily acknowledged that there were areas of government, like foreign policy, where they had no competence to determine the issues. They admitted: 'we have neither the brains nor the experience which are needed for furthering . . . such important work, referring it to his Majesty's consideration and well-informed prudence'. The rare individuals who did venture to express public criticism of the government put themselves in serious danger. In the remote provincial town of Torneå, a chaplain who had said in a sermon that there were 'many royal orders and statutes which twist and alter the laws' was brought before the magistrates and was lucky to escape by pleading it had been a slip of the tongue. Torneå had more than its share of indiscreet clergymen, though it is not recorded what happened to Mårten Kemp, who said while drunk: 'there is no sense at all in the king's Majesty's head'. There is no doubt what happened to Per Simonsson, who was found guilty before the Åbo High Court in 1682 'of an offensive speech about Our royal person'. On the direct order of the king, he was publicly whipped and exiled for life. This kind of reaction to public attacks on government was standard in the Europe of the day, as the experience of Titus Oates in the England of James II testifies.[1]

However, the intimidation of individual critics cannot explain why the Swedish nobility, an Estate of the realm with well-established legal rights and privileges, submitted to being deprived of nearly half of their landed properties, without any sustained effort to defend themselves. It was true that they could often recoup part of their losses through official salaries, that at the point of decision in 1680 the nobility were internally divided, and under threat from the unanimous support that the commoner Estates were giving to royal policies, and therefore vulnerable to political manipulation. And after reduktion had been decided on, there was solid good sense in the advice that Lindschöld gave to the Riddarhus in 1686, that in dealing with kings, as with God, prayer was more effective than argument. It lay wholly in the king's discretion how the reduktion would be applied. Those who submitted and collaborated could look for some mitigation of their losses. These pragmatic considerations were weighty, but are not sufficient to account by themselves for the failure of a powerful corporate group like the nobility to protect their interests more vigorously. Nor is it obvious why the commoner Estates were so eager to assist the king to build up a powerful administrative machinery, when all past experience suggested that this would result in increased tax burdens and services, and mounting central erosion of their traditional freedoms to run their local communities in accordance with traditional values and practices. To take an example, the military reforms of the absolutism did liberate the peasants from the lottery of the conscription system, but at the price of locking them inescapably into an alternative system of annual payments and services that were much more difficult to evade. The heavy hand of the reinvigorated government reached everywhere at the expense of traditional freedoms. The students of Uppsala University discovered this when they attracted the unfriendly attention of Charles XI in 1690, by doing what students had always done, getting drunk in the evenings and causing mayhem in the streets of the town. This was not acceptable in the Sweden of Charles XI, so a letter was sent to the Chancellor, directing him to enforce a curfew on the students throughout the year. Curfew breakers would spend a week in the castle prison on bread and

---

[1] Von Stiernman, ed., *Rikes commerce politie*, IV, pp. 322, 600; I. Mäntylä, *Tornion kaupungin historia; I osa; 1621–1809* (Tornio, 1971), pp. 191, 192; RA, Kongliga concept: vol. 287, Sept.–Nov. 1682, king's letter to Åbo *hovrätt*, 1 Dec. 1682.

water. If this failed to work, the king would send his guards to patrol the streets and establish martial law. The cost of this would be met by a deduction from student stipends. The students, like other unruly groups in society, were to experience the smack of firm government.[2]

Coercive force had its role to play in the establishment of the regime in the society, but it appears to have been a marginal one. There were few political prisoners in the Sweden of Charles XI, and in the post-war era nobody was executed for opposing the regime, which was more than could be said for Britain in that period. In order to find the reasons for the broad acceptability of the absolute monarchy it is necessary to start with religion, and to accept that the whole civilization of early modern Europe was a specifically Christian culture, and that the core values of established Christianity were, and always have been, authoritarian and repressive. This followed logically from the account in the Bible of the fall of mankind from grace through the sin of Adam. Because this original sin of Adam had corrupted all his descendants, man was inherently inclined to wickedness, and the whole structure of human society stood under the threat of a descent into anarchy. The danger could only be met by powerful authoritarian structures sanctioned by God. It was God who had ordained kings, priests and magistrates, and endowed them with authority, so that an orderly existence was still possible in a society of fallen men and women. Their function was repressive, their powers existed so that fallen man could be restrained, by whatever level of force was necessary, from indulging his ineradicable propensity towards sinful behaviour. Only through repression could any kind of civilized society be sustained.

It has been shown how in Sweden all education was in the hands of the clergy; only a very limited elite group could employ secular tutors and finish off the education of their offspring at overseas universities. The Swedish clergy taught a very clear and simple doctrine of authority, which they disseminated through the community in the catechism and by preaching. The catechism was summarized in a few basic rules, the *hustavlan*, which everyone was expected to learn by heart. On worldly authority the rules said, quoting relevant scripture, 'there is no authority but from God. The established authorities are sent by God. Therefore he who sets himself against authority, sets himself against God's decree.' On the duty of the subject it cited Romans 13:1: 'let everyone be obedient to authority, which has power, for there is no authority but from God'. The catechism explained why such compliance was in the interests of all, quoting Timothy 2:1 and 2: 'pray for kings and for all in authority, so that we may live a comfortable and quiet life, in honesty and in the fear of God'. The message was clear: giving unquestioning obedience to the powers that be was the price men had to pay if they wanted to live in peace and security. And, of course, the penalty for not doing so was not just insecurity in this world, but damnation in the next; the disobedient 'shall receive a judgement on

---

[2] KB, Engtrömska samlingen: B.II.1.12, king's letter to the Chancellor of Uppsala University 8 Sept. 1690.

themselves'. It has been noted that most of the clergy had been trained on the one basic textbook, the *Loci theologici* of the German Lutheran scholar Haffenreffer. This taught that a ruler was 'a person established by God to be . . . a faithful guardian of both tables of the Decalogue and other good and useful laws agreeable with this. Therefore it is customary in Scripture to call rulers gods, because they exercise an office conferred by God.' The subject's duty to honour authority, 'consists not only in external respect, but that a man inwardly acknowledges the ruler is of God's ordaining, loves him sincerely, is obedient and prays for him'. Haffenreffer does not assert that monarchy is the only form of government sanctioned by God, as a good Aristotelian he knew there were alternatives, approved models, but he simply assumed that monarchy was the form that God preferred. In his model of political society there were only two elements, the rulers, *magistratus*, and the subjects, *subditi*, and the latter had no share in authority at all. The copy of Haffenreffer that belonged to Archbishop Svebilius has survived, with his marginal notes. Svebilius was aware that the ruler was always subject to the law of God, and that if he breached that law he became a tyrant. But he also noted that tyrants too are ordained of God, to punish wickedness, and are to be obeyed; the duty of obedience was absolute. If anyone in lawful authority should command something against God's laws, then the subject must rather obey God than man, and be prepared to suffer the temporal consequences. But these subtleties were not part of the presentations to the subject at large. In these, kings were presented as superhuman beings. When Bishop Virenius preached at Lindschöld's funeral in 1690, he told the congregation: 'kings and rulers are God's officers and his anointed, so God has anointed them with wisdom and understanding, so that they often see, with their understanding eyes, when others are completely blind . . . so that we can say and conclude, not without cause, that kings are the most learned and wisest in the land'. Views like this are to be found not only in the utterances of careerists and sycophants; a preacher of proven integrity, like Jaspar Svedberg, also argued that through the anointing, kings acquire 'much greater and more glorious gifts than anyone else in the kingdom, and their wisdom, like their power, exceeds the wisdom of all the rest'. Finally it is to be remembered that most people had no access to any conflicting viewpoints on the matter. The educated among the elites would have read respected foreign authorities like Grotius and Pufendorff, who argued that in some cases, like in elective monarchies, power could be derived from the people, and then there would be a contract between the ruler and the subjects, but to the orthodox this was clearly an error, for the people had no power to confer. They might elect a king or other ruler, but his lawful authority as ruler was still conferred by God. The common folk had no such access. They did have their own oral culture, and this included ballads and stories recalling peasant rebels who had led the people against oppressive rulers. But most of these involved one of two scenarios, popular resistance to an alien usurper, or justified protest against evil Councillors or royal officers who concealed their misdeeds from a benevolent ruler, or prevented him hearing the grievances of his loyal subjects, which he would have redressed. They aimed to restore a failing system of government, not to challenge it. This tradition combined an age-old peasant resentment of landlords and gentry with an unshakeable belief in the institution of monarchy. In the circumstances of the later seventeenth century in Sweden, popular belief generated support for the absolutist programme. It would have been a very tough minded Swede who could stand out against the constant drip of indoctrination from above in the absence of any alternative view. The Land Law itself clearly established a strong executive kingship, limited only by the requirement to rule according to law and lawful custom.[3]

In seventeenth-century Europe there was a further force encouraging resort to strong authoritarian government. The society was struggling still to come to terms with the trauma of the Reformation, which had shattered centuries' old certainties, built round the concept of a universal Church. The legitimacy, which a divided Church could no longer convincingly confer, had to be sought through an alternative channel, through kings who were God's deputies on earth. Otherwise the anarchy, which was the worst of all fates, threatened. In Sweden, the attachment to monarchy, as the one sure guarantee of order and continuity, had been strikingly demonstrated by the occurrence of two long regencies. During these the government had had to be assumed by the magnates, and the monarchy was effectively in abeyance. Yet in neither case had the magnates tried to usurp power for themselves at the expense of the monarchy. And when, particularly after 1660, they were widely suspected of such intentions, they had been powerfully opposed by all four Estates in the Diet. In 1660, 1664 and 1668, the Estates had insisted on exercising close supervision and controls over an executive power vested in the regents. And when, in 1672, a faction among the magnates had proposed limiting royal power, by imposing a stricter coronation oath on Charles XI, or declaring the Form of Government to be fundamental law, these proposals had been firmly rejected in all the Estates. With an adult king on the throne, the attitude of the Estates towards the executive was reversed, and they put this on record in their sovereignty declaration of 1680, which affirmed that the kings of Sweden, as Christian rulers appointed by God, to whom alone they were accountable for their actions, had unlimited power to rule, according to law and lawful custom. The feelings of relief at the return to normality were apparent in the answer of the Clergy to the Propositions of 1680. They solemnly declared:

we cannot by hand or mouth, sufficiently describe and praise the king's Majesty's laudable actions . . . [or describe] with what obedient devotion and most humble thankfulness we, as honest patriots have taken to heart the king's happy progresses, glorious victories, heroic campaigns, most laudable administration and unwearying effort and innumerable burdens of government, and especially . . . the honourable peace . . . through the king's victorious arms.

[3] Normann, *Prästerskapet*, pp. 10, 13, 15, 18, 20, 31, 32.

They went on to say: 'our most humble devotion demands of us to hold the king's most gracious will and praiseworthy resolutions for our law, rule and guideline'.[4]

Authoritarian styles of government were as natural to seventeenth-century Europe as the weather, and Sweden was no exception. For the macro-absolutism of a king in his kingdom was reflected in the daily experience of his subjects, most of whom lived their lives in the micro-absolutisms of the paternal households, in which the master was king to his wife, family and servants, with the same right to unquestioned obedience as that ascribed to kings, and derived from the same source, the law of God. In innumerable books and orations, kings are depicted as the father writ large. Lindschöld made an eloquent speech on this theme to the Diet of 1686.

To be called a king, that is a great title, a glorious title, but *Pater patriae*, father of the country is a living title, the best title there can ever be . . . A king's nature is to attend to his power, his authority, his supremacy . . . but a father's duty is to attend to his childrens' well being, to protect them, to help them, to seek their progress, further their hopes, add to their bounties. A king, who is the highest God has set on earth, can approach nearer to Heaven through nothing so much as goodness, and can in no way be better likened to God than through a fatherly heart . . . This fatherly heart means that all your Majesty's subjects, the meanest as well as the greatest, can approach your Majesty's lofty throne, and come before your Majesty's mild countenance to lament his need, present his condition and beg help and support, with the same confidence and the same freedom as a child with a tender father. Therefore, most gracious king, the higher your Majesty rises in his grace, the deeper we ought to sink down in our humility and veneration.

The modern reader may dismiss Lindschöld's rhetoric as fantasy and experience its Baroque extravagance as repugnant. But his audience would not have done so. The conceit of kingship as patriarchy carried to its highest level would have fitted comfortably within the mental horizons of Charles XI's subjects.[5]

It would, however, be completely unrealistic to suggest that the acceptance of the absolutist regime in Sweden occurred only because the society had been conditioned to accept it. No amount of conditioning, even with techniques far superior to those available to seventeenth-century governments, can persuade any society to adopt ideas and values that are not consistent with the real life needs and experiences of its members. One major factor was the quite unusual homogeneity of the Swedish kingdom. Despite the obvious ethnic and linguistic divide between the king's Swedish and Finnish subjects, Sweden enjoyed a cohesion and stability based on a uniform legal system, a common religion, and with it a shared value system, supported by common administrative, social and economic norms and practices. These gave Swedish society a clear identity on which the loyalties of the subjects could focus. Sweden–Finland was a consensus society, whose basic aims and values were agreed by all. That meant it was an apolitical society. This can be

---

[4] *PR*, IV, pp. 141–2.   [5] *SRARP*, XV, p. 7.

seen when public issues were discussed critically; the discussion was usually in terms of personalities, not policies.

The only politicized area was foreign policy, where options had to be chosen, to ally with Louis XIV or oppose him, to enter the European war or stand aside from it, to sustain the duke of Holstein-Gottorp or seek conciliation with the king of Denmark. But in the seventeenth century, as in the twentieth, foreign policy was an elite interest, involving mysteries and matters of state which could not be exposed to broad public debate. That was why the concept of the Secret Propositions had developed in the Diet; originally they had been confined to foreign policy, and were not communicated to the Peasants. For the bulk of the king's subjects the only foreign policy issue that concerned them was peace or war, and they preferred peace. In each Diet, the Estates, after having referred the foreign policy issues back for the king's consideration, added the fervent hope that the peace could be maintained. Since this was the king's consistent aim, and after 1679 it was achieved, there was consensus on foreign policy as well. In a society where consensus prevails, and is shared by the ruler and the ruled, there is no role for an opposition, no point in an alternative government.

But to say that there was consensus in Sweden is not to say that there were no disputes or controversies within the society. On the contrary the records of the Courts reflect the great volume of litigation, and the working papers of the royal government, the minutes of the Estates, the king's legislative resolutions are all devoted to settling disputes between the subjects. Sweden did not have national politics; what it did have were individuals and groups, each pursuing their own particular interests, and coming into conflict with others. Swedish society at its highest level was formally divided into interest groups, like the four Estates, each with its well-defined functions and privileges, or liberties, as they were often called. In theory they were all supposed to function harmoniously for the common welfare. In practice there were marginal zones where interests clashed. These clashes could be provoked by royal policies: the clergy were resistant to the king's wish to revise the hymnal, the peasants were opposed to paying poll-tax on their adult children who stayed home, the nobility resisted full performance of their cavalry service obligations. But in such cases, the interest group concerned was pursuing issues specific to itself, which created no basis for a united opposition front. Almost the sole exception to this rule was the uniting of the three commoner Estates in 1680 and 1682 in support of the reduktion. Here they had a clear common interest in thrusting the financial burden of the king's reforms on to the nobility. But most disputes were between groups of subjects: the clergy clashed with the nobility over rights of church patronage, the burghers clashed with the peasants over the towns' monopoly of trade in peasant produce, and with the nobility over its economic privileges. The peasants disputed with the clergy the level of clerical fees; the clergy challenged the burghers over the system for paying the urban priesthood, and so on. These were perennial disputes, and generated the most embittered animosities, but subjects in dispute with one another over sectional interests were in a poor position to organize a common opposition to the proceedings of the royal government.

In reality, the existence of the disputes assisted and strengthened the position of the absolute king. For the only resolution of their controversies was to go up to the king and seek a ruling. A typical example can be followed from the minute of the Clergy Estate in the Diet of 1680. The Estate learned that a Peasant delegation had gone to the king and had alleged that the clergy were demanding excessive and unwarranted fees from the parishioners. It was the more alarming since the report said: 'the king showed impatience over such severe exactions'. The king then called on the parties to put their case. Deputations from the clergy went to the king; a conference was organized between delegates from each Estate, presided over by a member of the Council. It is known the king was genuinely concerned that the Peasant Estate was so incensed about the issue that it was threatening to refuse to sign the Diet Resolution if they did not get satisfaction. In the end, a settlement emerged, with the king urging the parish clergy to negotiate formal contracts with their parishioners to establish exactly what was due. Another example in 1680 arose when the Burgher Estate petitioned the king on behalf of the mining towns. Noblemen had been purchasing mines from commoners, and then claimed that their privilege exempted them from the requirement to market their product in the local staple town, to the detriment of its trade. Instead they claimed the right to sell directly to foreign exporters. The Burgher Estate requested the king to investigate the matter personally: 'this matter which so greatly concerns the towns . . . [and] not to remit the matter to anyone from the nobility, who for all sorts of reasons might have an interest in it'. This suggests how important it was that the king could be assumed to be above sectional interests. There are innumerable examples of the king intervening as arbiter. In November 1682 he ruled on a dispute between the professors of Uppsala University and the town of Uppsala. The town wanted to levy its normal marketing dues on produce from University's lands, while the professors claimed they were exempt from such payments by the terms of their endowment. The king ruled that the professors were in the right, 'since We have, no less than former kings and regents of Sweden caused their welfare to be taken into Our gracious consideration . . . in force of this, Our open letter, We thus exempt and free Our professors of Uppsala from the said taxes, now and for all time to come'. These instances all illustrate how a main function of a king of Sweden was to arbitrate over the disputes of his subjects. It followed from this that a king who was absolute, that is answerable to nobody but God, could perform this duty better than any other, and treat all his subjects impartially, because he owed no obligations to any of them, great or small. It was consistent with the character of Charles XI that he tried conscientiously to live up to this ideal. But it cannot have escaped his notice, and was certainly well appreciated by his advisers and officials, and by subjects, how the king's unique arbitral function inevitably created relationships of dependence and deference between the king and the subject, which could be exploited for the traditional politics of divide and rule.[6]

It is considerations of this kind that must be taken into account if the development and the wide acceptability of the absolute monarchy is to be fully understood. The system must be evaluated in contemporary terms, not in terms of the liberal values that become increasingly current in Europe after the French Revolution. If we seek to know why a society that had traditionally enjoyed a rule of law, and a wide measure of local autonomy, was induced or compelled to accept a boundless authoritarianism, vested by divine right in the sovereign ruler, it is necessary to consider how far the concept of the freedom and autonomy of the individual was valued in that society. In truth, the freedom of the individual was more likely to be seen as an anti-social threat to stability than as a necessary condition for personal fulfilment and the good life. An illustration of this can be found in the grievances of the Clergy Estate in the Diet of 1682. Their fifth grievance requested that 'since a large number of young and strong women stay at home and live in idleness, pleasing themselves . . . that such persons may be required to take up service, or compelled to work on the crown's farms'. It can be seen how the very idea of young persons, especially females, being free to determine their own way of life, was not only seen as undesirable, but it was an affront to the whole social order. For in a command society, there was no place for masterless individuals; they were always treated as a subversive force that must be repressed.[7]

Once the authoritarian ethos and structure of the society is understood, it then becomes apparent that absolute monarchy was well suited for the government of the society. It could deliver the kind of services that the society needed from government in an effective and economic way. There was much good sense and realism in the widespread peasant proverb: 'rather one master than a hundred'. In a world where everyone was subordinate to a higher power, the central problem for the subordinate majority was how they could be defended from oppression and exploitation by their ruling elites. It must have seemed plausible, at least, to believe that an absolute king, endowed with unlimited authority over all his subjects, and responsible to none of them, might be the only force capable of controlling, and where necessary punishing, the exploitative tendencies of the members of the elites. It is on record that Charles XI, throughout his reign, made an honest and consistent effort to do just that. And even the members of the elites, who were the potential targets of his campaigns, and who knew that there were working examples of alternative forms of government, could perceive them as potentially dangerous. It is apparent, from references in speeches and letters, that most educated Swedes knew about Oliver Cromwell and the English regicides. They never referred to them without a shudder of disapproval. That example demonstrated the awful conse-

---

[6] *PR*, IV, pp. 106, 107, 111, 115; Loenbom, ed., *Handlingar*, V, collection XIV, p. 149; KB, Engströmska samlingen, B.II.1.12, king's open letter 18 Nov. 1682.
[7] *PR*, IV, p. 161.

quences that followed from subjects challenging the authority of a lawful sovereign. Nobody wanted anything like that in Sweden.

In the general context of the dominant culture of early modern Europe, and the specific context of the kind of society that existed in Sweden–Finland, the emergence of the absolute monarchy was a wholly natural development. It had a firm ideological base that was philosophically coherent, and fitted well within the traditional Christian value system. Beyond that it was pragmatically justifiable; it did deliver effectively those services that the mass of the population needed from government. As managed by Charles XI, it preserved a rough equity of treatment between the different social groupings that made up the Swedish body politic. No realistic inhabitant of the early modern world expected life to be easy or comfortable, but they could hope that the discomforts would be equitably shared across society. There was, however, an unavoidable, but also an unthinkable flaw in the system: it depended for its successful operation on having a ruler with the right characteristics for his office. No one could have been better qualified than Charles XI. Here was a king, with proven ability as a warrior, who sought to avoid involvement in war, the universal sport of kings. He was cautious, conservative on most things, but willing to contemplate change, a pious, workaholic administrator, ruled by his conception of how God required him to guide and protect his subjects. By all accounts, Charles XI was not an easily lovable human being. But his dour integrity could evoke respect. Haqvin Spegel, who knew the king well, thought he was a paragon, 'by his great and numerous virtues, as like to God Almighty as any mortal can be'. Spegel, who had shown on several occasions his independence of mind, wrote a tract about monarchy, entitled *Konunga spegel* (A royal mirror) which took Solomon as a pattern of kingship. Spegel thought Charles XI compared well with Solomon, and was moved to poetry to express the comparison:

> If King Charles was not like Solomon in everything,
> Was not so eloquent as him, so wise, or so wealthy,
> So he was more chaste, more constant in God's teaching,
> More protective of his people, more accustomed to bear his Cross,
> And had the virtues which David and Joshua
> Are most admired for, his hopes were fixed on the Lord.

It was a typical irony of history that Charles XI, who learned his kingcraft on the job, acquired a reputation, by his successful performance of the role of God's Deputy on earth, for being a model of absolute kingship. His son and heir, Charles XII, who had been carefully trained for the role, was to demonstrate in a spectacular and brutal fashion the inbuilt fault in the system, its vulnerability to the hazards of the genetic lottery. He certainly demonstrated the strengths of absolutism, for through all the trials of the Northern War, Swedish society retained its cohesion, sustained a prodigious war effort and faithfully followed its king to the brink of destruction. At that point, a group of desperate conspirators had to adopt the only escape mechanism provided. It is almost certain that in 1718, Charles XII was discreetly assassinated, and the kingdom saved. In the aftermath, absolutism was formally repudiated and replaced by a different style of government through the Estates, set up and run by many of the same personnel who had served the absolutism to its catastrophic end. Yet the collapse of 1718 gives a quite false impression of the strength and durability of the absolutist idea. The major institutional achievements of Charles XI survived: the Church Law, the reformed state budget, the reduktion, the indelningsverk and the knektehåll and eventually the new Law Code confirmed by the Estates in 1734. But it also lived on in the hearts and minds of the majority of the kingdom's inhabitants. When the new Form of Government was being established, the two Estates that represented most of the ordinary Swedes, the Peasants and the Clergy, openly regretted its passing. In 1719, Jaspar Svedberg defied the prevailing faction and spoke on behalf of what was probably the silent majority. He recalled in his memoirs how

I stood up and declared the opinion of the Clergy with well-chosen words, saying, approximately, we have no permit to take from the ruler the power that God in His Word has ascribed to him . . . the King stands in God's place on earth. His power is of God. If he abuses it, so he shall answer before God, and not before his subjects. Here we have no Polish Republic, or some kind of English government. We have the power of a King, set out in the Royal Chapter of our old Law Book. They were no children who wrote that. And when, after that, kings ruled, and subjects got on with their lives, things went well in the kingdom . . . As wise men and true doctrine say, the ruler is given by the Lord and power from on high. A subject, a priest, a burgher, a peasant, yes and a nobleman should not question how a king behaves, and closely examine and judge what he is undertaking, that is to usurp God's office and judgement. We must believe and adhere to what the Spirit of God says: in the word of a king is power, and who shall say to him, what is it you are doing?[8]

Svedberg was probably the voice of the people in 1719. What was then happening in Sweden was a pattern endlessly repeated through human history. An elite minority of noblemen, bureaucrats and burghers contrived to establish their own oligarchic hegemony over the less advantaged majority of the common people, trampling on their expectations and opening the way for their unscrupulous manipulation and exploitation by the oligarchy. And in a bitter mockery of reality, they and the historians after them called the result an Age of Freedom.

[8] Normann, *Prästerskapet*, p. 169; Wetterberg, ed., *Svedbergs*, pp. 579–81.

Bibliography

UNPUBLISHED SOURCES

Archive du Ministère d'affaires ètrangéres, Quai d'Orsay, Paris: Correspondance diplomatique, Suède: vols. 61, 63, 64, 73

KB, Engströmska samlingen: B.III.12: Handlingar rörande Karl XIs regering
KB, Rålambska Manuskriptsamlingen: Fol. Nr. 5: 1680 års riksdagsärenden
KB, Rålambska Manuskriptsamlingen: Fol. Nr. 71, Politiska Pasquiller

RA, Diplomatica Danica 84, Ambassadören Frij. Johan Gyllenstiernas Bref till Kongl. Mjt. 1679–80
RA, Kanslikollegiets diarier 30: H. Hoghusens diarier 1677–82
RA, Kanslikollegiets Protokoll, 1686
RA, Kanslikollegiets Protokoll, A.II a. 7, 1687–9
RA, Kanslikollegium till KM: 1, 1656–95
RA, Kanslitjänstemäns koncept och mittagen skrivelser, 25, Karl XIs tid
RA, Kanslitjänstemäns koncept och mittagen skrivelser, 26, Karl XIs tid
RA, Kongliga concept, Karl XI, egenhandiga bref
RA, Kongliga concept: vol. 287, 1682
RA, Lagkommissionen 1686–1736: protokol
RA, Lagkommissionen 1686–1736: ÄK 15:8
RA, Lagkommissionen 1686–1736: ÄK 15:9
RA, Lagkommissionen 1686–1736: ÄK 15:10
RA, Lagkommissionen 1686–1736: ÄK 15:25, inkomna skrivelser från Kongl.Mjt.
RA, Rådsprotokoll 1680, vol. 72, Lillieflycht
RA, Rådsprotokoll 1680, vol. 73, Wattrang
RA, Rådsprotokoll 1681, vol. 74
RA, Rådsprotokoll 1686, Stenografiska rådsprotokoll av sekr. Svanhielm
RA, Rådsprotokoll 1694–5, vol. 91a, Bergenhielm, Protokoll hållna i KMts. kammar
RA, Rådsprotokoll 1696, vol. 91b
RA, Riksregistraturet 347, 1680
RA, Riksregistraturet 1681
RA, Riksregistraturet 357, 1682
RA, Riksregistraturet 367, 1683
RA, Riksregistraturet 1685

Bibliography

RA, Riksregistraturet 1688
RA, R 2375, Secreta Utskottets Protocoll 1686
RA, R 2377, Secreta Utskottets Protocoll 1689
RA, R 2378, Secreta Utskottets Protocoll 1693
RA, R 5956, Riksdag-journal, 1680, af Erik Benzelius
RA, R5957, Anon. Riksdagsjournalen, 1682
RA, Skrivelser till konungen, Karl XIs tid, Nils Bielke
RA, Skrivelser till konungen, Karl XIs tid, D
RA, Skrivelser till konungen, Karl XIs tid, Gyllenstierna
RA, Skrivelscr till konungen, Karl XIs tid, Erik Lindschölds skrivelser till KM
RA, Skrivelser till konungen, Karl XIs tid, Bengt Oxenstiernas skrivelser till KM
RA, Skrivelser till konungen, Karl XIs tid, Hans Wachtmeisters skrivelser till Kong.Mt.
   1677–90

UUB, E470, Kongl. brev till Greve Erik Dahlberg
UUB, E472, Kongl. brev till Fältmarskalken Rutger von Ascheberg 1656–90
UUB, E491, Handlingar till Sveriges politiska historia 1680–6
UUB, E518, Brev till Johan Rosenhane, II, 1668–81
UUB, E519, Brev till Johan Rosenhane, III, 1682–90
UUB, E520, Brev till Johan Rosenhane, IV, 1690–9
UUB, N879, Handlingar till Sveriges politiska historia 1677–80
UUB, N884, Nordiska Samlingen
UUB, N886, MSS *Le Dessein*

PRINTED SOURCES

Anon., *Les anecdotes de Suède ou histoire secrette des changemens arrivées dans ce royaume sous le règne de Charles XI* (Hesse-Cassel, 1718)
Arfwidsson, F., ed., *Erik Johan Mecks dagbok 1644–99* (Lund, 1948)
Baner, G. C., ed., *Ex Bibliotheca Trolleholmiae*, II.2: *Öfverstlöjtnanten friherre G. C. Baners Dagbok 1672–1697* (Lund, 1906)
Bergerström, O., ed., *Nils Skytte, Dagbok 1675–1720* (Stockholm, 1901)
Etienne-Gallois, A. A., ed., *Lettres inédites des Feuquières tirées des papiers de famille de madame la duchesse Décazes*, 5 vols. (Paris, 1845–64)
Fryxell, A., ed., *Handlingar rörande Sveriges historia ur utrikes arkiver samlade*, 4 vols. (Stockholm, 1836–43)
Gahm-Persson, S. F., ed., *Kongl. stadgar, förordningar, bref, och resolutioner, angående Swea Rikes landt-milicie til häst och fot*, 4 vols. (Stockholm, 1762–1814)
Handlingar rörande skandinaviens historia, 40 vols. (Stockholm, 1816–60), vols., III, V, VI, VIII, XIV, XVII, XVIII, XXVIII, XXIX, XXXI, XXXII, XXXIII, XXXIV, XXXV
Hildebrand, S., ed., *Haqvin Spegels Dagbok* (Stockholm, 1923)
   Karl XIs Almanacksanteckningar: från original ånyo utgivna (Stockholm, 1918)
   Sveriges Regeringsformer 1634–1809 (Stockholm, 1891)

Bibliography

Hildebrand, E. and Grimberg, C., eds., *Ur källorna till Sveriges historia under nyare tiden*, I: *1520–1721* (Stockholm, 1911)

Historiska handlingar befordrade af Kongl. Samfundet för utgifvande af handskriften rörande Skandinaviens historia (Stockholm, 1861ff)

Malmström, O., ed., 'Karl XIs bref till Nils Bielke', *Historiska Handlingar*, *18*, no. 2 (Stockholm, 1900)

Holmbäck, Å. and Wessen, E., eds., *Magnus Erikssons Landslag: i nysvensk tolkning*, Rättshistoriskt bibliotek 6 (Lund, 1962)

Liden, J. H., ed., *Handlingar om Riksdagen 1682* (Norrköping, 1788)

Loenbom, S., ed., *Anecdoter om namnkunniga och märkwärdiga svenska män*, 3 vols. (Stockholm, 1770–5)

Handlingar til konung Carl XI: tes historia, 8 vols. (Stockholm, 1763–7)

Historiskt archivum, innehållande märkwärdigheter, upplysningar och anecdoter i Svenska historien (Stockholm, 1774)

Lundström, H., ed., *E. Dahlberg: Dagbok 1625–1699* (Uppsala, 1912)

Ryden, A. J., ed., *Sveriges Kyrkolag af år 1686* (Göteborg, 1856)

Sjögren, C. J. V., ed., *Förarbetena till Sveriges rikes lag 1686–1736*, 4 vols. (Uppsala, 1900–2)

Stadshistoriska institutet, *Borgarståndets Riksdagsprotokoll före Frihetstiden* (Uppsala, 1933)

Stiernman, A. A. von, ed., *Alla Riksdagars och Mötens beslut*, 2 vols. (Stockholm, 1729–33)

Bihang utaf åtskillige allmena Handlingar ifrån år 1529 intil år 1698 (Stockholm, 1743)

Samling utaf kongl. Bref, Stadgar, och Förordningar angående Sveriges Rikes commerce, politie och oeconomie, IV (Stockholm, 1760)

Stille, Å., 'Bengt Oxenstiernas memorial våren 1690', *Historiska studier tillägnade Nils Ahnlund, 23.8.49* (Stockholm, 1949)

Styffe, C. G., ed., *Samling af intructioner för högre och lägre tjänstemän vid Landtregeringen i Sverige och Finland* (Stockholm, 1852)

Samling af instructioner görande den civila förvaltningen i Sverige och Finland (Stockholm, 1856)

Svensson, H., ed., 'Svenska riksrådets Protokoll: stenografiska protokoll tolkade av Hilding Svensson, 1678–79: 1682', in *Handlingar rörande Sveriges historia*, 3rd series, new edn, vol. XI (Stockholm, 1983)

Taube, B. and Bergh, S., eds., *Sveriges riddarskaps och adels riksdags-protokoll*, XIII: *1680* (Stockholm, 1896); XIV: *1682–3* (Stockholm, 1898); XV: *1686, 1689* (Stockholm, 1899); XVI: *1693, 1697* (Stockholm, 1900)

Thanner, L., ed., *Prästeståndets riksdagsprotokoll*, IV: *1680–1714* (Norrköping, 1962)

Wetterberg, G., ed., *Jaspar Svedbergs lefvernes beskrifning*, I Text (Lund, 1941)

SECONDARY SOURCES

Books

Åberg, A., *Indelningen av rytteriet i Skåne åren 1658–1700* (Lund, 1947)

Karl XI (Stockholm, 1958)

Når Skåne blev svenskt (Stockholm, 1958)

Rutger von Ascheberg (Malmö, 1950)

Snapphanarna (Lund, 1951)

Bibliography

Ågren, K., *Adelns bönder och kronans 1650–1680: skatter och besvär i Uppland* (Uppsala, 1962)

Ågren, S., *Karl XIs indelningsverk för armen: bidrag till dess historia åren 1679–1697* (Uppsala, 1922)

Almqvist, J. A., *Frälsegodsen i Sverige under storhetstiden: med särskild hänsyn till proveniens och säteribildning*, 2 vols. (Stockholm, 1931)

Almqvist, J. E., *Svenska lantmäteriet 1628–1928* (Stockholm, 1928)
Den svenska process rättens historia. Efter föreläsningar (Stockholm, 1944)

Anjou, L. A., *Svenska kyrkans historia ifrån Upsala möte år 1593 till slutet af sjuttande århundredet* (Stockholm, 1866)

Annerstedt, C., *Upsala universitets historia* (Uppsala, 1877–1910)

Arteus, G., *Den gamla krigsmakten: en översiktlig beskrivning av den svenska försvarsorganisationen 1521–1901* (Stockholm, 1985)

Asker, B., *Officernarna och det svenska samhället 1650–1700* (Uppsala, 1983)

Bååth, L. M. and Munthe, A., *Kungliga statskontoret 1680–1930* (Stockholm, 1930)

Barudio, G., *Absolutismus Zerstörung der 'Libertären Verfassung': studien zur 'Karolinischer Eingewalt', in Schweden zwischen 1680 und 1693* (Wiesbaden, 1976)

Blomdahl, R., *Förmyndarräfstens ekonomiska resultat* (Stockholm, 1973)
Förmyndarräfstens huvudskede: en studie i Stora Kommissionens historia, 2 vols. (Stockholm, 1963)
Förmyndarräfstens slutskede (Stockholm, 1968)

Böhme, K. R., *Bremische-verdische Staatsfinanzen 1645–1676: die schwedische Krone als deutsche Landesherren* (Uppsala, 1967)

Börjesson, H. J. and Wendt, E., *Svenska Flottans Historia*, 2 vols. (Malmö, 1942–3)

Brisman, S., *Den palmstruckska banken och riksens ständers bank under den karolinska tiden* (Stockholm, 1918)

Carlson, F. F., *Sveriges historia under konungarna af Pfalziska huset*, 7 vols. (Stockholm, 1855–89)

Carlsson, A. B., *Den svenska centralförvaltningen 1521–1809: en historiskt översikt* (Stockholm, 1913)

Carlsson, S., *Ståndssamhalle och ståndspersoner* (Stockholm, 1973)

Carisson, S. and Rosen, R., eds., *Den Svenska Historien* (Stockholm, 1967–8)

Cavallie, J., *Från fred till krig: de finansiella problemen kring krigsutbrottet år 1700* (Uppsala, 1975)
De höga officerarna: studier in den svenska militära hierarki under 1600-talets senare del (Stockholm, 1981)

Clemensson, G., *Flottans förlaggning till Karlskrona* (Stockholm, 1938)

Corin, C.-J., *Byråkrati och borgerlig självstyrelse i Stockholm under den karolinska tiden* (Stockholm, 1938)
Självstyre och kunglig maktpolitik inom Stockholms stadsförvaltning 1668–1697 (Stockholm, 1958)

Dahlgren, S., *Joel Grippenstierna* (Stockholm, 1969)

Dunsdorfs, E., *The Livonian estates of Axel Oxenstierna* (Stockholm, 1981)

Eden, N., *Kammarkollegiets historia: från Gustav Vasa till Karl XIIs död 1539–1718* (Stockholm, 1941)

Elgenstierna, G., *Den introducerade svenska adelns ättartavlor*, 9 vols. (Stockholm, 1925–36)

Bibliography

Ericson, E. and Vennberg, E., *Erik Dahlbergh: hans levnad och verksamhet: till 300 årsminnet 1625–1925* (Stockholm, 1925)

Ernby, E., *Adeln och bondejorden: en studie rörande skattefrälsehet i Oppunda härad under 1600-talet* (Uppsala, 1975)

Fabricius, K., *Skaanes overgang fra Danmark til Sverige: studier over nationalitetsskiftet i de Skaanske landskaber i de naermeste slaegtled efter Brömsebro og Roskildefriedene* (Copenhagen, 1952)

Fåhreus, R., *Magnus Gabriel de la Gardie* (Stockholm, 1936)
   Sverige och Danmark 1680–1682: ett bidrag till skandinavismens historia (Stockholm, 1897)

Fredriksson, B., *Försvarets finansiering: Svensk krigsekonomi under skånske kriget 1675–1679* (Stockholm, 1975)

Gaunt, D., *Utbildning till statens tjänst: en kollektivbiografi av stormaktstidens hovrättsauskultanter* (Uppsala, 1975)

Geijer, E. G., *Svenska folkets historia* (Malmö, 1929)

Grauers, S., *Bidrag till kännedom om det karolinska enväldets uppkomst* (Göteborg, 1926)
   Sveriges Riksdag: förre avdelningen Riksdagens historia intill 1865: fjärde bandet, Riksdagen under den karolinska tiden (Stockholm, 1932)

Grauers, S. and Stille, A., eds., *Historiske studier tillägnade Nils Ahnlund* (Stockholm, 1949)

Gullstrand, J. R., *Bidrag till den svenska sockensjälvstyrelsens historia under 1600-talet* (Stockholm, 1923)

Hallendorff, C., ed., *Riddarskapet och adeln och dess riddarhus* (Stockholm, 1926)

Hasselberg, G., *De karolinska kassationsakterna* (Lund, 1968)

Heckscher, E. F., *An economic history of Sweden* (Cambridge, Mass., 1954)
   Sveriges ekonomiska historia från Gustav Vasa, 2 vols. (Stockholm, 1936)

Hedar, S., *Enskilde arkiv under det karolinska enväldet* (Stockholm, 1935)

Helander, J., *Haqvin Spegel: hans lif och gärning intill år 1693* (Uppsala, 1899)

Herlitz, L., *Jordegendom och ränta: om fordelningen av Jordbrukets merprodukt i Skaraborgs län under frihetstiden* (Gothenburg, 1974)

Herlitz, N., *Grunddragen av det svenska statsskickets historia* (Stockholm, 1928)
   Om lagstifning genom samfällda beslut av konung och riksdag (Stockholm, 1926)

Hildebrand, E., *Den svenska statsförfattningars historiska utveckling från äldsta tider till våra dagar* (Stockholm, 1896)

Hjärne, E., *Från Vasa tiden till Frihetstiden: några drag ur den svenska konstitutionalismens historia* (Stockholm, 1929

Hjärne, H., *Sveriges statsskick i sjuttonde århundradet* (Stockholm, 1895)

Holmqvist, H., *Svenska kyrkans historia*, 3 vols. (Uppsala, 1933)

Holmqvist, K., ed., *Tre Karlar: Karl X, Karl XI, Karl XII* (Stockholm, 1984)

Ingers, E., *Bonden i svensk historia*, 2 vols. (Stockholm, 1949)
   Erik Lindschöld: biografisk studie (Lund, 1908)

Isberg, A., *Karl XI och den livländska adeln 1684–1695: studier rörande karolinska enväldets införande i Livland* (Lund, 1953)

Jägerskiöld, S., *Hovrätten under den karolinska tiden och till 1734 års lag: Svea Hovrätt: studier till 350-årsminnet* (Stockholm, 1964)

Johansson, K. H., *Svensk sockensjälvstyrelse 1686–1862* (Lund, 1937)

Bibliography

Katajala, K., *Nälkäkapina, veronvuokraus ja talonpoikainen vastarinta Karjalassa 1683–1697* (Helsinki, 1994)

Kleberg, J., *Kammarkollegium 1634–1718: svenska ambetsverk*, VI. 1 (Norrköping, 1959)

Kullberg, A., *Johan Gabriel Stenbock och reduktionen: godspolitik och ekonomiförvaltning 1675–1705* (Uppsala, 1973)

Lagerroth, F., *Statsreglering och finansförvaltning i Sverige till och med frihetstidens ingång* (Malmö, 1928)

Landberg, G., *Johan Gyllenstiernas nordiska förbundspolitik i belysning av den skandinaviska diplomatierns traditioner* (Uppsala, 1935)

Den svenska utrikespolitikens historia, I: *3 1648–1697* (Stockholm, 1952)

Larsson, L. O., *Bönder och gårdar i stormaktpolitikens skugga. Studier kring hemmanklyvning, godsbildning och mantalssättning i Sverige 1625–1750* (Växjö, 1983)

Lindahl, G., *Magnus Gabriel de la Gardie, hans gods och hans folk* (Stockholm, 1968)

Lindegård, S., *Consistorium regni och frågan om kyrklig överstyrelse: en studie i den svenska kyrkoförfattnings teori och praxis 1571–1686* (Lund, 1957)

Lindqvist, O., *Jakob Gyllenborg och reduktionen: köpe-, pante-, och restitionsgodsen i räfstepolitiken 1680–1692* (Lund, 1956)

Loit, A., *Kampen om feodalräntan: Reduktion och domänpolitik i Estland 1655–1710* (Uppsala, 1975)

Lövgren, A.-B., *Handläggning och inflytande: beredning, föredragning och kontrasignering under Karl XIs envälde* (Lund, 1980)

Magalotti, L., *Magalotti, L., Sverige under är 1674* (Stockholm, 1912)

Magnusson, L., *Reduktionen under 1600-talet: debatt och forskning* (Malmö, 1985)

Malmström, O., *Anteckningar rörande drottning Ulrika Eleonora, D.Ä. och Karl XIs hof* (Lund, 1898)

Nils Bielke såsom generalguvernör i Pommern 1687–1697 (Lund, 1896)

Mäntylä, I., *Tornionkaupungin historia; I osa; 1621–1809* (Tornio, 1971)

Mårtensson, L., *Förteckningen över bondeståndets ledamöter vid riksdagarna 1600–1697* (Stockholm, 1950)

Metcalf, M. F., ed., *The Riksdag: a history of the Swedish parliament* (Stockholm, 1987)

Munthe, A., *Joel Gripenstierna: en storfinansiär från Karl XIs tid* (Stockholm, 1941)

Kungl.Maj:ts kanslis historia, I: *Kansliet under det karolinska tidevarvet* (Uppsala, 1935)

'Likvidations kommissionen', in *Meddelanden från Svenska riksarkivet 1931* (Stockholm, 1931)

Nilehn, L., *Peregrinatio academica: det svenska samhället och de utrikes studieresorna under 1600-talet* (Lund, 1983)

Nilsson, S. A., *På väg mot reduktionen: studier i svenskt 1600-tal* (Stockholm, 1964)

De stora kigens tid: om Sverige som militärstat och bondesamhälle (Uppsala, 1990)

Nilsson, T., ed., *Den svenska historien*, VII: *Karl X, Karl XI, Krig och Reduktion* (Stockholm, 1978)

Nordmann, C., *Grandeur et liberté de la Suède 1600–1792* (Paris, 1971)

Normann, C. E., *Prästerskapet och den karolinska enväldet: studier över det svenska prästerskapets statsuppfattning under stormaktstidens slutskede* (Lund, 1948)

Norrhem, S., *Uppkomlingarna: Kanslitjänstemännen i 1600-talets Sverige och Europa* (Umeå, 1993)

Bibliography

Nygård, T., *Suomen palvelusväki 1600-luvulla: palkollisten määrä, työ, palkkaus ja suhteet isäntäväkeen* (Helsinki, 1989)

Östergren, P. A., *Till historien om 1734 års lagreform* (Stockholm, 1902)

Petersson, F., *Olaus Svebilius intill arkebiskopstiden* (Stockholm, 1940)

Petren, S., Jägerskiöld, S. and Norberg, T. O., *Svea hovrätt: studier till 350-årsminnet* (Stockholm, 1964)

Pleijel, H., *Svenska kyrkans historia; femte bandet: Karolinsk kyrkofromhet, pietism och herrnhutism, 1680–1772* (Stockholm, 1935)

Revera, M., *Gods och gård 1650–80: Magnus Gabriel de la Gardies godsbildning och godsdrift i Västergötland* (Motala, 1975)

Revera, M. and Torstendahl, R., eds., *Börder, bönder, börd i 1600-talets Sverige* (Uppsala, 1979)

Roberts, M., *Essays in Swedish history* (London, 1967)

Sweden as a great power 1611–1697: government, society, foreign policy (London, 1981)

The Swedish imperial experience 1560–1718 (Cambridge, 1979)

Roberts, M., ed., *Sweden's age of greatness* (London, 1973)

Robinson, J., *An account of Sweden as it was in the year 1688* (London, 1738)

Roos, J. E., *Uppkomsten av Finlands militiebeställen under indelningsverkets nyorganisation 1682–1700: en historisk-kameral undersökning* (Helsinki, 1933)

Rosen, J., *Johan Gyllenstiernas program för 1680 års riksdag* (Lund, 1945)

Skånska privilegier och reduktionsfrågan 1658–1686 (Lund, 1944)

Rudelius, K. O., *Sveriges utrikespolitik 1681–1684: från garantitraktaten till stilleståndet i Regensburg* (Uppsala, 1942)

Runeby, N., *Monarchia mixta: maktfördelnings debatt i Sverige under stormaktstider* (Stockholm, 1962)

Rystad, G., ed., *Europe and Scandinavia: aspects of the process of integration in the 17th. century* (Lund, 1983)

Johan Gyllenstierna (Stockholm, 1957)

Johan Gyllenstierna, rådet och kungamakten: studier i Sveriges inre politik 1660–1680 (Lund, 1955)

Sjödell, U., *Infödda svenska män av riddarskapet och adeln: kring ett tema i Sveriges inre historia under 1500 – och 1600-talen* (Västerås, 1976)

Kungamakt och hög aristokrati: en studie i Sveriges inre historia under Karl XI (Lund, 1966)

Riksråd och kungliga råd. Rådskarriären 1602–1718 (Lund, 1975)

Sjögren, O., *Karl den elfte och svenska folket på hans tid* (Stockholm, 1897)

Sjöstrand, W., *Grunddragen av den militära undervisnings uppkomst och utvecklings historia till år 1792* (Uppsala, 1941)

Sörndal, O., *Den svenska länsstyrelsen: uppkomst, organisation och allmänna maktställning* (Lund, 1937)

Steckzen, B., *Krigskollegii historia*, I: *1630–1697* (Stockholm, 1930)

Stille, Å, *Studier över Bengt Oxenstiernas politiska system och Sveriges förbindelser med Danmark och Holstein-Gottorp 1689–1692* (Uppsala, 1947)

Svedelius, J., *Nils Bielke: från Salsta till Capitolium* (Stockholm, 1949)

Svedelius, W. E., *Om reduktionen af krono- och adeliga gods under k. Carl X Gustafs och Carl XI:s regering* (Uppsala, 1851)

Bibliography

Swedlund, R., *Grev- och friherrskapen i Sverige och Finland: donationerna före 1686* (Uppsala, 1936)

Tarkiainen, K., *Se vanha wainooja: käsitykset itäisestä naapurista Iivana Julmasta Pietari Suureen* (Helsinki, 1986)

Tilly, C., ed., *The formation of national states in western Europe: studies in political development* (London, 1975)

Titz, C. A., *Bidrag till historien om riksdagen år 1686* (Uppsala, 1857)

Varenius, O., *Räfsten med Karl XIs förmyndarstyrelse*, 2 vols. (Uppsala, 1901–3)

Vasar,J., *Die grosse livländische Gutterreduktion 1678–84* (Tartu, 1930)

Viljanti, A., *Vakinaisen sotamiehenpidon sovelluttaminen Suomessa 1600-luvun lopulla erityisesti silmälläpitaen Turun läänin jalkaväki rykmenttia* (Turku, 1935)

Villstrand, N. E., ed., *Kustbygd och centralmakt 1560–1721: studier i centrum-periferi under svensk stormaktstid* (Helsinki, 1987)

Wahlberg, E., *Studier rörande Johan Gyllenstiernas verksamhet under krigsåren 1675–79* (Lund, 1934)

Weibull, M., *Samlingar till Skånes historia, förkunskap och beskrifning*, Tidskrift utgifven af Förening för Skånes Fornminnen och Historia genom M. Weibull, 3 vols. (Lund, 1868–71)

Wendt, E., *Amiralitetskollegiets historia*, I: *1634–1695* (Stockholm, 1950)

Westman, K. G., *Häradsnämnd och häradsrätt under 1600-talet och början av 1700-talet: en studie med särskilt hänsyn till upplandska domböcker* (Uppsala, 1927)

Wieselgren, O. H., ed., *Den svenska utrikesförvaltningens historia*, I: A. Munthe, *Utrikesförvaltningen 1648–1720* (Stockholm, 1935)

Wittrock, G., *Karl XI:s förmundares finanspolitik*, 2 vols. (Uppsala, 1914–17)

Ylikangas, H., *Suomalaisen Sven Leijonmarckin osuus vuoden 1734 lain naimiskaaren laadinnassa: kaaren tärkeimpien säännöstöjen muokkautuminen 1689–1694* (Helsinki, 1967)

Book chapters and periodical articles

Åberg, A., 'Rutger von Ascheberg och tillkomsten av den karolinska armen', *KFÅ* (1951)

Ågren, K., 'Gods och ämbete: Sten Bielkes inkomster inför riksdagen 1680', *Scandia* 31 (1965)

'The rise and decline of an aristocracy: the Swedish social and political elite in the 17th century', *Scandinavian Journal of History* 1 (1976)

Ahnlund, N., 'Bidrag till problemet *Anecdotes de Suède*', *HT* 43 (1923)

Almqvist, J. E., 'Till belysning av skatteväsendet i Skåne, Blekinge och Bohuslän under den karolinska tiden', *Historiske Tidskrift för Skåneland* (1921)

Asker, B., 'Aristocracy and autocracy in 17th century Sweden: the decline of the aristocracy within the civil administration before 1680', *Scandinavian Journal of History* 15 (1983)

'Officers ideal, rekrytning och större samhälls förändring', *HT* 112 (1992)

Back, P.-E., 'Striden om *nebenmodus*. En studie i Karl XI:s pommerska finanspolitick', *KFÅ* (1958)

Berggren, E., 'Jacob Boethius och hans opposition mot det karolinska enväldet', *KFÅ* (1942)

Bergh, S., 'Rangstriderna inom adeln under 1600- talet', *HT* 16 (1896)

Blomdahl, R., 'Karl XI, förmyndarräfesten och enväldet', *HT* 85 (1965)

Bibliography

Brolin, P. E., 'Ståndsutjämningen som historiskt problem', *HT* 71 (1951)

Buchholz, W., 'Schwedische-Pommern als Territorium des deutsches Reichs 1648–1806', *Zeitschrift für neuere Rechtsgeschichte* (1990)

Carlgren, W., 'Kungamakt, utskott och stånd på 1680 och 1690-talenriksdagar', *HT* 41 (1921)

Carlsson, S., 'Ståndsutjämning och ståndscirkulation', *HT* 70 (1950)

Corin, C.-F., 'Slottsfogden Georg Stiernhoff och Stockholms magistrat 1675–1690', in *Historiske studier tillägnade Nils Ahnlund* (Stockholm, 1949)

Elmroth, I., 'Generationsväxlings problematick i den svenska nyadeln under 1600 och 1700-talen', *Scandia* 45 (1979)

'Repliker kring en avhandling', *HT* 89 (1969)

Fahlberg, B., 'Det senare 1600-talets svenska utrikespolitik', *HT* 74 (1954)

Fåhreus, R., 'Sverige och förbundet i Augsburg år 1686', *HT* 16 (1896)

Fredriksson, B., 'Krig och bönder', in M. Revera and R. Torstendahl, eds., *Börder, bönder, börd i 1600-talets Sverige* (Uppsala, 1979)

Grauers, S., 'Bidrag till kannedom om det karolinska enväldets uppkomst', *Göteborgs högskolas årsskrift* (1926)

'Kring förspelet till 1680 års riksdag', in *Historiska studier tillägnade Nils Ahnlund* (Stockholm, 1949)

Hammarström, I., 'Kronan, adeln och bönderna under 1600-talet. Några problemställninga', *HT* 84 (1965)

Hasselberg, G., 'De karolinska kungabalksförslagen och konungars makt över beskattningen', *KFÅ* (1943)

Hessler, C.-A., 'Aristokratfördömandet. En riktning i svensk historieskvrivning', *Scandia* 15 (1943)

'Den svenska ståndsriksdagen', *Scandia* 8 (1935)

Hildebrand, E., 'Enväldets tilltänkta grundlagar i Sverige', *HT* 15 (1895)

Jägerskiöld, O., 'Studier över Bengt Oxenstiernas politiska system och Sveriges förbindelser med Danmark och Holstein-Gottorp 1689–1692', *HT* 67 (1947)

Jägerskiöld, S., 'Eric Lindeman – Lindschöld I', *KFÅ* (1983)

Josephson, R., 'Karl XI och Karl XII som esteter', *KFÅ* (1947)

Jutikkala, E., 'Large-scale farming in Scandinavia in the 17th century', *Scandinavian Economic History Review* 23 (1975)

Lagerroth, F., 'Revolution eller rättskontinuitet?', *Scandia* 6 (1933)

Lagerroth, R., 'Svensk konstitutionalism i komparative belysning', *HT* 86 (1966)

Landberg, H., 'Kungamaktens emancipation. Statsreglering och militärorganisation under Karl X Gustav och Karl XI', *Scandia* 35 (1969)

Lindqvist, O., 'Claes Fleming, räfstepolitiken och den samtida propagandan', *Scandia* 25 (1959)

Losman, A., 'Tre Karlars studier', in K. Holmqvist, ed., *Tre Karlar: Karl X, Karl XI, Karl XII* (Stockholm, 1984)

Lundqvist, S., 'The experience of empire', in M. Roberts, ed., *Sweden's age of greatness* (London, 1973)

Lövgren, A.-B., 'Kan man lita på riksregistraturet vid 1600-talets slut?', *Scandia* 40 (1974)

'Kring en tidangivelse. Erik Lindschölds åter inträde i kansliet efter onåden', *KFÅ* (1975)

Bibliography

Mäntylä, I. 'Kronan och undersåtarnes svält', *KFÅ* (1988)

Munthe, A., 'Ett stycke karolinsk vardag. Ur Henrik Henriksson Horns dagboksantecknin-gar . . . januari 1684–juli 1685', *KFÅ* (1946)

'Till förmyndarräfstens historia', *HT* 56 (1936)

Nilsson, S. A., 'Från förläning till donation', *HT* 88 (1968)

'Krig och folksbokföring under svenskt 1600-tal', *Scandia* 48 (1982)

'Landbor och skattebönder', in M. Revera and R. Torstendahl, eds., *Bördor, bönder, börd i 1600-talets Sverige* (Uppsala, 1979)

'Reduktion eller kontribution. Alternativ inom 1600- talets svenska finanspolitik', *Scandia* 24 (1958)

Nordensvan, C. G., 'Svenska armen under senare hälften av 1600-talet', *KFÅ* (1923)

Olsson, H. A., 'Karl XI och lagen: några synpunkter mot bakgrunden av 1693 års suveränitetsförklaring', *KFÅ* (1969)

'Laguppfattningen i Sverige under 1600- och det tidiga 1700-talet: en huvudlinja', *KFÅ* (1968)

'Ständernas förklaring år 1682 rörande lagstiftningen', *KFÅ* (1971)

Österberg, E., 'Bönder och centralmakt i det tidigmoderna Sverige', *Scandia* 55 (1989)

'Folklig mentalitet och statlig makt: perspektiv på 1500-och 1600-talens Sverige', *Scandia* 58 (1992)

Palme, O., 'Bazins besckickning till Sverige 1682', *HT* 30 (1910)

Persson, F., 'Att leva på hoppet – om den misslyckade klienten', *HT* 112 (1992)

'En hjälpande hand: principiella aspekter på patronage i förhållande till nepotism och meritokrati under stormaktstiden', *Scandia* 59 (1993)

Rivera, M., 'Hur bönders hemman blev säterier', in M. Revera and R. Torstendahl eds., *Börder, bönder, börd i 1600-talets Sverige* (Uppsala, 1979)

Rosen, J., 'Johan Gyllenstierna, Hans Wachtmeister och 1680 års riksdag', *Vetenskapssocietet i Lund, Årsbok* (1948)

'Johan Gyllenstiernas program för 1680 års riksdag', *Scandia* 16 (1944)

'Rutger von Aschebergs ämbetsberättelse 1693', *Scandia* 17 (1946)

'Sjättepenningen och den svenska godspolitiken i Skåne på 1600-talet', *Scandia* 15 (1943)

Statsledning och provinspolitik under Sveriges stormaktstid: en forfattningshistorisk skiss', *Scandia* 17 (1946)

Rystad, G., 'Claes Rålambs memorial 1655 och rådsoppositionen mot Karl XIs förmyndare', *KFÅ* (1963)

'Tjänster och löner', *HT* 86 (1966)

Schück, H., 'Karl XI och förmyndarräfsten', *HT* 84 (1964)

Sjöberg, M. T., 'Staten och tinget under 1600-talet', *HT* 110 (1990)

Sjödell, U., 'Gamla lågfrälset och 1600-tals byråkratien', *HT* 94 (1974)

'Kring de *Bondeska anekdoterna*', *Scandia* 31 (1965)

'Kungamakt och aristokrati i svensk 1900-tals debatt', *HT* 85 (1965)

Sörensson, P. K., 'Adelns rustjänst och adelsfanans organisation', *HT* 42 and 44 (1922 and 1924)

Stavenow, L., 'Sveriges politik tiden för Altona kongressen 1686–1689', *HT* 15 (1895)

Stille, Å., 'Bengt Oxenstiernas memorial våren 1690', *Historiska studier tillägnade Nils Ahnlund 23.8.49* (Stockholm, 1949)

Bibliography

Thanner, L., 'Carl Gustav Gyllencreutz memorial om suvereniteten, *KFÅ* (1957)
'1680-års statsförklaring', *Historiskt arkiv 11* (Lund, 1961)
'Suveränitetsförklaring år 1693. Tillkomst och innebörd', *KFÅ* (1954)
Upton, A. F., 'Absolutism and the rule of Law: the case of Karl XI of Sweden', *Parliaments, Estates and Representation* 8 (1988)
'The Riksdag of 1680 and the establishment of royal absolutism in Sweden', *English Historical Review* 102 (1987)
'The Swedish nobility, 1600–1772', in H. M. Scott, ed., *The European nobilities in the seventeenth and eighteenth centuries, II: Northern, central and eastern Europe* (London, 1995)
Wernestedt, F., 'Bidrag till kännedom om den karolinska armens tillkomst', *KFÅ* (1954)
Wittrock, G., 'Riksskattsmästaren Gustav Bondes politiska program 1661', *HT* 33 (1913)

Index

Index

Taubenfeldt, G., 15
Thegner, O., Burgomaster of Stockholm, 39, 52,
    54, 112, 131, 164
    as coordinator of the commoner estates in
    1682 Diet, 44, 45, 46, 50, 58
Törne, M., Burgomaster, 144, 164, 232
Torneå, 152, 251–2
towns in Swedish society, 4, 163–6
trade and manufactures, Swedish, 127–8, 231–5
    reports on the Diets 1693, 1697, 144, 232–3
    Trade Commission established in 1686 Diet,
    127, 234–5

Ulrika Eleonora, Danish princess, queen of
    Charles XI, 29, 140–3, 148, 213, 220
United Provinces/Dutch Republic, 24, 93, 95,
    96, 98, 100, 104, 202, 205, 208
Uppland, 67, 79, 81, 163
Uppsala town, 164, 227, 252–3, 258
Uppsala University, 12, 167, 216, 252, 258
    role of in training bureaucrats and clergy, 167,
    173

Värmland, 73, 82
Västerås, 227
Västerbotten, 235
Västergotland, 227
Viborg, 189

Wachtmeister, A., 15, 32, 35, 94, 137, 138

Wachtmeister, H., Admiral, 15, 32, 40, 70, 83,
    96, 108, 216, 230–1, 249
    appointed General Admiral 1681, 84
    directs naval reconstruction programme, 83–7
    government manager in Riddarhus 1680, 28,
    35, 36, 38
    leads fleet to sea in 1689 crisis, 84, 203
    see also navy
War College, 7, 57
    reduced remit of after 1680, 41
war contingency taxation, 135–6, 144, 145–6,
    245, 247
Wellingk, M., Swedish diplomat, 100, 203, 204,
    232
Westphalia, treaties of 1648, 7, 11, 92, 185, 210
Wallenstedt, 196
William III of Orange, stadholder and king of
    Great Britain, 101, 105, 202, 203, 205, 206,
    207, 210
Wismar, 7, 11, 161, 185, 188
    Tribunal in, 185, 187
Wrangel, C. G., Field Marshal, 24, 65
Wrede, F., president of the Chamber College,
    44, 49, 104, 119, 131, 163, 192, 194, 196,
    218, 220
    marshal of the nobility in the 1682 Diet, 44–7,
    49

Zweibrücken, principality of, 95–6, 102, 104,
    202, 206, 210

CAMBRIDGE STUDIES IN EARLY MODERN HISTORY

The King's Army: Warfare, Soldiers, and Society during the Wars of Religion in France, 1562–1576
JAMES B. WOOD
Spanish Naval Power, 1589–1665: Reconstruction and Defeat
DAVID GOODMAN
State and Nobility in Early Modern Germany: The Knightly Feud in Franconia, 1440–1567
HILLAY ZMORA
The Quest for Compromise: Peace-Makers in Counter-Reformation Vienna
HOWARD LOUTHAN

Titles available in paperback marked with an asterisk*

The following titles are now out of print:
French Finances, 1770–1795: From Business to Bureaucracy
J. F. BOSHER
Chronicle into History: An Essay in the Interpretation of History in Florentine Fourteenth-Century Chronicles
LOUIS GREEN
France and the Estates General of 1614
J. MICHAEL HAYDEN
Reform and Revolution in Mainz, 1743–1803
T. C. W. BLANNING
Altopascio: A Study in Tuscan Society 1587–1784
FRANK MCARDLE
Gunpowder and Galleys: Changing Technology and Mediterranean Warfare at Sea in the Sixteenth Century
JOHN FRANCIS GUILMARTIN JR
The State, War and Peace: Spanish Political Thought in the Renaissance 1516–1559
J. A. FERNÁNDEZ-SANTAMARIA
Calvinist Preaching and Iconoclasm in the Netherlands, 1544–1569
PHYLLIS MACK CREW
The Kingdom of Valencia in the Seventeenth Century
JAMES CASEY
Filippo Strozzi and the Medici: Favor and Finance in Sixteenth-Century Florence and Rome
MELISSA MERIAM BULLARD
Rouen during the Wars of Religion
PHILIP BENEDICT
The Emperor and his Chancellor: A Study of the Imperial Chancellery under Gattinara
JOHN M. HEADLEY
The Military Organisation of a Renaissance State: Venice c. 1400–1617
M. E. MALLETT AND J. R. HALE
Neostoicism and the Early Modern State
GERHARD OESTREICH